P. Duff

Duff's Book-Keeping

By single and double entry. Practically illustrating merchants', manufacturers',

private bankers', railroad, and national bank accounts. Twentieth Edition

P. Duff

Duff's Book-Keeping
By single and double entry. Practically illustrating merchants', manufacturers', private bankers', railroad, and national bank accounts. Twentieth Edition

ISBN/EAN: 9783337117399

Printed in Europe, USA, Canada, Australia, Japan

Cover: Foto ©Andreas Hilbeck / pixelio.de

More available books at **www.hansebooks.com**

DUFF'S

BOOK-KEEPING,

BY

Single and Double Entry.

PRACTICALLY ILLUSTRATING

MERCHANTS', MANUFACTURERS', PRIVATE BANKERS', RAIL ROAD, AND NATIONAL BANK ACCOUNTS,

INCLUDING ALL THE LATE IMPROVEMENTS IN THE SCIENCE.

WITH A COPIOUS INDEX.

By **P. DUFF,**

FORMERLY MERCHANT,

FOUNDER AND PROPRIETOR OF DUFF'S MERCANTILE COLLEGE, OF PITTSBURGH, PA.

Let no man enter into business while he is ignorant of the manner of regulating books. Never let him imagine that any degree of natural ability will supply the deficiency, or preserve multiplicity of affairs from inextricable confusion.—DR. JOHNSON.

TWENTIETH **EDITION**, ENLARGED AND REVISED.

NEW YORK:

HARPER & BROTHERS, PUBLISHERS,

FRANKLIN SQUARE.

1871.

☞ Blank books, ruled complete to match this work, manufactured by R. C. ROOT, ANTHONY & CO., Stationers and Account-Book Manufacturers, 21 Nassau Street, New York. These books are made of fine extra size-paper, with the author's directions to teachers printed upon each cover.

STEREOTYPED BY MACKELLAR, SMITHS & JORDAN,
PHILADELPHIA.

DUFF'S BOOK-KEEPING.

REMARKS UPON THE TWENTIETH EDITION.

THE early editions of this work were the result of nearly twenty years' accumulated experience in American and European commerce; and there is no undue assumption in asserting that it introduced improvements in Commercial Education previously unknown in schools. Experienced business men in all quarters promptly sanctioned these improvements; and the Legislature of Pennsylvania recognized the public value of them. in promoting the ends and purposes of Commerce, by granting the author an Act of Incorporation, with perpetual Charter, for establishing one of the first Commercial Colleges in America.

The favorable reception and extensive sale of the former impressions, have induced the author to prepare a new, revised and enlarged edition, in which he has spared neither labor nor expense, having added nearly two hundred pages of new matter, including a full set of Joint Stock Bank Books, exemplifying all the changes required for conducting bank accounts under the new National Banking law, now adopted by nearly all American banks. He has also given all the most approved forms of modern Railroad accounts; and, as no system of accounts has yet appeared for the use of Private Bankers, he has added a full set of books expressly adapted to their business.

The work now includes all the improvements for assisting the teacher and perfecting the education of the Commercial Student, suggested by upwards of twenty-seven years' daily experience in instructing large classes in this branch of education.

Referring to the testimonials appended to its pages, he feels confident that Clerks, Merchants, Bankers, and all persons who buy or sell, or have any thing to do with accounts, will find the study of this work contribute to their advancement. In this hope, it is again respectfully submitted to the public by

THE AUTHOR.

3

DUFF'S BOOK-KEEPING.

INTRODUCTORY REMARKS UPON THE FIRST EDITION.

To MERCHANTS:—

In announcing a new work to the public, it is obviously the writer's first duty to state to his readers wherein he offers improvements in the subject upon which he treats. The author's objects in adding to the publications upon this subject are briefly these:—

FIRST. To provide instructors with the means of imparting more perfect and practical instruction than can be given from any work now in use.

SECOND. To introduce several new and important modern improvements, having for their object, the abbreviation of the process, and greater security against error.

THIRD. To supply all classes of merchants, mechanics, &c., with a complete book of reference. Nearly all the works now in use being prepared almost exclusively for the use of the wholesale merchant, leaving the mechanic and retailer with no other assistance than such as they can draw from books prepared for another department of commerce—a fact which may account for the imperfect knowledge of book-keeping among certain classes of traders.

Among houses conducting the more extensive and complicated operations of commerce, irregularity in the management of their accounts is now becoming, perhaps, a rare occurrence. The conductors of such establishments, no doubt, strongly impressed with the disastrous consequences of any confusion in this department, take effectual means to guard against it, by informing themselves of the most accurate and most improved methods of management. But this is far from being the case among the middle and smaller class of dealers and mechanics. The frequent failures among them often disclose the most culpable ignorance and negligence in the management of their accounts: and as the extensive dealers are, themselves, often among the severest sufferers by these events, they should consider it their duty to make proper inquiry into the business qualifications, as well as the solvency and integrity of those to whom they extend confidence. And they should use their influence to impress it strongly upon the minds of such persons, that the want of that knowledge, which is to be obtained alone from systematic accounts, must always more or less increase the hazard of ultimate miscarriage in business; and that it is, therefore, the first and most obvious duty of every dealer and trader, small and great, to keep a precise and methodical account of his transactions. If young merchants had one-tenth part of the author's experience in winding up and adjusting deranged books of account, especially in partnership business, they would guard against confusion in their books with as much vigilance as they do against fire or shipwreck.

In some countries, this duty of the merchant is watched over by the government, and enforced by many anxious legislative provisions.* But with us it is left to be impressed solely by public opinion; and by the dread of that reproach, loss of credit and loss of character, that must ever follow the detection of ignorance and irregularity in the manner of recording business transactions.

---

* The French *Code de Commerce* gives a minute description of the several books which every tradesman must keep.

5

TO TEACHERS.

THIS work is divided into two parts; the FIRST PART containing in a cheap and convenient form for teachers, a complete course of instruction and practice upon Single and Double Entry, embracing all that is necessary for the learner to understand thoroughly, before he attempts to write in business books.

The SECOND PART is designed for the assistance of merchants and accountants in the counting-room. Both parts may be had bound together, or the first part in a separate volume when required.

This work is, by its minuteness and simplicity of illustration, intended to assist the learner, and thereby to assist his teacher. No pains have been spared to bring down the principles of the science to the level of the humblest capacity. In perusing the work, persons unacquainted with the labors of the class-room, will perhaps be struck with the repetition of references, back to the same rules and definitions; but those who understand the art of directing the progress of the human mind—experienced preceptors—know well how much successful and efficient instruction depends upon making those principles already acquired explain new difficulties.

It has always been my opinion, that a course of school instruction in Book-keeping might be so framed, that the teacher would have little to do but to see that his pupils followed the directions laid down for their guidance, which should leave them no means of getting through the exercises without mastering the subject. And if teachers would strictly follow my directions, in teaching from this work, I shall be satisfied to allow an impartial examination of their pupils to stand as a test of the merits of this attempt to effect that purpose.

The teacher will of course instruct those persons only in Single Entry who purpose to keep their books in that way and who desire to learn the science no farther. Those who learn the science upon the Double Entry principle always understand Single Entry; it therefore requires no attention from the Double Entry student, except a perusal. The introductory set of the Double Entry course is only intended for those having no previous knowledge of the subject. Those who are partially acquainted with it, may commence with the rules and oral exercises on page 38. In this set they will obtain a full knowledge of all the principles of the science.

To persons engaged in business, time is often a great consideration. To such persons you can give, from this treatise, a perfectly effective course of instruction by omitting all writing except the Journal and Ledger. Direct them to journalize the transactions from the printed Day Book. But all the other directions, in reference to the oral exercises upon the rules and the auxiliaries, oral journalizing, &c., must be strictly carried out to ensure thorough instruction.

The two sets of books embraced in the second part, though different in form, comprehend no departure from the governing principle of the science, and will not, therefore, be difficult to acquire by those who are well versed in the principles of the science. But I would recommend a course of exercise upon them, before attempting to put them in practice in business.

In transcribing our Single Entry Day Book, or any of those books where our Ledger folios are inserted as post marks, the learner must be cautioned to leave the columns blank, to insert his own post marks.

Farther directions for teaching will be found interspersed throughout the work, whenever they are deemed necessary to guide the instructor in his progress.

NEW YORK, *August, 1866.*

6

SINGLE ENTRY
BOOK-KEEPING,

EXEMPLIFIED IN A PARTNERSHIP BUSINESS, CONCLUDING WITH
AN ILLUSTRATION OF THE PARTNERSHIP SETTLEMENT
AND DIVIDEND OF THE PROFITS.

PRESENTING, ALSO, THE REQUISITE STEPS FOR TRANSFORMING THE SAME
LEDGER INTO A DOUBLE-ENTRY ONE.

PRELIMINARY REMARKS.

It may perhaps be asked why Book-keeping by Single Entry is presented in a work containing the explanation of the science by Double Entry, since. the acquirement of the latter must necessarily bring a knowledge of the former. This is perfectly true; and I have embodied my views in reference to it, in my directions to the teacher, on the last page. Those who have the means, capacity, and inclination to learn the science upon the double entry principle, will not, therefore, do more than merely peruse this set, for I do not imagine that any person thoroughly versed in the double entry process will ever keep his books in any other way. But it is, at the same time, equally certain, that there is a large class of persons, both in town and country, such as farmers, mechanics, retailers, milliners, and other dealers, who, for various reasons, are not inclined to keep their accounts by double entry; and, as every person who buys or sells any thing must keep accounts in some way, the author feels confident that the following illustration of this simple but useful form of accounts will prove serviceable and acceptable to this class of dealers. The managers and teachers of public schools will also find it worthy of their attention; for, however limited a young man's education may be, a knowledge of Book-keeping, to this extent at least, should form a part of it. In this set will be found a practical illustration of a process not to be found in any other work that we have seen—transforming the Single Entry Ledger into a double entry one. All simple as this process may appear after it is explained, it will be found that many accountants are not aware that there is any way of changing the principle of keeping the books but by the laborious and tedious process of transferring all the accounts to a new Ledger,—an operation that is seldom necessary until the old Ledger is filled.

GENERAL RULES FOR DEBITING AND CREDITING ACCOUNTS.

1. Give the Rule for opening books in private business.

1. I credit the stock account, which represents my own name, for what I invest in business, and if I owe any thing I debit it for the amount.

2. Give the Rule for opening books in partnership business.

2. I credit each partner for what he pays in, and debit him for what he draws out.

3. When is a person Dr.?

3. When he gets into my debt, he is Dr. for the amount, and
When I get out of his debt, he is Dr. for what I pay or cease to owe him.

4. When is a person Cr.?

4. When I get into his debt, he is Cr. for the amount, and
When he gets out of my debt, he is Cr. for what he pays or ceases to owe me.

5 What is the rule respecting orders, bills, drafts, &c.?

5. Credit a person always when you draw on him on your own account, and debit him when he draws on you.

6. Which side of the Ledger is used for the Drs. and Crs.?

6. The Drs. always on the left. and the Crs. always on the right.

7

SINGLE ENTRY BOOK-KEEPING.

NAMES, DESCRIPTION, AND USES OF THE BOOKS REQUIRED.

THE Day Book and **Ledger** are **the** only books generally used in this **mode** of keeping accounts. If Bill Books, or any other auxiliaries, should, in any case, be required, the form and directions for keeping them will be found in our Double Entry Set (p. **45**). I would, however, **recommend** Single Entry Book-keepers to keep a CASH BOOK, and, **in some** cases, a CASH SALES BOOK. In order **to** make these books thoroughly understood, we subjoin an exemplification **of each, in connection with each** other, and with **tho** following Day Book. We begin **with**

THE CASH SALES BOOK.

In this book **is** recorded a detailed account of all sales for ready cash ; also for cash received for sales entered upon **the** Day Book, and collected before posting to the Ledger— see third Day Book Entry, Sept. 10, p. 10. From this book the amount is transferred weekly **to** the Cash Book, or as much oftener as we wish **to balance** that book, at the same **time** noting the amount on this book—"Ent'd C. B., p. 00." **This is** more convenient **than** the common way of entering every sale **upon** the Cash Book, **or** entering them first upon a slate—a practice that can never be recommended, as it is about the same trouble to write upon slate as upon paper, and all future reference to entries made in this way is forever prevented by rubbing them out. **When** the nature **of** the business renders it too difficult to keep a record of every sale, the **usual course is** to keep the money received for sales during the day in a **drawer,** separate from **that** entered in the Cash Book, and to count it out and enter it **in one sum in** the evening " Rec'd for sales this day."

The **following** illustration will sufficiently explain the **nature and** use of this book :—

NEW YORK, September 1st, 1866.

1866. Sept.						
	1	Sold for Cash, viz.—				
		1 Vest and 2 pr. Pants,	to R. Carpenter,	22		
		4 yds. Fine Blk. Cloth, @ $6,	J. Manly,	24		
		1 Silk Hat, $5. Box, 25 cts.,*		5	25	
	4	1 pr. fine Boots, $6. Silk Hat, $5,	J. Toole,	11		
		1 Mahogany Sofa,	do.	20		
	5	1 Dining Table, $50. 1 Toilet do., $10,	F. Le Roy,	60		
	6	1 Rosewood Piano,		150		
		Music Stool,		5		
			Entered Cash Book, p. 1.			297 25
	8	Sold for Cash,—				
		1 Saddle, $15. Bridle, $2,	R. Trotter,	17		
	9	1 Gig Harness complete,	do.	14		
		1 Travelling Trunk,		12		
	11	2 Leather Hat-boxes,		3		
	15	1 Bbl. Flour, and cartage,	F. Howe,	6	25	
			Ent'd Cash Book, p. 1.			52 25
	16	Sold for Cash,—				
		2 Braid Bonnets,	Mrs. Mason,	12		
		1 Velvet Bonnet, $8. Ribbon and trimming, $4,		12		
	18	Making 2 Silk Bonnets,		5		
		Making a Mantilla, $4. 4 yds. Fringe for do., $4,	Mrs. Hill,	8		
	20	4 Lace Collars, @ $4,		16		
			Ent'd Cash Book, p. 1.			53
		Sold for Cash,—				
	25	1 Silver Watch, No. 4445,	Samuel Gray,	40		
	27	Repairing a Gold Repeater,	G. W. Smith,	2		
	29	Engraving 1 dozen Tablespoons,	F. Robb,	1	50	
			Ent'd Cash Book, p. 1.			43 50

* When a sale is made to an unknown person, the name may be left blank.

THE CASH BOOK.

[1]This book is kept for the purpose of recording all moneys received and paid. This is done[2] by debiting this account for all sums received, and crediting it for all sums paid away. Every evening, or as often as the nature of the business may render it necessary, the balance in hand is known[3] by finding the difference between the debit and credit sides, as shown by the small figures in the margin. This difference must always agree[4] with the amount of cash found in hand by counting. Any discrepancy must arise from error, which must be sought out and rectified before the account is balanced. When all is correct,[5] enter the balance in hand at the credit side in red, to distinguish it from sums paid away. The lines should be red, and neatly drawn with a ruler, exactly as below. They serve to keep the new account distinctly separated from the old account—a matter of greater importance than young book-keepers generally imagine. It also adds much to the appearance of your book to begin the words "Rec'd" and "Paid" all upon a perpendicular line, either by a fold in the paper or a pencil line. As nobody can pay away more money than he receives, the credit side of this account can never exceed the debit, but by an error. When the money is all paid away, the account must balance.

Dr. CASH (Received).

1866. Sept.			
1	To P. Duff	Rec'd on his capital	1100
	" W. Gordon.	Rec'd " "	900
6	" Merchandise.	Rec'd sales, S. B. 1.	297 25
			2297 25
15	To Merchandise.	Bal. brought down, S.B.1	1160 75
20	"	Rec'd sales, S. B. 1.	52 25
	"		53
			1266
29	To Merchandise.	Bal. brought down	841 50
		Rec'd sales, S. B. 1.	43 50

Cr. ACCOUNT (Paid).

1866. Sept.			
1	By Merchandise.	Pd. Fox's bill	450
	"	Pd. Dunn's do.	300
	"	Pd. Carr's do.	280
5	By Expense.	Pd. for Coal	8 50
6	" Merchandise.	Pd. Freight	98 75
		Bal. to new acct.	1160
			2297 25
20	By J. Day.	Paid him on acct.	25
30	" Cope & Son.	Remitted them	200
	" W. Hay.	Remitted him	200
		Bal. to new acct.	841
			1266

1. What is the use of the Cash Book?
2. How is the account of all moneys received and paid kept?
3. How do you know, at a front the book, the balance of cash in hand?
4. What must the difference between the two sides of this account agree with

5. When all is found correct, how do we balance the account?
* As this illustration will sufficiently explain the nature and use of this book, it is deemed unnecessary to continue it through the whole set.

9

1

1	P. Duff and William Gordon having this day entered into copartnership under the firm of Duff & Gordon, they pay as capital as follows:—		
	[1]P. Duff is credited for—		
	Cash paid in per Cash Book	1100.	
	James Wood owes him on account	200.	
	[2]David Cutler owes him on his note	150.	1450
1	James Wood (Carpenter), Dr.		
	For the above balance due P. Duff		200
1	W. Gordon is Cr.		
	For Cash paid in per Cash Book	900.	
	" Balance due him from R. Martin, 270 Bowery	95.	
	" Merchandise and Store fixtures per Inventory*	890.	1885
1	Robert Martin (270 Bowery), Dr.		
	For the above Balance due W. Gordon		95
1	William Gordon, Dr.		
	For bal. due by him to Wm. Hay assumed by firm	250.	
	" " " T. P. Cope & Sons, de.	265.	515
2	William Hay, Cr.		
	For balance due him by W. Gordon as above		250
2	T. P. Cope & Sons, Cr.		
	For the above balance due them by W. Gordon		265

10.

1	James Wood, Cr.			
	For his bill of Carpenter work for repairing store		105	
1	James Wood, Dr.			
	For amt. paid his order for Merchandise to John Toole		12	
Paid, Sept. 15.	[3]Frederick Howe, Dr.			
	For 1 barrel Fine Flour. (Cartage, 25 cts.)		6	25

20.

2	James Carter, Dr.			
	For 1lb Tea, $1; 12lb Sugar, $1; 1lb Raisins, 25,	$2 25		
	" 1 bag 160lb Rio Coffee @ 10.	16	18	25
Returned Sept. 22.	[4]Robert Manly, Dr.			
	For 1 best Silk Hat		5	
2	James Day, Dr.			
	For Cash on account		25	

1. Duff is here credited for the reasons given in Rule 2.
2. Cutler is not debited on book account for this sum, because we hold his note for it.
3. We do not require to open an account with Howe for this entry, because it was paid before posting.—See *Cash Sales Book.*
4. If he had returned this after posting, we must then credit him **for** the amount, when returned, on the Day Book, and afterwards post as usual.
* The form of an inventory can be seen on pages 59 and 61.

2	T. P. Cope & Sons, Dr.				
	For bill remitted them				200
2	William Hay, Dr.				
	For amount of bill remitted him				200

Oct. 5.

2	Robert Barclay, Dr.				
	For 4 yds. Satin Ribbon,	@ 50 cts.,	$2.		
	" 1 pr. Silk Gloves,		.75		
	" 16 yds. Fig'd Satin,	@ 1 50,	24.		26	75
2	¹ William Hay (to close acct.), Dr.				
	For our order on James Wood				50
1	James Wood, Cr.				
	For the above order				50
1	James Wood, Dr.				
	For 1 pr. Waterproof Boots, $6. 1 Silk Hat, $5,				11

10.

2	² Robert Barclay, Dr.				
	For Sundries .				25
2	³ James Carter, Dr.				
	For 1 Fine Black Dress Coat		$28.		
	" 1 full circle Cloak, velvet trimmed		45.	73.	
	Received cash on account of the same .			50.	
	Balance to his debit				23

20.

1	Jas. Wood (per order to J. Pine), Dr.				
	For 1 barrel Fine Flour,			$6.50	
	" 1 gal. Molasses, 50 cts. 1lb Tea, 75 cts. 1lb Pepper, 25 cts.,			1.50	
			Per bill		8
1	P. Duff, Dr.				
	For 1 Velvet Vest, $8. 1 Fine Black Dress Coat, $28,				36
1	W. Gordon, Dr.				
	For 1 pr. Ladies' Boots, $2. 1 pair Men's do., $6.50,				8	50

30.

2	James Carter, Cr.				
	For his invoice of Flour,				258
2	Robert Barclay, Cr.				
	For his invoice of Cloths, &c.				150.
2	James Day, Dr.				
	For a full suit of Clothes, $35. A ¾ circle Cloak, $30				65

1. When this entry is posted, Hay's account must be closed, as you see on our Ledger.
2. This is an imperfect entry. On the Day Book always specify what you sell.—See note 6, p. 24.
3. If this $50 had been paid on account of a former debt, it must appear at Carter's credit; but as it
    was paid on account of this particular purchase, this entry is sufficient.—See note 4, p. 25.

1	[1] Robert Martin (to close acct.), Cr.				
	For his invoice of Silks . . . . . . 67.				
	" cash in full . . . . . . 28.			95	
	5.				
2	Robert Barclay, Dr.				
	For 30 barrels Superfine Flour . . . . @ $6.			180	
	"				
2	T. P. Cope & Sons, Dr.				
	For our note in full for balance of account . . .			65	
	"				
2	[2] Robert Barclay (to close acct.), Cr.				
	For his note for balance of his account in full . . .			81	75
	10.				
1	Robert Martin, Dr.				
	For 1 barrel of Sugar, 241 ℔.				
	Tare, 21 Nett 220℔, @ 5cts., $11.				
	" 2℔ Sperm Candles, ... @ 37½ cts., .75			11	75
	"				
2	T. P. Cope & Sons, Cr.				
	For their invoice of Dry Goods and Groceries . $800.				
	Less paid them on account cash . . . . 300.				
	. Balance to their credit .			500	
	20.				
2	[3] Robert Evans (Buffalo), Dr. @ 4 months.				
	For 12 pair Waterproof Boots . . @ $8. 96.				
	" 24 *" "* Light . . @ 6. 144.				
	" 24 *"* Boys' Shoes . . . @ 1.25 30.				
	" Packing Case and Cartage 1.25			271	25
	"				
2	James Carter, Dr. @ 3 months.				
	For 1 ps. S. Fine Black Cloth, No. 1288. 24½				
	" " " Blue *"* 1299. 25½ 50 yds., @ $4. $200.				
	" End *"* Green *"* 1320. 7 *"* 3. 21.				
	" Wrapper and Cartage 25			221	25
	30.				
1	Robert Martin, Cr.				
	For his account of Hosiery against William Gordon			2	25
	"				
1	[4] William Gordon, Dr.				
	For amount assumed with R. Martin, as above, .			2	25
	"				
2	James Day, Cr.				
	For 3 months' wages from 1st Sept. to date, as foreman, @ $50 ℞ mo.			150	
	"				
2	[5] James Day, Dr.				
	For Cash on account Forty-one Dollars			41	
	JAMES DAY.				

1. See that you close Martin's account. When this is posted it will balance.
2. Barclay's account must now be credited for this note and closed.
3. It is well to specify the terms of sale both upon your Day Book and the **Invoice.—See Form 3,** p. 20.
4. Gordon is Dr. because he gets in debt to the firm for assuming his debt to Martin.
5. Business men will find this a convenient way of taking receipts.

2	James Day (to close acct.), Dr. For cash in full		19	
1	P. Duff, Dr. For a Winter Frock, $35. Hat, $5 . . . 40. " Cash paid George Cutler's bill . . . 21.		61	
1	P. Duff, Cr. For Cash Received for his bill on Gibson, Bright & Co., London .		983	
	10.			
2	T. P. Cope & Sons, Cr. For their invoice of Broad Cloths and Silks . . .		2000	
2	William Hay, Cr. For his invoice of Prints, &c.		800	
	15.			
1	James Wood, per Mrs. W. Dr. For 20 yards Figured Silk . . . @ 1.50 30. " 16 " English Prints . . . @ 25 4.		34	
1	James Wood, Cr. For his bill of new door and window shutters . . .		37	
	20.			
1	W. Gordon, Dr. For 12 yards Fine Black Cloth . . . . @ $6.		72	
3	James Wood (to close acct.), Cr. For 8 yards Prints returned, $2. Cash in full, $71 . . .		73	
	31.			
1	P. Duff, Dr. For Cash paid House Rent to date, $140. Taxes, $17.88 . .		157	88
1	William Gordon, Dr. For Cash paid House Rent to date, $100. Taxes, $4.13 . .		104	13

STATEMENT exhibiting our Profits and Dividends.

			Effects.		Liabilities.	
	P. Duff	f. 1	254	88	2488	
	W. Gordon	"	701	88	1885	
	Robert Martin	"	11	75	2	25
	Wm. Hay	2			800	
	T. P. Cope & Sons	"			2500	
	James Carter	"	262	50	258	
	Robert Evans	"	271	25		
	Cash	3	3694	75		
	Merchandise	"	3369	25		
	Bills Receivable	"	81	75		
	Bills Payable	"			65	
			8582	01	7948	25
			7948	25		
	Surplus effects		633	76		
1	P. Duff's half gain to his credit . .				316	88
1	W. Gordon's " to his credit . .				316	88

REMARKS UPON THE DAY BOOK.

ALL our transactions are generally first entered upon the Day Book; hence it is called[1] the book of original entries, and is always referred to when full particulars or explanations are called for. It is therefore obvious that all copying into it from slates or waste pieces of paper [2] is liable to destroy its testimony. If the nature of the business requires original entries to be made upon Time Registers or other memorandum books, these books ought always to be paged and the Day Book entry should show its reference to them.

Pass-books are often useful between persons having very frequent transactions with each other; but we must caution the Accountant against placing any dependence upon another person's pass-book. His Day Book must record every transaction as if no such book existed.

Though the preposition To is correctly used in their Journal by Double Entry Book-keepers, yet in the Single Entry Day Book the expression is unmeaning and ungrammatical. I have therefore substituted FOR, as more correct and agreeable to the idiom of our language. As you post the entries from the Day Book to the Ledger, [3] insert the page of the Ledger in the marginal column on the left of the page. This serves as a post mark, and shows how far your posting is completed. You must afterwards [4] compare all the entries in the Ledger with those in the Day Book, check-marking them thus √ with a pencil both on the Day Book and Ledger. No person can expect to keep his books perfectly correct without this precaution.

ON OPENING THE LEDGER.

The following Ledger is ruled in the common form, and it is the most suitable for any kind of business. The page is divided by a perpendicular line making what is called a folio, or if the paper be small it will be better to take two pages for a folio. The space intended for each person's Account is headed in large text hand with his name, or, if it be a firm, with its legal title. Every Account occupies both folios, the left or Dr. side representing [5] our Account against him, and the right or Cr. side [6] his Account against us. The difference represents [7] the Balance we owe him or which he owes us, as the case may be. The abbreviations Dr. and Cr. are [8] never required except at the head of the page. In opening a business Ledger always index each Account before you head it, as an omission in the Index often causes much trouble and sometimes mistakes. In business the Index generally has a page allotted to each letter of the alphabet. The following illustration will here be sufficient to explain it.

INDEX TO THE LEDGER.

1. What is the Day Book called?
2. What objections are there to copying from a slate into the Day Book?
3. What is to be done as you post the entries from the Day Book to the Ledger?
4. What is to be done after you have posted the Day Book into the Ledger?
5. What does the left folio of an Account in the Ledger contain?
6. What does the right one contain?
7. What does the difference represent?
8. Where are the abbreviations Dr. and Cr. required?

14

1866.						1866.					
Oct.	20	For Coat and Vest	2	36		Sept.	1	For Sundries paid as cap.	1	1450	
Dec.	1	" a Coat, $35. Hat, $5	4	40		Dec.	1	" Cash for bill on Lond.	4	988	
		" Cash p'd, Cutler's bill	4	21			31	" his ½ net profit		316	88
	31	" Taxes & Rent 254.88		157	88							
		Balance fol.	3	2500							
				2754	88					2754	88

1. What is to be done with this and the following account when closing the Ledger?
2. How are they then closed?

1. They remain open until the gain or loss is ascertained (see Day Book 3) and entered.
2. They then close into balance like any other account.

WILLIAM   GORDON.

1866.						1866.					
Sept.	1	For his debts assumed	1	515		Sept.	1	For Sundries paid as cap.	1	1885	
Oct.	20	" 2 pr. Boots	2	8	50	Dec.	31	" his ½ net profit	4	316	88
Nov.	30	" Martin's bill	3	2	25						
Dec.	20	" 12 yds. Cloth	4	72							
	31	" Cash p'd taxes & rent 701.88		104	13						
		Balance fol.	3	1500							
				2201	88					2201	88

1. What does the balance entry at this and the preceding account represent, and when are they transferred to the balance account?
2. How are these balances found?
3. How are they disposed of in re-opening the books?

1. They represent each partner's present net capital, and are the last transfers to the balance account.
2. By taking the difference between the two sides of the account *after they are credited for their share of the gain.*
3. These balances are carried to the respective partners' credit.

ROBERT   (270 Bowery.)   MARTIN.

1866.						1866.					
Sept.	1	For bal. due W. Gordon	1	95		Nov.	1	For Sundries	3	95	
Nov.	10	Sugar, $11. Candles, 75	3	11	75	Dec.	30	For acct. ag't W. Gordon	3	2	25
						Dec.	31	Balance fol.	3	9	50
				11	75					11	75

1. For what purpose is the line drawn across this account under the $95?
2. What is the balance $9.50 at the credit side, and what is to be done with it in the new account?

1. Because the payment on the 1st November squared the account.
2. It is what he owed us when balancing our books, and will be carried to his debit in re-opening them.

JAMES   (Carpenter, 18 Cliff.)   WOOD.

1866.						1866.					
Sept.	1	For bal. due P. Duff	1	200		Sept.	10	For bill of work	1	105	
	10	Paid order to Toole		12		Oct.	5	Our order favor W. Hay	2	50	
Oct.	5	Pair Boots, $6. Hat, $5	2	11		Nov.	1	Bal. to debit in new acct.		76	
	20	Paid on order, J. Pine		8							
				231						231	
Nov.	1	Bal. due per acct. rend.		76		Dec.	15	For bill of work	4	37	
Dec.	15	For Silk, $30. Print, $4	4	34							
		Forward, fol.	3	110				Forward, fol.	3	37	

1. What is the meaning of the above balance entry of $76?
2. What is the meaning of the last footing of this account?

1. It was the balance due us on settlement.
2. When an account fills up, always reserve a line at the bottom and foot both sides down upon the same line, noting them as above, "Forward."—See the Account continued, fol. 3.

1866.					1866.				
Sept.	30	For Bill remitted	2	200	Sept.	1	For Bal. due by Gordon	1	250
Oct.	5	" our order on Wood		50					
				250					250
Dec.	31	Balance	fol.	3	800	Dec.	10	For Invoice of Goods	4	800
								For Bal. bro't down		800

1. Why was this account footed on the 5th October?
2. Why is the above $800 brought down to credit side?

1. We balance this account on the 5th October for the reasons given in note 1, at R. Martin's account, last page.
2. This is the way the account re-opens if continued on this page.

T. P.   (Philadelphia.)   COPE & SONS.

1866.					1866.				
Sept.	30	For Bill remitted	2	200	Sept.	1	For Bal. due by Gordon	1	265
Nov.	5	" our note in full	3	65					
				265					265
Dec.	31	Balance	fol.	3	2500	Nov.	10	For Bal. on Invoice	3	500
						Dec.	10	" Invoice of Cloths	4	2000
				2500					2500

JAMES   CARTER.

1866.						1866.					
Sept.	20	For Mdse. per Bill	1	18	25	Oct.	30	For Invoice of Flour	2	258	
Oct.	10	" Bal. on Bill	2	23		Dec.	31	" Balance fol.	3	4	5
Nov.	20	" Invoice of Cloth	3	221	25						
				262	50					262	50

ROBERT   BARCLAY.

1866.						1866.					
Oct.	5	For Mdse. per Bill	2	26	75	Oct.	30	For Invoice of Cloth	2	150	
	10	" Sundries		25		Nov.	5	" his note in full	3	81	75
Nov.	5	" Mdse. per Bill	3	180							
				231	75					231	75

ROBERT   (Buffalo.)   EVANS.

1866.						1866.					
Nov.	20	For Invoice of Shoes	3	271	25	Dec.	31	Balance fol.	3	271	25

JAMES   (Foreman.)   DAY.

1866.					1866.				
Sept.	20	For Cash on account	1	25	Nov.	30	For 3 mos. wages to date	3	150
Oct.	30	Clothes, $35. Cloak, $30	2	65					
Nov.	30	For Cash	3	41					
Dec.	1	" "	4	19					
				150					150

Dr.   JAMES   WOOD.   **Cr.**   **3**

1866. Dec.	Bro't forw'd,	f.	1	110		1866. Dec.		Bro't forw'd,	f.	1	37
						20	8 yds Print ret'd, @ 25		4		2
						"	Cash in full				71
				110							110

CASH   ACCOUNT.

1866. Dec.	31	For am't on hand	4	3634	75		1866. Dec.	31	Balance	fol.	3	3634	75

1. What is the use of this and the four following accounts in Single Entry Book-keeping?
2. How do we find the amount of cash on hand?

1. This and the four following accounts are never opened in Single Entry Book-keeping until we are closing the Ledger.
2. The amount of cash in hand is found by counting it.

MERCHANDISE   ACCOUNT.

1866. Dec.	31	For am't on hand ⅌ Inv.	4	3363	25		1866. Dec.	31	Balance	fol.	3	3363	25
		For Bal. bro't down		3363	25								

1. How is the amount of goods on hand ascertained?
2. What is to be done with the Cash Merchandise and Bill Accounts, if the books are to be hereafter kept by Single Entry?
3. What if they are to be kept by Double Entry?

1. The Merchandise on hand is found by inventory.
2. The Cash Merchandise and the two following accounts remain closed.
3. The balances of these four accounts are all brought down.

BILLS   RECEIVABLE.

1866. Dec.	31	For notes on hand	4	81	75		1866. Dec.	31	Balance	fol.	3	81	75

BILLS   PAYABLE.

1866. Dec.	31	Balance	fol.	3	65		1866. Dec.	21	For our notes unpaid	4	65

1. What constitutes the distinction between a Double and Single Entry Ledger?
2. Why, then, are these accounts opened here?

1. The five last accounts belong to Double Entry books. No accounts are kept in Single Entry books but personal accounts.
2. These accounts are opened here only for the purpose of recording the partners' settlement, and to illustrate the manner of re-opening the Ledger by Double Entry.—See notes 1 and 2, p. 19.

BALANCE   ACCOUNT.

1866. Dec.	31	Am't due by Martin	f.	1	9	50		1866. Dec.	31	Bal. due W. Hay	2	800
		" " Jas. Carter		2	4	50				" T. P. Cope & Sons	"	2500
		" " R. Evans			271	25				" on our notes 3365.	3	65
		Cash in hand		3	3634	75				" P. Duff, net cap'l	1	2500
		Mdse. in hand			3363	25				" W. Gordon, do.	"	1500
		Bills Receivable	7365.		81	75						
					7365							7365

1. What does the Dr. side of this account represent?
2. How is the present net capital found?
3. Where is the list of debts owing by the concern, and what do they amount to?
4. What is the partners' present joint capital?
5. What portion of this $4000 belongs to each partner?
6. How do we ascertain the amounts they have paid in and drawn out?
7. How do we ascertain if our operations are all correct?
8. What is the reason of this?

1. A complete inventory of all the effects of the firm.
2. By deducting what they owe from the amount of their property—see the small figures in the margin above.
3. The three first entries on the credit side, amounting to $3365.
4. This leaves the present net joint capital $4000.
5. That depends upon the amounts which they have paid in and withdrawn.
6. This can only be known by their accounts.
7. If the operations are all correct, the balances due them or their accounts must, as above, exactly close this account.
8. The balances due to other persons and the balances due the proprietor or proprietors of a concern must exactly use up all its effects, neither more nor less

    17

CONCLUDING REMARKS UPON THE LEDGER.

It may be necessary to state that the object for closing the Ledger [1] may be: 1st, To ascertain and record a division of the gain or loss between the partners; or, 2d, To prepare the books for a partner to come in; or, 3d, To prepare for transferring the contents of the old Ledger to a new one; or, 4th, For transforming the Single Entry Ledger into a Double Entry one, or transferring the Accounts to a new Double Entry Ledger.

In closing the Ledger, every Account is made even by a Balance Entry at the lesser side, of the amount requisite to make it equal to the other side. These balance entries all represent [2] either effects or liabilities of the concern, and are all transferred as fast as the Accounts are closed, to the Balance Account [3] for the purpose of exhibiting the amount total of each, and thereby to ascertain what the concern is at present worth. There is no way of knowing this but by making up one list of every thing we possess and another list of every thing we owe. Now, this leads us to the most simple and rational explanation of the Balance Account; for the Dr. side is simply this list of our effects and the credit side the list of our Liabilities. The Difference, if the Dr. side be the largest, [4] is what we are now worth. If the Cr. side be the largest, [5] the difference is what we are insolvent.

The closing entries of the Ledger need not appear on the Day Book. They may all be made upon the face of the Ledger. They ought, however, both letters and figures, to be in red ink. All transfers from one folio to another on the Ledger should also be noted *fol.* or *folio*,[6] to distinguish the pages from those which refer to the Day Book. But the Accountant must avoid the practice of making any other entries upon the Ledger without an original entry with full particulars upon the Day Book.

If an entry affecting a personal Account cannot be found upon the Day Book, its correctness may be questioned, and in case of litigation it is liable to be rejected altogether.—See Note 2, page 14, and Note 2, page 25.

The statement at the foot of Day Book, p. 4, will always give the correct gain or loss, provided it includes all the effects and liabilities. The rule is—

ALL DEBITS ARE EFFECTS; ALL CREDITS ARE LIABILITIES.

If the amount of effects exceeds that of the liabilities, the surplus is gain, passing to credit of the Stock account, or to the credit of the partners. If the liabilities exceed the effects, the deficiency is loss, and passes to the debit of Stock, or the partners' accounts if the business belongs to a firm.

---

1. What are the objects for closing the Ledger?
2. What do all Balance Entries represent?
3. What are they all transferred to the Balance Account for?
4. If the Dr. side of the Balance Account be the largest, what does the difference between its sides represent?
5. What if the Cr. side be the largest?
6. Why must the transfers on the face of the Ledger be noted folio?

IT has already been explained—see Cash Account, Note 1, and Merchandise Account, Note 2—that these and the other property accounts were not opened until we were closing the Ledger. They were then opened for the purpose of recording the different species of property the firm possessed when the dividend was made. If the books are re-opened by Single Entry these accounts remain closed; but if they re-open by Double Entry their balances as well as all the others are brought down. But whether the books are afterwards to be kept by Single or Double Entry, no dividend ought to be made between the partners without a record of all their effects and liabilities, and that record and Balance Account ought always to be in the Ledger, or in a book for the purpose, not on loose sheets of paper, as is the practice with many business people. As the Ledger now stands, if you desire to re-open it by Single Entry, you have only to bring[1] all the balances of the personal accounts down as we have done with Hay's account—Ledger folio 2—leaving only the Cash, Merchandise, and two Bill Accounts on folio 3 closed. If you desire to open the same accounts in a new Single Entry Ledger, leave them all closed upon the old Ledger, and transfer every account under date of the old Balance Account, to the new Ledger, entering " Balance from Ledger A (or B) folio"—giving the folio of the old Ledger.

If you desire to re-open by Double Entry in the old Ledger, bring down[2] the balances of the Cash, Merchandise, and the two Bill Accounts, with all the balances of the personal accounts, and your Ledger is open by Double Entry. A glance at the Balance Account proves this, for there we see every debit and credit that we have brought down into new account, and they being equal in amount $7,365, our basis for a Double Entry Ledger is as complete as if it had been kept upon that principle from the beginning.

If you wish to transfer the contents of the old Balance Account to a new Double Entry Ledger, it can be done direct from the Balance Account in the old Ledger to the respective accounts in the new Ledger, giving reference to the folio of each account in the old Ledger as above directed in transferring to the Single Entry Ledger. Those who prefer passing the transaction through the Journal will make the following entry :—

SUNDRIES, DR. To SUNDRIES, $7365.

Robert Martin, bal. per Ledger A, folio 1,			.	.	.	$9.50
James Carter,	do.	do.	2,	.	.	4.50
Robert Evans,	do.	do.	2,	.	.	271.25
Cash in hand,	do.	do.	3,	.	.	3,034.75
Mdse. do.	do.	do.	3,		.	3,363.25
Bills Receivable in hand,	do.	3,	.			81.75
To William Hay, for bal. due him,	2,					$800.
" T. P. Cope & Sons, do.	2,		.			2,500.
" Bills Payable, bal. due on our Notes, 3,						65.
" P. Duff, for his Net Capital,	1,	.				2,500.
" W. Gordon, do.	1,					1,500.

When this entry is posted into the new Ledger, the transfer to it is completed. The learner will not expect to understand what we have said here in reference to re-opening his Ledger by Double Entry until he has acquired a knowledge of that method in the next Chapter. He will then refer back to this matter, which could only be explained here in connection with the Single Entry Ledger.

He will also refer to our directions for correcting errors in the next Chapter, p. 98.

---

1. If the Ledger is re-opened by Single Entry, what balances are to be brought down?
2. What balances do you bring down to re-open by Double Entry?

SINGLE ENTRY BOOK-KEEPING.

EXERCISES IN MAKING OUT ACCOUNTS, INVOICES, &c. IN CONNECTION WITH THE PRECEDING SET.

(1.) FORM OF AN ACCOUNT.—See J. Wood's Account, Ledger folio 1.

MR. JAMES WOOD,

To DUFF & GORDON. Dr.

1866				
Sept.	1	For bal. due P. Duff on old %		200
	10	" Paid your order in favor of John Toole		12
Oct.	5	" 1 pr. Boots, $6. Hat, $5		11
	20	" Paid your order in favor of J. Pine		8
1866.		Cns.		231
Sept.	10	For your bill of carpenter work	$105.	
Oct.	5	" our order on you in favor of Wm. Hay	50.	155
		Bal. due Duff & Gordon		76

NEW YORK, 1st Nov. 1866.

Note.—Accounts current are always drawn from the Ledger, referring by the dates to the Day Book when particulars are wanted. See that the account and the Ledger balance alike, and as soon as Wood admits the correctness of the account, you must close his account on the Ledger, as we have done, and bring the balance down, requesting him to make his books also conform to the settlement. Many persons keep their books in such a slovenly manner that they never show their settlements; in consequence of which, they are perpetually pestering their neighbors in business for statements of old settled accounts. Attention to our directions in this matter will save trouble to both parties.

(2.) FORM OF A BILL OF PARCELS.—See Day Book, p. 2. October 10.

MR. JAMES CARTER,

BOT. OF DUFF & GORDON

1 Fine Black Dress Coat		28
1 Full Circle Cloak, trimmed with velvet		45
		73
Received cash on account		50
	Balance due	23

NEW YORK, 10th Oct. 1866.

(3.) FORM OF AN INVOICE.—See Day Book, p. 3. November 20.

MR. ROBERT EVANS,

Terms, net cash in 4 months.) BOT. OF DUFF & GORDON.

12 pair strong Waterproof Boots	@ $8.	96	
24 " fine "	@ 6.	144	
24 " Boys' Shoes	@ 1.25	30	
Packing Case and Cartage		1	25
		271	25

NEW YORK, Nov. 20, 1866.

Before forwarding this invoice, compare it carefully in every particular with your Day Book.

SINGLE ENTRY BOOK-KEEPING.

MERCANTILE TERMS AND ABBREVIATIONS USED IN THIS WORK.

Account current, a running account, embracing all transactions from one date to another.

Account sales, an account of goods sold on consignment.

Amt., for amount.

Acct., for account.

@, for at.

Bal., for balance.

Bbls., for barrels.

B. B., for Bill Book.

Bottomry Bond, a mortgage or lien upon a vessel.

C. B., for Cash Book.

Co., for Company.

C. S. B., for Commission Sales Book.

Cr., for Credit.

Closing an account, to make it even.

Closing lines, the lines which separate the old from the new account.

Counter Entry, an entry made to balance one on the opposite side.

Counter Error, an error balanced by another one on the opposite side.

Counter Order, to recall an order.

Dr., for Debtor.

Do., or ditto, for the same.

Dft., for draft.

Ds., for days.

Defalcation, deficit, diminishing or cutting off.

Disct., discount, a sum or rate per cent. deducted from the principal amount.

Doz., for dozen.

Dishonored, when a note or bill remains unaccepted or unpaid.

Del Credere, an Italian mercantile term signifying guarantee.

Days of grace the time allowed by law and custom to pay a note after it is due.

Dividend, the profit to be divided.

Drawer, the maker of a draft.

Drawee, the person upon whom it is drawn.

E. E., for errors excepted.

E. and O. E., for errors and omissions excepted.

Exch., for Exchange.

Endorse, to write your name on the back.

Full extend, to extend figures into the money columns.

Footing an account, to add it up.

Folios, the pages of the Ledger.

Gal., for Gallon.

Hhd., for Hogshead.

Honor a draft, to accept it.

I. B., for Invoice Book.

Inventory, a list of goods or debts.

Insolvent, not having sufficient effects to pay one's debts.

£, for pound sterling.

Lighterage, a charge for conveying goods to a vessel in the harbor.

Mos., for Months.

Mdse., for Merchandise.

Maturity, the day upon which a note or bill is payable.

Mart, a place for public trade.

N. A., a new account.

N. P., net proceeds, the amount remaining after all charges are deducted.

No., for number.

N. G., net gain, the gain remaining after all losses are deducted.

N. C., net capital, the capital, clear of all debts.

N. L., net loss, the loss above all gains.

O. A., old account.

Per Ct., for per cent., as 5 Per Ct.

Ps., for pieces.

P., for per or by.

Prox., for proximo, next month.

P. B. P., for Bill of Parcels.

Pd., for paid.

Prem., for premium, an advance upon the face of the Bill.

Par, the face of the Bill.

Protecting, accepting or taking up a Bill.

Policy, the contract with an Insurance Office.

Protest, legal notice of the non-payment of a note or bill; which notice holds the endorsers liable for its payment.

Rec'd, for Received.

Renewal of a Note, extending its time upon a new Note.

Re-consign, to send our employer's consignment to another market, for sale.

Solvent, able to pay debts.

Short extend, to extend figures to the left of the money columns.

S. B., Sale Book.

Stg., Sterling.

Signature, a person's name in his own handwriting.

Sgt., sight.

Ulto., ultimo, last month.

Yds., yards.

21

INTRODUCTORY SET.

PRELIMINARY REMARKS.

HAVING in the last Chapter explained Single Entry Books, we have now to treat of the science upon the Double Entry principle. We purpose to introduce it as if the learner had no previous knowledge of the subject. For such persons we have prepared the following INTRODUCTORY SET.

The purpose of this set is to explain the initial difficulties of the science. We have found by experience that it is difficult to make a pupil, who has no previous knowledge of the subject, understand the language of the Journal until he is made acquainted with the nature and disposition of the accounts in the Ledger. How, for instance, can we explain to a beginner the meaning of such expressions as "Cash to Sundries," or "Sundries to Cash," but by taking him to the Ledger and there explaining to him the Cash Account and the manner and object for keeping it? Until he has the Ledger explained to him in some way, the language of the Journal must remain unintelligible to him: and to this may be ascribed the difficulty and ill success in teaching Book-keeping from some of the most popular treatises in use; in which, after bewildering the pupil with Rules and Lectures upon Journalizing, they conclude with what ought to be first explained,—the Ledger.

We here introduce our pupils at once to that book, by first defining its nature and use, and then by posting a few entries into it, sufficient to afford an explanation of the balance sheet. He then brings it to a close and determines the gain or loss upon these transactions,—an operation that can hardly fail to awaken his interest and create a taste for the science.

He next brings down the balances, and, after recording a few more entries, closes his Ledger as before, ascertains the increase or decrease of capital, and prepares for transferring his balances to a new set of books. This already affords him a commanding view of the whole subject; particularly of that part of the process which is so seldom understood by young accountants,—viz. transferring the contents of old books to new ones.

The light thrown upon the subsequent parts of the process, by this early acquaintance with the nature and purposes of the different accounts in the Ledger, will render the pupil's progress less difficult and perplexing and more effective.

The teacher will not omit to require answers to all the questions given at the foot of each page, for the pupil's examination as he proceeds.

22

SET I.—DOUBLE ENTRY BOOK-KEEPING.

DEFINITION OF THE LEDGER.

ALL the other books used in business may be considered as tributaries to this Book. Every transaction affecting our affairs must come to some accounts in the Ledger for final adjustment. It therefore follows that a distinct knowledge of the nature of the accounts in it and the manner of conducting them is indispensable to enable a person to record an entry intelligibly upon the other Books.

In the infancy of commerce,[1] the LEDGER was the only book used; and where the transactions are few, it still may be made to answer the same purpose, by making the entries on it at once, without the intervention of any other book. Thus, when a sum is to be entered, by the index you find the account headed, in a large distinct hand, with the name of the person with whom the transaction has occurred, and at the proper side we enter the date, particulars, and amount.

This book[2] is generally kept in folios of two pages to a folio. Of late, however, each page is generally made to serve for a folio by a dividing line down the middle. On the left side of each folio are the date columns, and on the right those for the money. [3]One folio is allowed to each person's account, the left side being assigned to the debits,[4] which means your account against the person, and the right side receives the credits or the person's account against you. Thus, your account against him and his account against you are brought together under one head, yet arranged on opposite sides, in such a manner that, if once correctly placed, no doubt can afterwards arise as to what sums belong to his account or to your account. When either party pays the other in full,[5] after the payment is entered, the account must be closed. [6]When the two sides of an account are found to be equal, place the sum at the foot of each and draw ink lines below them in such a way as to keep the figures distinctly separated from those of the transactions that may follow after the settlement, and which may be kept under the same head—see our Cash and Merchandise accounts in the Introductory Ledger, pages 33 and 34.

In addition to persons' accounts, in Double Entry Books,[7] we also keep accounts of every kind of PROPERTY we own and deal in. This is done under different heads precisely as we have just described in personal accounts;[8] making each property account Dr. for what we pay for it, that is what it gets in debt to us; and CREDIT for what it brings us in; that is what it pays us or gets out of our debt. In fact we may say that such accounts are personified and are dealt with in all respects like persons. Thus, if you own a house, ship, or steamer, let each have an account in your Ledger. [9]This account is debited for the cost or value of the property,[10] and credited for the freight or rent it has brought you in, and also for the proceeds of the sales if you have sold. Then an inspection of the account will show what we have made or lost by that piece of property. Thus, if the cost[11] (the Dr. side) be more than what it has brought us in (the Cr. side), then we have lost by it. But if the Credit side be the largest, then we have gained by it. In the same manner the gain or loss is determined upon the purchases and sales of Merchandise or any other property.—See Merchandise Account, 1st Set.

---

1. What was the first book used in Commerce? 2. How is the Ledger generally kept? 3. How many folios for each account, and which side is used for the debit and which for the credit side? 4. What do you mean by the debits and credits of an account? 5. When either party pays the other off, what is to be done with the account? 6. What do you mean by closing an account? 7. What other accounts besides personal accounts are kept in Double Entry Books? 8. How are property accounts kept? 9. To which side of the property account do you place its cost or value? 10. What do you place to the credit side of a property account? 11. How do you determine what you have made or lost by a property account?

23

SET I.—DOUBLE ENTRY LEDGER AND DAY BOOK.

The third class of accounts[1] kept in Double Entry Books may be called PROFIT AND LOSS ACCOUNTS, as they receive no entries but gains and losses. [2]They are kept for the purpose of recording all expenses and losses, and all gains. They may be kept all under one head— PROFIT AND LOSS; which is kept like all other accounts with a Dr. and Cr. side. [3]The Dr. side receives all entries of Expense and Loss, and the credit side all entries of gain. [4]But where the gains and losses are thus thrown together in one account, we deprive ourselves of the means of determining the gain or loss arising out of particular sources. But if we subdivide this account and open branches for Interest, Commissions, Expenses, &c., and debit each of these branches for all we lose upon it, and credit it for all we gain by it, it is obvious that each of these accounts will at any time present an important and interesting piece of information. And the longer we keep them, the more interesting and instructive they become, as they can be made to present a tabular view of their respective results for comparison at different periods of our business.

Presuming that our attentive learner has now obtained some idea of the Ledger, we will next endeavor to explain the

DAY BOOK.

This book is by some called THE BLOTTER, and it is not an inappropriate name for some people's Day Books. But for obvious reasons, scratching out, scoring or blotting entries upon this book ought to be avoided. If an entry be made wrong, it ought to be corrected, as we shall direct when speaking of the correction of errors, page 98, Note 11.

This book is ruled in single pages, never in folios like the Ledger. There is a marginal column on the left and money columns on the right.—See our Day Book in the following Set, page 28.

This book becomes necessary as soon as the business transactions become so numerous as to render it inconvenient to turn to the proper account in the Ledger and to record them there separately. [5]On the Day Book we enter them down one after another as they occur, like so many different memorandums. We reserve no spare space for each man's account here as we do in the Ledger. We have, however, to take care that every entry embraces the following particulars. [6]1st, the date; 2d, the person or account; 3d, what you have bought or sold, paid or received; 4th, the terms of payment; 5th, the articles, quantities, prices, and amounts. By inspecting any of our Day Books it will be seen that entries for different persons' accounts are all intermixed upon the same page; but are separated by ink lines in such a manner that there is no difficulty in distinguishing what belongs to each person's entry.

At our first leisure time we POST the contents of the Day Book into the Ledger. [7]Posting signifies the process of transferring each Day Book entry to the proper side of its proper account in the Ledger, in the same order of date as they occurred upon the Day Book. In order to show distinctly how far the posting has proceeded, when the post or transfer is made to the Ledger,[8] the entry is marked off or the Ledger page inserted in the margin of the Day Book, as we have done upon the first page of the following Day Book.

WHEN a Day Book is kept it is called the Book of original Entry, [1]and will always be referred to in any case of doubt or dispute about the correctness of any entry upon the Ledger. It then becomes a matter of importance to have every entry made upon the Day Book[2] in such a way as to explain itself, and also that every entry affecting other persons' accounts should originate[3] upon this book. The practice of making some entries originate upon the Ledger where a Day Book is kept, often leads to perplexing consequences. The original entry ought also to be made [4]by the clerk with whom the transaction occurred. The next Book requiring explanation is the

JOURNAL.

This Book[5] becomes necessary as soon as the nature and extent of the business introduces many long and intricate entries upon the Day Book. When one Day Book entry affects a number of accounts in the Ledger, posting such entries direct from the Day Book becomes difficult and liable to error. [6]The purpose of the Journal is to arrange all the transactions from the Day Book in such a manner that each Ledger title shall be affixed to its respective Debit or Credit, and thus render the posting into the Ledger less liable to omissions and errors. The transactions of a very extensive business may be stated upon the Day Book in the Journal form in such a manner as to be posted without difficulty and without the intervention of a Journal. This, however, can only be done by those who have learned to keep the Journal; and a correct knowledge of the language and principles of this Book is an important and somewhat difficult part of the science of accounts to acquire. We embody our instruction for making the entries of this book in rules upon the next page, which are immediately afterwards put in practice in the introductory Day Book and Journal. We hope our attentive learner will now have but little difficulty in answering his teacher the following

GENERAL QUESTIONS ON THE PRECEDING LESSONS.

QUEST. 1. When a person buys of you on credit, to which side of his account in the Ledger do you place the amount?
2. If you buy on credit, to which side of the person's account do you place the amount?
3. If you afterwards pay him this amount?
4. How does the account then stand and what is to be done with it?—See Note 5, p. 23.
5. When you receive money, to which side of the Cash Account do you place it?
6. When you pay money away?
7. When you buy Merchandise, to which side of the account do you place the amount?
8. When you sell Merchandise?
9. If you buy Houses, Ships, or Steamboats?
10. If they bring you in freight or rent, or if you sell the whole or part of any of them?
11. If you lose money, pay rent, clerks' wages, or other expenses, to which side of the Profit and Loss Account do you place the amount?
12. If you receive money for storage, or by renting part of your premises, to which side of the Profit and Loss Account do you place the amount?

THE TEACHER'S EXAMINATION.—1. What book is always referred to in case of dispute about the correctness of the Ledger? 2. How should an entry be always made upon the Day Book? 3. Where should all entries affecting other persons' accounts be first made? 4. By whom ought an original entry to be made? 5. When does the Journal become necessary? 6. What is the use of the Journal?

SET I.—DOUBLE ENTRY.

RULES FOR JOURNALIZING.

THE following rules must be committed to memory. For the convenience of the teacher we give them in the interrogative form. The learner will find it useful, in exercising himself, to cover the answers.

QUEST. 1. What is the general rule for regulating the debits and credits in Double Entry Book-keeping?

ANS. 1. The Debits and Credits arising out of every transaction must, in amount, be equal.

2. What is the rule for opening Books?

2. The Stock Account represents myself, and must therefore be debited for what I now owe and credited for what I now possess.*

3. When is a personal account debited?

3. When he gets into my debt, or I get out of his debt, he is Dr. for the amount.

4. When is a personal account credited?

4. When I get into his debt, or he gets out of my debt, he is Cr. for the amount.

5. What is the general rule for receiving and delivering property?

5. The thing received is Dr. to the thing delivered.†

6. Repeat a more particular rule for debiting property accounts.

6. When property becomes mine, it is Dr. for its cost or value; and when it costs me any thing afterwards, it is Dr. for that cost.

7. When are property accounts always credited?

7. When property brings me in any thing, it is credited for the amount, and when it ceases to be mine it is credited for its value or what I receive for it.

8. When is the Profit and Loss Account to be debited and credited?

8. Always debit loss and credit gain.

9. What is a Bill Receivable?

9. Any obligation on paper which I hold against others.

10. What is a Bill Payable?

10. The same description of obligations held by others against me.

---

* The term STOCK is universally used by Accountants for this purpose; but it is rather an ill-chosen title, as young Book-keepers are apt to confound it with the Merchandise Account. The term CAPITAL or some other title that would better express the nature of the account would be more appropriate. The author has not, however, thought proper to change the title of the account, it being his object to introduce all his improvements by conflicting as little as possible with established usages.

† Or, the receiving account Dr. to the imparting account.

THE DAY BOOK AND JOURNAL.

INTRODUCTORY REMARKS.

'. THESE two Books are here bound together. This is done, both here and with the principal set, for the mutual convenience of the learner and the teacher; but they will recollect that these Books are never kept so in business. There they are always bound separately.

DIRECTIONS TO TEACHERS AND LEARNERS.

2. After committing to memory the preceding Rules for Journalizing you will transcribe into your Day Book the first page of the one following. Then study the Journal entries, applying the preceding rules for that purpose, and refer from each entry in the Journal to its final disposition in the Ledger. Endeavor to understand the nature of all the Accounts there before you go farther, for it is that book that regulates the Journal. Therefore the first thing to be known is what accounts in the Ledger are entitled to debits and credits out of the transaction. Afterwards you can frame your Journal entry without difficulty.

3. The teacher will then take the printed Journal and hear the class, each pupil in turn, give the Journal entries verbally from their own manuscript Day Books, requiring their answers at the same time to the interrogatories at the bottom of the page.

4. When they can do this satisfactorily, they are prepared to write the Journal. This must first be done from their own manuscript Day Book, without any farther assistance from the printed Journal, upon slates or loose sheets of paper ruled to the Journal pattern, taking care to extend the debit and credit amounts in their proper columns and upon the same line with their respective accounts. The teacher should require each pupil to repeat this operation on the slate or waste paper until he can write the Journal correctly without farther assistance from his teacher. His printed book ought to be laid aside during this operation. After this they will have no difficulty in Journalizing their Day Book direct into their Journal, in all respects as they will afterwards have it to do in business. When this is done with the first page of the Day Book, they will open their Ledgers; directions for which will be found preceding the Introductory Ledger.—p. 32.

5. After posting the first page of the Journal and Balancing the Ledger according to the directions, the class will transcribe the next page of the Day Book and proceed with it in all respects as before.

6. Teachers will observe that all our directions are given for instructing in classes, but they at the same time serve for individual instruction.

7. Let me caution all teachers against allowing their students to make their Journals or their postings in the Ledger from the printed book. They might as well expect to learn Arithmetic by copying off the questions and answers, as to acquire the art of Book-keeping by such means.

8 All transfers from one book to another must be carefully compared and check-marked on both books thus √. On the Ledger a small point (·) is best, as it does not deface the page. No person can keep his work correct long without checking. When you have no figures for your cent columns avoid the useless practice of filling them with ciphers, which are in your way when adding the column.

¹ My effects, commencing business this day, consist of—

Cash in hand		$1000.	
Charles Page owes me on his note	$500.		
R. Manly owes me on his bond and mortgage	1500.	2000.	3000

5.

Bought for Cash of William Hay Merchandise per Invoice   600

"

Sold James Carter for Cash—

60 pieces of two Blue Prints		@ $3.	$180.	
70 " Fancy Stripes		" 4.	280.	460

10.

² Rec'd Cash from R. Manly for his mortgage $1500.
Also Interest due on the same   90.   1590

14.

Bo't of A. Stuart & Co. on my note @ 60 days Merchandise ⅌ Invoice   300

"

³ Bought of Warden & Bell Merchandise ⅌ Invoice $800.
Paid them Cash on account of the same   200.

The balance to their account @ 2 months   600

25.

⁴ Sold William Hay—

5 hhds. Sugar, 1180, 1220, 1300, 1100, 1200 = 6000 lbs.
Tare 10 per cent. off   600

Net 5400 lbs., @ 5 cts., $270.
120 pieces Furniture Prints   @ $3.   360.   630.

Rec'd Cash on account of the same   330.

The balance to his account @ 2 months .   300

30.

⁵ Paid Cash for Store Rent, Advertising, &c.   150

"

Sold for Cash to J. Beck & Co. the remainder of my Merchandise in hand

240 pieces Merrimac Prints		@ $3.	$720.	
30 " Furniture "		" 2.	60.	780

"

Paid Cash Jennings & Co.'s account for Clothing for my private use   130

1. Stock must be here credited for the amount of my property according to Rule 2, and Cash and Bills Receivable are debited by Rule 5, these amounts being now received into these books.
2. Cash, the thing received, is here debited for the whole amount; but there being nothing delivered for the $90, Profit and Loss is credited according to Rule 8. Bills Receivable can only be credited for the face of the bill.
3. Although Warden & Bell might have been here credited for the whole Invoice, and debited for the payment upon it, yet the Journal entry we have given is more concise and equally correct.
4. For the reasons given in the last note, Hay is here only debited for the balance due on this purchase. If he had made this payment on a former account, then it must appear at his credit, and the whole of this invoice at his debit.
5. We have received nothing in exchange for this cash, and there being no person responsible to us for it, we must debit Profit and Loss.
6. The figures in the left marginal column of the Journal are the pages of the Ledger, and are written as the posting proceeds. They serve as post marks to show how far that operation is completed.
7. As the Day Book entries are journalized, EACH IS MARKED OFF IN THE MARGIN, as the above two first entries.

L. F.		Drs.	Cas.
1	[1] Sundries, Dr. to Stock account		3000
2	Cash account	1000	
1	Bills Receivable account*	2000	
	5.		
1	Mdse., Dr.	600	
2	To Cash		600
	"		
2	Cash, Dr.	460	
1	To Mdse.		460
	10.		
2	[2] Cash, Dr. to Sundries	1590	
1	To Bills Receivable		1500
3	" Profit & Loss		90
	14.		
1	Mdse., Dr.	300	
2	To Bills Payable		300
	"		
1	[3] Mdse., Dr. to Sundries	800	
2	To Cash		200
2	" Warden & Bell		600
	25.		
1	[4] Sundries, Dr. to Mdse.		630
2	Cash	330	
2	William Hay	300	
	.30.		
3	[5] Profit & Loss, Dr.	150	
2	To Cash		150
	"		
2	Cash, Dr.	780	
1	To Mdse.		780
	"		
3	Profit & Loss, Dr.	130	
2	To Cash		130

1. Why is Stock account **credited**, **and** Cash and Bills Receivable account **debited** for this amount?
2. Why is Cash here debited for the whole amount, and Bills Receivable credited for only $1500?
3. Why not credit Warden & Bell **for** the whole Invoice, and debit them for the payment?
4. Why not debit Hay for the whole Invoice, **and carry** the payment to his credit on account?
5. Why debit Profit & Loss for this amount?
6. What are the figures in the left hand **marginal** column of the Journal, **and** when are they inserted?
7. What is done to show how far the Day Book is journalized?

* The learner will observe, that, although the word *account* is *understood* after every Ledger title, it is never written. And in a business journal we seldom write the abbreviation Dr.; but, for the purposes of instruction, we deem it advisable to retain it.

[1] Received by the packet Gladiator, Pratt, master, from London, an Invoice of Prints, shipped me by R. Morris, by my order and for my account, amounting, per invoice, to £450 sterling, due 31st inst. . . 2000.		
Paid freight and duty in Cash . . . . 500.	2500	

10.

Received Cash from Charles Page for his note in my favor . . .	500	

14.

[3] Sold James Day—		
300 pieces London Chintz Muslin, @ $4 . . . $1200.		
30 " Cambric Handkerchiefs, @ $10 . . 300.	1500	
Received Cash on account of the same . . $1000.		
" his note @ 3 months for the balance . . 500. $1500.		

"		
[5] Received from the Executors of my Father's Estate, House and Lot 44 Broadway, valued at . . . . . . $15000.		
Cash . . . . 10000.	25000	

21.

[4] Discounted for C. Banks his note @ 1 month for $1000.		
" " C. Murray " " 9 months for 1500. $2500.		
Deduct 33 days' Interest on Banks's note 5.50		
" $9\frac{3}{10}$ months' Interest on Murray's note 68.25 73.75		
Net proceeds paid them in Cash . . .	2426	25

"		
Bought of Charles Page Mdse. per Invoice . . $2100.		
Paid him Cash on account . . . . $2000.		
[6] Gave him my order on William Hay, payable in Mdse. for the balance . . . . 100.	2100	

25.

Paid Cash my bill for boarding at the Astor House to date . . .	50	

31.

[6] Paid William Hay Cash on loan for 30 days . . . $2200.		
Sold him, on account, 3 pieces best black Broadcloth, viz., No. 1144. 24², 1004. 22³, and 909. 23. = 70 yards, @ $10 700.	2900	

"		
[7] Gave Warden & Bell my order on William Hay, payable in Cash, for	**100**	

"		
Paid Rents, Clerks' Wages, &c., in Cash	103	75

1. We debit Merchandise for what it costs to bring it home, as well as the purchase money—recollect Rule 6. Morris is only credited for $2000, because that is all we get in debt to him. (Rule 4.)
2. We do not debit Day on Book account for the balance of his purchase, because we received his note for it. We cannot record two claims for the same sum.
3. The Profit and Loss account is only intended to record our gains and losses by business; and as we have not earned this property by our business, it would not be proper to carry it to that account, although our doing so would make no difference in the final closing of the Stock account.
4. The discount upon these notes is a gain to us, we therefore credit Profit and Loss for it.
5. Hay must be credited for this order, because we get in debt to him for paying this amount for us.
6. Hay must here be debited for both the Cash and Merchandise, because he gets into our debt for the amount—recollect Rule 5.
7. Here Warden & Bell is Dr., because we got out of their debt for **that amount, and** Hay is credited, because we get into his debt for the same amount.

		Dne.		Cns.	
1	¹ Mdse., Dr. to Sundries	2500			
2	To R. Morris			2000	
2	" Cash			500	

10.

2	Cash, Dr.	500			
1	To Bills Receivable			500	

14.

1	² Sundries, Dr. to Mdse.			1500	
2	Cash	1000			
1	Bills Receivable	500			

"

1	² Sundries, Dr. to Stock			25000	
3	House and Lot 44 Broadway	15000			
2	Cash	10000			

21.

1	⁴ Bills Receivable, Dr. to Sundries	2500			
2	To Cash			2426	25
3	" Profit & Loss			73	75

"

1	⁵ Mdse., Dr. to Sundries	2100			
2	To Cash			2000	
2	" William Hay			100	

25.

3	Profit & Loss, Dr.	50			
2	To Cash			50	

31.

2	⁶ William Hay, Dr. to Sundries	2900			
2	To Cash			2200	
1	" Mdse.			700	

"

2	⁷ Warden & Bell, Dr.	100			
2	To William Hay			100	

"

3	Profit & Loss, Dr.	103	75		
2	To Cash			103	75

1. Why is Merchandise debited for **any more** than the amount for which we credit Morris?
2. Why is not Day debited for the unpaid balance of this invoice?
3. This amount being a gain, why not credit Profit & Loss for it?
4. Why is Profit & Loss credited for this $73.75, it being a deduction from the notes?
5. Why do we credit Hay for this order?
6. Why is Hay debited in this case?
7. Why debit Warden & Bell and credit Hay for this order?

ON OPENING AND CLOSING THE LEDGER.

WHEN the pupil has Journalized the first Day Book and afterwards carefully compared his Journal with it, he will open his Ledger. In a clean text hand write the title of each Account, giving it five or six more lines of space than on the printed Ledger. Insert the abbreviations Dr. and Cr.[1] at the top of the page only. Then post the Journal into the Ledger. Before attempting this, it will be well to compare the entries from the printed Journal to the Ledger. In expressing the entry upon the Ledger, it will be seen that a debit is always To that Account which receives credit for this sum, and the Cr. Account expresses the same entry By the Account that was made Dr. for the same sum. Where several accounts are referred to, the expression is either To or BY Sundries. But the learner will acquire the process more readily by seeing it done on his printed Ledger than by any other means. But let the amount always be first inserted, the date and other particulars afterwards. When the Journal is posted,[2] compare and check every entry from it to the Ledger, check-marking them thus √ with a pencil on the inner left-hand marginal line of the Journal and on the double line on the left of the money column on the Ledger. Then add up all the Accounts[3] and take off a Trial Balance, both sides of which must come out equal.—See form at the end of the Ledger, page 36.

After studying the oral exercises under each Account upon the Ledger until he can answer them readily, the pupil is prepared to close his Ledger. Though this is the most difficult part of the process of Book-keeping to understand, I think the following method of elucidating it will make the matter intelligible.

By closing a Ledger we make every Account upon the face of it even. 'The purpose of this is to dispose of all the Balances in such a manner as to EXHIBIT and RECORD the increase or decrease of Capital up to the present time.

I have found by experience that the most simple and rational explanation of the Balance Account will be found in the following process.* Let the pupil be required to make up from his Ledger, upon waste paper, a list of his effects thus:—

From the Bills Receivable Account I find I have Notes in hand amounting to $500.
By the Cash Account, I find cash in hand . . . . . . 3,080.
By W. Hay's Account, I perceive he owes me . . . . 300.

Making the total amount of my effects . . 3,880.

By Bills Payable Account, I find I owe on my Notes 300.
And to Warden & Bell, By their Account, I owe . 600. Am't I owe, 900.

Leaving my present Net Capital . . . . . 2,980.

Now, compare this statement with our Balance Account, and I shall be much mistaken if it does not give you a clear insight into the nature and object of that Account. You will now close all the Personal and Property Accounts, ruling them off to the same pattern given on our Ledger, transferring the Balances at the same time to the proper side of the Balance Account. When this is completed you will find the present Net Capital exhibited by the Balance Account as in the above statement, $2,980, which according to the Stock Account is $20 less than the Capital we opened the books with. You find the particulars of this loss at the Profit & Loss Account. Close that Account into Stock and then you will find that the Stock and Balance will exactly close each other—a result that must always take place when the operations are correct, because all gains must produce a corresponding increase of property, at the Dr. side of Balance, and through the Profit & Loss Account the credit side of the Stock is increased exactly to the same amount. Losses affect these two Accounts through the same channels also precisely to the same extent.

These remarks apply to the first set of the following Books. After bringing all the Balances down and posting the second set, the process of closing is the same as in the first Balance.

---

1. Where are the abbreviations Dr. and Cr. placed?
2. What is the first thing to be done after posting the Journal?
3. What next?
4. What is the purpose of closing the Ledger?
* See also Notes 2 to 6, page 18. And directions for ruling, pp. 56 and 57.

STOCK ACCOUNT.

1866.					1866.				
Nov. 20	To Profit & Loss*	f.	3	20	Nov. 1	By Sundries 3000. / 20. / 2980.		1	3000
	" Balance	f.	3	2080					
				3000					3000
Dec. 31	To Balance	f.	3	28500	Dec. 30	By Bal. bro't down			2080
					14	" Sundries 27,980.		2	25000
					31	" Profit & Loss	f.	3	520
				28500					28500

1. What is posted to the Dr. side?	1. What I owe.
2. What to the Cr. side?	2. The amount of my capital.
3. When is the account closed?	3. After the Profit & Loss is closed.
4. How does it then close?	4. To or By Balance.
5. How do we mark the transfers?	5. F. or Folio.
6. Why are the balance entries red?	6. Because they begin the new account.

MERCHANDISE.

1866.					1866.				
Nov. 5	To Cash		1	600	Nov. 5	By Cash		1	460
14	" Bills Payable			200	25	" Sundries			630
	" Sundries 1700.			800	30	" Cash 1870. / 1700.			780
30	" Profit & Loss	f.	3	170			Gain 170.		
				1870					1870
Dec. 1	To Sundries		2	2500	Dec. 14	By Sundries		2	1500
21	" " 4000.			2100	31	" Wm. Hay 2200. / 5000.			700
31	" Profit & Loss	f.	3	600		" Balance 5200. / 4600.	f.	3	3000
				5200			Gain 600.		5200

1. What is posted to the Dr. side?	1. The cost and charges of purchases.
2. What to the Cr. side?	2. The sales made.
3. How does it close if all be sold?	3. To or By Profit & Loss.
4. How if part is unsold?	4. By Balance, and To or By Profit & Loss.
5. How do we find the $3000 balance?	5. Inventory. See p. 59.

BILLS RECEIVABLE.

1866.					1866.				
Nov. 1	To Stock 2000. / 1500. / 500.		1	2000	Nov. 10	By Cash		1	1500
					20	" Balance	fol.	3	500
				2000					2000
Dec. 30	To Bal. bro't down			500	Dec. 10	By Cash		2	500
14	" Mdse.		2	500	31	" Balance	fol.	3	3000
21	" Sundries 3000. / 500. / 3500.			2500					
				3500					3500

1. What does the Dr. side of this account show?	1. The notes received.
2. What does the Cr. side show?	2. Those passed away or lost.
3. How will it stand when all notes are passed away?	3. Self balanced.
4. How does it always close?	4. By Balance for the notes on hand.

* The rules for posting do not apply to the closing entries.

1866. Nov.						1866. Nov.					
	1	To Stock	1	1000			5	By Mdse.	1	600	
	5	" Mdse.	"	460			14	" "	"	200	
	10	" Sundries	"	1500			30	" Profit & Loss	"	150	
	25	" Mdse.	"	330				" " 1080.	"	130	
	30	" " 4100. 1080. 3080.	"	780				" Balance fol.	3	3080	
				4160						4160	
		To Bal. bro't down		3080		Dec.	1	By Mdse.	2	500	
Dec.	10	" Bills Receivable	2	500			21	" Bills Receivable	"	2426	25
	14	" Mdse.	"	1000				" Mdse.	"	2000	
		" Stock 14580. 7280. 7300.	"	10000			25	" Profit & Loss	"	50	
							31	" William Hay	"	2200	
								" Profit & Loss 7280.	"	102	75
								" **Balance** fol.	3	7300	
				14580						14580	

1. What does the Dr. side of this account show?
2. What does the Cr. side show?
3. What does the difference represent?
4. How does the account close?
5. How will it stand when all your money is paid away?
6. Why can the credit side never exceed the debtor?

1. The Dr. side shows all cash received.
2. The Cr. side shows all cash paid away.
3. The difference represents the balance in hand.
4. It always closes By Balance.
5. When all is paid away the account must be even.
6. Because we cannot pay away more than we receive.

(My Notes Paid.) **BILLS PAYABLE.** (My Notes passed away.)

1866. Nov.						1866. Nov.				
	30	To Balance fol.	3	300			14	By Mdse.	1	300
Dec.	31	To Balance fol.	3	300			30	By Bal. bro't down		300

1. What do the Dr. and Cr. sides of this acc't show?
2. What does the difference represent?
3. How does the account always close?

1. The Dr side is the amount taken up, the Cr. side the notes passed away.
2. The balance I still owe on my notes.
3. Always To Balance, never By Balance.

(My Acct. against him.) **WILLIAM HAY.** (His Acct. against me.)

1866. Nov.						1866. Nov.				
	25	To Mdse.	1	300			30	By Balance fol.	3	300
	30	To Bal. bro't down		300		Dec.	21	By Mdse.	2	100
Dec.	31	" Sundries 3200. 300. 3500.	2	2900			31	" Warden & Bell 300.	"	100
								" Balance fol.	3	3000
				3200						3200

1. What does the debit and credit side of this account show?
2. How does it close?

1. Explained in the parenthesis at the head.
2. All personal accounts close either To or By Balance.

WARDEN & BELL.

1866. Nov.						1866. Nov.				
	30	To Balance fol.	3	600			14	By Mdse.	1	600
Dec.	31	To Wm. Hay	2	100			30	By Bal. bro't down		600
		" Balance fol.	3	500						
				600						600

ROBERT MORRIS.

1866. Dec.						1866. Dec.				
	31	To Balance fol.	3	2000			1	By Mdse.	2	2000

Dr. (Its Value or Cost.) **HOUSE, 44 BROADWAY.** (What it brings me in.) **Cr**

1866.					1866.					
Dec.	14	To Stock	2	15000	Dec.	31	By Balance	fol.	3	15000

1. How does this account close if the property be on hand?
2. How if sold?

1. By Balance if you still own the property.
2. If sold close To or By Profit & Loss.

(Expenses and Losses.) **PROFIT & LOSS.** (Gains.)

1866.						1866.						
Nov.	30	To Cash		1	150	Nov.	10	By Cash		1	90	
		" "	250.	1	130		30	" Mdse.	360. fol.	1	170	
		Net Loss	20.					" Stock, net loss	fol.	1	20	
					280						280	
Dec.	25	To Cash		2	50	Dec.	21	By Bills Receivable		2	73	75
	31	" "	153.75	2	103	75	31	" Mdse.	672.75 153.75 fol.	1	600	
		" Stock for net gain, f.		1	520			Net Gain 520.				
					673	75					673	75

1. What do the Dr. and Cr. sides of this account show?
2. What accounts close into it?
3. When is it closed, and into what account does it close?
4. What does the difference between the sides represent?

1. The Dr. side shows all expenses and losses, and the Cr. side all gains.
2. All accounts exhibiting gain or loss are closed into this account.
3. This is the last account closed but two. It always closes into Stock, never into Balance.
4. The difference represents the net gain or loss.

BALANCE
(My Effects and Debts due me.)

ACCOUNT.
(What my concern owes.)

1866.						1866.					
Nov.	30	To Bills Receivable f.	1	500	Nov.	30	By Bills Payable	fol.	2	300	
		" Cash	2	3080			" Warden & Bell	300.		600	
		" Wm. Hay	2980. 900.	300			" Stock for net capital		1	2980	
		Net capital 2080.		3880						3880	
Dec.	31	To Mdse.	fol.	1	2000	Dec.	31	By Bills Payable	fol.	2	500
		" Bills Receivable "		3000			" Warden & Bell		500	
		" Cash	2	7300			" R. Morris	2000.	2000	
		" Wm. Hay	31300. 2500.	3000			" Stock for net capital		1	28500
		" House	3	15000						
		Net cap. 28500.		31300					31300	

1. What is transferred to the Dr. side?
2. What to the Cr. side?
3. What does the difference represent?
4. How does the account close?
5. Is Stock or Balance first closed?

1. All my effects.
2. All amounts that I owe.
3. Net capital or net insolvency.
4. By Stock for net capital, or To Stock if I am insolvent.
5. Usually the Stock first.

Proof Sheet Nov. 30, 1866. Drs.   Crs.   Proof Sheet **Dec. 31, 1866.** Drs.   Crs.

Stock	f.	1				Stock	f.	1			
Mdse.						Mdse.					
Bills Receivable						Bills Receivable					
Cash		2				Cash		2			
Bills Payable						Bills Payable					
Wm. Hay						Wm. Hay					
Warden & Bell						Warden & Bell					
Profit & Loss		3				R. Morris					
						House in Broadway		3			
						Profit & Loss					

NOTE.—These proof sheets or trial balances are taken off for the purpose of ascertaining if both sides of the Ledger are alike in amount. If this sheet comes out correct, your Ledger will be sure to balance; but if there should be a difference between its sides, the Ledger will certainly not balance until the errors are sought out and rectified.

TEACHER'S EXAMINATION.—After closing the first of the preceding sets, the pupil should be able to answer his teacher the following questions. If he cannot readily do so, he should refer again to the instructions under the accounts. If he does not wish to cheat himself out of the instruction that he desires to obtain, he should by no means consult the key,—that being intended for teachers only, those who teach themselves included.

Q. 1.—What was your **net capital at the time of closing, and which of** the accounts show it?

2.—What was your net gain **or loss, and which of** the accounts show it?

3.—What was the whole **amount of your gain,** and what was the whole amount of your loss.

4.—What did you gain or lose on your Merchandise account?

5.—What was the amount of Merchandise purchased?

6.—What was the amount of your sales?

7.—What amount of Merchandise was there on hand, or was there any?

8.—What amount of Cash on hand?

9.—What amount of Bills Receivable on hand?

10.—What do you owe on your Notes?

11.—What is the whole amount of your debts, and what account shows it?

12.—What is the whole amount of property you now possess, and what account shows it?

13.—What amount of property did you possess at the time of opening the books, and what account shows it?

14.—What were your average daily sales for the month of November, the time your books were open, allowing there were twenty-six business days in it?*

15.—What was the gain per cent. on your total sales?†

The pupil should, when he balances his Ledger the second time, answer the same questions upon the balance of each account.

---

* Found thus—Total sales per Merchandise, Crs. is $1870 ÷ 26 = 71¾ average daily sales.

† Found thus—The cost per Dr. side $1700 : $100 :: $170 (gain) : 10, the gain per cent. Or such operations may be shortened by making a common fraction, with the GAIN or LOSS for a numerator, and the cost for a denominator. Change this fraction into a decimal, carrying it to two places, and it is always the GAIN or LOSS per cent.

NOTE.—In the second balance of our Merchandise account, part of the goods remain unsold. The difference between the cost of the whole (per Dr. side) and the amount on hand per inventory, is THE COST OF THE PART SOLD, with which proceed to find the gain per cent. as above. But observe, the result of this operation will only be correct when the inventory of goods on hand is taken at cost and charges.—See Note 3, p. 61.

EXEMPLIFYING THE TRANSFER OF BUSINESS

FROM THE PRECEDING TO THE PRESENT SET.

THIS SET EMBRACES ALL THE MOST APPROVED FORMS OF

AUXILIARIES.

CONNECTED AS SUCH WITH THE PRINCIPAL BOOKS.

Also, concise and comprehensive rules for Journalizing, practically illustrated with ORAL EXERCISES.

The written exercises embrace—

Illustrations of Buying and Selling Merchandise on private Account and on Account of others.

Buying and selling the same on joint Account.

Importing and Exporting on private Account, on Account of others, and on Account of ourselves and others in Company.

Receiving and forwarding Merchandise.

The management and settlement of Executors' Accounts.

Buying, Selling, Remitting, Collecting, Discounting, Accepting, and Paying Bills of Exchange.

SHIP OWNERS' ACCOUNTS.

As sole owner, as part owner, and as agent for the owners, exemplifying a dividend and settlement of their Accounts, the adjustment and settlement of Marine Losses, and of Loss by Fire.

We have so studiously avoided lengthening the process of instruction by any unnecessary entries, that probably no two entries can be found in the set which do not illustrate a different application of the principles of the science. On the other hand, the utmost care has been taken to carry instruction into every department of the most extensive and diversified commerce, to omit no information necessary for forming the most accomplished Accountant. The whole is condensed into about twelve pages of Day Book and Journal, accompanied with such mental exercises as, if attended to, will leave the learner no means of getting through the written exercises without mastering the subject.

DIRECTIONS TO TEACHERS.

It has been before stated that the preceding set is only designed as an introduction for those altogether uninitiated. Those who understand the disposition of the debits and credits in the Ledger, will, after a perusal of the initiatory set, commence with the study of the following RULES AND ORAL EXERCISES. They afterwards study the definitions and answer the interrogatories upon the Auxiliaries. In some cases it may be necessary to write the Cash Book and Bill Books, but most of learners will find no difficulty in applying them without this trouble. The process of teaching those who have been through the introductory set and those who commence here, is hereafter in all respects the same.

RULES FOR JOURNALIZING, WITH ORAL EXERCISES.
LESSON I.

Note.—The pupil should lay a sheet of paper over the answers while he reads the questions to himself.

Give the general rule for debits and credits.

Repeat the general rule for opening books.

EXAMPLES.

QUES. 1. If you begin business with a capital of $7000 cash, what will be your Journal entry?

2. If you have cash $7000, merchandise $3000, W. Hay owes you $5000, and you own the brig Troy worth $5000?

3. Suppose you owe at this time on your notes and bonds $2000, to R. Morris on acct. $3000.

4. State more particularly what is meant by the term "Sundries to Stock."

5. Explain the full meaning of the expression "Stock to Sundries," in your 3d answer.

Repeat the rule for debiting persons.

EXAMPLES.

6. If W Hay buys $600 worth of mdse. of you on Book acct.?

7. If you pay R. Morris $1000 cash which is at his credit on your Books?

8. If Morris make an abatement of $100 from the above acct. and pay him $900 in full for balance?

Repeat the rule for crediting personal accounts.

EXAMPLES.

9. Suppose W. Hay pays you the above $600 in cash?

10. If he fail and you receive $300 cash and lose the balance?

RULE I.—The debits and credits arising out of every transaction must be equal in amount.

RULE II.—The Stock account represents myself, and must therefore be debited for what I now owe and credited for what I now possess.

ANS. 1. Cash, Dr. $7000
    To Stock, . . . $7000

2. Sundries to Stock, . . . 20000
    Cash, ... 7000
    Mdse. 3000
    W Hay, ... 5000
    Brig Troy, . . . 5000

3. Stock to Sundries, . . . 5000
    To Bills Payable, . . 2000
    R. Morris, . . 3000

4. It may be stated more fully thus: Several accts. are Dr. to the Stock acct. which is credited for $20000
The Cash acct. is Dr. for . . $7000
And the mdse. acct. is debtor for 3000
And Wm. Hay's acct. debtor for 5000
And the Brig Troy's account is debtor for 5000

5. To express it in full we might say: The Stock account is debtor to several accts. for $5000, viz., it is Dr. to the Bills Payable account, which is credited for . . . $2000
And it is Dr. to R. Morris's account, which is credited for . . 3000*

RULE III.—When he gets into my debt he is Dr. for the amount. When I get out of his debt he is Dr. for what I pay or cease to owe him.

ANS. 6. Wm. Hay, Dr. . . . $600
    To mdse. sold him on acct. . $600

7. R. Morris, Dr. . . 1000
    To Cash paid him in full, . 1000

8. R. Morris to Sundries, to close . 1000
    To Profit & Loss, . . 100
    " Cash paid him in full, . 900
Here we only pay Morris $900, but we debit him for $1000—what we cease to owe him.

RULE IV. When I get into his debt he is Cr. for the amount. When he gets out of my debt he is Cr. for what he pays or ceases to owe me.

ANS. 9. Cash, Dr. $600
    To Wm. Hay in full, . . 600

10. Sundries to Wm. Hay, to close acct 600
Profit & Loss for abatement, . 300
Cash received in full, . . 300
Here you have only received $300, but the rule requires you to credit him for $600—the amount he ceases to owe you.

---

* While this and the preceding answer will give the learner a distinct conception of the meaning of all similar Journal expressions, these expositions at the same time show how much accountants have abbreviated common language without obscuring their meaning; for while the rules are observed no language is less liable to be misunderstood than that used by accountants

SET II.—DOUBLE ENTRY RULES.

Quest. 11. If Hay balance his Book account by giving you his note for $600?

12. If he afterwards fail and you lose the am't of the note? Repeat the general rule for receiving and delivering property.

EXAMPLES.

13. If you sell merchandise for cash $500?

14. If you sell it for the purchaser's note?

15. If you pay your own note for $1000, half in cash and half in merchandise?

16. If you buy merchandise for cash $100?

17. If you give your note for the same purchase?

18. If you buy $400 worth of merchandise and pay the amount in other merchandise from store?

Give a more particular rule for debiting property accounts.

EXAMPLES.

19. If you buy the brig Tribune for $12,000 and pay $6000 in cash, and give a Bottomry bond on the vessel for the balance?

20. Suppose this vessel becomes yours by the legacy of a deceased friend?

21. If you pay cash $1000 for repairing her?

Give the rule stating when property accounts are always credited.

EXAMPLES.

22. If you receive $1000 cash for freight of Brig Tribune?

23. If your agents Taylor & Co. advise you that they have received $1500 cash for freight to New Orleans?

24. If you sell the Brig Tribune for $16,000 and receive in payment a dwelling-house in 2d street and a Bill of Exchange on London for $6000?

25. If you lose the Brig Tribune by fire or shipwreck before she is insured?

26. If you present $500 cash to a friend?

Ans. 11. Bills Receivable **Dr.** . . 600
  To Wm. Hay for his note to close acct. 600

12. Profit and Loss Dr. . . 600
  To Bills Receivable, . . . 600

Rule V. The thing received Dr. to the **thing delivered.**

13. Cash Dr. . 500
  To Merchandise, . 500

14. Bills Receivable Dr. · 500
  To Merchandise, . 500

15. Bills Payable to Sundries, . 1000
  To Cash for money paid, . . 500
  " Merchandise for sale, . . 500

16. Merchandise Dr. . . 100
  To Cash, . . 100

17. Merchandise Dr. . . 100
  To Bills Payable, . . 100

18. Merchandise Dr . 400
  To Merchandise, . 400

Some contend that any entry of such transactions is unnecessary—that it is like giving change for a $50 bank note. But if such **transactions** are not recorded your merchandise account will not show the amount of your purchases nor the amount of your sales.

Rule VI. When property becomes mine it is Dr. for its cost or value. When it costs me any thing afterwards it is Dr. for that cost.

19. Brig Tribune to Sundries, . 12,000
  To Cash, ... 6000
  " Bills Payable, . . . 6000

20. Brig Tribune Dr. . . . 12,000
  To Stock, ... 12,000

Here the property is Dr. for its value although it costs you nothing.

21. Brig Tribune **Dr.** . 1000
  To Cash, . . 1000

Rule VII. When it brings me in any thing it is Cr. for the amount. When it ceases to be mine it is Cr. for its value or what I receive for it.

22. Cash **Dr.** . . . 1000
  To Brig Tribune for Freight, . 1000

23. J. Taylor & Co. Dr. . . 1500
  To Brig Tribune, for freight collected, 1500

24. Sundries to Brig Tribune, . 16,000
  House in 2d street, . . 10,000
  Bills Receivable, . 6,000

25. Profit and Loss **Dr.** . . . 10,500
  To Brig Tribune, to close account, 10,500

26. Profit and Loss **Dr.** . . 500
  To Cash, . . . 500

Thus, you perceive, when property ceases to be yours, either by sale, loss, or giving away, it is to be credited

39

RULES FOR JOURNALIZING, WITH ORAL EXERCISES.

LESSON II.

Repeat the Rule for debiting and crediting Profit and Loss accounts.

EXAMPLES.

QUES. 1. If you lose your purse with $100 cash in it?

2. If you find $500 cash and cannot find the owner?

3. If you pay cash for a new suit of clothes $50 and $100 for new house furniture.

4. If you lose $1000 worth of mdse. by fire, uninsured?

Repeat the Rule respecting Bills of Exchange, Drafts, Orders, &c.

5. What is a Bill Receivable?

6. What is a Bill Payable?

7. If you draw on R. Morris for $100 and sell the bill for cash at par?

8. If you sell at 5 per cent. premium?

9. If you sell at 5 per cent. discount?

10. What will be Morris's entry when he accepts this bill?

11. If Morris draw on you at sight in favor of S. King, for $1000, and you pay the bill in cash?

12. If he draw at 60 days' sight in favor of Wm. Hay, and you accept?

13. Afterwards you take up this acceptance with cash?

14. If Wm. Hay draw an order on you for $50 in favor of J. Toole, which you pay in mdse. from store?

15. If you owe James Day $20 and give him an order on Hay payable in mdse. for $20?

16. If you buy a Bill of Exchange for $1000 for cash at par?

17. If you buy at 5 per cent. premium?

18. If you buy at 5 per cent. discount?

RULE VIII. Profit and Loss accounts are always debited when I lose and credited when I gain.

ANS. 1. Profit and Loss, Dr. . . . $100
To Cash, ... $100

2. Cash, Dr. 500
To Profit and Loss, . . . 500

3. Sundries to Cash, ... 150
Profit and Loss or Expense acc't for the clothes, ... 50
House furniture for the articles bo't 100

4. Profit and Loss, Dr. . . . 1000
To Merchandise, . . . 1000*

RULE IX. Credit a person always when you draw on him on your own account, and debit him when he draws on you on his account.*

5. Any obligation on paper which I hold against others.

6. The same kind of obligations which I have given to others, and which they are holding against me.

7. Cash, Dr. 100
To R. Morris, ... 100

8. Cash to Sundries, . . . 105
To R. Morris for the bill, . . 100
Profit and Loss or Exchange acc't. for the premium, ... 5

9. Sundries to R. Morris, . . 100
Cash for the net proceeds, . . 95
Profit and Loss or Exchange for Discount, ... 5

10. Duff, Dr. 100
To Bills Payable, . . . 100

11. R. Morris, Dr. . . . 1000
To Cash, ... 1000

12. R. Morris, Dr. . . . 1000
To Bills Payable, . . . 1000

13. Bills Payable, Dr. . . . 1000
To Cash, ... 1000

14. W. Hay, Dr. 50
To Merchandise, . . . 50

15. James Day, Dr. . . . 20
To William Hay, ... 20

16. Bills Receivable, Dr. . . 1000
To Cash, ... 1000

17. Sundries to Cash, . . . 1050
Bills Receivable for the Bill, . 1000
Profit and Loss or Exchange for the Premium, ... 50

18. Bills Receivable to Sundries, . 1000
To Cash for money paid, . . 950
Profit and Loss for Discount, . 50

---

* Let the learner's mind be thoroughly impressed with the meaning of this rule and the two following questions; otherwise it will take him a long time to divest himself of the idea that every draft or bill he draws upon his correspondent must appear on one or the other of the Bill Accounts.

DOUBLE ENTRY RULES.

Quest. 19. If you sell this bill at 10 per ct. premium for cash?
20. If you sell it at 10 per ct. discount?
Give the rule for keeping the accounts of consignments received.
21. What do you do with the Invoice of the property?

EXAMPLES.

22. If you receive $1000 worth of goods from Morris for sale on his acct. You give bonds for $500 duties and pay frt., &c. in cash, $100?
23. If you sell $100 worth of these goods for cash?
24. If Morris draw on you at sight for $300 and you pay the draft, $100 in his own goods, $100 worth of your own goods, and $100 in cash?
25. How is the net proceeds found on any account sales?
26. Suppose Morris's goods all sold for $2000. You have paid charges $700, your commission is $100, leaving the net proceeds $1200. How do you close the sales?
27. Where should this entry be first made?
28. Why not credit Morris for the amount of the Invoice of the above consignment?
29. If he draw on you for $500 on acct. of the sales?
Give the rule for keeping acct. of property you consign to others.

EXAMPLES.

30. If you ship by the Herald and consign to R. Morris, London, for sale on your own acct. Mdse. 4000, pay charges in cash, $400, give your note for insurance, 600: = $5000?
31. If you draw on Morris for $500 on % of this consignm't?
32. If he return you acct. sales $6000, with a remittance in specie in full for same?
33. If he send you the acct. sales without the remittance?
34. If you receive acct. sales, $6000, and before making an entry of the returns draw on him and sell the bill for cash at 8 per ct. premium?

Ans. 19. Cash to Sundries . . 1100
To Bills Receivable . . 1000
" Profit & Loss, for premium . 100
20. Sundries to Bills Receivable . . 1000
Cash for net proceeds . . . 900
Profit & Loss for the 10 per ct. Discount 100

Rule X.—Debit the owner's Sales for all charges incurred, and credit the same account for what the property sells for.

21. I enter a copy of it on the Invoice Book, but make no other entry of it.
22. R. Morris's Sales to Sundries . . 600
To Bills Payable for the bonds . 500
" Cash paid for freight, &c. . 100
23. Cash, Dr. 100
To Morris's Sales . . 100
24. R. Morris, Dr. to Sundries . . 300
To Morris's Sales . . 100
" Merchandise . . . 100
" Cash 100
25. By deducting all charges, including my commission, from total sales.
26. R. Morris, Sales to Sundries to close acct. 1300
To Commission 100
" R. Morris, for net proceeds . 1200
27. The particulars of such entries must always appear upon the Day Book.
28. Because I do not get in debt to him for any thing but the net proceeds of what the goods sell for.
29. I debit his private account for all advances made on account of the consignment, and never the consignment account.

Rule XI.—Debit Shipment or Adventure to such a place for the cost and charges of the investment, and credit the same account for what it brings me in.

30. Shipment to London to Sundries . 5000
To Mdse. 4000
" Cash 400
" Bills Payable . . 600
31. I credit his private account for it—not the shipment to London.

32. Cash, Dr. 6000
To Shipment to London . . 6000
33. R. Morris, Dr. 6000
To Shipment to London . . 6000
34. Cash, Dr. 6480
To Shipment to London . . 6480

41

SET II.—DOUBLE ENTRY BOOK-KEEPING.

RULES FOR JOURNALIZING, WITH ORAL EXERCISES.

LESSON III.—ON JOINT ACCOUNTS.

JOINT ACCOUNTS [1] or special partnerships imply those operations in which several individuals or commercial houses unite in the purchase and sale of a particular article on speculation. Their joint interest is confined solely to these transactions, and the parties give themselves no joint title, neither do they become publicly known as a firm. Their sales, and sometimes their purchases, are effected by a manager, who generally keeps the account of the same in his own private books; and the partnership terminates for the time with the sale of the joint property. The learner must understand that although we cannot avoid calling these connexions partnerships, yet they differ essentially from GENERAL PARTNERSHIPS, [2] where the parties are legally and publicly known under a firm or title, as Hay, Wood & Co., and who contribute a certain capital for the purpose of carrying on a general business for a specified period.

The manager of the joint sales keeps the account [3] in his own private books under the title of Sales in Co. [4] If he have more than one in hand, he distinguishes them by prefixing to the title numbers, as, 1st Co., 2d Co., &c. [5] The manager debits his joint account FOR HIS OWN SHARE ONLY of the first cost, and for all charges incurred while in his hands, and [6] credits the same account for the total sales, for the other partners' shares in the property as well as his own.*

The following remarks will be useful in enabling the student to comprehend the transactions to which this rule is to be applied. The manner of opening the accounts by the manager as well as the silent partners, will vary according to the manner of making up the joint stock put in speculation. When the manager or any of the partners purchases or furnishes property to the concern, [7] each of the other partners must be immediately furnished with a copy of the invoice; and when the sales are completed, [8] each one must have a copy of the account sales. The joint stock is generally made up in one or the other of these three ways.

1. WHEN EACH PARTNER ADVANCES HIS OWN SHARE—Each silent partner keeps his account under the title of [9] "ADVENTURE IN Co.," debiting it for its cost, and crediting it for what it brings him in, precisely as he would a private adventure or consignment.

The manager makes his [10] SALES IN Co. Dr. for his own share only, and receives the other partners' shares as he would consignments..

2. IF THE MANAGER PURCHASES OR FINDS THE WHOLE STOCK— [11] As before he debits "Sales in Co." for his own share, and he debits each of the silent partners for their share; they at the same time crediting him and debiting their "Adventures in Co."

3. IF THE MANAGER'S SHARE BE PAID OR PUT IN BY ONE OR MORE OF THE SILENT PARTNERS—The manager's debit entry will be as before, [12] and he credits him or them, to whom he becomes indebted for his share, they at the same time debiting him for the same amount. Their own "Adventures in Co.," they debit as before.

---

1. What are Joint Accounts or special partnerships? 2. What are general partnerships? 3. Where does the manager of the joint sales keep the account? 4. How does he distinguish them if he have several? 5. For what does the manager debit his joint account? 6. What does he credit it for? 7. What is to be done when property is bought on joint account? 8. What is the manager's duty when the sales are completed? 9. Under what title do the silent partners keep their accounts? 10. What title does the manager use? 11. When the manager finds the whole joint stock, what accounts does he debit for it? 12. If the manager's share be paid in by the other partners, whom does he credit for it?

* The author of the "National System of Book-keeping," a recent publication, and in some respects an ingenious work, takes a different view of this matter. By his rule the manager debits the joint account for the whole stock. He adduces some ingenious arguments in favor of his theory, but he appears to overlook the fact that his reasoning only applies where the transactions are entered in books belonging to the joint business, and not when entered in the private books of the manager. Here he does not seem to perceive that his theory will often inevitably compel the Book-keeper to debit his joint account for what the silent partners are legally responsible to him, and to credit the same parties for what he is NOT responsible to them. This is certainly, at all times and under all circumstances, an awkward and dangerous principle to admit in accounts. We have laid down a rule that can never lead the Book-keeper into such a dilemma. By its provisions a person is always held responsible in his private account from the time that that responsibility commences. And the fact of his having property in our hands for sale on his account, gives no pretext for a deviation from the rule—not even though his responsibility or indebtedness be created by advances made to him expressly on account of the property so placed in our hands for sale.—See Question 29, p. 41.

DOUBLE ENTRY RULES.

Repeat the rule for conducting a joint account as manager of the sales

EXAMPLES.

QUEST. 1. How does the silent partner keep his account?
2. If you purchase on your note for your joint acct. with Wm. Hay, $1000 worth of Mdse.?
3. Why not debit sales in company for the whole amount?
4. What would be your entry, supposing Hay gave you his note for the $500 before you made the above entry?
5. What would be Hay's entry in Answer 2?
6. If he gave Duff his note, as in Answer 4?
7. What will be your entry where Hay puts $2000 worth of goods in your store for sale on joint acct.?
8. Why not credit Hay for the whole $2000?
9. What will be Hay's entry in Answer 7, if he purchase the goods on his note?
10. If you sell $2000 worth of the above goods, receiving in payment cash $1000, and the buyer's note for $1000?
11. If you barter the remainder for goods on your own acct.?
12. The property being all sold for $3000, and the whole first cost $2000, and your 5 per ct. commission being $150, what entry will close sales?
13. Explain how you find the amts. composing this entry?
14. If you receive from R. Morris, of London, $6000 worth of Mdse. for sale on acct. of himself, J. Taylor & Co., of New Orleans, and yourself, upon which you pay cash for duties $1000?

RULE XII.—Debit Sales in Co. for my own share only of the first cost and for the whole charges incurred while in my possession, and credit the same account for the total sales.

RULE XIII.—Debit Adventure in Co. for its cost, and credit for what it brings him in.

ANS. 2. Sundries to Bills Payable . $1000
    1st Co. Sales, for my half   500
    W. Hay, for his half . . 500
3. Because Hay becomes legally responsible to me from this date for $500, and must, by Rule III., be made Dr. for the amount. It becomes his property by virtue of our agreement, is at his risk, and if lost by fire or perish by any other means, not in consequence of my carelessness, he will have to pay me this $500.
4. Sundries to Bills Payable . . . 1000
    1st Co. Sales, for my half. . 500
    Bills Receivable, for Hay's Note for
      his half 500
5. 1st Co. Adventure, Dr. . . . 500
    To Duff 500
6. 1st Co. Adventure, Dr. . . . 500
    To Bills Payable 500
7. 1st Co. Sales, Dr. . . . 1000
    To Wm. Hay . . . 1000
8. Because I do not get in debt to him for any more than my own half. He is still the owner of one-half the amount, and if the property never sells I shall never be accountable to him for any thing but my own share.
9. Sundries to Bills Payable . . 2000
    1st Co. Adventure, for his own share 1000
    Duff,   for his share . 1000
10. Sundries to 1st Co. Sales . . 2000
    Cash 1000
    Bills Receivable . . . 1000
11. Merchandise, Dr. . . . 1000
    To 1st Co. Sales . . 1000
12. 1st Co. Sales to Sundries, to close acct. 2000
    To Commission . . . 150
    " W. Hay, for his half N. P. . 1425
    " Profit & Loss, for my half gain . 425
13. The $2000 debit is the difference between the debit and credit sides of the account on the Ledger after the sales are completed: from the Cr. side we have the total sales $3000 — 150 charges = $2850 net proceeds, and $2850 ÷ 2 = $1425, each share; and $1425 — $1000 (my half first cost) = $425, my half net gain.*
14. 2d Co. Sales to Sundries . . 3000
    To R. Morris, for my ⅓ Invoice 2000
    " Cash paid duties . . 1000

NOTE.—This being a new speculation, we give it a new title: 2d Co.
* No pupil can expect to understand the settlement and closing of these accounts without repeated study. He must analyze them and find out the results for himself.

RULES AND ORAL EXERCISES.

QUEST. 15. What entry will Taylor & Co., New Orleans, make when they receive a copy of the Invoice?

16. What entry will they make when they receive your acct. sales without remittance, their ½ being $3300?

17. What will be Morris's entry when he receives your copy of the sales, supposing you send with it a remittance in specie for the net proceeds?

18. Suppose William Hay sends you $6000 worth of Mdse. for sale on joint acct., and you make up the joint property to $10000 by adding $4000 worth of tea, what will your entry be as manager, each partner's share being $5000?

19. What will be Hay's entry in this case?

20. Supposing the whole of the above speculation only produce $5000, leaving the acct. in your Ledger even when the sales are completed, what entry will you make to settle the transaction with Hay?

21. Suppose the goods had produced $8000, and your charge for commission is 5 per ct., how would the acct. close?

22. Explain how you find the amounts composing this entry?

23. Supposing the whole speculation of $10000 was sold for $4000,—the first cost and your commission being the same as before,—how will you close the account?

24. Explain how the amounts composing this entry are found?

ANS. 15. Shipment from London to New York in Co., Dr.. . . . 2000
  To R. Morris for their ⅓ Invoice   2000

16. Duff, Dr. 3300
  To shipment from London to New York in Co. . . . 3300

17. Cash, Dr. 3300
  To Shipment to New York in Co. 3300

18. 1st Co. Sales, Dr. to Sundries, my half first cost . . . 5000
  To Mdse. 4000
  " Wm. Hay for amt. paid in on my acct. . . . 1000
                                       6000

19. Sundries to Mdse. . . . 6000
  1st Co. Adventure, for his half   5000
  Duff, for amt. paid in for him .   1000

20. One-half of what the goods have produced belongs to Hay, and must be credited or paid to him, which only leaves me $2500 for what cost me $5000, I have therefore lost $2500, just the amt. I owe Hay, therefore, Profit & Loss Dr. for my loss 2500
  To W. Hay, for his half N. P. . 2500

21. Sundries to Sundries, $4200.
  1st Co. Sales, for bal. of acct. . . 3000
  Profit & Loss, for my half loss . . 1200
  To W. Hay, for his half N. P. . 3800
  " Commission, for my commission   400

22. The $3000 bal. of acct. is the difference between the two sides of the acct. upon the Ledger after all the sales are posted. The total sales are 8000 — 400 charges = 7600 ÷ 2 = $3800, each share, and my half first cost 5000 — 3800 = 1200, my loss.

23. Profit & Loss to Sundries to close 1st Co. Sales 3100
  To W. Hay, for his half N. P. . 1900
  " 1st Co. Sales, for bal. of acct. on the Ledger . . . 1000
  " Commission, for my 5 per cent. in total sales . . . 200

24. They are found as before by deducting the charges from the total sales (Rule 12); then the difference between my half net proceeds and my half first cost is gain or loss.

The learner should now analyze a number of similar entries and find the correct amounts to form the Journal entry, which, when correct, will always close the account on the Ledger

Learners can never readily understand the closing entry of either joint accounts or consignments without having before them the position of the account upon the Ledger. The closing entry must always exactly fill up the lesser side of the account there.—See Note 1, Morris's Sales, p. 107, and Notes 5 to 12, p. 220

REMARKS ON NOTES AND BILLS AND THE BILL BOOK.

THE heading of these books so perfectly explains their nature, use and manner of entering Bills Received and passed away, that any farther explanation seems unnecessary. Learners, however, often experience difficulty in determining the precise day upon which notes and acceptances will fall due. We shall endeavor, in the following directions, to make the matter understood.

When the term of a Note is expressed in days, the day of date and the day of maturity are always counted as one, or, in other words, [1]the day after drawing or accepting is the first day counted in the time to run. Thus, a bill drawn or accepted on May 1st, at 20 days, will fall due May 24th—including three days' grace. A bill drawn or accepted on the 29th of April, at 60 days, has to run—

In April .	.	.	1 day.
In May	.	.	31 "
In June	.	.	30 "
In July	.	.	1 "
			63 days. [2]Due, July 1st.

Again, a Bill drawn or accepted 30th April, at 90 days, has to run—

In May .	. . .	.	31 days.
In June	. .	.	30 "
In July .	. ,	.	31 "
In August .		.	1 "
			93 days. [2]Due, Aug. 1st.

It will be observed in the last example that no time is allowed for April, although the date is on the last day of that month; as, according to the rule laid down above, the day following the date is the first day counted in the time to run.

When the last day of grace falls upon Sunday, the note must be paid the preceding Saturday. Accountants do not, however, generally notice this in recording their bills upon their Books.

When the term of a note or bill is expressed in months, [3]CALENDAR MONTHS are always understood, and it becomes due in the last month of its term, upon the day corresponding with its date, to which are added the days of grace. It is contrary to the established usage of Merchants and Bankers to extend the time of payment for any deficiency in the length of the months of which the term of the note is made up. For instance, a note drawn on the 31st March, at three months, and another note drawn on the 30th March, also at three months, will [4]both fall due on the same day—viz. 3d July. [5]The custom of merchants not permitting the term of the note to extend beyond the end of June, except for the days of grace.

The following statements will disclose to persons operating extensively in notes and acceptances the importance of attending to this matter when drawing or accepting. It will be seen that bills of different dates running the same time, will sometimes fall due the same day, and thus occasion unexpected inconvenience.

TEACHER'S EXAMINATION.—1. Give the rule for computing the time when notes and bills fall due.
2. A note dated 29th April having 60 days to run, what day will it be due?
3. When the term of a note is expressed in months, what kind of months is understood?
4. If one note be dated the 30th and another 31st March, at 3 mos., upon what day will they fall due.
5. Why do they both fall due on the same day?

It will also appear that by obtaining one day's advance in the date, two, three, and sometimes four days are gained in the time of payment. For example, a note or bill drawn or accepted on the 28th February, at six months, is due August 31st; but if dated on the 1st March, only one day later, it would not be due until the 4th September, thus extending the term of payment four days for one day's difference in the date; and this difference in the date is frequently a matter of little consequence to the payee of the bill.

In all our computations in reference to Notes and Bills, three days' grace are in every instance included.

In the following instances, one day's advance in the date will give the day of payment three and four days later.[1] Notes drawn or Bills accepted February 28th,*

At	1 month,	are due	Mar.	31,	but if	dated 1st March	are not due till	April 4.
At	2 months,	"	May	1,	"	"	"	May 4.
At	3	"	"	May	31,	"	"	"	June 4.
At	4	"	"	July	1,	"	"	"	July 4.
At	5	"	"	July	31,	"	"	"	Aug. 4.
At	6	"	"	Aug.	31,	"	"	"	Sept. 4.
At	7	"	"	Oct.	1,	"	"	"	Oct. 4.
At	8	"	"	Oct.	31,	"	"	"	Nov. 4.
At	9	"	"	Dec.	1,	"	"	"	Dec. 4.
At	10	"	"	Dec.	31,	"	"	"	Jan'y 4.
At	11	"	"	Jan'y	31,	"	"	"	Feb. 4.

One day's advance in the date will in the following cases give *two additional days in the time of payment. Notes drawn or bills accepted April 30th,

At	1 month,	are due	June	2,	but if	dated 1st May	will not become due till	June 4.
At	3 months,	"	Aug.	2,	"	"	"	Aug. 4.
At	4	"	"	Sept.	2,	"	"	"	Sept. 4.
At	6	"	"	Nov.	2,	"	"	"	Nov. 4.
At	8	"	"	Jan'y	2,	"	"	"	Jan'y 4.
At	9	"	"	Feb.	2,	"	"	"	Feb. 4.
At	11	"	"	April	2,	"	"	"	April 4.

The above illustrations will serve to disclose the principle upon which we desire to fix the attention of our students and all commercial persons having any thing to do with bills. An error of one day in recording the maturity of a note or acceptance may cause the holder to lose his remedy against the endorsers; and perhaps cause him to lose the note altogether.

---

1. Notes drawn or Bills accepted on the last day of February, with a running time, in months, will advance the day of payment three and four days, by dating forward one day.
2. Notes drawn or Bills accepted on the last day of a thirty-day month, with a running time in months, expiring in a thirty-one day month, will advance the day of payment two days, by dating forward one day.
* Our calculations are all made for ordinary years. When February intervenes, leap-year makes a day's difference.

We have next to point out the other inconsistency we have alluded to, viz. those instances in which several notes or acceptances, dated or accepted on different days and having the same time to run, in months, will fall due upon the same day.

Suppose you give four notes dated—

August 28, at 6 months,
August 29, at 6 months,
August 30, at 6 months,
August 31, at 6 months.

You will find these notes, although of different dates and all of the same running time, will become due on the same day.[1]

Again, suppose you give two notes dated—

March 30, at 3 months,
March 31, at 3 months.

Both these notes will be presented to you for payment on the same day.[2]

The author trusts that the importance of the subject will be a sufficient apology for the length of this article. With the exception of Bankers, the greater part of business men have no definite principle for determining the precise day upon which notes and bills will, in some cases, become due.

---

1. Notes drawn or Bills accepted on the last three days of thirty-day months, and the last four days of thirty-one day months, with a running time, in months, expiring in February, will all become due on the same day.
2. Notes drawn or Bills accepted on the last two days of thirty-one day months, with a running time, in months, expiring in a thirty-day month, will both fall due on the same day.

47

BILLS

DATE.	NO.	DRAWER'S NAME.	ON WHOM OR IN WHOSE FAVOR DRAWN.	ON WHAT ACCOUNT.	TIME TO RUN
1866					
Dec. 14	1	James Day,	Favor of Myself,	Merchandise,	3 months.
21	2	C. Banks,	"	Cash Lent,	1 month.
1867.	3	C. Murray,	"	Do.	9 months.
Jan. 10	4	Thomas Edwards,	"	Merchandise,	30 days.
19	5	James Carter,	"	On account,	20 days.
30	6	William Hay,	"	Balance of account,	60 days.
31	7	W. Morris,	"	My note,	30 days.
	8	J. Warden,	"	Do.,	30 days.
Feb. 9	9	William Park,	Warden & Bell,	Morris's sales,	4 months.
12	10	James Carter,	William Hay,	An old note,	1 month.
25	11	J. Bowline,	Myself,	Cash Lent,	Bottomry.
	12	Baker & Fox,	On R. Morris,	Cash,	60 days' s'gt
28	13	Warden & Bell,	Myself,	My Bill on London,	1 month.
Mar. 12	14	J. Taylor & Co.,	Barclay, Hope,	R. Morris's sales,	60 days' s'gt
	15	W. Wallace,	Favor of Myself,	Estate of A. Lenox,	2 months.
	16	Joel Post,	"	" "	3 months.
17	17	James Day,	"	Renewing an old note,	60 days.
20	18	H. Parnell,	"	Estate of A. Lenox,	60 days.
April 6	19	James Walker,	Warden & Bell,	Money Lent,	6 months.
May 13	20	Warden & Bell,	Bill on Landis,	2d Co. Sales,	30 days' s'gt
18	21	Austin & Co.,	Favor of Myself,	Do.	60 days.
	22	W. Wallace,	"	An old note for A. Lenox,	3 months.
June 18	23	Joel Post,	Bill on Baring,	For Cash, &c.,	60 days' s'gt
25	24	Geo. Barron,	My favor,	Refined Sugars,	30 days.
26	*	William Hay,	"	Hay's accommodation.	3 months.
1866.					
Dec. 21	3	C. Murray,	Favor of Myself,	Cash Lent,	9 months.
1867.					
May 18	21	Austin & Co.,	"	2d Co. Sales,	60 days.
	22	W. Wallace,	"	Old note to A. Lenox est.	3 months.
June 18	23	Joel Post,	Exchange on Baring	Cash, &c.,	60 days' s'gt
25	24	Geo. Barron,	My favor,	Refined Sugars,	30 days.

1. When a note or acceptance is received, it is entered, with all the particulars, in the left-hand amount column.
2. When it is passed away, the date, when and how it is disposed of, are inserted in the columns indicated, and the amount is extended into the right-hand amount column.
3. Note No. 4 above is paid in two instalments. Such entries may occasionally be made here; but it will be found more convenient in practice, when a note is not paid at maturity, to [a] charge it in account to the party we look to for payment, at the same time writing it out of this book as we have done above with No. 10.—See notes 3 and 4, p. 52. Before we balance the
4. bill account on the Ledger, [b] we must see that the difference between the two sides of it, and the difference between the two
5. sides of this book, agree. The above notes "carried down" [c] are the notes in hand at the time of balancing.
6. The left-hand amount column is footed and noted "forward" when it is filled, the amount appearing in the head of the same column on the next page "bro't forward." The right-hand amount column cannot be carried forward until the spaces are all filled at the time of balancing.
* All notes which you endorse for accommodation may be entered in this manner in red ink; but they do not pass through the books.

RECEIVABLE.

WHEN DUE.	AMOUNT.	WHEN	AND HOW DISPOSED OF.	AMOUNT.
		1867.		
17	500	Mar 17	Rec'd $100, Ren'd $400,	500
24	1000	Jan. 24	Rec'd in Cash and Mer.,	1000
24	1500	June 30	Carried down,	1500
12	3000	Feb. 12	Cash $2000, Mdse. $1000	3000
11	600	Feb. 12	Ren'd $300, Lost $300,	600
3	1515 75	Apr. 22	Rec'd in Cash,	1515 75
5	800	Feb. 6	Discounted in City Bk.,	800
5	600	Jan. 31	Discounted in City Bk.,	600
12	2100	June 12	Rec'd in Cash,	2100
15	300	Mar. 16	Charged to W. Hay,	300
	2000	Mar. 20	Collected by R. Morris,	2000
31	4444	Feb. 28	Sold to R. Irvin & Co.,	4444 44
14	2011	Apr. 20	Rec'd in Cash,	2011
15	4500	Apr. 5	Passed to P. Nevius,	4500
15	1200	May 18	Renewed for,	1200
19	500	June 18	Rec'd in Bill on Lond.,	500
22	400	May 31	Ch'd to Profit & Loss,	400
9	1340	31	Ch'd to Estate of Lenox,	1340
	2063	June 18	Rec'd in Cash and Mer.,	2063
20	7000	May 25	Sold to C. Hartwell,	7000
21	3000	June 30	Carried down,	3000
28	1200	" "	" "	1200
	2000	" "	" "	2000
29	980	" "	" "	980
	1000	June 26	Endorsed & ret'd to Hay,	1000
	45554 19			45554 19
24	1500			
21	3000			
21	1200			
	2000			
28	980			

1. How do we enter a note or acceptance when received?
2. How when it is passed away?
3. How are notes most conveniently disposed of when not paid at maturity?
4. What has to be attended to before balancing the Bill account on the Ledger?
5. What are those notes carried down?*
6. How is this book continued from one page to another?

* If you are re-entering those notes upon a new page, "carry forward" will be the proper **expression.**

BILLS

DATE OF ACCEPTANCE.	NO.	DRAWER'S NAME.	IN WHOSE FAVOR.	ON WHAT ACCOUNT.	TIME TO RUN.
1866.					
Nov. 14	1	Myself,	A. Stuart & Co.,	Merchandise,	60 days.
1867.					
Jan. 3	2	Taylor on Myself,	Ryan & Dale,	"	10 days.
15	3	Myself,	W. Bayard & Co.,	"	1 month.
15	4	"	Capt. W. Rivers,	Ship Hudson,	3 months.
31	5	"	W. Morris,	His Note,	30 days.
	6	"	J. Warden,	His Note,	30 days.
Feb. 1	7	"	U. States,	Merchandise,	3 months.
	8	"	"	"	6 months.
	9	"	"	Morris's Goods,	3 months.
	10	"	"	"	6 months.
20	11	Morris, on Myself,	R. Banks,	R. Morris,	10 days' s'gt
Mar. 4	12	Myself,	W. Hay,	Insurance of ship Roscoe,	4 months.
Apr. 5	13	"	W. Morris,	Shipment to Liverpool,	30 days.
	14	"	"	R. Morris's Ship't to Bost.	30 days.
10	15	Taylor, on Sydney,	S. Coates,	Honor of J. Taylor & Co.,	10 days.
	16	Myself,	J. Walker,	Insurance 2d Co. Ship't,	3 months.
20	17	"	U. States,	Duties 2d Co. Sales,	6 months.
May 31	18	"	Wm. Hay,	Insurance for R. Morris,	2 months.
June 18	19	"	Warden & Bell,	Purchase of Flour,	60 days.
1867.					
Feb. 1	8	Myself,	U. States,	Merchandise,	6 months.
	10	"	"	Morris's Goods,	6 months.
Mar. 4	12	"	W. Hay,	Insurance of ship Roscoe,	4 months.
Apr. 10	16	"	J. Walker,	Insurance 2d Co. Ship't,	3 months.
20	17	"	U. States,	Duties 2d Co. Sales,	6 months.
June 18	19	"	Warden & Bell,	Purchase of Flour,	60 days.

Note.—The directions respecting the Bills Receivable Book apply in all respects to this book.
The notes "carried down" are the notes we have out unpaid, and, like the other Bill Book, must agree with the balance or its representative in the Ledger, at the time of balancing.

PAYABLE.

1	2	3	4	5	6	7	8	9	10	11	12	AMOUNT.	WHEN	AND HOW PAID.	AMOUNT.
													1867.		
16												300	Jan. 16	Pd. City Bank,	300
16												1000	" "	1000
	18											1600	Feb. 18	Pd. in Cash and Mdse.,	1600
		18										8000	Apr. 22	Pd. in Cash and Mdse.,	8000
			5									800	Mar. 4	Pd. in City Bank,	800
			3									600		Pd. in Merchants' Bk.,	600
				4								1111 11	May 4	Pd. the Custom House,	1111 11
							4					1111 11	June 30	Carried down,	1111 11
				4								1111 11	May 4	Pd. the Custom House,	1111 11
							4					1111 11	June 30	Carried down,	1111 11
				5								2500	Mar. 5	Pd. in Mdse.,	2500
						7						400	June 30	Carried down,	400
							8					161 45	May 8	Pd. in Cash,	161 45
							8					41 25		Do.	41 25
		23										601	Apr 23	Pd. in Cash,	601
									13			145	June 30	Carried down,	145
											23	3000	June 30	Do. Do.	3000
								3				112 30	June 18	Pd. Insurance Co.,	112 30
									20			1160	June 30	Carried down,	1160
												24865 44			24865 44
							4					1111 11			
							4					1111 11			
						7						400			
									13			145			
											23	3000			
									20			1160			

51

CONCLUDING REMARKS ON THE BILL BOOKS.

1 ALL practical accountants who have seen the principle upon which I have kept the Bill Books have given it their unqualified approbation. In the operations of some houses, the Bill account is nearly as heavy and voluminous as the Cash account, and there is no way in which accuracy can be so easily preserved or errors so readily found as upon the principle of balancing these books like the Cash Book. In a business where any considerable number of bills or notes are received or given, this precaution appears to me almost indispensable for maintaining harmony between these books and their representatives in the Ledger.

2. Although I have here only balanced them once,—at the time of closing the Ledger, —yet, in a business of any magnitude, it will be advisable to do so much oftener, at the same time balancing their representatives in the Ledger, or at least seeing that they conform to these books, and also to the amount of Bills and acceptances in hand. Any discrepancy in this particular is a conclusive proof of error existing somewhere, which must be found out and rectified before you go farther. You will notice that those notes which have been renewed at the face—see Wallace's note, No. 15—are not passed into the Ledger, neither are accommodation notes, such as that of William Hay's on the 26th June. You will not therefore expect the account in the Ledger to *add up* the same as this Book; but if every thing is correct it will conform to it in the BALANCE. Cross accommodation bills, like Bills Receivable No. 7 and 8, where you have given a consideration for them—your own notes—must of course appear on your Bill Book like any other note.

Another species of accommodation is when you grant your signature as security upon a note or acceptance without any consideration, as in the case of Hay's note—see Bills Receivable, June 26. I have recommended the entry of all such notes with their particulars and amounts in RED INK. Such a practice may make the Bill Book a useful monitor to those who do much of this kind of business.

3. I have before given directions—Note 3, p. 49—respecting the payment of notes by instalments. The prevailing practice is to credit the Bill account with every instalment, however trifling, endorsing it at the same time upon the note. Notwithstanding its long established general usage, this practice is often attended with great inconvenience to the Book-keeper. A more fruitful source of confusion could hardly be devised. After getting a number of these partial payments upon different notes posted to the account, in any attempt to trace out errors afterwards, it will be found a perfect labyrinth.

4. When a note is overdue, it ought either to be renewed or charged to the promisor in book account, and as he makes payments upon it pass them to his credit. Those who have been pursuing a different course will risk nothing by giving what I here suggest a trial.

SET II.—DOUBLE ENTRY BOOK-KEEPING.

THE CASH BOOK.

INTRODUCTORY REMARKS.

This book [1] is kept for the purpose of ascertaining every evening, or as often as is necessary, that all money received and paid has been kept account of,

This is done by debiting this account for [2] all money received, hence we find by the Dr. side the total amount received. When [3] money is paid out we credit this account, and thereby find by the credit side the total amount paid away. [4] And the difference between the amount paid away and the amount received must be the balance in hand. When the money in hand is counted it must agree with [5] the balance as shown by this book. Any difference is conclusive proof of error, which should be immediately sought out and an entry made to rectify it.

All cash transactions are generally first entered [6] upon this book, and afterwards transferred to the Day Book, when [7] they are marked off this book upon the left hand side of the money column thus 1/. But there is no objection to making the entry occasionally first on the Day Book and the collateral entry afterwards on this book.

As the Cash Book is generally referred to [8] as the book of original entry for all such transactions as are entered upon it, great care is necessary in making these entries. [9] They should be made in such a manner as will enable any one afterwards to determine what account was intended to be debited or credited for the money paid or received. For this purpose accountants adopt the following RULE:

When money is received, [10] write the NAME of the account to be credited for it, next the date column on the left side,—the words of explanation on the same line a little to the right.

When money is paid away, [11] write the NAME of the account to be debited for it, next the date column on the right side,—the words of explanation on the same line a little to the right.

The Ledger titles are by this means kept in a perpendicular column, separated by a slight space from the explanatory words—refer to our cash book and see. By this arrangement no doubt can afterwards arise as to what accounts were intended to be debited or credited. And it adds much to the appearance of the book to begin these words of explanation all upon a perpendicular line, either by a fold in the paper or a pencil line. [12] Every thing except the dates and names of accounts must be kept to the right of this line.

Nothing shows a man's ignorance of accounts more effectually than beginning his entries here with the title of the book "To Cash" or "By Cash." Nothing but cash is entered here, and that title is never written in the book except in the heading of it.

The Bank account, check-book, &c., are exemplified in the second part of this work.

TEACHER'S EXAMINATION.—1. For what purpose is the Cash Book kept?
2. What is placed to the Dr. side?
3. What to the credit side?
4. How do we ascertain the balance in hand?
5. What must the money in hand agree with?
6. Where are all cash transactions generally first entered?
7. What is done with them when they are entered in the Day Book?
8. For what purpose is the Cash Book generally referred to?
9. How should entries be made on this book?
10. How is money received to be entered?
11. How money paid?
12. What is kept to the right of the perpendicular line spoken of?

53

1867.					
Jan.	1	To Stock	For Bal. on hand, per Ledger A, fol. 2	7300	
	3	" Mdse.	Rec'd for sale to A. Stuart & Co.	300	
	16	" James Carter	Rec'd amount of his % in full	560	
	18	" House 44 Broadway	Rec'd of Carver a quarter's rent	150	
	24	" Bills Receivable	Rec'd of Banks on % of his note	500	
	30	" Wm. Hay	Rec'd on %	1500	
	31	" Bills Payable	Rec'd n/p. of Warden's note discounted	596	70
			10906.70 * 6600. 4726.70	10906	70
			Bal. bro't down	4226	70
Feb.	5	To Morris's Sales	Rec'd for sale to J. Lorillard	360	
	6	" Bills Receivable	Rec'd n/p. of Morris's note discounted	796	40
	12	" " "	Rec'd of T. Edwards on his note	2000	
	25	" R. Morris	Rec'd n/p. of draft on Barclay	1995	
		" Commission	Rec'd for collecting same	5	
		" Profit & Loss	Rec'd a purse found in the Park	400	
	28	" Bills Receivable	Rec'd for Baker & Fox's Bill $4444.44		
		" Profit & Loss	Rec'd 8½ per ct. prem. on same 377.78	4822	22
		" Sundries	Rec'd of Warden on my Bill	2810	16
			27415.48 10952.78 6462.70		
				17415	48
			Bal. in hand bro't down	6462	70
Mar.	1	To Wm. Hay	Rec'd on 1st Co. account	2500	
	2	" Ship Hudson	Rec'd for freight	1850	
	5	" Mdse.	Rec'd of R. Banks	255	
		" Ship Roscoe and Owners	Rec'd for freight and passages	1800	
	12	" N. Y. Insurance Office	Rec'd in full	3690	
		" Estate A. Lenox	Rec'd deposit in Manhattan Bank	7500	
	17	" Bills Receivable	Rec'd on J. Day's note	100	
		" Profit & Loss	Rec'd interest on same	4	20
	28	" Mdse.	Rec'd of Wm. Hay bal. of Invoice	500	
			24661.90 13020. 11641.90		
				24661	90
			Bal. bro't down	11641	90
Apr.	20	To Bills Receivable	Rec'd amount of Warden & Bell's note	2011	
		" Profit & Loss	Rec'd 20 days' interest on same	6	70
			Forward . . .	13659	60

* Note.—The learner should place these figures in his manuscript in pencil.

ACCOUNT.

Cr.   )

1867					
Jan.	3	By Mdse.	Paid M. Hunter & Co. for Inv. of Flour	1800	
	16	" Bills Payable	Pd. my note to A. Stuart & Co.	300	
		" " "	Pd. my acceptance for Taylor & Co.	1000	
	18	" House 44 Broadway	Pd. J. Carpenter's Bill for repairs	280	
	20	" Ship Hudson	Pd. Capt. Rivers on % of purchase money	2100	
	30	" "	Pd. disbursements	1200	
			Bal. to n/a.	4226	70
				10906	70

Feb.	1	By Mdse.	Pd. freight, per "Herald"	85	
		" Morris's Sales	Pd. " " "	167	78
	5	" " "	Pd. Cooperage, &c. on Wines	5	
	12	" " "	Pd. freight of Wine to New Orleans	28	
		" Shipm't to New Orleans	Pd. freight, per "Jersey"	33	
		" J. Taylor & Co.	Pd. " " "	11	
	18	" House in Broadway	Pd. Insurance $200, Policy $1	201	
		" Profit & Loss	Pd. Insurance on Mdse. in Store	181	
		" R. Morris	Pd. on % of his Bill	3400	
		" Bills Payable	Pd. on my note to W. Bayard	20	
	20	" Morris's Sales	Pd. R. Banks for overgauged Wine	21	
	25	" Bills Receivable	Pd. J. Bowline on Bottomry Bond	2000	
		" " "	Pd. for Baker & Fox's Bill 4444.44		
		" Profit & Loss	Pd. 8 per cent. Prem. on same 355.56	4800	
			Bal. to n/a. 10922.78	6462	70
				17415	48

Mar.	2	By Ship Roscoe, my ¼	Pd. Capt. Manly bal. of purchase	2120	
	4	" Ship Roscoe and Owners	Pd. disbursements	850	
		" Bills Payable	Pd. my note favor W. Morris	800	
		" " "	Pd. " " " J. Warden	600	
	12	" Mdse.	Pd. freight of Cotton from New Orleans	180	
	16	" Estate A. Lenox	Pd. note in the Manhattan Bank	2500	
	17	" " "	Pd. for Law Expenses	10	
		" House 49 Cedar Street	Pd. Insurance and Policy	160	
	25	" 1st Co. Sales	Pd. my half Invoice of Cotton	4500	
	31	" Charlotte Lenox	Pd. her on % of Legacy	500	
		" Robert Lenox	Pd. him on % of Legacy	800	
			Bal. to n/a. 13,020	11641	90
				24661	90

Apr.	1	By Bills Receivable	Pd. J. Walker in loan on his note	2000	
	5	" Shipm't to Liverpool	Pd. Shipping charges	348	55
		" R. Morris	Pd. charges on shipment to Boston	20	
	10	" John Taylor & Co.	Pd. their draft on S. Wood & Co. protested	1204	
		" Sundries	Pd. charges on 2d Co. shipm't to London	300	
		" 1st Co. shipm't to Boston	Pd. Shipping charges	60	
	15	" Sundries	Pd. charges on 1st Co. shipm't to Liverpool	133	
			Forward . . .	4065	55

1867.					
			Bro't forward	13659	60
Apr.	22	To Bills Receivable	Rec'd amount of Wm. Hay's note	1515	75
		" Profit & Loss	Rec'd interest on same	5	05
				15180	40
			Bal. bro't down	7121	89
May	1	To House in Cedar Street	Rec'd a quarter's rent	300	
		" City Bank Stock	Rec'd Dividend	500	
		" Merchant's "	Rec'd "	250	
		" House 44 Broadway	Rec'd Rent	150	
	4	" Ship Hudson	Rec'd Freight	3500	
		" Ship Roscoe and Owners	Rec'd freight and passage money	4200	
		" Merchants' Bank Stock	Rec'd of Finlay & Co. on % of sale	500	
	8	" R. Morris	Rec'd of Walker bal. on my Bill of Exch.	4200	
	13	" Mdse.	Rec'd of J. Walker ½ 3d Co. Adventure	1500	
		" 2d Co. Sales	Rec'd on % of sale to Warden & Bell	1640	
	18	" " "	Rec'd of Austin & Co. on Sales at Auction	560	
		" Profit & Loss	Rec'd of W. Wallace, for interest	18	90
	25	" Bills Receivable	Rec'd for Warden & Co.'s draft on Landis	7000	
		" Profit & Loss	Rec'd 1 per ct. prem. on the same	70	
				31510	70
			Bal bro't down	28785	78
June	12	To Bills Receivable	Rec'd of Warden & Bell, for their note	2100	
	18	" " "	Rec'd of J. Walker bal. due on note	563	
		" R. Morris	Rec'd Insurance for loss per "Columbia"	5452	70
				36901	48
			Bal. bro't down	8891	

DIRECTIONS FOR RULING.

1. What are the lines called footing lines?
2. How are they drawn under the longest column?
3. How are they drawn upon the other side, where there is a blank space in the money column?
4. What are the closing lines, and what is the use of them?
5. Where are they drawn?
6. How far do you bring the balance below the closing line, and what must this balance agree with?

The author has been thus precise in his directions in this matter, hoping thereby to inspire his learners with an early taste for neatness and uniformity in a matter which contributes so much to the appearance of their books, and which is of more importance in preserving accuracy and order than many persons imagine.

The directions here given apply to the Ledger, and all other books upon which balances are struck.

1867.					
			Bro't forward	4065	55
Apr.	20	By 2d Co. Sales	Paid Freight, &c. per "Vixen"	185	
	22	" Sundries	Pd. on my note to Capt. Rivers	8207	05
	23	" Bills Payable	Pd. my acceptance for honor of Taylor & Co.	601	
			Bal. to n/a. 8058.60	7121	80
				15180	40
May	4	By Bills Payable	Pd. my bonds in the Custom House	2222	22
	8	" " "	Pd. my notes to the Insurance Office	202	70
	31	" R. Morris	Pd. charges on shipment per "Columbia"	300	
			Bal. to n/a. 2224.92	28785	78
				31510	70
June	12	By R. Morris	Pd. for Bank's Bill of Exchange	7200	
	18	" Warden & Bell	Pd. them on %c	10000	
		" Bills Receivable	Pd. for J. Post's Bill on London	1660	
	25	" " "	Pd. for Sugars sold to G. Barron	800	
		" 1st Co. Sales	Pd. Wm. Hay his half net proceeds	6971	25
	28	" House 49 Cedar Street	Pd. Carpenter & Co.'s Bill of Repairs	280	
	30	" Profit & Loss	Pd. Expenses 1st Jan'y to date	1099	23
			Bal. to n/a. 28010.48	8891	
				36901	48

1. The footing lines are those drawn under the amounts before adding up.
2. They are drawn close under the foot of the column.
3. Directly opposite the line footing the longest column, touching the same line lightly inside the date column.
4. The closing lines are those drawn after the columns are added up, to keep the old account separate from the new account.
5. They are always drawn on the first faint line below the figures, touching it lightly inside the date columns, and doubling across the money columns, but never running through the date columns.
6. The balance brought down always occupies the first faint line below the closing line, and it must always agree with the cash in hand and the balance of the cash account in the Ledger.

THE INVOICE BOOK.

PRELIMINARY REMARKS.

In this book [1] we enter copies or abstracts of all invoices of goods received on our own account, on account of others, and on account of ourselves and others in company.

This is the general practice among merchants, but the author has found it more convenient in extensive business [2] to paste the original invoices into a book made of some description of paper of a larger size than the invoices. By means of an index to this book, it will be found more convenient to refer to the original invoices than by seeking them from files.

The first entry of an invoice [3] may be either here or on the Day Book, but when it is entered on the Day Book, each entry should be marked off this book as we have done on the following page.

Exporters sometimes use an "INVOICE OUTWARD BOOK," but we have shown that invoices of this kind as well as inland invoices may be entered on the Sales Book.

The particulars of an invoice need not be entered on the Day Book. [4] The amount only is required.

We have not considered it necessary to extend this book through the whole set; most learners will easily learn its nature and use from these remarks. It will seldom be necessary to transcribe the book.

As far as our exemplification of this book extends, the learner will find its examples all in connexion with the Day Book.

---

1. What is the use of this book?
2. How may invoices be most conveniently kept for reference?
3. Where is the first entry of an invoice to be made?
4. How is an invoice to be entered upon the Day Book?

D. B. 1.　300 pieces best 4-4 London Chintz Prints　.　. @ $ 4.　1200.
　　　　　100　″　　″　27 inch Furniture Prints　.　. @ $ 3.　300.
　　　　　　8　″　　French Cambric Handkerchiefs .　. @ $10.　80.
　　　　　100　″　　India Pongees　.　.　.　.　. @ $ 6.　600.
　　　　　50　″　　″　　″　Figured　.　.　. @ $ 7.　350.
　　　　　50　″　　″　Bandannas　.　.　.　. @ $ 7.　350.
　　　　　20 Canton Crape Shawls　.　.　.　. @ $ 6.　120.　　3000

D. B. 1.　INVOICE of 24 Bales Cotton shipped by **J. Taylor & Co.** on board
　　　　the Brig Jersey, Spencer, Master, for New York, and consigned to
　　　　P Duff, Merchant, by his order and for his account and risk.

P D　　1.450　4.420　7.390　10.410　13.560　16.580　19.550　22.510
1 to 24　2.400　5.430　8.380　11.450　14.540　17.500　20.590　23.540
　　　　3.410　6.500　9.410　12.500　15.520　18.500　21.500　24.560

　　　　1260 + 1350 + 1180 + 1360 + 1620 + 1580 + 1640 + 1610
　　　　　　　　　　　　　　　　= 11600, @ 8 cents.　　928

------------------ CHARGES. ------------------

　　　　Commission purchasing $928 @ 2½ per cent. .　.　. $23.20
　　　　Cartage, &c. .　.　.　.　.　.　.　.　.. 1.80
　　　　Freight and Insurance　.　.　.　.　.　47.　　72
　　　　　　　　　　　　　　　　　　　　　　1000
　　　E. E. NEW ORLEANS, }
　　　　Dec. 10, 1866.　 }　.　　　　　J. TAYLOR & Co.

　　　　　　　　　　　　　　NEW YORK, Jan. 3, 1867.
　　　MR. P. DUFF,
　　　　　　　　Bo't of MARTIN HUNTER & CO.

D. B. 1.　400 bbls. Superfine Flour　.　.　. @ $4.50　1800

　　　　　　　Rec'd Payment,
　　　　　　　　　　MARTIN HUNTER & Co.
　　　　　　　　　　Per J. MANLY.

D. B. 1.　MR. P. DUFF,
　　　　　　　　Bo't of WALTER BAYARD & Co.
　　No. 1444.　1 ps. 24?
　　″　1448.　1 ″ 25?
　　″　1450.　1 ″ 19?
　　　　　── 70 yds. Super Wool Black Broadcloth, @ $ 8.　560
　　″　2280.　1 ″ 25 yds. Super Blue Broadcloth　.　″　8.　200
　　　D. F.　2 ″ finest Saxon Flannel　.　.　. ″ 20.　40
　　　F.　80 ″ Common　.　.　.　. ″ 10.　800

　　　　　　　Rec'd Payment,　　　　　　　　　　　1600
　　　　　　　By Note @ 1 month,
　　NEW YORK,　　　　　WALTER BAYARD & Co.
　　　January 15, 1867.

D. B. 2.	1 ps. 20½ yds. Super Black Broadcloth . . . @ $5. 102.50 1 " 20½ " " Brown " . . . " 4. 83. 1 Dress Coat . . . . . . " 14.50	200

New York, Jan. 20, 1867.

Mr. P. Duff,

Bo't of C. Banks,

D. B. 2.	100 bbls. Genesee Superfine Flour . . . . . @ $5. Rec'd Payment by my note due this day, C. Banks.	500

New York, Jan. 24, 1867.

Invoice of Merchandise shipped by R. Morris on board the Ship
Herald, Chase, Master, for New York, by order and for account and
risk of P. Duff, merchant there.

P. D.
N. Y.

4 Packages, No. 1 to 4. No. 1, containing 50 pieces, 3000 yds., Figured Satins . @ 5s " 2, " 600 " Rolled Jaconets . . " 5s. " 3, " 600 " Fancy 2-color Fur. Prints . " 10s. " 4, " 600 " " 5- " " . " 20s.	£750 150 300 600

————— CHARGES. —————
Commission, 5 per ct. on £1800 . . . . . £90.
Export duty and entry, £12 10s. Cartage, Wharfage, and
Lighterage, £8 10s. . . . . . . 21.
Insurance and Policy . . . . 89. | 200

Amount due in Cash April 10th next, sterling | £2000
In Federal currency, $8888.88
London, Dec. 30, 1866.   R. Morris.

Invoice of 30 Pipes Port Wine, shipped by R. Morris on board
the Ship Herald, Chase, Master, for New York, consigned to P. Duff,
merchant there, for sale on account of the shipper.

P. D.
R. M.

30 Pipes, 3600 galls., Best Old Port . . @ 10s.   £1800.
————— CHARGES. —————
Export duty, entry, &c., £44 10s. Cartage and
Wharfage, £11 10s. . . . . . £56.
Insurance and Policy . . . . . 96.
Cooperage, Lighterage, &c. . . . . 48.   200. | 200
————
£2000.

London, Dec. 30, 1866.   • R. Morris.

Mr. P. Duff,

(Terms, 3 mos.)   Bo't of William Hay,

20 ps. 400 yds. 10-4 Damask Table Linens, . . @ $3. $1200. 4 " 54½ " 12-4 " " " . " 4. 218. 3 " 40½ " 8-4 " " " . " 2. 81. Packing-box . . . . . 1.	1500

New York, Feb. 12, 1867.

Mr. P. Duff,

Bo't of T. Edwards,

200 bbls. Genesee Flour . . . . . . @ $5.	1000

New York, Feb. 18, 1867.

2423	Barrels	Flour	.	.	.	.	.	.	@	85.	12115	
6	Pieces,	240 yds., Brussels Carpet	.	.	.	.	"	1.50			360	
70	"	Merrimac Prints,	.	.	.	.	.	"	3.		210	
40	"	" Furniture	.	.	.	.	.	"	4.		160	
420	"	English Prints	.	.	.	.	.	"	5.		2100	
365	"	" Furniture	.	.	.	.	.	"	6.		2190	
8	"	161 yds. Fine Broadcloth	.	.	.	.	"	6.			966	
1	"	Fine Saxon Flannel	.	.	.	.	.	.			11	62
1	"	Scarlet "	.	.	.	.	.	.			15	60
		Entered Ledger, folio 1.	.	.	.	.	.	.			18128	22

CONCLUDING REMARKS.

1. In business the Inventory generally makes a pretty long document, but the above will sufficiently explain its nature, and a reference to it will serve to explain the balancing of the merchandise account in the Ledger.

2. Teachers who use treatises on Book-keeping which give no example of the inventory of the merchandise on hand at the opening and closing of the Ledger, will find it a difficult task to make the closing of the merchandise account fully understood. A learner who has never seen an inventory, will form so vague an idea of it from a mere verbal description, that he will probably forget even the name of it before he has balanced his account. But give him an exemplification of it, and he will ask no more questions about it.

3. I would suggest that the inventory be always taken as near the cost and charges of the goods as possible. Having it upon this principle enables us, as we have shown,—Note 15, page 36—to ascertain the average gain per cent. upon the AMOUNT OF GOODS SOLD, which is at all times an important matter for the merchant to know. But I shall perhaps be told that taking the inventory upon this principle will, in some instances, produce a false result in the balance sheet. I admit that in some cases it will. But take it upon any principle you please, and it is only an estimated value. The actual value can only be determined by sale: and as a general rule the cost and charges form a pretty correct estimate for the balance sheet. But if circumstances render it necessary to deviate from this rule of estimate, I would still, for the purpose above referred to, take the account upon the same principle, and afterwards let an estimated deduction or addition be made to it for the balance sheet.

4. On the last page there are two invoices from Morris. The first is on our own account, and the second on consignment. The learner will perceive from this that there is not, in general, any use for a COMMISSION INVOICE BOOK. Such a book is only required in a few of the most extensive commission houses. All invoices of goods received may be entered upon this book. When the business is extensive, an index will be found useful.

THE SALES BOOK.

PRELIMINARY REMARKS.

THE purpose of keeping this book [1] is to avoid entering the particulars of long invoices upon the Day Book.

In extensive business the full particulars of every sale [2] are first entered on this book, and the amount afterwards transferred to the Day Book, when it is marked off this book as we have done on the next page.

By referring to our entry of the 12th February, it will be seen that invoices outward may be entered here as well as inland ones.

In a limited business the [3] Day Book serves for entering all sales upon: in this case the Sales Book is dispensed with.

The following exemplification extends only through two months of our Day Book. But this will be found quite sufficient to explain its use, and it is so easily understood that the learner will hardly find it necessary to transcribe it.

In a very extensive business there is often a Sales Book required in each department, in which the salesman in that department enters all his sales. From hence it is transferred afterwards to the Day Book or to the Journal by the book-keeper.

It may be proper to observe here that the Journal may be composed direct from the auxiliaries without passing the entries into the Day Book. By this course a considerable amount of writing is saved. But the author will not attempt the explanation of that method of journalizing in this Set, the object of which is to make the PRINCIPLES of the science thoroughly understood by the simplest and most efficient plan of teaching, leaving details that would embarrass the learner and hinder his teacher to be explained hereafter.

Persons who are unacquainted with the labors of the class-room, generally form but an imperfect idea of the nature of the teacher's task in first inducting the uninitiated pupil into the science of accounts. It is sufficiently difficult when the entries are all arranged for journalizing in the Day Book, but let the pupil's attention be divided between the Day Book and some five or six auxiliaries, and the matter becomes infinitely more difficult and perplexing. We have tried this plan of teaching. These remarks are therefore dictated by experience.

This plan of journalizing will, however, be found fully explained in the second part of this work, where, after having fully mastered the principles of the science, the pupil can understand and apply them with all desirable ease.

---

1. What is the object for keeping the Sales Book?
2. When this book is kept, where are the particulars of each sale first entered?
3. When no Sales Book is kept, where are the particulars of the sales first entered?

	Sold A. Stuart & Co., for Cash—		
	20 pieces London Prints . . . @ $5.	100	
D. B. 1.	10 " plain Pongees . . . @ $8.	80.	
	10 " figured . . . @ $9.	90.	
	10 " Merrimac Prints . . . @ $3.	30.	300

10.

D. B. 1.	Sold Thomas Edwards, on his note @ 30 days—		
	400 barrels Flour . . . @ $5.	2000.	
	200 pieces London prints . . . @ $5.	1000.	3000

"

D. B. 1.	**Sold James** Carter, on account—		
	3 hhds. Sugar, viz. 1204, 1196, 1100 = 3500lb.		
	Tare 10 per ct. . . 350 3150lb @ 8c. 252.		
	50 pieces Merrimac Prints . . . @ $4. 200.		452

15.

D. B. 1.	Sold Henry Pryor, in payment for James Carter's order on me—		
	6 pieces Flannel . . . @ $15.	90.	
	2 yards fine Broad Cloth . . . @ $9.	18.	108

16.

D. B. 1.	Sold James Carter, **on account**—		
	100 barrels Flour . . . . . @ $5.	500.	
	10 " Corn Meal . . . . @ $3.	30.	
	15 " Rye " . . . . @ $3.	45.	
	5 " Herring . . . . @ $5.	25.	600

19.

D. B. 2.	Sold James Carter, on account—		
	4 pieces fine Blue Broad Cloth, 19², 20, 20², 20 = 80 yds., @ $5.		400

20.

D. B. 2.	Sold Capt. Rivers, in part payment of the Ship Hudson—		
	240 barrels Genesee S. F. Flour . . . $5.	1200.	
	60 hhds. N. O. Sugars, 71,111lb		
	Less Tare 10 per ct. 7,111 Net 64,000lb @ 6¼,	4000.	
	10 chests H. S. Tea . . Net 1000lb @ 70,	700.	5900

Feb. 12.

J. T. & Co.	INVOICE of Cloths, Silks, &c., shipped on board the Brig Jersey, Spencer, master, for New Orleans. Consigned to J. Taylor & Co., for sale on my account—		
	20 pieces, 1200 yds., Figured Satins . . @ $1.50 $1800.		
	4 " 80² " Best Black Cassimere . @ $2.	161.	
	8 " 160 " S. W. Black Broad Cloth @ $5.	800.	
	20 " 400 " 10-4 Damask Table Linen @ $3.	1200.	
	4 " 54² " 12-4 " " " @ $4.	218.	
	3 " 40² " 8-4 · " " " @ $2.	81.	
	———— CHARGES. ————	4260	
	Packing Boxes $4.50, Cartage $1 . $5.50		
	Freight and Insurance . . 27.50	33.	
			4293

E. E. NEW YORK, }
12th Feb., 1867. }   P. DUFF

INVOICE of Tea shipped by the Brig Jersey, Spencer, master, for New Orleans, by order and for account and risk of J. Taylor & Co., and to them consigned.

2

J. T. & Co.	10 chests H. S. Tea, wt.	915lb.			
	Tare . . .	115	Net 800lb @ 75	$600.	

——————————— CHARGES ———————————

Cash Paid Freight and Cartage		.	$11.		
Comm'n 5 per cent. on $600		. .	30.		
Comm'n ½ per cent. for effecting Insurance	3.	33.		44.	
E. E. NEW YORK, } 12th Feb., 1867. }			P. DUFF.		644

18.

Sold R. Banks, in part payment of R. Morris's draft on me in his favor—

40 barrels S. F. Flour	.	. @ $5.	200

Sold W. Bayard & Co., in part payment of my note due this day—

100 barrels fine Flour	. . . . . @ $5.	500

28.

The following articles were destroyed by fire in my store in Front Street, yesterday :—

100 barrels Corn Meal	. . . . .	Cost $3.	300.	
200 " Rye Flour	. . . . .	" $3.	600.	
300 " Wheat	. . . . .	" $4.	1200.	
Amount of Damages upon Sugars and other goods, agreed upon by the appraisers	. . .		1590.	
Amount claimed upon my policy, and admitted by the Insurance Office	. . . . .			3690

This entry marks out the course that we would in general recommend in case of loss by fire, particularly in a partial loss. In some kinds of business it is often found more difficult to prove the loss and damage, than inexperienced persons generally imagine. Although the author has nothing himself to complain of in his past transactions with insurance offices, enough has come under his notice to convince him that the greater part of insurers do not sufficiently study the terms of their contract as embraced in their policy. Every office has a form of policy of its own, and these forms are so various, and sometimes so worded, that it is very difficult to make out how you are to proceed in case of loss, or indeed whether you can maintain an action at all upon the policy. Unless the nature and position of the property are very accurately described, a part, or even the whole of it, may fall without the scope of the policy; for every condition inserted in that instrument, either in the printed proposals or in writing, are parts of the contract, and must be strictly and literally observed. A person of our acquaintance once insured his goods in the first and second floors of the building, the only parts he then occupied. He either did not notice the terms of his policy, or forgot its restriction to those particular parts of the building, and afterwards removed a great part of his goods to the cellar and the third floor. A fire afterwards occurred, and he could recover nothing upon his loss in the cellar or the third story. In another case the insurer accepted of a policy in which was inserted the condition, that in case of loss the money was not to be payable until the insured produced a certificate of character from the minister of the parish. It was afterwards decided that he could not recover, although the minister wrongfully withheld the certificate; for it seems to be a settled legal maxim, that if you undertake for the act of a stranger you must see it done.

Although these remarks do not strictly belong to our subject, yet they cannot be far out of place in connection with the last transaction recorded in our Sales Book. They may, at least, serve to put the young and inexperienced upon their guard in entering into these important contracts.

COMMISSION SALES BOOK.

INTRODUCTORY REMARKS.

THIS book [1] is only required in extensive commission warehouses. It is kept in folios: [2] to the Dr. side are placed the particulars of all charges attending the sales: [3] and at the Cr. side the particulars of each sale. When the goods are all sold [4] the account is debited for the net proceeds, which is at the same time carried to the credit of the owner, or to the credit of cash if you pay him at the time you render account sales. The form of this account will be found among the mercantile forms—p. 117.

All the entries of both sides this book pass regularly to [5] the Day Book (refer by the dates and see) and are then marked off this book in the manner we have directed in the Cash Book.—Note 7, p. 53.

In a limited commission business, [6] the sales of each consignment, as well as the charges attending it, may be entered at once upon the Day Book without a sales book: and when an account sales is required it can be readily made out [7] by reference from the sales account in the Ledger to the Day Book.

There can be no entry of the invoice of a consignment upon this book. That must be entered upon the Invoice Book only.[8]—See Invoice Book, p. 60: also Rule 10, Questions 21 to 28.

In the second part of this work will be found another method of keeping consignment accounts: but the principle is essentially the same as this. The sales of Merchandise on acct. of ourselves and others in company is kept also upon this book [9] in all respects as we have just described for the sales of others.

The ORDER BOOK is used for entering orders received for goods. It is so simple that I have not considered it necessary to give an exemplification of it.

The EXPENSE BOOK, as also an improved form of Check Book, will be found in the second part of this work.

SALES OF WINES SOLD BY ORDER AND

1867.										
Feb.	1	¹ For my two bonds passed to the Custom House, viz.								
		one at 3 months, for . .	1111.11							
		one at 6 ⁄⁄ ⁄⁄ . .	1111.11	2222	22					
		For Cash paid freight and primage .		167	78					
	5	⁄⁄ ⁄⁄ ⁄⁄ for gauging . . .		1	50					
	1	⁄⁄ ⁄⁄ ⁄⁄ for carting and cooperage		3	50					
	12	⁄⁄ ⁄⁄ ⁄⁄ for cartage, freight, and insurance on 10 Pipes Wine consigned to J. Taylor & Co., New Orleans . .		28						
	20	⁄⁄ Cash refunded R. Banks, 6 galls. overgauged Wine sold 18th inst. . .		21		2444				
Mar.	12	⁄⁄ Storage		3	50					
		⁄⁄ Advertising		14	50					
		⁄⁄ Commission on $12,120, @ 5 per cent.		606		624				
		² n/p. to R. Morris's credit due by average, May 2*				9052				
						12120				

1. We find the entry of this and all the **others on the** Day Book by their respective dates.
2. This is found by deducting the charges from **the** total sales. See small figures in the margin.
3. The entries are generally first made here and afterwards transferred to the Day Book, when they are marked off this book thus √ to show how far **the** transfers have been made. There is no objection, however, to making the first entry of some of the transactions on the Day Book, and the corresponding entry afterwards here.

Sales of 40 Bales Brussels Carpeting for the Joint

1867.										
Apr.	20	For Bonds passed to the Custom House for duties		3000						
		Paid freight and primage per "Vixen" .	150.							
		⁄⁄ Insurance against fire, and policy	33.							
		⁄⁄ Cartage . . .	2.	185		3185				
May	18	For Storage, $3; Advertising, $10 .		13						
		⁄⁄ Commission 2½ per cent. on $15874		396	85	409	85			
		⁄⁄ R. Morris's ⅓ net proceeds is		4093	05					
		⁄⁄ J. Taylor & Co.'s do. .		4093	05					
		⁄⁄ My do. .		4093	05	12279	15			
						15874				

NOTE.—The learner will find forms of the account sales of both the above consignments among the Mercantile Forms at the end of the Ledger—pp. 117 and 118.

* The rule for finding this average time is given on the next page.

1867.					
Feb.	5	Sold for cash to J. Lorillard,			
		1 Pipe, 120 galls., Port Wine . . @ $3.			360
	9	Sold Wm. Park on his note @ 4 mos.—due June 12,			
		5 Pipes, 600 galls., Port Wine . . @ $3.50			2100
	"	Sold to W. Bayard & Co., as cash, this day,			
		3 Pipes, 360 galls., Port Wine . . @ $3.			1080
	12	Shipped to New Orleans, per Brig Jersey, and consigned to J. Taylor & Co., for sale on account of Morris's Sales, 10 Pipes Port Wine, 1200 galls., invoiced at $3.50 per gallon.*			
	18	Sold to R. Banks, as cash, this day,			
		2 Pipes, 240 galls., Port Wine . . @ $2.50			840
Mar.	12	Rec'd for n/p. of the above consignment to J. Taylor & Co., Barclay & Co.'s Acceptance @ 60 days, due May 14, for		4500	
		Taken to my own acct. at market prices, the remaining 9 Pipes, 1080 galls., @ $3, @ 60 days, due May 14		3240	7740
			12120.		
			$960.		12120
			9652.		

TEACHER'S EXAMINATION.

1. How do you find the entry of this upon the Day Book?
2. How is the net proceeds found?
3. Are the entries first made here or first on the Day Book?

* No farther entry can be made of this, it being a re-consignment, until returns are received—See March 12.

		Account of R. Morris, J. Taylor & Co., and myself, each ⅓.			
1867.					
May	13	Sold to Warden & Bell for draft on New Orleans,			
		120 pieces, 4250 yards, . . . @ $2.			8500
	18	Net proceeds of 55 pieces sold at Austin & Co.'s auction		3560	
		Taken to my own account,			
		55 pieces, 1907 yards, . . . @ $2.		3814	7374
			15874.		
			$594.95		
			N. P. 3)11278.15		
			6093.05		
					15874

CONCLUDING REMARKS ON CONSIGNMENTS.

1. As the average time upon which the sales of a consignment will fall due is almost always required, the accountant must be prepared to work out the solution promptly and accurately. A course of practical exercises will be found hereafter under the head of Commercial Calculations. We subjoin the solution of the preceding sales. The following is the

2. RULE.—Multiply each sum by the time that intervenes between its maturity and that of the first sum due. Divide the sum of these products by the total amount of sales, the quotient is the equated time COUNTED FORWARD from the day upon which the first sum falls due.*

Let us illustrate this rule by the sales on the last page. Three days of grace are allowed upon all notes and acceptances, but no grace is allowed upon cash sales or sales on Book account.

SOLD.	DUE.		DAYS.		
Feb. 5.	Feb. 5.	$360. ×	0.		
9.	June 12.	2100. ×	127,	=	266.700.
9.	Feb. 9.	1080. ×	4,	=	4.320.
18.	18.	840. ×	13,	=	10.920.
Mar. 12.	May 14.	7740. ×	98,	=	758.520.
		12,120.		)1,040,460.(86 days.	

Gives 86 days, nearly, to count forward from Feb. 5, making the sales fall due by average May 2.

Fractional parts of a day are never counted, unless the fraction amounts to a half day or upwards: it then counts another day.

3. As inexperienced persons are apt to mix up consignments, charges, and advances upon the consignments all into one account, I must again direct particular attention to Rule X., page 41. I have there marked out the course for conducting these accounts, sanctioned by the most experienced accountants. A regular account of sales drawn out upon this plan enables the owner of the consignment to see what the adventure has produced him, and thus determine at sight his gain or loss by the speculation. This will not be shown by your account, if you mix up advances and other matters in it.

4. When consigned goods are retailed, it is hardly possible to keep a detailed account of each sale. You may, in such cases, credit the sales to your own merchandise account; and when the account sales is required, the difference between the quantity received and the quantity on hand, will be the quantity sold, for which render account sales, closing the sales account, and entering on the Invoice Book the articles on hand when this account was rendered.

---

* PROOF.—Multiply each sum by the time that intervenes between its maturity and that of the last sum falling due. Divide the sum of these products by the whole amount of sales, the quotient is the equated time COUNTING BACK from the day upon which the latest sum falls due.

DAY BOOK AND JOURNAL.

SET II.

PRELIMINARY DIRECTIONS TO TEACHERS AND LEARNERS.

THE opening Day Book entry of this set is drawn from the 'balance account of the preceding set. By referring back to it, and attentively comparing it, the learner cannot fail to obtain a distinct conception of the process of opening new books from old ones,—an operation seldom well understood by young book-keepers.

He must also understand that the cash in hand ²must be entered in the Cash Book.

The Merchandise on hand ³must be entered in the Invoice Book.

The Notes and Bills in hand ⁴must be recorded in the Bills Receivable Book.

The Notes and acceptances he has outstanding ⁵must be recorded in the Bills Payable Book.

The teacher will now follow the directions given on page 27 for inducting his pupils thoroughly into the language and form of the journal. Those who patiently submit to that course will seldom experience any difficulty after the first one or two pages. Students will also find it a useful exercise to give verbally, the journal entries to be made in their books by each of the persons named in our entries.

As some business men require their journals to embody brief explanations of their transactions, I have journalized the month of May in this manner as a specimen. But I have not given the whole journal upon this plan, because, in his incipient steps, every thing that takes his attention off the LEDGER TITLES has a tendency to perplex and embarrass the learner.

We have adhered to that form of Journal in most general use, and it is to be observed that it is a form, the practice upon which, prepares the student for using any other without difficulty.

It will be found useful to have some copies of the text-book prepared with blank paper pasted over all the Journals. From these books require each pupil, in turn, to journalize all the Day Book entries of the month upon the black-board, before writing them in his books. This compels them to study each lesson well mentally before attempting to write it. If the learner does not wish to cheat himself out of thorough instruction, he should never copy any part of the printed Journal.

NEW YORK, January 1, 1867.

¹Inventory of my Effects ⅌ Balance account, Ledger A. fol. 3.—
  Mdse. in hand . . . ⅌ Invoice Book, p. 1. $3000.
  Cash in hand . . . Ledg. A. fol. 2. 7300.
  Due me on notes . . . ⅌ Bill Book, p. 1. 3000.
  William Hay owes me . . Ledg. A. fol. 2. 3000.
  House and Lot 44 Broadway " " 3. 15000. | 31300

"

¹Debts owing by me ⅌ Balance account Ledger A. fol. 3.—
  Due on my notes ⅌ Bill Book, p. 2. . . . 300.
  Due Warden & Bell . . . . Ledg. A. fol. 2. 500.
  " R. Morris, London, due 31st ult. . " " 2000. | 2800

3.

Sold A. Stuart & Co. for Cash—
  Mdse. ⅌ Sales Book, p. 1. . . . . | 300

"

²Received ⅌ Brig Jersey, Spencer, Master, from J. Taylor & Co.,
  New Orleans, for my acct.—
  24 bales Cotton, ⅌ Invoice Book, p. 1. | 1000
  Accepted their draft on me for amt. of the Invoice in favor of
  Ryan & Dale, @ 10 days' sight, $1000.

"

Bought for Cash of Martin Hunter & Co., Flour ⅌ I. B. 1. . | 1800

10.

Sold Thomas Edwards, on his note @ 30 days, Mdse. ⅌ S. B., p. 1. | 3000

"

Sold James Carter on account, Mdse. ⅌ S. B., p. 1. . . | 452

15.

Bought of Walter Bayard & Co., on my note @ 1 month, Mdse.
  ⅌ I. B. 1. . . . . | 1600

"

³Paid James Carter's order on me in favor of H. Pryor, in Mdse.
  ⅌ Sales Book 1. . . . . | 108

16.

⁴Received from James Carter Cash in full . . . . . | 560

"

⁵Paid Cash in the City Bank for my note in favor of A.
  Stuart & Co. . . . . 300.
  Also, my acceptance of J. Taylor & Co.'s draft in favor of
  Ryan & Co. . . . . 1000. | 1300

"

Sold James Carter on account, Mdse. ⅌ Sales Book 1. . | 600

1. You may journalize direct from the old Balance account without a Day Book entry, thus:—
  SUNDRIES DR. TO SUNDRIES, $31,300,
  per Balance account, Ledg. A. f. 3.
  Mdse. . . . . 3000.
  Cash . . . . 7300.
  Bills Receivable . . . . 3000.
  William Hay . . . . 3000.
  House and Lot 44 Broadway . . . . 15000.
    To Bills Payable . . . . 300.
    " Warden & Bell . . . . 500.
    " R. Morris ½ . . . . 2000.
    " Stock . . . . 28500.
2. We do not here credit Taylor & Co., because we have accepted their draft for the amount,
3. We have paid Carter's order upon us, he therefore gets in debt to us.
4. When a person pays us in full, we ought to close his account.—See notes 5 and 6, page 23.
5. Neither the Bank nor any of the parties named here are to be debited, because they do not
  get in debt to us.
  As the entries are journalized they should all be marked off this book, as in the margin of
  the first entry above.

1	¹ Sundries, Dr. to Stock				21390
1	Mdse.			3000	
2	Cash	Ledger A. fol. 2.*		7300	
3	Bills Receivable	" " 1.		3000	
3	Wm. Hay	" " 2.		3000	
4	House and Lot 44 Broadway	" " 3.		15000	
	"				
1	¹ Stock, Dr. to Sundries			2800	
4	To Bills Payable	Ledger A. fol. 2.			300
5	" Warden & Bell	" " 2.			500
5	" R. Morris, London	" " 2.			2000
	3.				
2	Cash, Dr.			300	
1	To Mdse.				300
	"				
1	Mdse., Dr.			1000	
4	² To Bills Payable				1000
	"				
1	Mdse., Dr.			1800	
2	To Cash				1800
	10.				
3	Bills Receivable, Dr.			3000	
1	To Mdse.				3000
	"				
5	James Carter, Dr.			452	
1	To Mdse.				452
	15.				
1	Mdse., Dr.			1600	
4	To Bills Payable				1600
	"				
5	³ James Carter, Dr.			108	
1	To Mdse.				108
	16.				
2	Cash, Dr.			560	
5	⁴ To James Carter, to close acct.				560
	"				
4	⁵ Bills Payable, Dr.			1300	
2	To Cash				1300
	"				
5	James Carter, Dr.			600	
1	To Mdse.				600

TEACHER'S EXAMINATION.

1. Cannot these two entries be made direct from the old Balance account?
2. Why not credit Taylor & Co.?
3. Why debit Carter for this amount?
4. What is to be done with Carter's account when this is posted?
5. Why not debit some of the parties named, or the Bank?

* Although it is not generally done, book-keepers will find the convenience of making the opening entries of a new Ledger always give a direct reference to the old one. See that every journal entry conforms to the Book-keeper's FIRST RULE—equal debits and credits.

¹ Paid Cash for Repairing House 44 Broadway .	280
"	
² Received Cash for a Quarter's Rent of House 44 Broadway . .	150
"	
Received of James Carter his note @ 20 days in full . . .	600
19.	
Sold James Carter on acct. Mdse. ℔ Sales Book 1..	400
20.	

Bought of Captain Rivers the ship Hudson for $16000.

Sold him in part payment Mdse. ℔ Sales Book 1. . . .	5900.	
Paid him in Cash	2100.	
Gave him my note, dated 15th inst., @ 3 months, for the balance	8000.	16000

³ James Carter has failed, and I have compounded with him at 50 cents on the dollar. Rec'd the same in Mdse. I. B., p. 2. . .	200.	
The Balance is lost	200.	400
24.		
Gave Warden & Bell my Order on James Walker for the balance I owe them		500
"		
Received of C. Banks in payment for his note due this day—		
Mdse. ℔ Invoice Book, p. 2.	500.	
Cash, ...	500.	1000
30.		

⁴ Received of William Hay payment of his account of $3000 now due—			
Cash		1500.	
His note @ 60 days for the balance . .	1500.		
63 days' interest included . .	15.75	1515.75	3015 75

"	
Paid Cash for disbursements of Ship Hudson	1200
31.	
Exchanged notes with W. Morris for our mutual accommodation, each note drawn at 30 days, for	800
"	

⁵ Exchanged notes with J. Warden for our mutual accommodation, each note drawn at 30 days, for $600, and I have discounted his note in the City Bank. Rec'd Cash net proceeds of same . .	596.70	
30 days' discount	3.30	600

1. Here House in Broadway is Dr., because it cost us this sum.
2. House in Broadway must be credited for what it brings us in for sale or rent.
3. Carter must be credited for what he gets out of my Debt.
4. We only credit Hay for what he gets out of our Debt. Profit & Loss or Interest account is credited for the gain on the transaction.
5. As we disposed of Warden's note immediately, it is not necessary to debit Bills Receivable for it, as in the preceding entry, where we retain the note. No property account can be credited until it has been PREVIOUSLY DEBITED. The Bills Receivable account must show that we received the note before we can show that we passed it away. Bills Payable, the first thing delivered, must be credited.

4	¹ House 44 Broadway, Dr.	280			
2	To Cash			280	
	"				
2	Cash, Dr.	150			
4	² To House 44 Broadway			150	
	"				
3	Bills Receivable, Dr.	600			
5	To James Carter			600	
	19.				
5	James Carter, Dr.	400			
1	To Mdse.			400	
	20.				
6	Ship Hudson, Dr. to Sundries	16000			
1	To Mdse.			5900	
2	*"* Cash			2100	
4	*"* Bills Payable			8000	
	"				
5	³ Sundries, Dr. to James Carter, to close account			400	
1	Mdse.	200			
6	Profit & Loss	200			
	21.				
5	Warden & Bell, Dr.	500			
7	To James Walker			500	
	"				
3	Sundries, Dr. to Bills Receivable			1000	
1	Mdse.	500			
2	Cash	500			
	30.				
	⁴ Sundries, Dr. to Sundries $3015.75.				
2	Cash	1500			
3	Bills Receivable	1515	75		
3	To William Hay, to close account			3000	
6	*"* Profit & Loss			15	75
	"				
6	Ship Hudson, Dr.	1200			
2	To Cash			1200	
	31.				
3	Bills Receivable, Dr.	800			
4	To Bills Payable			800	
	"				
4	Sundries, Dr. to Bills Payable			600	
2	Cash	596	70		
6	Profit & Loss	3	30		

TEACHER'S EXAMINATION.

1. Why debit House in Broadway?—Repeat Rule VI.
2. Why credit House in Broadway?—Repeat Rule VII.
3. Why is Carter credited for $400 when he has only paid $200?—Repeat Rule IV.
4. Why not credit Hay for $3015.75, the amount he has paid?—Repeat Rule IV.
5. Why not credit Bills Receivable, Warden's note being the thing delivered to the bank?

¹Received by the Ship Herald, Chase, master, from London, Mdse. p. I. B. 2, shipped to me by R. Morris by my order and for my account, amounting ⅌ Invoice, due in London 10th April next, to $8888.88

Gave my bonds to the Custom House for duties @ 3 and 6 mos.   2222.22

Paid freight in Cash   85. | 11196 | 10

---

²Received from R. Morris, by the Ship Herald, Chase, master, from London, 30 pipes Port Wine, ⅌ Invoice Book, £2000 sterling, for sale on his account.

Gave my bonds to the Custom House for duties @ 3 and 6 mos. $2222.22

Paid freight in Cash   167.78 | 2390

5.

Paid Cash for Cooperage and Cartage of Morris' Wines | 5

Sold for Cash to Jacob Lorillard,
120 gallons R. Morris' Wines.   C. S. B. 1.   @ $3 ⅌ gallon   . | 360

6.

³Discounted in the City Bank W. Morris' note of $800.
Received Cash net proceeds $796.40
27 days' discount   3.60 | 800

9.

Sold Wm. Park on his note @ 4 mos., endorsed by Warden & Bell,
5 pipes R. Morris' Wines, p. C. S. B. 1 | 2100

12.

⁴James Carter, who lately failed, compounds with me for 50 cents on the dollar for the note which I hold against him due yesterday.
Received a new note endorsed by W. Hay for $300.
The balance is lost   300. | 600

Rec'd Cash of T. Edwards on account of his note due this day   . | 2000

⁵Shipped by the Brig Jersey, Spencer, master, and consigned to J. Taylor & Co., New Orleans, 10 pipes 1200 gallons R. Morris' Wines, for sale on account of his consignment.   C. S. B. 1.
Paid freight, &c., in cash | 28

⁵Shipped by the same vessel, consigned to J. Taylor & Co., for sale on my account, Mdse. from store, p. Sales Book $2760.
Invoice of Table Linens, bo't of Wm. Hay on acct. @ 3 mos.   1500.
Freight and charges paid in cash   33. | 4293

⁶Shipped by the same vessel, and consigned to J. Taylor & Co., by their order and for their account, an Invoice of Tea from store, p. S. B. (due this day) $600.
Paid Freight and Insurance in cash   11.
Commission on $600 at 5 per cent. is $30.
Commission for effecting insurance ½ per cent. is   3.   33. | 644

---

1. We credit Morris only for what we get into debt to him—see note 1, p. 36.
2. We never credit any account for the invoice of a consignment—see Questions 21 and 28, p. 41.
3. Bills Receivable was debited (Jan. 31), therefore we must now credit that account.
4. Bills Receivable must be credited for the am't of the note given up; Profit & Loss is Dr. for the loss.
5. The first of these shipments is a re-consignment, and cannot be debited to any account.
   The second is an adventure of our own; we debit shipment to N. Orleans—Rule XI, p. 41.
   The third being shipped by Taylor & Co.'s order, and on account, they are debited.

1	¹ Merchandise, Dr. to Sundries	11196	10		
5	To R. Morris			8888	88
4	" Bills Payable			2222	22
2	" Cash			85	
	"				
7	² R. Morris' Sales, Dr. to Sundries	2390			
4	To Bills Payable			2222	22
2	" Cash			167	78
	5.				
7	R. Morris' Sales, Dr.	5			
2	To Cash			5	
	"				
2	Cash, Dr.	360			
7	To R. Morris' Sales			360	
	6.				
3	³ Sundries, Dr. to Bills Receivable			800	
2	Cash	796	40		
6	Profit and Loss	3	60		
	9.				
3	Bills Receivable, Dr.	2100			
7	To Morris' Sales			2100	
	12.				
3	⁴ Sundries, Dr. to Bills Receivable			600	
3	Bills Receivable	300			
6	Profit and Loss	300			
	"				
2	Cash, Dr.	2000			
3	To Bills Receivable			2000	
	"				
7	⁵ Morris' Sales, Dr.	·28			
2	To Cash			28	
	"				
7	⁵ Shipment to New Orleans, Dr. to Sundries	4293			
1	To Mdse.			2760	
3	" Wm. Hay			1500	
2	" Cash			33	
	"				
8	⁵ John Taylor & Co., Dr. to Sundries	644			
1	To Mdse.			600	
2	" Cash			11	
8	" Commission			33	

[1] Received from T. Edwards for the balance of his note due 12th instant, an invoice of Flour 🏷 I. B. 2	1000
n	
Insured my house in Broadway, for one year, in the Sun Office, for $10,000, @ 2 per ct.; policy $1. Amt. paid in cash . . .	201
n	
[2] Insured in the New York Office, $12,000 for one year on my stock of mdse. in my store in Front street, @ 1½ 🏷 ct.; policy $1. Amt. paid in cash	181
n	
[3] Pd. R. Morris' Bill on me at sight for $4440, in favor of R. Banks,	
In Mdse. 🏷 Sales Book 3 . . . . 200.	
R. Morris' goods 🏷 C. S. B. 1 . . . . . 840.	
Cash . . . . . 3400.	4440
n	
Pd. my note due this day in favor of W. Bayard Co. for 1600, . .	
In R. Morris' Wines 🏷 C. S. B. 1, sold him 9th inst. $1080.	
Mdse. 🏷 Sales Book 3 . . . . . . 500.	
Cash for balance . . . . . . 20.	1600
20.	
[4] Accepted R. Morris' Bill on me at 10 days' sight in favor of R. Banks, for	2500
n	
Refunded cash to R. Banks for 6 galls. overgauged Wine belonging to R. Morris, sold him 18th inst., twenty-one dollars. R. BANKS.*	21
25.	
Collected for R. Morris Ryan & Dale's draft on Barclay, Fox & Co., for $2000. Net Proceeds Rec'd in Cash . . . . 1995.	
Also my commission on same, ¼ 🏷 ct. . . . . 5.	2000
n	
[5] Lent Cash to Capt. John Bowline on the Bottomry Bond of his Ship, the Hunter, payable with 20 🏷 ct. prem. to my agent, R. Morris, in London, 10 days after the arrival of his Ship in England	2000
n	
[6] Bought for Cash of Baker & Fox their Bill at 60 ds. on R. Morris for £1000 Sterling 4444.44	
Premium on the same, 8 🏷 ct. 355.56	4800
n	
[7] Found in the Park a purse containing eighty half eagles, which I have advertised but no owner has claimed it	400

1. I have here followed the usual practice; but I prefer the course recommended in Note 3, page 48.
2. I have made it a rule to debit Merchandise only for the cost and charges of bringing it into store and for manufacturing. The cost of keeping the store I carry to Expense or Profit and Loss.
3. We here pay this amount for Morris; it is the same as paying it to him; he gets into our debt and is therefore Dr.
4. We should never debit a consignment account for any thing but the charges. All advances made on acct. of it should be debited to the owner's private acct.—Rule X., Note 29, p. 41.
5. This is a Bill Receivable, that account is therefore Dr.
6. We can only debit Bills Receivable for the face of the bill, not for what it costs.
7. We debit property for its value when it becomes ours, whether it costs us any thing or not.
* This is Banks' signature, making a receipt of the entry.—See Note 5, **p. 12.**

1	Mdse., Dr.	1000	
3	¹ To Bills Receivable		1000
	"		
4	House in Broadway, Dr.	201	
2	To Cash		201
	"		
6	² Profit & Loss, Dr.	181	
2	To Cash		181
	"		
5	³ R. Morris, Dr. to Sundries	4440	
1	To Mdse.		200
7	" Morris' Sales		840
2	" Cash		3400
	"		
4	Bills Payable, Dr. to Sundries	1600	
7	To R. Morris' Sales		1080
1	" Mdse. "		500
2	" Cash "		20
	20.		
5	⁴ R. Morris, Dr.	2500	
4	To Bills Payable		2500
	"		
7	R. Morris' Sales, Dr.	21	
2	To Cash		21
	25.		
2	Cash, Dr. to Sundries	2000	
5	To R. Morris		1995
8	" Commission		5
	"		
3	⁵ Bills Receivable, Dr.	2000	
2	To Cash		2000
	"		
2	Sundries, Dr. to Cash		4800
3	⁶ Bills Receivable	4444 44	
6	Profit & Loss	355 56	
	"		
2	⁷ Cash, Dr.	400	
6	To Profit & Loss		400

TEACHER'S EXAMINATION.

1. When a note is thus paid by instalments, is it not liable to complicate and confuse the Bill account to credit it in different payments?
2. Why not debit Merchandise?
3. Why debit Morris?
4. If this bill is drawn on account of the consignment, would it not answer as well to debit that account for it? See Form xxi., p. 120.
5. What is a Bottomry Bond? Repeat Question 5, Rule IX., p. 46.
6. Why not debit Bills Receivable for $4800, what it cost?
7. Why debit Cash for this, seeing it cost us nothing?

¹Sold for Cash, at 8½ per cent. prem., to R. Irvin & Co., Baker &
  Fox's Bill on R. Morris for £1000 sterling, equal to .   4444.44
Premium 8½ per cent. .   .   .   .   .   377.78 | 4822|22

¹Sold Warden & Bell, by C. Murray, Broker, my Bill of
  Exchange, @ 60 days' sight, on R. Morris, for £1000 stg. . 4444.44
Prem. on the same 8½ per. ct. . $377.78
Murray's Brokerage ¼ per ct. off .   12.06 gain 365.72.

Add 33 days' Int. included in Warden & Bell's note   11.
              Whole gain on the transaction .   376.72 | 4821|16

Received in payment
  Warden & Bell's note   .   . 2000.
  33 days' Interest included .   .   11.   2011.
  Cash for the balance .   .   2810.16
                        4821.16

²At the fire which broke out in my store in Front Street yesterday,
  goods were destroyed amounting, ⅌ Sales Book, 3, to .   . | 3690

March 1.

1st Co. William Hay and myself have entered into an arrangement for the purpose of buying and selling Merchandise on joint account, each partner's
interest in such speculations to be equal. He now advances me cash
to be invested under this arrangement .   .   .   . | 2500

⁴William Hay has sent to my store for sale on joint acct.
  5 pipes, 900 gals., Madeira Wine .   .   @$1. $900.
    My half, due June 1st, is .   .   . | 450

2.

⁵Bo't of James Walker on Book acct., @ 30 days, for the
  joint acct. of myself and Wm. Hay, 20 tierces, 24,000 lb.,
  Rice .   .   .   .   @ 5 c. $1200.
    W. Hay's half, due April 1st, is . $600.
    My half,   " " " " is   . 600.   . | 1200

Received Cash, freight of the Ship Hudson . | 1850

Being appointed Agent for the Ship Roscoe, I have purchased of Capt.
  Manly ¼ of the vessel for $5000. Sold him, in payment—
  5 pipes, 900 gals., 1st Co. Wine . @ $1.⅓ $1200.
  20 tierces, 24,000 lb., 1st Co. Rice @ 7 cts. 1680.   2880.
  Balance paid in Cash .   .   .   .   2120. | 5000

4.

⁶Paid Cash for Disbursements of Ship Roscoe .   850.
Passed my note at 4 mos. for her Ins. on 20,000 @ 2 p. ct. 400. | 1250

1. Here we sell two bills, both drawn on Morris. Bills Receivable is credited for the first, that account
    having been debited when we received the bill and gave value for it—note 6, p. 76. We credit
    Morris for the other bill, because we have drawn it ourselves, and therefore get into his debt.
2. See Day Book, February 18, and Sales Book, February 28. We debit the Insurance Office, as we
    hold it responsible for this amount.
3. We are not responsible to Hay for any thing more than our own share—$450.
4. Here we debit Hay for his half, because he becomes owner of half the purchase, and has not paid
    us for it.
5. The advances we make as Agent for the vessel, must not be mixed up with the cost of our own
    share of her; therefore we must have two separate accounts.

2	Cash, Dr. to Sundries		4822	22		
3	¹ To Bills Receivable				4444	44
6	ʳ Profit & Loss				377	78
	″					
	Sundries, Dr. to Sundries $4821.16					
3	Bills Receivable		2011			
2	Cash		2810	16		
5	¹ To R. Morris				4444	44
6	″ Profit & Loss				376	72
	″					
8	² New York Insurance Office, Dr.		3690			
1	To Mdse.				3690	

Mar. 1.

2	Cash. Dr.		2500			
3	To Wm. Hay				2500	
	″					
9	1st Co. Sales, Dr.		450			
3	³ To Wm. Hay				450	

2.

7	Sundries, Dr. to James Walker		1200			
3	Wm. Hay		600			
9	⁴ 1st Co. Sales		600			
	″					
2	Cash, Dr.		1850			
6	To Ship Hudson				1850	
	″					
9	Ship Roscoe my ½, Dr. to Sundries		5000			
9	To 1st Co. Sales				2880	
2	″ Cash				2120	

4.

9	⁵ Ship Roscoe & Owners, Dr. to Sundries		1250			
2	To Cash				850	
4	″ Bills Payable				400	

TEACHER'S EXAMINATION

1. Why is Bills Receivable account not credited alike for both these bills?—Repeat Rule IX., p. 40.
2. Where are the particulars of this entry for holding the insurance office responsible for this amount?
3. Why should not Hay have a credit for the whole amount of goods which he put into my hands?—Repeat Rule XII., and note 8, p. 43.
4. Why not debit Sales in Co. for the whole amount?
5. Why not debit the account of Ship Roscoe my ½ for the amount?

Paid Cash to the City Bank for my note due to-morrow in favor
of W. Morris . . . . 800.
Also paid Cash to the Merchants' Bank for my note in favor of
J. Warden 600.   1400

5.

[1] Sold R. Banks 5 hhds. Havana Sugar, viz.—
    1050, 1150, 1000, 1200, 1100   5500 lbs.
    Less Tare, 10 per cent.   550   4950 lbs., @ 10 cts.   495.
    5 chests Y. H. Tea, viz.—
     80, 85, 75, 90, 70 . . . 400 lbs. net.   @ 90 cts.   360.
    6 ps., 20^2, 19^2, 20, 21, 19, 20,   120 yds. S. F. Cloth, @ $10. 1200.
    6 doz. pair best 12-4 Bath Blankets . . . @ $120.   720.
150 pieces 3-color Merrimac Prints . . . . @ $3.   450.
 20 yds. Super Saxon Flannel . . . . . @ .75   15.
 10 " Finest Green Broadcloth . . . . @ $9.   90.
 16 " Fancy Fig'd Satin . . . . . @ $1.50   24.
      2 Packing Cases 1.   3355
Received in Payment my acceptance for R. Morris, due
    this day . . . . 2500.
Banks' Order at sight on J. Walker, which I deposit on
    acct. with Walker . . . . 600.
Cash for Balance . . . . 255. $3355.

//

[2] Received Cash for Freights and Passages ⅌ Ship Roscoe   1800

//

[3] 1st Co. Mdse. being all sold, I render Wm. Hay acct. and close the sales
    as follows:—Total Sales, $2880.   My 2½ Commission is . 72.
Storage . . . . 8.
W. Hay's half net proceeds due this day is . . . . 1400.
My net gain is 350.   1830

12.

Received from J. Taylor & Co., New Orleans, acct. sales of Morris' Wines.
    Net proceeds, $4500, for which I have received their bill @ 60 days
    on Barclay, Hope & Co., which is accepted   4500

//

[4] Received from J. Taylor & Co., N. Orleans, acct. sales of my consignment
    ⅌ Brig Jersey. Net proceeds, $5800, for which received their Invoice
    of Sea Island Cotton, amounting to . . . . 5800.
Paid freight and charges on the same in cash 180.   5980

//

Taken to my account the remaining 9 pipes, 1080 galls., Morris' Wines,
    @ $3 ⅌ gall., as cash in 2 months 3240

//

Received from the New York Insurance Office Cash in full . . 3690

//

[5] Shipment to N. Orleans closes with a gain of . . . 1507

---

1. This entry shows how a sale must appear on the Day Book when no Sales Book is kept.
2. I have to account to the Ship Roscoe and Owners for this sum, therefore I credit their account.
3. The total sales per Ledger is $2880, less charges $80 = $2800, half of which is Hay's share, $1400.
    Our half first cost per Ledger was $1050, and our share net proceeds being $1400, leaves our gain
    $350.
4. Taylor & Co. having remitted the proceeds of the sales, the transaction is not carried to their account.
    We have only to debit the thing received, and credit the account that brought that thing in.—Rule
    V. and VII., p. 39.
5. Always close property accounts when all is sold, as we do with personal accts. when we settle with the
    parties.—Note 4, p. 70. The gain or loss must appear in the Profit & Loss acct., for reasons given
    Mdse. acct.—Note 4, p. 53.

4	Bills Payable, Dr.	1400	
2	To Cash		1400

5.

1	¹ Sundries, Dr. to Merchandise		3355
4	Bills Payable	2500	
7	James Walker	600	
2	Cash	255	

"

2	Cash, Dr.	1800	
9	² To Ship Roscoe & owners		1800

"

9	1st Co. Sales, Dr. to Sundries, to close account	1830	
8	To Commission		72
6	" Profit & Loss $8 and $350		358
3	³ " W. Hay		1400

12.

3	Bills Receivable, Dr.	4500	
7	To Morris' Sales		4500

"

1	Merchandise, Dr. to Sundries	5980	
7	⁴ To Shipment to New Orleans		5800
2	" Cash		180

"

1	Merchandise, Dr.	3240	
7	To Morris' Sales		3240

"

2	Cash, Dr.	3690	
8	To New York Insurance Office, to close account		3690

"

7	⁵ Shipment to New Orleans, Dr., to close account	1507	
6	To Profit & Loss		1507

TEACHER'S EXAMINATION.

1. Why are all these particulars given in the Day Book **Entry**?
2. Why credit Ship Roscoe and owners for this sum?
3. How is Hay's half net proceeds and our half net gain found here? Repeat Question 25, page 41.
4. Why credit Shipment to New Orleans for this $5800?
5. Why should this account be debited for this sum?

[1] Morris' Consignment being all sold, I render him account; closing the sales as follows:—Total sales $12,120, charges posted to date, $2444.

My commission on the sales @ 5 ⅌ cent., is	$606.	
Storage and advertising .	18.	
Net proceeds at Morris' credit, due 2d May	9052.	**9676**

//

[2] As Executor of the estate of the late A. Lenox I have received possession of the following property for the use of his heirs, viz.

Cash in deposit in the Manhattan Bank	7500.	
Notes in hand, No. 15 and 16, ⅌ Bill Book .	1700.	
House and lot 49 Cedar Street, valued at	12000.	
100 Shares City Bank Stock	10000.	**31200**

16.

[3] James Carter's Note for $300 endorsed by W. Hay, fell due in my hands yesterday and remaining unpaid, I value the same in account with Hay as cash due this day **300**

//

Pd. Cash for A. Lenox's Note in the Manhattan Bank . . . **2500**

17.

[4] James Day's Note for $500 falls due in my hands to-day.

Rec'd in payment his new Note @ 60 days for .		400.	
// Cash for the balance .	100.		
63 days' interest on new Note .	4.20	104.20	**504	20**

//

Paid Cash Attorney's fees for Estate of A. Lenox .	10.	
[5] *// // * Insurance of house 49 Cedar Street .	160.	**170**

20.

Received H. Parnel's Note @ 60 days for balance due the Estate of A. Lenox **1340**

//

[6] W. Hay has put into my store for sale on joint acct. 9 pipes Wine, 1080 gallons . . . . @ $3, $3240.

I have added the same quantity at same price from store .	3240.	
	$6480.	
My half is		**3240**

25.

[6] Wm. Hay and myself have bought for cash on joint acct. 200 Bales Cotton, amounting ⅌ invoice to . . . . $9000.

Each partner has paid his own share in cash **4500**

---

1. The total sales were $12,120, less the whole charges $3068, leaves net proceeds $9052.—Form IV. p. 117.

2. We must here debit the several kinds of property we receive and credit the account of the estate for the whole, which property must be disposed of hereafter according to instructions, when the estate will be debited for it.—Note 3, Lenox Estate, p. 119.

3. I have here done as recommended in Note 3, page 48.—I look to Hay for the amount.

4. The things received are Dr. to the things delivered, and Interest or Profit & Loss is credited for the gain.

5. This building belongs to the Lenox Estate, and we debit it for what we expend upon it, and credit it for the returns.

6. For the reasons given in Rule XII. neither of these entries affects Hay's acct. in our Books.

7	Morris' Sales, Dr. to Sundries, **to close acct.** .	9676	
8	To Commission . .		606
6	" Profit & Loss .		18
5	¹ " R. Morris .		9052
	"		
10	² Sundries, **Dr. to Estate of A. Lenox** .		31200
2	Cash	7500	
3	Bills Receivable	1700	
10	House 49 **Cedar** Street . . .	12000	
10	City Bank **Stock**	10000	

16.

3	³ Wm. Hay, Dr.	300	
3	To Bills Receivable		300
	"		
10	A. Lenox Estate, Dr. . .	2500	
2	To Cash.		2500

17.

	⁴ **Sundries, Dr. to Sundries** . . $504.20			
3	Bills Receivable.	400		
2	Cash	104	20	
3	To Bills Receivable		500	
6	" Profit & Loss		4	20
	"			
2	Sundries, **Dr. to Cash** . .	170		
10	⁵ Estate of A. **Lenox** . . .	10		
10	House 49 Cedar **Street** .	160		

20.

3	Bills Receivable, Dr. . . .	1340	
10	To Estate of A. Lenox . .		1340
	"		
9	⁶ 1st Co. Sales **Dr.** . . .	3240	
1	To Mdse.		3240

25.

9	⁶ 1st Co. Sales Dr.	4500	
2	To Cash		4500

[1] Placed to 1st Co. Account 500 bbls. Flour from store @ $5 $2500.
William Hay has sent in 300 bbls.   @ $5 1500.
  My half is . . . . . $2000.
  Rec'd Bal. of Wm. Hay's share in cash 500. . . . 2500

31.

[1] Paid Cash to Charlotte Lenox on acct. of her legacy 500

"

[2] Paid Cash to Robert Lenox on acct. of his legacy 800

April 1.

Lent Cash to James Walker on his note @ 6 months, endorsed by Warden & Bell, and dated the 6th instant, for . . . 2000.
6$\frac{3}{10}$ months' Interest included in the note . . . 63. 2063

5.

Shipped by the Columbia, Gray, Master, consigned to Baring & Co.,
 Liverpool, for sale on my account—
 40 bales Cotton from store . . . . 2500.
 100 bbls. Flour from do. . . . @ $5 500. 3000.
 4500 bush. Wheat @ $1, Bought of P. Nevius on
  Barclay, Hope & Co.'s acceptances . . 4500.
Shipping Expenses paid in Cash . . . 348.55
Passed my note to the Marine Insurance Co. for premium [3] on $8010 @ 2 per ct. (covering the pre-
 mium and policy), Policy $1.25 . . . . 161.45 8010

"

[4] Shipped by the Brig Cherub, consigned to Hartwell & Thorndike, Bos-
ton, by order and for account of R. Morris, London—
240 bbls. Mess Pork, Bought of Wm. Hay @ 30 days, due
 May 5th . . . . $2000.
Paid Shipping Expenses in Cash . . . . 20.
Passed my note @ 30 days for Insurance . . 41.25
Commission on purchase of $2000 @ 5 per cent . . 100.
 $\frac{1}{4}$ per ct. for effecting Insurance . . . 5. 105. 2166 | 25

10.

[5] Paid Cash for honor of John Taylor & Co., their draft on Sidney Wood
& Co. being Protested for non-payment. *
Bill $1200, Protest, &c., $4 . . . . 1204.
My $\frac{1}{2}$ per ct. Brokerage 6. 1210

"

Received from the Executors of my father's Estate 50 shares Merchants'
Bank [6] Stock, valued at 5000

---

1. Hay does not here get in debt to us, nor we to him. Therefore we have no entry for his acct.
2. These persons being Legatees, we must debit their private accounts for all payments we make them, until the final settlement.—Note 3, Lenox Estate, p. 110.
3. The invoices, shipping expenses, and policy, amount to $7849.80. Then 98 : 100 : : 7849.80 : $8010, the sum upon which to cast the 2 per ct. premium, which amounts to $160.20 + 7849.80 = 8010, thus insuring both premium and policy with the shipment.
4. Morris gets in debt to us for this amount, therefore he is Dr.—not Hartwell & Thorndike.
5. We were not obliged to pay this draft. We have done it to save the credit of our N. Orleans correspondents, Taylor & Co.
6. We might credit Profit and Loss, but such additions to our capital belong more properly to Stock, for reasons given in note 3, page 30.

1	¹ Sundries, Dr. to Mdse. .		2500
9	1st Co. Sales .	2000	
2	Cash .	500	

31.

2	Sundries, Dr. to Cash		1300
10	² Charlotte Lenox .	500	
10	² Robert Lenox .	800	

April 1.

3	Bills Receivable, Dr. to Sundries .	2063	
2	To Cash . . * .		2000
6	" Profit & Loss .		63

5.

7	³ Shipment to Liverpool, Dr. to Sundries .	8010	
1	To Mdse. .		3000
3	" Bills Receivable .		4500
2	" Cash .		348	55
4	" Bills Payable .		161	45

"

5	⁴ R. Morris, Dr. to Sundries .	2166	25
3	To Wm. Hay .		2000
2	" Cash .		20
4	" Bills Payable .		41	25
8	" Commission .		105

10.

8	⁵ John Taylor & Co., Dr. to Sundries .	1210	
2	To Cash .		1204
8	" Commission .		6

"

4	Merchants' Bank Stock, Dr. .	5000	
1	⁶ To Stock .		5000

TEACHER'S EXAMINATION.

1. Why is there no entry here for Hay's account? Repeat Rule XII., p. 43.
2. Why not debit the Estate of Lenox, these being payments to the Legatees?
3. How do we find the amount upon which to cast the premium?
4. Why are Hartwell & Thorndike not debited for these goods, they being shipped to them?
5. Why should we pay this draft, it being drawn on Sidney Wood & Co.?
6. Why not credit Profit & Loss for this $5000?

[1] Accepted *supra protest* for the honor of J. Taylor & Co., their bill at
10 days, on Sidney Wood & Co., for $600; protest $1 . $601.
My ¼ ℔ cent. Brokerage—due 23d inst. . . 3. | 604

"

[2] Shipped by the Cambria, Adams, master, and consigned to R. Morris,
London, for sale on his acct., J. Taylor & Co., and myself, each ⅓.

60 Bales Sea Island Cotton from store			. $4000.	
100 Barrels Flour	from do.	@ $6.	. 600.	4600.
200 Bales 1st Co. Cotton	.	.	.	9500.
Shipping Expenses paid in Cash	.	.	.	300.
Passed my Note @ 3 mos. for insurance	.	.	.	145.
My commission on $14400 @ 2½ ℔ ct. is	.	". $360.		
" " Effecting Insurance ¼ ℔ ct.	.	. 36.	396.	14941

J. Taylor & Co.'s ⅓ is   4980.33
R. Morris'   "   4980.33
My (2d Co.)   "   4980.34 $14941. Due this day.

"

[3] Shipped by the Brig Tribune, Speer, master, and consigned to C.
Hartwell, Boston, 18 Pipes Wine belonging to 1st Co., amounting
℔ Invoice to $6480. My half is . . . $3240.
Paid shipping expenses in cash . . . . 60. | 3300

15.

[4] Shipped by the Erie, Truck, master, and consigned to Baring & Co.,
Liverpool, for sale on 1st Co. account,
400 Barrels Flour from store, @ $6, ... $2400.
150 " " put on board by Wm. Hay, @ $6, $900.
Wm. Hay passes his Note for insurance . . 165. 1065.
I have paid the other expenses in Cash . . . 133. | 3598

My half is . . 1799.
Wm. Hay's do. is . 1799. $3598, as cash this date.

"

[5] Received from J. Taylor & Co., of New Orleans, invoice of 100 Bales
Cotton shipped to London on the 2d inst., consigned to R. Morris
for sale on their acct., Morris' acct., and on my acct., each ⅓.
My (2d Co.) ⅓ due in cash 2d inst., is . . . . . | 1660

20.

Received Cash amt. of Warden & Bell's note due 31st ulto., 2011.
" 20 days' interest on the same . 6.70 | 2017 | 70

"

3d Co. | [6] Received from J. Walker invoice of sugars amounting to $4000 which
he has purchased to sell on our joint acct. My half is . . . | 2000

---

1. This means accepting after protest—after Sidney Wood & Co. refused to accept. The bill is then
in the same situation as that in Note 5, last page, and if not protested here will return under
damages against our New Orleans correspondents, Taylor & Co. We of course debit them for
the amount.—Form XXI., p. 120.
2. We have paid for the whole shipment, and Taylor & Co. and Morris are each responsible to us
for their respective shares from this date.
3. This is part of the 1st Co. property shipped to another market, and our share is charged to a new
acct.: therefore 1st Co. Sales must be credited for our share.
4. We debit Hay for his share of the adventure, and credit him for what he has paid upon it. It
would have been equally correct to have debited him for the balance only.—Note 4, p. 28.
5. We credit Taylor & Co. for our share of this adventure because they have paid the amount for
us, and we still owe them for it.
6. We call this an adventure because we do not manage the sales.

8	[1] John Taylor & Co., Dr. to Sundries	604		
4	To Bills Payable		601	
8	*n* Commission		3	
	n			
	[2] Sundries, Dr. to Sundries . . . . $14941.			
8	J. Taylor & Co.	4980	33	
5	R. Morris	4980	33	
11	2d Co. Shipment to London	4980	34	
1	To Mdse.		4600	
9	*n* 1st Co. Sales		9500	
2	*n* Cash		300	
4	*n* Bills Payable		145	
8	*n* Commission		396	
	n			
11	[3] 1st Co. Shipment to Boston, Dr. to Sundries	3300		
9	To 1st Co. Sales		3240	
2	*n* Cash		60	
	15.			
	Sundries, Dr. to Sundries . . . . $3598.			
11	[4] 1st Co. Shipment to Liverpool	1799		
3	Wm. Hay	1799		
1	To Mdse.		2400	
3	*n* Wm. Hay		1065	
2	*n* Cash		133	
	n			
11	2d Co. Shipment from N. Orleans to London, Dr.	1600		
8	[5] To J. Taylor & Co.		1600	
	20.			
2	Cash, Dr. to Sundries	2017	70	
3	To Bills Receivable		2011	
6	*n* Profit and Loss		6	70
	n			
11	[6] 3d Co. Adventure, Dr.	2000		
7	To J. Walker		2000	

TEACHER'S EXAMINATION.

1. What does accepting *supra protest* mean?
2. Why debit Taylor & Co., and Morris, for their shares at this time?—Repeat note 3, p. 43.
3. Why is 1st Co. Sales credited for this amount, seeing the goods are not yet sold?
4. Why is Hay both debited and credited in the same entry?
5. Why credit Taylor & Co., seeing we have not received any thing from them?
6. Why do we call this an adventure?—See note 9, p. 42.

[1] Received by the Vixen, Chase, Master, from R. Morris, London, **40** bales Brussels Carpeting, amounting ⅌ Invoice to £2700 sterling, consigned to me for sale on **2d** Co. account. My ⅓ is £900, due 10th instant, equal to . . . . . . $4000.
Gave my bonds @ 6 mos. to the Custom-House for duties . 3000.
Paid Freight and other charges in Cash 185.   7185

22.

[2] Paid my note in favor of Capt. Rivers, which has lain over under protest since the 18th instant, for . . . . . $8000.
4 days' Interest, $5.33, protest, &c., $1.72 . . . . 7.05   8007 | 05

Sold him on account 800 bbls. 1st Co. Flour @ $6 . 4800.
Paid the balance in Cash 3207.05

8007.05

*

[3] Received Cash from W. Hay for his note due 3d inst. . . 1515.75
19 days' Interest on same $4.80, postages 25 . . . 5.05   1520 | 80

23.

Paid Cash for J. Taylor & Co.'s draft on Sidney Wood & Co. Accepted by me on the 10th instant, for 601

25.

[4] Received advice from R. Morris that on the 20th ultimo Capt. Bowline cancelled his Bottomry Bond on the Ship Hunter, by paying Morris the amount on my account . . . . . . $2000.
Also the premium upon the same 400.   2400

30.

[5] Received from J. Walker account sales of the Invoice of Sugars bought by him on the 20th instant; net proceeds $5000.
My half is 2500

*

3d Co. Adventure now closes with a gain of . . . 500

May 1.

[6] Rec'd Cash for a Quarter's Rent of House 49 Cedar St. . 300.
"   5 per ct. dividend on City Bank Stock . 500.
"   5 per ct.   "   on Merchants' " . 250.
"   Quarter's Rent of House 44 Broadway . 150.   1200

4.

[7] Received Cash Freight of Ship Hudson . . 3500.
Freight and Passage money of Ship Roscoe 4200.   7700

*

[8] Paid Cash for two Bonds to the Custom-House for $1111.11 each .   2222 | 22

---

1. We are only accountable to Morris for our own share of this shipment.
2. We can never debit the Bill account for more than the face of the note—the same as it was credited.
3. If we credit the Bill account for any more than it was debited when the note was received, it will throw the account that much out of balance.
4. R. Morris gets in debt to us for the amount he acknowledges to have received for us.
5. We credited him for our share of the purchase money when he bought the goods; now, as he has sold the property, and got our share of the net proceeds in his hands, we debit him.
6. These different accounts must have credit for these sums, because they have brought us in these amounts.
7. I am sole owner of the Hudson, but only part owner and agent of the Roscoe.
8. These are Bills Payable: we have opened no Custom-House bonds account.

12	2d Co. Sales, Dr. to Sundries	7185		
5	¹ To R. Morris		4000	
4	" Bills Payable		3000	
2	" Cash		185	

22.

Sundries, Dr. to Sundries, $8007.05.

4	² Bills Payable	8000		
6	Profit & Loss	7	05	
9	To 1st Co. Sales		4800	
2	" Cash		3207	05

"

2	Cash, Dr. to Sundries	1520	80	
3	³ To Bills Receivable		1515	75
6	" Profit & Loss		5	05

23.

4	Bills Payable, Dr.	601	
12	To Cash		601

25.

5	⁴ R. Morris, Dr. to Sundries	2400	
3	To Bills Receivable		2000
6	" Profit & Loss		400

30.

7	⁵ J. Walker, Dr.	2500	
11	To 3d Co. Adventure		2500

"

11	3d Co. Adventure, Dr. (to close acct.)	500	
6	To Profit & Loss		500

May 1.

12	Cash, Dr. to Sundries	1200	
10	⁶ To House 49 Cedar Street, Received Rent		300
10	" City Bank Stock " Dividend		500
4	" Merchants' do. " do.		250
4	" House 44 Broadway " Rent		150

4.

12	⁷ Cash, Dr. to Sundries	7700	
6	To Ship Hudson . . . Rec'd Freight		3500
9	" Ship Roscoe and owners " "		4200

"

4	⁸ Bills Payable, Dr.	2222	22
12	To Cash . . . Paid my two Custom-house bonds	2222	22

1. Why not credit Morris for the whole shipment?—Repeat note 8, page 43.
2. As it cost me $8007.05 to take up this note, why not debit the Bill account for that amount?
3. Why not credit Bills Receivable for the $1520.80, having received that amount for the note?
4. Why is Morris Dr.?
5. Why debit Walker in this case?
6. Why is this sum credited to so many different accounts?
7. Why not credit the Ship Roscoe and the Ship Hudson alike here?
8. Why not debit Custom-house Bonds account?

[1]Sold Finlay & Co. my 50 shares Merchants' Bank Stock @ 110, $5500.		
Bought of them in part payment 500 bbls. Mess Pork for the joint account of myself and Wm. Hay . @ $10 . . . 5000.		
Received the balance in Cash . . . . . 500.		5500
Wm. Hay's half is 2500		
My half is . . . . . 2500 $5000 as cash this day.		

Merchants' Bank Stock now closes with a gain of . .		750

8.

Paid Cash for my notes in the Insurance Office . $161.45		
and . . . 41.25		202 70

Sold James Walker my Bill at 60 days' sight on R. Morris for £1000		
sterling 4444.44		
8 per ct. Premium 355.56		4800
[2]Received in payment Walker's Receipt for the balance I owe		
him . . . . 600.		
Cash for the balance . . . . . . 4200.		
4800.		

13.

Delivered to James Walker, for sale on our joint account, an Invoice of		
Sugars, amounting to $3000. My half is . . . 1500.		
Received Walker's Check on the Bank for his half . . 1500.		3000

Sold Warden & Bell 120 pieces, 4250 yds., 2d Co. Carpeting, @ $2, $8500.		
Received in payment their draft at 30 days' sight on J. Landis & Co., [3]of		
New Orleans, for $7000, at 2 per ct. disct. . . 6860.		
Cash for the Balance . . . . 1640. $8500.		
2 per ct. Discount on the Bill is . . . . 140.		8640

18.

Sold in Austin & Co.'s Auction Room, 55 pieces 2d Co. Carpeting.		
Net proceeds ⅌ their acct. sales $3560.		
Received in payment their note at 60 days, for . . $3000.		
Cash for Balance . . . . 560.		
I take the remaining 55 pieces to my account at market prices 3814.		7374

I close 2d Co. Sales, rendering each partner a copy of the account.		
Total Sales $15,874, Charges posted $3185.		
[4]My Storage is $3, Advertising $10 . . . $13.		
" Commission 2½ per ct. on $15,874 . . . 396.85		
R. Morris's ⅓ net proceeds due this day is . . . 4093.05		
J. Taylor & Co. ⅓ do. do. . . . 4093.05		
My ⅓ do. 4093.05		
My ⅓ first cost was 4000. gain . . 93.05		8689

1. Merchants' Bank Stock is the thing delivered, and is therefore credited.
2. We debit Walker, because we get out of his debt for this amount.—See Led., p. 167.
3. The rule is always to debit or credit a bill for its face—not for what it passes in payment.
4. We deduct the whole charges, $3594.85, from the total sales, $15,874, which leaves $12,279.15 net proceeds, divided by 3 gives each partner's share $4093.05.—See Form V., p. 118.

4	¹ Sundries, Dr. to Merchants' Bank Stock				5500	
12	Cash Received of Finlay & Co. .	500			
3	Wm. Hay, for his half invoice	2500			
9	1st Co. Sales for my half do.	2500			

"

| 4 | Merchants' Bank Stock, Dr. (to close) . | 750 | | |
| 6 | To Profit and Loss, for net gain . | | 750 | |

8.

| 4 | Bills Payable, Dr. | 202 | 70 | | |
| 12 | To Cash Paid my two notes in the Marine Office | | 202 | 70 |

"

	Sundries, Dr. to Sundries, . . . $4800.			
7	² James Walker, for his Receipt in full	600		
12	Cash Received of Walker	4200		
5	To R. Morris, for my bill on him		4444	44
6	" Profit and Loss for 8 ℔ ct. Premium on the same .		355	56

13.

1	Sundries, Dr. to Mdse. delivered J. Walker on joint acct. .		3000	
11	3d Co. Adventure for my half	1500		
12	Cash Rec'd for Walker's half	1500		

"

	Sundries, Dr. to Sundries, . . . $8640.			
3	³ Bills Receivable for draft on Landis & Co.	7000		
12	Cash for balance	1640		
12	To 2d Co. Sales for sale of carpeting		8500	
6	" Profit and Loss for 2 ℔ ct. discount on draft		140	

18.

12	Sundries, Dr. to 2d Co. Sales		7374	
3	Bills Receivable, for Austin & Co.'s Note	3000		
12	Cash Received of Austin & Co.	560		
1	Mdse. for carpets taken to my acct.	3814		

"

12	⁴ 2d Co. Sales, Dr. to Sundries, to close acct.	8689		
6	To Profit and Loss, for storage and net gain .		106	05
8	" Commission 2½ ℔ ct. on $15874 .		396	85
5	" R. Morris, for his ½ net proceeds .		4093	05
8	" J. Taylor & Co. for " "		4093	05

1. Why credit Merchants' Bank Stock?
2. Why debit Walker?
3. Why should not Bills Receivable be debited for $6860 only, what it was received in payment for?—Note 2, B. Receivable acct., p. 103.
4. How do we settle this transaction and find each partner's share?

NOTE.—As some merchants desire their Journals to exhibit a brief recapitulation of the Day Book entries, we are journalizing the month of May in this manner as an illustration. The learner will perceive from this, that by particularizing the transactions more minutely, he can construct his Day Book on the Journal form, and post direct from it to the Ledger, without the use of a Journal: which in any ordinary business is, therefore, not required.

[1] Renewed W. Wallace's Note of $1200 due 15th inst., for the same amount for 3 months. Received Interest, &c., in cash . . .	18	90

25.

Sold for cash at 1 ℘ ct. premium to C. Hartwell, Warden & Bell's draft on Landis & Co. of New Orleans . . . . . 7000.			
1 ℘ ct. premium is . . . . . . 70.		7070	

31.

[2] H. Parnell has failed, and the note which I hold against him for Lenox's Estate, due 22d instant, is lost . . . . . 1340.		
J. Day has also failed, and the note which I hold against him due 19th, is lost . . . . . . 400.	1740	

"

Shipped by the Columbia, Gray, Master, by order and for account of R. Morris, London, due in cash this day.		
1000 Barrels Flour from store, @ $5 . . $5000.		
Shipping charges paid in cash . . . . 300.		
Passed my note to the National Insurance Co. for premium 112.30		
Commission for shipping 5 ℘ ct. on $5300 . . 265.		
" for effecting insurance ¼ ℘ ct. on $5565 13.92 278.92	5691	22

"

Shipped by the same vessel and consigned to R. Morris 80 packages Mdse. received from Hartwell & Thorndike, Boston		
My comm. receiving and forwarding 50 cts. ℘ package, due June 30	40	
Forwarded Hartwell & Thorndike particulars for Insurance		

June 1.

Bot. of Warden & Bell 2400 Barrels Genesee Flour @ $5. Amt. ℘ Invoice $12000. Sold them in part payment			
50 pieces English Prints @ $4 . . . . $200.			
8 pieces 320 yards Brussels Carpet @ $2 . . 640. 840.			
I am to pay them cash on the 18th instant . 10000.			
[3] And to give my note at 60 days for the balance 1160. 11160.	12000		

"

Received from R. Morris his Account Sales of 2d Co. Shipment from [4] New Orleans to London. Net proceeds £1435 10s. sterling.		
. My ⅓ is £478 10s. due April 15, equal to . 2126.66		
Also sales of 2d Co. Ship't. to London, ℘ "Cambria." N.P.		
£3800 5s. stg. My ⅓ £1266 15s. due Apr. 30, equal to 5630.	7756	66

"

I now close the following accounts, viz.:		
2d Co. Shipment, New Orleans to London, with a gain of 526.66		
2d Co. Shipment to London, with a gain of . . 649.66	1176	32

"

Received from C. Hartwell Account Sales of 18 Pipes Wine shipped to him for sale on 1st Co. acct. 10th Apr. last. N. P. due June 10	6480	

1. The note being renewed at the face, there is no occasion for passing it through the books, though it must appear on the Bill Book.—See Bill Book May 18, p. 48.
2. Parnell's note was credited to Lenox's Estate, and is, therefore, not our loss.
3. We must for the present credit Warden & Bell for this $11160, and they will be debited for the cash and note when delivered them.—See June 18, p. 94.
4. He has sold the goods and got our money in his hands.

12	¹ Cash, Dr.	18	90
6	To Profit & Loss, for Interest, &c., received for renewing Wallace's note for $1200		18	90

25.

12	Cash, Dr. to Sundries	7070	
3	To Bills Receivable for Warden & Bell's bill sold to C. Hartwell		7000
6	ɴ Profit & Loss for 1 per ct. Premium received on the same		70

31.

3	Sundries, Dr. to Bills Receivable		1740
10	² Lenox's Estate for H. Parnell's note lost by his failure	1340	
6	Profit & Loss for J. Day's note lost by his failure	400	

5	R. Morris, Dr. to Sundries for Shipment per "Columbia"	5691	22
1	To Mdse. for 1000 bbls. Flour from store @ $5		5000
12	ɴ Cash paid Shipping Charges on the same		300
4	ɴ Bills Payable for my note passed for Insurance		112	30
8	ɴ Commission for Shipping 5 per ct. on $5300 $265.		
	ɴ ɴ for effecting Ins. on 5565 ½ per ct. 13.92		278	92

5	Robt. Morris, Dr.	40	
8	To Commission for Receiving and Forwarding 80 **packages** of goods from Hartwell & Thorndike		40

June 1.

1	Mdse., Dr. to Sundries	12000	
1	To Mdse.		840
5	³ ɴ Warden & Bell		11160

5	⁴ R. Morris, Dr. to Sundries	7756	66
11	To 2d Co. Shipment from New Orleans to London		2126	66
11	ɴ 2d Co. Shipment to London		5630

6	Sundries, Dr. to Profit & Loss		1176	32
11	2d Co. Shipment from New Orleans to London, to close	526	66
11	2d Co. Shipment to London, to close	649	66

12	C. Hartwell, Dr.	6480	
11	To 1st Co. Shipment to Boston		6480

1. Why is not Bills Receivable debited for this renewal, like that on March 17?
2. Why not debit Profit & Loss for both of these losses?
3. Why credit Warden & Bell for this amount, when it is to be paid in a particular way?
4. **Why** is Morris debited for these sums?

¹1st Co. Shipment to Boston now closes as follows—
Total Sales $6480; Charges Posted $60.
My Commission on $6480 @ 2½ per ct. is   .   .   .   162.
Wm. Hay's half net proceeds due this day is   .   .   3129.   **3291**
The balance of the acct. on the Ledger is $3180.
My half first cost is   .   .   . $3240.
My half net proceeds is   .   .   3129.   Loss 111. $3291.

12.

Received Cash from Warden & Bell for their note due this day   **2100**

"

²Bought for Cash at 8 per ct. premium, of R. Banks & Co., for the account
of R. Morris, their Bill @ 60 days' sight on Gibbs, Son & Bright, London, for £1500 sterling, which I remit to Morris   .   . $7200.
My ¼ per ct. for Investing, due this day   .   .   18.   **7218**

18.

Paid Warden & Bell balance due them on purchase of Flour 1st instant.
Check on the City Bank for   .   .   .   10000.
My note @ 60 days for the balance   .   .   1160.   11160

"

James Walker has returned the whole invoice of goods which I placed in
his hands for sale on joint account 13th May last   .   .   3000.
My half is   .   .   . $1500.
³Walker's half is.   .   .   . $1500. $3000.
Walker takes up his note of $2063, due 9th October next,
and pays me the balance in Cash   .   .   .   563.   **3563**

"

⁴The Ship Columbia in which I shipped and insured on May 31, for R.
Morris, goods amounting to $5565, is lost. Received payment for the
loss from the National Insurance Office as follows—
My Premium note held by the office for   .   . $112.30
Cash for the balance—due Morris this day   .   .   5452.70   5565

"

⁵Bought of Joel Post, his Bill on Baring & Co. @ 60 days' sight for £450
sterling $2000
Premium 8 per ct. 160.   2160
Paid him in his note due 15th instant   .   500.
Cash for the balance   .   .   .   1660. $2160.

25.

⁶Bought 10 tierces Refined Sugars at Austin's auction room
for Cash   .   .   .   .   . $800.
Sold them at the same place to G Barron on his note at 30
days for $980.   Gain on the transaction   .   .   180.   980

1. The Rule is always to deduct all charges, including commission, from total sales.—See note 4, p. 90.
2. Our Profit & Loss account is not to be debited for this premium—we paid it for Morris.
3. We have taken back Walker's share of these goods in part payment of his note.
4. We got in debt to Morris, having collected this money for him of the Insurance Office.
5. We have here received one Bill Receivable, and given up another.
6. Property can never be delivered or credited, until it is received and debited: this merchandise having been sold before it was brought home or entered, the transaction cannot affect that account. Bills Receivable—the thing received—is Dr.; Cash and Profit & Loss, Cr.

	Sundries, Dr. to Sundries . . . . . $3291.				
11	¹ 1st Co. Shipment to Boston, to close acct. . .	3180			
6	Profit & Loss	111			
3	To Wm. Hay			3129	
8	" Commission			162	

12.

12	Cash, Dr.	2100			
3	To Bills Receivable			2100	

5	² R. Morris, Dr. to Sundries	7218			
12	To Cash			7200	
8	" Commission			18	

18.

5	Warden & Bell, Dr. to Sundries, to close acct. . .	11160			
12	To Cash			10000	
4	" Bills Payable			1160	

	Sundries, Dr. to Sundries . . . . . $3563.				
1	³ Mdse.	3000			
12	Cash	563			
3	To Bills Receivable			2063	
11	" 3d Co. Adventure, to close acct. . . .			1500	

5	⁴ Sundries, Dr. to R. Morris			5565	
4	Bills Payable	112	30		
12	Cash	5452	70		

	Sundries, Dr. to Sundries . . . . . $2160.				
3	⁵ Bills Receivable	2000			
6	Profit & Loss	160			
3	To Bills Receivable			500	
12	" Cash			1660	

25.

3	Bills Receivable, Dr. to Sundries	980			
12	⁵ To Cash			800	
6	" Profit & Loss			180	

1. Explain how the net proceeds is found here. The student will not understand this entry without repeated study.
2. Why is Profit & Loss not debited for the premium we paid on this Bill?
3. Walker paid us for this $1500 worth of goods on the 13th May, why is he not now credited for the amount, having returned the goods?
4. Why credit Morris for this money?
5. Why is the Bills Receivable account both debited and credited in the same entry?
6. Why is the Merchandise account not to be credited for this $980, seeing merchandise is the thing delivered?

¹ William Hay and myself having agreed to close our speculations on joint account, he has taken delivery of his half Invoice of Pork, bought 4th May last, and which remained unsold, and I carry my half to my own Merchandise account .   .   .   . | 2500

² Close 1st Co. Sales.   Total sales effected for 200 bales Cotton and 800 bbls. Flour, $14300.
My Commission, 2½ per cent., on the same is 357.50
Wm. Hay's half net proceeds paid him in cash is .   .   .   6971.25
My net gain is   .   .   .   .   471.25 | 7800

28.

Paid Cash J. Carpenter & Co.'s Bill for Repairs of House 49 Cedar Street | 280

My Commission for collecting $800 for Estate A. Lenox, @ 5 per cent., is | 40

³ Received advice from Baring & Co., of Liverpool, of the Sale of 1st Co. Shipment of Flour, shipped by the "Erie" 15th April last, net proceeds £900 sterling. $4000, which they remitted agreeably to my orders to R. Morris, London, on my account, 10th ultimo   .   . $4000.
Premium on Exchange is 8 per ct..   .   .   .   .   .   .   320. | 4320
    Wm. Hay's half is   .   .   .   2160.
    My half is   .   .   .   2160. $4320.

Received advice from R. Morris that he received Cash £562 10s. on the 20th ultimo, Freight of Ship Roscoe   .   .   .   . $2500.
⁴ The present rate of Exchange on London is 8 per ct. prem.   .   200. | 2700

⁴ I close the acct. of Ship Roscoe and owners.   Total receipts of Freight is $8700.   Disbursements to date $1250.
My 2½ Commission on Freights and Passages collected is .   .   217.50
C. Hartwell's ½ net proceeds is 3616.25
My   ¼   do. 1808.13
Wm. Hay's   ¼   do.   .   .   .   .   .   1808.12 | 7450

30.

Received advice from R. Morris that he has sold my ¼ of Ship Roscoe. Net proceeds due 30th August, £1462 10s.   .   .   .   .   . | 6500

I now close 1st Co. Shipment to Liverpool with a gain of   .   361.
Also   Ship Roscoe my ¼ with a gain of   .   .   .   3308.13 | 3669 | 13

Paid Cash for Expenses, ⅌ Expense Book, from 1st January to date   .   . | 1099 | 23

⁵ Balance of Interest due R. Morris, ⅌ acct. current rendered, is   £ | 33 | 06

1. Hay has paid for his share of these goods, therefore cannot be debited when he takes them away.
2. Deduct all charges from the total sales.—See Note 3, p. 86, and Note 4, p. 90.
3. Profit & Loss or Exchange must be debited for both these sums, because the gain on the exchange forms part of the profits, for which we are accountable to our associates in the transactions.
4. This is a settlement of all our transactions as agent for the ship up to this date. We close her acct. and carry the dividends to the credit of the other owners.
5. This is found by drawing out his account current.—See Form 1, p. 114.

1	¹ Mdse., Dr.	2500		·	
9	To 1st Co. Sales			2500	
	"				
9	² 1st Co. Sales, Dr. to Sundries, to close acct.	7800			
8	To Commission			357	50
12	*"* Cash			6971	25
6	*"* Profit & Loss			471	25
	28.				
10	House 49 Cedar Street, Dr.	280			
12	To Cash			280	
	"				
10	Estate of A. Lenox, Dr.	40			
8	To Commission			40	
	"				
	³ Sundries, Dr. to Sundries $4320.				
5	R. Morris	4000			
6	Profit & Loss	320			
3	To Wm. Hay			2160	
11	*"* 1st Co. Shipment to Liverpool			2160	
	"				
9	Sundries, Dr. to Ship Roscoe & owners			2700	
5	R. Morris	2500			
6	³ Profit & Loss	200			
	"				
9	⁴ Ship Roscoe & owners, Dr. to Sundries, to close account	7450			
8	To Commission			217	50
12	*"* C. Hartwell			3616	25
9	*"* Ship Roscoe, my ¼			1808	13
3	*"* Wm. Hay			1808	12
	30.				
5	R. Morris, Dr.	6500			
9	To Ship Roscoe, my ¼			6500	
	"				
6	Sundries, Dr. to Profit & Loss			3669	13
11	1st Co. Shipment to Liverpool, to close acct.	361			
9	Ship Roscoe, my ¼, to close account	3308	13		
	"				
6	Profit & Loss, Dr. to Sundries	1132	29		
12	To Cash			1099	23
5	⁵ *"* R. Morris			33	06

1. Why is Hay not debited for **the proportion of these** goods that he has taken away?
2. How is the net proceeds and Hay's share found?
3. Why should we debit our Profit & Loss account for these premiums on Exchange?
4. What is the object of this entry?
5. How is this balance of interest ascertained?

ON THE DETECTION OF ERRORS.

1. If the Day Book, Journal, and Ledger have been carefully checked according to our previous directions, we may presume that all is thus far correct. If our trial comes out incorrect, our attention will, therefore, be first directed to its own additions and those of the Ledger. Then see that all the accounts are taken off correctly, and upon the proper side of the sheet—that the amounts are correctly forwarded from one page to another. Then examine the additions of all the Journal entries, to be certain that the debits and credits are equal upon that book. If the error is not found by these means, the posting from the Journal to the Ledger since the last balance will have to be all checked over again—a formidable undertaking in a business of any magnitude; but there is no other means of finding the error.

2. ON THE CORRECTION OF ERRORS IN THE LEDGER.—It is not easy to lay down precise directions for correcting errors in all cases. But it may be useful to the learner to have some general directions, and also to be guided in all cases by the following general rule—always to make the correction explain itself, by distinctly referring to the place of the error, and the error to refer to the place of correction. It is not sufficient merely to write "To Error" or "By Error," because either the book-keeper, or his successor, may be called upon for an explanation of an entry of this kind.

3. If a post be omitted at the proper date, enter it under the date of the last entry, with the back date in the title column, in a parenthesis, thus (July 19); the page of the Journal in its own column.

4. If two accounts be opened with the same person, close the one into the other, "To," or 'By A. B.'s acct., fol."—footing and ruling off the closed account, as a settled account; stating the particulars of such transfers at A. B.'s open account with the Journal reference.

5. If you have posted an entry to the wrong side of an account, erase the figures in the amount column, leaving a couple of ciphers to fill up the space, and leave the rest of the line without erasure: it serves to explain the alteration and does not deface the page. Then make the post to the proper side.

6. If you have posted to a wrong account, dispose of the error as directed in the last paragraph; then post the entry to the proper account.

7. If the same entry be twice posted, leave ciphers in the money column of the last entry as before directed. If you have room in the title column, insert (see last entry) or such explanation as the case require, on the same line with the correction.

8. I do not approve of correcting errors by counter entries if it can be avoided, as it gives the account a distorted appearance. The merchandise account, for instance, may by this means be made to exhibit an amount of purchases and sales far beyond the reality; while the chief object for keeping this account is to show these amounts correctly. If, however, the error is discovered after the account is footed and forwarded (a thing that ought never to be done until it is checked), then the correction can only be made by a counter entry, or by footing the column and deducting the error from it.

9. If you have discovered an error in the addition after the account is footed and forwarded, note it "short" or "over added, $—corrected June —, fol."—and make the entry of the correction, as usual, refer to the folio of the error. If there be many of them, it may be proper to make a Day Book entry of them; but this can only be done with those errors requiring a *double entry* for their correction.

10. ON CORRECTING ERRORS IN THE JOURNAL.—This book, like the Ledger, not being a book of original entry, when it can be done without defacing the page, there is no objection to correcting an entry by erasing a figure or two, and writing over them again. But if the error make it necessary to cancel the whole entry, it must not be scored nor scratched out, but mark it in the margin "void, corrected page,"—then make the corrected entry in the first vacancy, giving reference to the place of error.

11. ON CORRECTING ERRORS IN THE DAY BOOK.—It should be a rule never to erase any essential particular of a record on this or any other book of original entry. If an error admits of correction without cancelling the whole entry, it may be done by running the pen lightly through the name or figures, leaving them legible, and writing the correct ones over them.

12. If the error makes it necessary to cancel the whole entry, you will proceed as just directed for the same purpose in the Journal.

ON OPENING AND CLOSING THE LEDGER.

AFTER journalizing a page or a month of the Day Book, the learner will open his Ledger according to the directions in note 1, page 32. Then proceed as there directed with the posting and checking, until the whole business of the set is posted into the Ledger. Then add up all the accounts that remain open, inserting the amounts on each side in pencil in the margin. From these amounts make up your trial balance, referring to those on page 36 for the form, and to our directions for detecting errors on the last page if it comes out wrong.

It may be proper here to fix the pupil's attention distinctly upon the OBJECT for closing the ledger, which is not only [1] to ASCERTAIN the gain or loss, but to RECORD it upon the face of the Ledger in such a manner as to afford satisfactory evidence, at any future period, of the true state of the business at this time.—See Notes 1 to 4, p. 18.

For this purpose the Double Entry Ledger furnishes the particulars for making up [2] two statements, both of which will exhibit the same result. 1st, a detailed statement of gains and losses in the Profit & Loss account, from whence the stock, or original capital, receives the result, and then immediately shows the PRESENT NET CAPITAL. The second statement, which must always confirm the correctness of the first one, is made up by presenting a detailed account of Effects and Liabilities in the Balance Account, upon the principles before explained, Notes 2 to 6, p. 18, and Note 4, p. 32. The difference between the amount of the Effects and that of the Liabilities must be the present net capital, and if the operations are all correct will always agree with the result produced by the first statement.—See Notes 1 to 6, Balance acct., p. 35. This agreement between the Stock and Balance account is always a certain consequence of this mode of keeping accounts, because the net gain or loss, which is finally made to show itself in the Stock account, must always produce a corresponding increase or decrease of property, which affects the Balance account to precisely the same extent that it does the Stock account. Therefore, as the balances of property agreed with the credit side of stock (Rule II.) at the opening of the books, they must continue to do so ever after, so long as all the steps of the process are strictly correct. The learner will now derive farther assistance from the following

RULES FOR CLOSING THE LEDGER.

RULE I. All personal accounts close To or By BALANCE.

II. All accounts of property belonging to ourselves, close as follows :—
  Case 1st.—If all be sold, paid away or lost, and the account remaining open, close it To or By PROFIT & LOSS.
  Case 2d.—If all or part remain on hand, credit the account first By Balance for the value remaining in hand, and if this entry does not close it, close as in Case 1st—To or By PROFIT & LOSS.

III. All accounts representing gain or loss, close To or By PROFIT & LOSS.

IV. When Profit & Loss has received all its transfers, IT CLOSES INTO STOCK—never into Balance—and after all other accounts are closed, Stock finally CLOSES INTO BALANCE.

V. Bills Payable always closes To BALANCE for the amount we owe on our notes. When they are all paid, the account must be SELF-CLOSED.

It may be stated also as a general rule, that no property account can close To Balance. This part of Book-keeping is rarely ever understood, without repeated and attentive study; but as no person is entitled to call himself an accountant who cannot close a Ledger, the author trusts that all learners who desire to excel in the profession, will give this part of the subject that attention which its importance deserves. If they will but take half the pains to study it, that he has taken to explain it, their perseverance will be amply repaid.

---

1. What is the object of closing the Ledger?
2. What particulars does it furnish for the purpose of ascertaining the present net capital?
I. How do all personal accounts close?
II. How do property accts. belonging to ourselves close when all is sold, paid away, or lost, and the acct. still remaining open?
  How if all or part of the property remain in hand?
III. How do all accounts representing gain or loss close?
IV. How does the Profit & Loss account close, and when does it close?
V. How does the Bills Payable account close while we owe any thing on our notes?
  How does it close when all our notes are paid?

INDEX TO LEDGER B.

CAUTION TO YOUNG BOOK-KEEPERS.—Always index an account before you head it in the Ledger. Without this precaution you are liable to forget it occasionally, and afterwards to open a second account with this same individual: and unimportant as this may appear to the inexperienced, they will find it will sometimes lead them into very troublesome and vexatious mistakes.

1867.					1867.				
Jan.	1	To Sundries	1	2800		Jan.	1	By Sundries	1	31300	
June	30	" Balance	fol. 13	61544 50		Apr.	10	" Mer's Bank Stock	8	5000	
				64344 50		June	30	" Profit & Loss fol.	6	28044 50	
								64344.50 / 2800. / 61544.50		64344 50	
						June	30	By Bal.		61544 50	

The learner is referred to the Introductory Ledger for all the exercises that will apply to this one.—See Stock acct., p. 33.
1. Is this acct. not usually kept without any entries from the time of opening until closing?
2. If some part of the Liabilities were left out at the opening of the Books, what account should it be afterwards carried to?
3. When collections of doubtful debts (usually left behind in the old Ledger when opening new books) are made, is this not the proper account to credit for them?

1. It is; but there is no irregularity in carrying an entry to it like that on the 10th April, above.
2. Either to this or the Profit & Loss account. It would not be advisable to encumber this account with trifles.
3. It will make no difference in the final balance, whether entered here or at the Profit & Loss acct.; but, for reasons before given, large amounts of this kind ought to appear in the Profit & Loss.—See note 3, p. 30.

MERCHANDISE.

1867.						1867.					
Jan.	1	To Stock	1	3000		Jan.	3	By Cash	1	300	
	3	" Bills Payable		1600			10	" Bills Receivable		3000	
		" Cash		1800				" James Carter		452	
	15	" Bills Payable		1600			15	" "		108	
	20	" J. Carter	2	200			16	" "		600	
	24	" Bills Receivable		500			19	" "	2	400	
Feb.	1	" Sundries	3	11196 10			20	" Ship Hudson		5900	
	18	" Bills Receivable	4	1000		Feb.	12	" Shipm't to N. Orl's	3	2760	
Mar.	12	" Sundries	6	5980				" J. Taylor & Co.		600	
		" Morris' Sales		3240			18	" R. Morris	4	200	
May	18	" 2d Co. Sales	11	3814				" Bills Payable	4	500	
June	1	" Sundries	12	12000			28	" N. Y. Ins. Office	5	3690	
	18	" "	13	3000		Mar.	5	" Sundries	6	3355	
	25	" 1st Co. Sales *6083.10*	14	2500			20	" 1st Co. Sales	7	3240	
	30	" Profit & Loss fol.	6	13743 12			28	" Sundries	8	2500	
						Apr.	5	" Ship't to Liverpool		3000	
							10	" Sundries	9	4600	
							15	" "		2400	
						May	13	" "	11	3000	
							31	" R. Morris	12	5000	
						June	1	" Mdse. *4645. / 18128.22*		840	
							30	" Bal. p.I.B.p.	13	18128 22	
				64573 22				*187.413*		64573 22	

See Mdse. acct. p. 33, and directions for ruling, p. 56.
1. What difference is there between the closing of this account and any other account of property?
2. Supposing it is required to know the gain or loss upon Flour, Cotton, or any other branch of your Merchandise, how is it to be done?

1. There is no essential difference, except in the manner of finding the balance in hand.
2. Open an Account for the Flour or whatever branch of this account you desire to show its own gain or loss, and conduct and close it in every respect like the Merchandise account.

Note.—Be particular to write the "BALANCE" closing entries in red. No others are brought down or forward, and no others should be written in this color.—Note 5, Stock acct., p. 33.

1867 Jan.		Dr.	f	Amount		1867 Jan.		Cr.	f	Amount
Jan.	1	To Stock Led. A. f. 2.	1	7300		Jan.	3	By Mdse.	1	1800
	3	" Mdse.		300			16	" B. Payable	1	1300
	16	" J. Carter		560			18	" House 44 Broad'y	2	280
	18	" House 44 Broad'y	2	150			20	" Ship Hudson		2100
	24	" B. Receivable		500			30	" " 6695.		1200
	30	" Sundries		1500				" Bal. carried down		4226 70
	31	" B. Payable 10906.70 6695. 4226.70		596 70						
				10906 70						10906 70
Feb.		To Bal.		4226 70		Feb.	1	By Mdse.	3	85
	5	" R. Morris' Sales	3	360				" R. Morris' Sales		167 78
	6	" B. Receivable		796 40			5	" "		5
	12	" "		2000			12	" "		28
	25	" Sundries	4	2000				" Ship't to N. Orl's		33
		" Profit & Loss		400				" J. Taylor & Co.		11
	28	" Sundries	5	4822 22			18	" House in Broad'y	4	201
		" " 17415.48 10902.78 6462.70		2810 16				" Profit & Loss		181
								" R. Morris		3400
								" Bills Payable		20
							20	" R. Morris' Sales		21
							25	" Bills Receivable		2000
								" Sundries 10902.78		4800
							28	" Bal. carried down		6462 70
				17415 48						17415 48
Mar.	1	To Bal.		6462 70		Mar.	2	By Ship Roscoe my ¼	5	2120
		" Wm. Hay	5	2500			4	" Sh. Roscoe & Owners		850
	2	" Ship Hudson		1850				" Bills Payable	6	1400
	5	" Mdse.	6	255			12	" Mdse.		180
		" Sh. Roscoe & Owners		1800			16	" Estate A. Lenox	7	2500
	12	" N. Y. Ins. Co.		3690			17	" Sundries		170
		" Estate A. Lenox	7	7500			25	" 1st Co. Sales		4500
	17	" Sundries		104 20			31	" Sundries 17099	8	1300
	28	" Mdse. 24661.90 13020. 11641.90	8	500				" Bal. carried down		11641 90
				24661 90						24661 90
	31	To Bal.		11641 90		Apr.	1	By B. Receivable	8	2000
Apr.	20	" Sundries	9	2017 70			5	" Ship't to Liverpool		348 55
	22	" "	10	1520 80				" R. Morris		20
							10	" J. Taylor & Co.		1204
								" Sundries	9	300
								" 1st Co. Ship't to B'n		60
							15	" Sundries		133
							20	" 2d Co. Sales	10	185
							22	" Sundries		3207 05
		Forward to fol. 12		15180 40				Forward to fol. 12		7457 60

1. The learner's attention is here particularly directed to the operation of continuing an account upon a new page. If we were balancing the account here, the expression of the closing entry would be, "Balance in hand carried forward,"—not "carried down;" and the new account would open, "Balance Bro't" forward. The columns should never be footed in ink until checked. Never forget to leave a line to foot the columns upon. The same directions apply to all other accounts.—Note 2, Wood's acct., p. 15.

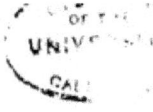

Dr.   **BILLS**   **RECEIVABLE.**   **Cr.**   3

1867.					1867.				
Jan.	1	To Stock,	1	3000	Jan.	24	By Sundries,	2	1000
	10	" Merchandise,		3000	Feb.	6	" "	3	800
	18	" J. Carter,	2	600		12	" "		600
	30	" Sundries,		1515 75			" Cash,		2000
	31	" Bills Payable,		800		18	" Mdse.,	3	1000
Feb.	9	" Morris' Sales,	3	2100		28	" Cash,	5	4444 44
	12	" Bills Receivable,		300	Mar.	16	" Wm. Hay,	7	300
	25	" Cash,	4	2000		17	" Sundries,		500
		" "		4444 44	Apr.	5	" Ship't to Liverpool,	8	4500
	28	" Sundries, .	5	2011		20	" Cash,	9	2011
Mar.	12	" Morris' Sales,	6	4500		22	" "	10	1515 75
		" Estate of A. Lenox,	7	1700		23	" R. Morris,		2000
	17	" Sundries,		400	May	25	" Cash,	12	7000
	20	" Estate of A. Lenox,		1340		31	" Sundries,		1740
Apr.	1	" Sundries,	8	2063	June	12	" Cash,	13	2100
May	13	" "	11	7000		18	" Sundries,		2063
	18	" 2d Co. Sales,		3000			" "	3602,19	500
June	18	" Sundries,	13	2000		30	" Balance,	f. 13	8680
	25	" "		980					
		42754.19 / 3602.19 / 8680.		42754 19					42754 19
	30	To Balance,		8680					

See Bills Receivable account, p. 33.
1. Is it not better to post the debit and credit of each note on the same line opposite each other?

2. Does the manner of conducting this account not form an exception to Rules VI. and VII.?

3. Why is this deviation from the rule for conducting other property accounts?

1. It is, where there are no endorsements; but it is better not to occupy the learner's attention with this mode of posting it until he has learned the principles—See p. 167.
2. It does so; it is always debited and credited for the *face of the bill only*; not for what it costs or what it brings in.
3. It is done for the purpose of making the balance of the acct. agree with the balance of notes on hand.

WILLIAM   **HAY.**

1867.					1867.				
Jan.	1	To Stock Ledger A, f.	2	3000	Jan.	30	By Sundries,	2	3000
Mar.	2	To J. Walker,	5	600	Feb.	12	By Ship't to N. Orleans	3	1500
	16	" Bills Receivable,	7	300	Mar.	1	" Cash,	5	2500
Apr.	15	" Sundries,	9	1799			" 1st Co. Sales,		450
May	4	" Merch. B'k Stock,	11	2500		5	" " "	6	1400
June	30	" Balance, 5199. fol.	13	10813 12	Apr.	5	" R. Morris,	8	2000
						15	" Sundries,	9	1065
					June	1	" "	13	3129
						28	" "	14	2160
							" Ship Roscoe & Own.		1808 12
							16012.12 / 5199. / 10813.12		
				16012 12					16012 12
					June	30	By Bal. ⅌ % rendered,		10813 12

See Form III., p. 116, and
Morris' account, p. 193.

4 Dr. BILLS   **PAYABLE. Cr.**

1867.					1867.				
Jan.	16	To Cash,	1	1300	Jan.	1	By Stock,	1	300
Feb.	18	" Sundries,	4	1600		3	" Mdse.,		1000
Mar.	4	" Cash,	6	1400		15	" "		1600
	5	" Mdse.,		2500		20	" Ship Hudson,	2	8000
Apr.	22	" Sundries,	10	8000		31	" Bills Receivable,		800
	23	" Cash,		601			" Sundries,		600
May	4	" "		2222 22	Feb.	1	" Mdse.,	3	2222 22
	8	" "	11	202 70		"	" R. Morris' Sales,		2222 22
June	18	" R. Morris, 17938.22	13	112 30		20	" R. Morris,	4	2500
	30	" Balance, f.	13	6027 22	Mar.	4	" Sh. Roscoe & own'rs	5	400
					Apr.	5	" Ship't to Liverpool,	8	161 45
							" R. Morris,		41 25
						10	" John Taylor & Co.	9	601
							" Sundries,		145
						20	" 2d Co. Sales,	10	3000
					May	31	" R. Morris,	12	112 30
					June	18	" Warden & Bell,	13	1160
				24865 44			24865.44 / 17938.22 / 6927.22		24865 44
					June	30	By Balance,		6927 22

See Bills Payable, p. 34.
1. Is it not found convenient to post the debits and credits upon the same line, as described in the Bills Receivable acct.?
2. Why then was it not introduced here?
3. How does this account close and re-open when posted in this way?

1. I recommend this mode of posting both bill accounts, in all kinds of business.
2. Because it is desirable to avoid distracting the pupil's attention with too many matters at once, and we have exemplified it in our Bill Accounts, p. 167.
3. Precisely like the Bill Book, p. 50.

HOUSE 44   BROADWAY.

1867.					1867.				
Jan.	1	To Stock Ledger A, fol.	3	15000	Jan.	18	By Cash,	2	150
	18	" Cash,	2	280	May	1	" "	10	150
Feb.	18	" "	4	201	June	30	" Balance, f.	13	15000
			15481. / 15300.			30	" Profit & Loss, f.	6	181
			181.	15481					15481
June	30	To Balance,		15000					

1. What is this account debited and credited for?
2. How does it close?
3. How is the first closing entry of $15000 found?
4. How is the second closing entry found?
5. What does this difference represent, and what is done with it?

1. It is debited for its cost and credited for what it has brought me in.—Rules VI. and VII., p. 39.
2. By Rule II., p. 99.
3. It is what we value the house at.—See first debit entry.
4. It is the difference between the two sides after the first closing entry is made.
5. It is the loss upon the property, and we debit Profit & Loss for it.

MERCHANTS'   BANK STOCK.

1867.					1867.				
Apr.	10	To Stock,	8	5000	May	1	By Cash,	10	250
May	4	" Profit & Loss,	11	750		4	" Sundries,	11	5500
				5750					5750

1. How is this account kept and closed?

1. This is a property account, and is conducted by the same rules as all other property accounts. The property being all sold on the 4th of May, the account was then closed by a Day-Book entry.—See Note 5, p. 80.

1867.					1867.				
Feb.	18	To Sundries	4	4440	Jan.	1	By Stock, Led. A. fol.	2	2000
	20	" B. Payable		2500	Feb.	1	" Mdse.	3	8888 88
Apr.	5	" Sundries	8	2166 25		25	" Cash	4	1995
	10	" "	9	4980 33		28	" Sundries	5	4444 44
	25	" "	10	2400	Mar	12	" Morris' Sales	7	9052
May	31	" "	12	5691 22	Apr.	20	" 2d Co. Sales	10	4000
		" Commission		40	May	8	" Sundries	11	4444 44
June	1	" Sundries		7756 66		18	" 2d Co. Sales		4093 05
	12	" "	13	7218	June	18	" Sundries	13	5565
	28	" "	14	4000		30	" Profit & Loss	14	33 06
		" S. Roscoe & owners		2500			" Bal. fol.	13	5676 59
	30	" S.Roscoe.my¼		6500					
				50192 46					50192 46
June	30	To Bal. ⅌ acct. Rend.		5676 59					

1. What does the debit and credit side of this account show?
2. How do they close?
3. Why is the expression "Rendered" annexed to the Balance brought down?

1. All personal accounts are alike, and are debited for your account against them, and credited for their account against us.—Note 3, p. 23.
2. To or By Balance.
3. Because a statement of his account has been sent him.—See p. 114.

WARDEN   &   BELL.

1867.					1867.				
Jan.	24	To James Walker	2	500	Jan.	1	By Stock, Led. A. fol.	2	500
June	18	" Sundries	13	11160	June	1	" Mdse.	12	11160
				11660					11660

1. When was this account footed and ruled off?
2. Is it always necessary to close an account every time it is settled?

1. On June 18, when we paid him off.
2. There may be cases when it is not absolutely necessary to do so; but as the omission of it sometimes leads to very troublesome consequences, our advice is, always to make it a rule to do so.—See note 1, Wood's Account, p. 15, and note p. 20.

JAMES   CARTER.

1867.					1867.				
Jan.	10	To Mdse.	1	452	Jan.	16	By Cash	1	560
	15	" "		108					
				560					560
	16	To Mdse.	1	600		18	By B. Receivable	2	600
	19	" "	2	400		20	" Sundries		400
				1000					1000

1. This account was closed on the 15th and 19th; would the balance struck on the 19th not have served for both?

1. It would; but it is better to close the old account every time it is paid.

105

6 Dr.   SHIP   HUDSON.   Cr.

1867						1867						
Jan.	20	To Sundries		2	16000		Mar.	2	By Cash		5	1850
	30	" Cash	1700.		1200		May	4	" "	3350.	10	3500
June	30	" Profit & Loss fol.		6	4150		June	30	" Balance	3350. 1700. 4150	f.13	16000
					21350							21350
June	30	To Balance			16000							

1. How is this account kept, and how are the first and second closing entries found?

1. This account is in every respect like "House in Broadway," and closes by the same rule.—See that account, p. 104.

PROFIT · &   LOSS.

1867						1867						
Jan.	20	To J. Carter		2	200		Jan.	30	By Sundries		2	15 75
	31	" B. Payable			3 30		Feb.	25	" Cash		4	400
Feb.	6	" B. Receivable			3 60			28	" "		5	377 78
	12	" "		3	300				" Sundries			376 72
	18	" Cash		4	181		Mar.	5	" 1st Co. Sales		6	358
	25	" "			355 56			12	" Shipm't to N. Orl's			1507
Apr.	22	" Sundries		10	7 05				" Morris' Sales		7	18
May	31	" B. Receivable		12	400			17	" Sundries			4 20
June	1	" Sundries		13	111		Apr.	1	" Bills Receivable		8	63
	18	" "			160			20	" Cash		9	6 70
	28	" "		14	320			22	" "		10	5 05
		" S. Roscoe & owners			200			25	" R. Morris			400
	30	" Sundries	3373.80		1132 29			30	" 3d Co. Adventure			500
		" Amount to date			3373 80		May	4	" Mer'ts Bank Stock		11	750
		" Ho. in Br'dway 3634.60 f.		4	181			8	" Sundries			355 56
		" Stock for net gain f.		1	28044 50			13	" "			140
								18	" 2d Co. Sales			106 05
									" Cash		12	18 90
								25	" "			70
							June	1	" Sundries			1176 32
								25	" Bills Receivable		13	180
									" 1st Co. Sales		14	471 25
								30	" Sundries	10969.41		3669 13
									" Amount to date			10969 41
									" Mdse. fol.		1	13743 12
									" Ship Hudson "		6	4150
									" Commiss'n 31599.30 2634.80 28044.50 "		8	2736 77
					31599 30							31599 30

See PROFIT & LOSS ACCOUNT, p. 35.

1. Why is this account footed on both sides June 30?
2. What are these transfers, and why is the note "fol." annexed to them?
3. What is the object for **bringing these** transfers **to this** account?
4. As a general rule, no entry passes from Balance to this Account: neither has it any balance to bring down into new account: is there no exception to this rule?

1. These were the additions for the Trial Balance, and are placed there to save the trouble of adding up the whole column again after the transfers are made.
2. They are the gains and losses found by closing the different accounts named. "Folio" distinguishes the Ledger pages from those of the Journal, which are placed together in the same column.
3. To complete our account of gains and losses, and thereby ascertain our net increase or decrease of capital, shown by the small marginal figures.—Note 4, Mdse. p. 33.
4. There are but few exceptions, save those created by partnership settlements.—Part II., p. 177.

1867.					1867.				
Mar.	5	To Mdse.,	6	600	Jan.	24	By Warden & Bell,	2	500
Apr.	30	" 3d Co. Adventure,	10	2500	Mar.	2	" Sundries,	5	1200
May	8	" Sundries,	11	600	Apr.	20	" 3d Co. Adventure,	9	2000
				3700					3700

R. MORRIS'   SALES.

1867.					1867.				
Feb.	1	To Sundries,	3	2390	Feb.	5	By Cash,	3	360
	5	" Cash,		5		9	" Bills Receivable,		2100
	12	" "		28		18	" R. Morris,	4	840
	20	" " 2444.	4	21			" Bills Payable,		1080
Mar.	12	" Sundries,	7	9676	Mar.	12	" Bills Receivable,	6	4500
						"	" Mdse., 2122. 2444.		3240
				12120			9676.		12120

Repeat Rule X., p. 41, and see Note 3, p. 68.
1. How is Morris' net proceeds found when all the goods are sold?
2. How are consignment accounts closed and reopened when the Ledger is closed with part of the property on hand, and no sales rendered?
3. How if you render account sales of the part sold?

1. There was $9676 Balance at the credit of the account when the sales were completed. Our commission is $006, storage and advertising $18. After deducting these charges the remainder belongs to Morris. It is therefore evident that this balance of $9676 belongs to these three accounts.—See Journal entry March 12, p. 83, and Account Sales, p. 117.
2. They close and re-open by Double Balance.—See Commission Sales acct., Part II., p. 169.
3. The acct. closes as above, and does not re-open until the sale of the goods on hand recommences.—Note 4, p. 68.

SHIPMENT TO   (J. Taylor & Co.)   **NEW ORLEANS.**

1867.					1867.				
Feb.	12	To Sundries,	3	4293	Mar.	12	By Mdse.,	6	5800
Mar.	12	" Profit & Loss,	6	1507					
				5800					5800

Repeat Rule XI., p. 41, and Rule II., p. 99.
1. What kind of an account is this, and why was it closed on the 12th March?

1. It is a property account, and was closed on the 12th March because full returns were then received.—Note 5, p. 86.

SHIPMENT TO   (Columbia)   **LIVERPOOL.**

1867.					1867.				
Apr.	5	To Sundries,	8	8010	June	30	By Balance,	f. 13	8010
June	30	To Bal. bro't down,		8010					

1. When the accounts are to continue in the same **Ledger**, would it not have been answered as well to have made the entry in the Balance account, without closing and re-opening this acct.?

1. It would; but I wish to show the universal application of my rule for closing all property accounts belonging to ourselves. This example differs from any previous one, as the property has produced no returns.—Rule II., p. 99.

107

1867.						1867.						
Feb.	12	To Sundries,		3	644		Apr.	15	By 2d Co. Shipm't New			
Apr.	10	" "		8	1210				Orleans to London,		9	1600
		" "		9	604		May	18	" 2d Co. Sales, ₅₆₉₃.₀₅		11	4093 05
		" "	7438.33 5693.05	9	4980 33		June	30	" Balance,	f.	13	1745 28
			1745.28		7438 33							7438 33
June	30	To Bal. ⅌ ℀ rendered,			1745 28							

See Form II., p. 116, Morris' acct., p. 105.

COMMISSION   ACCOUNT.

1867.							1867.						
June	30	To Profit & Loss,	fol.	6	2736	77	Feb.	12	By J. Taylor & Co.,		3	33	
								25	" Cash,		4	5	
							Mar.	5	" 1st Co. Sales,		6	72	
								12	" R. Morris' Sales,		7	606	
							Apr.	5	" R. Morris,		8	105	
								10	" J. Taylor & Co.,			6	
									" "		9	3	
									" Sundries,			396	
							May	18	" 2d Co. Sales,		11	396	85
								31	" R. Morris,		12	278	92
									" "			40	
							June	1	" Sundries,		13	162	
								12	" R. Morris,			18	
								25	" 1st Co. Sales,		14	357	50
								28	" Estate of A. Lenox,			40	
									" Sh. Roscoe & owners			217	50
					2736	77			2736.77			2736	77

1. To what class of accounts does this belong?
2. Why not carry the entries to Profit & Loss at once?
3. How is this account kept?
4. How is it closed?
5. Are there not sometimes entries made at this account that have to be brought down into new account?

1. It is a branch of the Profit & Loss acct.
2. We could not then know what we made by this branch of our business.—See Note 4, p. 24.
3. By debiting it for returned commissions, and for what we may lose by guaranteeing, and crediting it for all we earn by agencies.
4. Always to Profit & Loss—never To Balance.
5. Very seldom, except in partnership settlements: these are explained in the next part, p. 177.

NEW YORK   INSURANCE OFFICE.

1867.						1867.					
Feb.	28	To Mdse.,		5	3690	Mar.	12	By Cash,		6	3690

1. To which class of accounts does this belong?

1. Although it is not with a person, yet it is a personal acct and is kept in every respect similar.

1867.					1867.				
Mar.	1	To Wm. Hay,	5	450	Mar.	2	By Sh. Roscoe, my ½,	5	2880
	2	" J. Walker,		600					
	5	" Sundries,	6	1830					1890.
				2880					2880
	20	To Misc.,	7	3240	Apr.	10	By Sundries,	9	9500
	25	" Cash,		4500		"	" 1st Ship't to Bost'n,	9	3240
	28	" Mdse.,	8	2000		22	" Sundries,	10	4800
May	4	" Merch. B'k Stock,	11	2500	June	25	" Mdse.,	20040. 12240.	14	2500
June	25	" Sundries, 12240.	14	7800				7800.	
				20040					20040

See Notes 5 and 6, p. 42, and Rule XII., p. 43.

1. Why was this account closed on the 5th of March?

2. How and where does this account close when all is sold?

3. How if there be none sold, or if the sales are not more than enough to cover the charges you have advanced?
4. How if there be more than enough sold to cover charges?

5. Why is this distinction made after the charges are covered?
6. What is done with the balance entry?

1. Because we rendered account sales and settled with our partner at that date.—Note 5, p. 80.
2. It closes To Sundries, by a Day Book entry.—See Note 3, p. 80, and Note 2, p. 96.
3. It closes By Balance, the charges being payable out of the first sales.
4. Credit the account first By Balance for our proportion of the part unsold, then close To Sundries as if all were sold.
5. The amount sold afterwards is partly ours and partly our associate's.
6. It is brought down or transferred like all other balance entries.—See Part II., p. 177.

SHIP　　(My ½)　　ROSCOE.

1867.					1867.				
Mar.	2	To Sundries,	5	5000		June	28	By Sh. Roscoe & own'rs	14	1808	13
June	30	" Profit & Loss,	14	3308	13		30	" R. Morris,	"	6500
				8308	13					8308	13

1. To what class of accounts does this belong?

1. It is a property account, and is conducted and closed by the same rules as all other property accounts.

SHIP ROSCOE　　AND OWNERS.

1867.					1867.				
Mar.	4	To Sundries,	5	1250	Mar.	5	By Cash,	6	1800
June	28	" "	14	7450	May	4	" "	10	4200
					June	28	" Sundries,	14	2700
				8700					8700

1. What kind of an account is this?
2. How is it closed?

3. Could this and the last account not be kept under one head upon the same principle as 1st Company Sales?
4. Why?

1. It is conducted under the rules for personal accounts.
2. If the debit side be the largest, close By Balance; but if the credits be the largest, close To Sundries, as on the 28th of June.—See Part II., p. 177.
3. Not without the risk of much confusion.

4. Because the credits of the former account are private property; but the credits of the latter are joint property, and could not therefore be placed in one account.

1867.					1867.					
Mar.	16	To Cash,	7	2500	Mar.	12	By Sundries,	7	31200	
	17	" "		10		20	" B. Receivable,	12340.	1340	
May	31	" Bills Receivable,	12	1340	June	30	" City Bank Stock, £	10	500	
June	28	" Commission, 5%.	14	40						
	30	" House 49 Cedar St	10	140					29010.	
	"	" Balance, f.	13	29010						
				33040					33040	
							By Balance,		29010	

1. What is the object of this account, and how is it kept?

2. How does it close and reopen?

3. Suppose the time has arrived when we have to pay over the above balance, $29010, to the two legatees, to each one half, and R. Lenox takes the house in Cedar Street at its valuation as part payment, and C. Lenox the bank stock, also at our valuation, as part payment of her legacy; and we pay over each the remaining balance due them in cash, how do we close all these accounts?

1. It is to show the **details of our** administration of the Lenox Estate, and is **opened and** conducted like a personal account.

2. After it has received its transfers from its branches—see the two next accounts—then close as a personal acct.

3. By a Day Book entry, thus—

LENOX ESTATE TO SUNDRIES TO CLOSE ACCT., $29010.

To House 49 Cedar St., conveyed to R. Lenox for 12000
" R. Lenox, amount already paid per acct. . . . 800
" Cash paid R. Lenox for balance of his Legacy . . 1705
" City Bank Stock, conveyed to C. Lenox for . . . 10000
" Charlotte Lenox, for amount paid per acct. . . . 500
" Cash, now paid balance of her Legacy 4005

HOUSE 49   (Lenox Estate)   CEDAR STREET.

1867.					1867.					
Mar.	12	To Estate of A. Lenox,	7	12000	May	1	By Cash,	10	300	
	17	" Cash,		160	June	30	" Balance, 12300. f.	13	12000	
June	28	" " 12440. 12000. 160.	14	280			" Estate of A. Lenox,	10	140	
				12440					12440	
June	30	To Balance,		12000						

1. What is this account debited and credited for?
2. How does it close?
3. Why not close To or By Profit & Loss?

1. Debit first for its value, and for what it costs afterwards; credit for what it brings in by sale or rent.
2. If unsold, credit first By Balance for the value; then close To or By Lenox Estate.
3. The gain or loss is not ours; it belongs to the estate.

CITY   (Lenox Estate)   BANK STOCK.

1867.					1867.					
Mar.	12	To Estate of A. Lenox,	7	10000	May	1	By Cash,	10	500	
June	30	" " " f.	10	500	June	30	" Balance, f.	13	10000	
				10500					10500	
June	30	To Balance,		10000						

CHARLOTTE   (Legatee of Lenox Estate)   LENOX.

1867.								
Mar.	31	To Cash,	8	500				

You may, if you choose, close this and the following account By Balance, like "Shipment to Liverpool," p. 107; but I have shown at Hartwell's Account, p. 112, that there is no necessity for it.

ROBERT   (Legatee of Lenox Estate)   LENOX.

1867.								
Mar.	31	To Cash,	8	800				

Dr. 2d Co. Shipment to　(R. Morris)　London.　Cr. 11

1867.						1867.					
Apr.	10	To Sundries,	9	4980	34	June	1	By R. Morris,	12	5630	
June	1	″ Profit & Loss,	12	649	66						
				5630						5630	

See Note 2, p. 86, and Note 4, p. 92.
1. How is this account kept?

1. It is kept and closed in all respects like any other consignment or property account.

1st Co. Shipment to　(C. Hartwell)　Boston.

1867.					1867.				
Apr.	10	To Sundries,	9	3300	June	1	By C. Hartwell,	12	6480
June	1	″ ″	13	3180					
				6480					6480

See Note 3, p. 86.
1. What is this account debited and credited for?
2. Why not credit for our own share of the returns only as in the last account?

1. It is debited for our proportion of the first cost and the whole charges, and credited for the WHOLE returns.
2. Because Hartwell accounts to us here for Hay's share as well as ours. In the last account Morris accounted to each partner for his share.

1st Co. Shipment to　(Baring & Co.)　Liverpool.

1867.					1867.				
Apr.	15	To Sundries,	9	1799	June	28	By Sundries,	14	2160
June	30	″ Profit & Loss,	14	361					
				2160					2160

See Note 3, p. 96.
1. This account, like the last, was debited for our share of the first investment, why not also credit it for the WHOLE returns?

1. In the last account we had charges to deduct from the returns; in this we have none, we therefore carry Hay's half net proceeds at once to his credit.

2d Co. Shipment from　(R. Morris)　New Orleans to London.

1867.						1867.					
Apr.	15	To J. Taylor & Co.,	9	1600		June	1	By R. Morris,	12	2126	66
June	1	″ Profit & Loss,	12	526	66						
				2126	66					2126	66

See Note 5, p. 86.
1. What is this account debited and credited for?

1. It is debited, like "2d Co. Shipment to London," for our share of the first cost, and credited for our proportion of the returns.

3d Company　(J. Walker)　Adventure.

1867.					1867.				
Apr.	20	To J. Walker,	9	2000	Apr.	30	By J. Walker,	10	2500
	30	″ Profit & Loss,	10	500					
				2500					2500
May	13	To Mdse.,	11	1500	June	18	By Sundries,	13	1500

1. Why is this account called an ADVENTURE in Co.?

1. To distinguish it from those joint accounts of which we are the managers of the sales.—See Notes 9 and 10, p. 62.

1867.						1867.					
Apr.	20	To **Sundries**,	10	7185		May	13	By **Sundries**,	11	8500	
May	18	" "	11	8689			18	" "		7374	
				15874						15874	

See Note 4, p. 90.
1. How is this account **conducted**?

1. **In** all respects like 1st Co. Sales, p. 109. We account to each partner for his share of the net proceeds. See form of account, p. 116.

CASH   ACCOUNT.

1867.						1867.					
		Bro't forward, fol.	2	15180	40			Bro't forward, fol.	2	7457	60
						Apr.	23	By Bills Payable,	10	601	
							30	" Bal. carried down,		7121	80
				15180	40					15180	40
Apr.	30	To Bal. bro't down,		7121	80	May	4	By Bills Payable,	10	2222	22
May	1	" Sundries,	10	1200			8	" "	11	202	70
	4	" "		7700			31	" R. Morris,	12	300	
		" Merh. Bank Stock,	11	500			"	" Bal. carried down,		28785	78
	8	" Sundries,		4200							
	13	" Merchandise,		1500							
		" Sundries,		1640							
	18	" 2d Co. Sales,		560							
		" Profit & Loss,	12	18	90						
	25	" Sundries,		7070							
				31510	70					31510	70
	31	To Bal. bro't down,		28785	78	June	12	By R. Morris,	13	7200	
June	12	" Bills Receivable,	13	2100			18	" Warden & Bell,		10000	
	18	" Sundries,		563				" Sundries,		1660	
		" R. Morris,		5452	70		25	" Bills Receivable,		800	
								" 1st Co. Sales,	14	6971	25
							28	" House 49 Cedar St.		280	
							30	" Profit & Loss,		1099	23
							"	" Balance, f.	13	8891	
				36901	48					36901	48
June	30	To Balance		8891							

See Cash Account, p. 31, and Note 6, p. 57.
1. Why is this account balanced every month?

1. Because it must always conform to the Cash Book, and it is easier to make it do so by frequently comparing them.

C.   (Boston)   HARTWELL.

1867.						1867.					
June	1	To 1st Co. Ship't to Boston,	12	6480		June	28	By Sh. Roscoe & owners	14	3616	25

1. Why is this account not closed like all the rest, and what is done with the balance?
2. Would there be any irregularity in closing it?

1. We find the balance by the small pencil figures in the margin, and transfer it as usual to the balance account; but there is no occasion for closing a person's account until you have a settlement with him, or wish to transfer his account to New Books.
2. None: the pupil may **close** it if he chooses.—See Note 3, p. 113.

1867.						1867.				
June 30	To Mdse.	fol.	1	18128	22	June 30	By Wm. Hay	fol.	3	10813 12
	" Bills Receivable		3	8680			" Bills Payable		4	6927 22
	" House in Br'dway		4	15000			" Estate of A. Lenox		10	29010
	" R. Morris		5	5676	59		" Stock for n/c		1	61544 50
	" Ship Hudson		6	16000						
	" Ship't to Liverpool		7	8010						
	" John Taylor & Co.		8	1745	28					
	" House 49 Cedar st.		10	12000						
	" City Bank Stock			10000						
	" Charlotte Lenox			500						
	" Robert Lenox			800						
	" Cash		12	8891						
	" C. Hartwell			2863	75					
				108294	84					108294 84

See Notes to Balance Account, page 17 and 25.
The teacher will now apply the examination on page 56 to this Ledger.

1. REMARKS.—Referring to our previous instruction in closing and re-opening accounts—Notes 5 and 6, p. 9—1 to 7, p. 18—4, p. 32—6, Stock acct., p. 33, and 7, Mdse. acct., p. 33: we may repeat that re-opening a Ledger means, MAKING A NEW ENTRY OF ALL THE EFFECTS AND LIABILITIES, in the heads of the new accounts: and the new accounts recommence immediately under the closing lines of the old ones—Note 6, p. 56—or, if there be no space there, forward under a new head.*

2. We have closed this Ledger, as we first closed the introductory one, under the supposition that the accounts are to continue in the same book. All those accounts that have closed into Balance, are therefore re-opened by bringing the balance (entered in red in the old account) down into the heads of the new accounts in black. If we had closed with the view of transferring the balance to a new Ledger, then this one must remain closed, as you perceive at the second closing of the introductory Ledger.

3. We may observe here, that though we cannot well avoid doing so in teaching, in making up the Balance Account in business, it is unnecessary to close any personal accounts but those with whom you have had settlements; all that is necessary, is to find their correct balances in pencil in the margin—see Hartwell's account last page—and transfer them, as if the accounts were closed, to the Balance Account; and after all is found correct, go over all those accounts requiring addition, and in place of closing them, only foot them, noting the footing on each side "amt. to date," as we have done with our Profit & Loss account before the transfers were made—see p. 106. Leave all the personal accounts open in this manner, to receive any new entries that may occur until you settle with them; then they must always be balanced—Note 1, Carter's acct., p. 105. To exemplify this matter fully, I have left open the two Lenox's and Hartwell's accounts—p. 110 and 112; but I have found it answer the purposes of instruction better to direct the student, for the first time, to close all the accounts without distinction. This is indeed the readiest way to explain what we are referring to.

4. Some authors pass all their closing entries into the Journal, and post them from thence into the Ledger. In business, this must incur additional labor without any apparent advantage.

5. Before proceeding with the general balance, the proof or trial sheet must always be first taken off, in business practice. I always take my trial as follows: transfer all the balances from the pencil figures in the margin of each account, to their respective places in the Profit & Loss and Balance accounts; leaving all the accounts open for the present. Forward the footings of the Balance account only, in pencil. Then pencil the difference of Profit & Loss into Stock, and Stock in the same manner into Balance, which must then be even, if all be correct: if not, the errors have to be sought and corrected in the usual manner. In taking a trial by this method in any extensive business, much labor is saved; but it requires great care and accuracy in every step of the process.

* As with our merchandise account, page 101, which is left closed for the student to re-open upon a new page.

Dr.   R. Morris, Esq., in Acct. Current and

Date.	Items.	Principal.	When Due.	Time.	Interest.-
1867.			1867.		
Feb. 18	For amt. paid your Bill at sight favor R. Banks	4440	Feb. 18	4.12	97 68
20	*v* accept'g your Bill @ 10 days, favor of R. Banks	2500	Mar. 5	3.25	47 92
Apr. 5	*v* Invoice of Merchandise per "Cherub"	2166 25	May 5	1.25	19 86
10	*v* your ⅓ Invoice of joint Ship't ⅌ "Cambria"	4980 33	Apr. 10	2.20	66 40
25	*v* amt. collected from Capt. Bowline	2400	Mar. 20	3.10	40
May 31	*v* Invoice of Shipment to you ⅌ "Columbia"	5691 22	May 31	1.	28 46
	v Com'n forwarding 80 packages from Hartwell & Thorndike, of Boston	40	June 30		
June 1	*v* My ⅓ your Acct. Sales joint Shipment from New Orleans	2126 66	Apr. 15	2.15	26 58
	v My ⅓ your Acct. Sales joint Shipment ⅌ "Cambria"	5630	30	2.	56 30
12	*v* Banks' Bill on Gibbs, Son & Bright	7218	June 12	.18	21 65
28	*v* Baring & Co.'s Remittance on my acct.	4000	May 10	1.20	33 33
	v Freight collected by you for ship Roscoe	2500	May 20	1.10	16 67
30	*v* n. proceeds my ⅓ Ship Roscoe	6500	Aug 30	2.	65
	v Bal. of Int. Acct. at cr. in Acct. Current 50192.46 44315.87			$454.85	33 06
	5676 59	50192 46			487 91
	Balance due P. Duff this day	5676 59			

Errors Excepted, }
New York, June 30th, 1867. }   P. Duff.

1. All well-managed mercantile houses render statements of accounts to all their customers and correspondents, and settle and close their accounts every time they make out their balance sheet. The above, and the two next forms, are illustrations : this one embraces all transactions between us and Morris since our last settlement—from the time that we last balanced our books, down to the time of closing them—30th June.

2. There are various ways of stating interest accounts, but we have seen none that presents all the particulars with so much clearness and simplicity, and in so little space, as this form.

3. The heading of the columns explains sufficiently the use of each of them. The statement is drawn from Morris' account in the Ledger, referring from there by the dates to the Day Book for particulars, when due, &c. The dates, items, principal, and when due columns, are filled up on both sides first. Then compute the time of each entry from the date in the WHEN DUE COLUMN to the time of settlement—30th June, allowing three days' grace only where notes or acceptances are given or received.—See notes 1 to 5, page 45. Extend this time into the TIME COLUMN, and then compute and extend the interest into its column. Those entries which we do not know the day upon which they fall due—such as that on May 8th, Cr. side—are left blank in the interest column, and a Day Book entry will be made to adjust the matter as soon as we learn the particulars.

4. Observe, the date in the WHEN DUE COLUMN, and the figures in the columns to the right of it, in the first entry on the 30th June, Dr. side, are to be written in red, because this $65 interest belongs to Morris, and is not therefore added in our interest column, but, as you perceive, is carried over to Morris' interest column. By the terms of sale which he has effected of our ⅓ Ship Roscoe, the money is not due until the 30th August.—See Day Book, June 30, p. 96. This account is made out, and interest upon every transaction so

MERCANTILE FORMS.

See R. Morris' Acct., page 105, and Form XX., p. 120.

Interest Acct. to 30th June, 1867, with P. Duff.*   Cr.

Date.	Items.	Principal.	When Due.	Time.	Interest.
1867. Jan. 1	For Bal. due you ⅌ acct. rendered	2000	1866. Dec. 31	6.	60
Feb. 1	″ your invoice goods ⅌ "Herald"	8888 88	1867. Apr. 10	2.20	118 52
25	″ Proceeds Ryan & Co.'s Bill on Barclay	1995	Feb. 25	4.5	41 56
28	″ my dft. to Warden & Co., due ⅌ your Advice	4444 44	May 30	1.	22 22
Mar. 12	″ n. proceeds my Acct. Sales your goods ⅌ Herald	9052	2	1.28	87 50
Apr. 20	″ my ¼ your joint Invoice ⅌ "Vixen"	4000	Apr. 10	2.20	53 33
May 8	″ my dft. favor of Walker	4444 44			
18	″ your ¼ my Acct. Sales ⅌ "Vixen"	4093 05	May 18	1.12	28 65
June 18	″ Ins. recovered upon Ship't ⅌ "Columbia"	5565	June 18	.12	11 13
30	″ Interest in Red at Dr. side				65
	″ Balance of Interest Acct.	33 06			
	″ Balance to debit in new acct.	5676 59			
		50192 46			487 91

adjusted, that the balance will fall due in cash on the 30th day of June. Therefore, though this principal of $6500 is a debit, yet its interest from the 30th June to 30th August must be carried over to Morris' credit. When sums fall due in this manner, subsequent to the date of the account on both sides, extend the time and interest in red; then, before you balance, carry over the balance of the " red interest" to the proper side.

5. By looking attentively at the small marginal figures above, you will see how the balance of the interest is found and disposed of. For the Day Book entry of it, see note 5, p. 96. It is put to the debit of our interest column, to close it, and at the same time to Morris' credit. Afterwards the account closes in all respects like his account in the Ledger. As there is no entry in any book to show by what process this balance of interest is found, a letter press copy of all such accounts should be preserved in a book kept for the purpose. We have left the exchanges to be computed at the end of the year, as is often done in business.

6. In stating an account current of any kind, always use such words as will express, in the most concise and perspicuous terms, the origin of the transactions, without any regard to the technical expressions used for the same entries in your Ledger.

Those who desire to become expert at making out accounts of this kind, must persevere in repeating the operation several times from their own books, without assistance from our forms.

* In this and all the forms let the student use his own name, not ours.—See note, p. 75.

115

SET II.—DUFF'S BOOK-KEEPING.

(Form II.)   Messrs. JOHN TAYLOR & CO.

IN ACCT. CURRENT WITH P. DUFF, Dr.

1867.					
Feb.	12	For our invoice of Teas ⅌ "Jersey"			644	
Apr.	10	" Protecting your draft on Wood & Co. for . . .	$1200.		
		" Paid Protest, &c., $4. My ½ ⅌ ct. commission $6. .	10.	1210	
		" Accepting your draft at 10 days on Wood & Co. .	$600.		
		" Protest, $1. My ½ ⅌ ct. commission $3. . .	4.	604	
		" Your ½ Joint Shipment to London ⅌ "Cambria" . .		4980	33
				7438	33

Crs.

1867.					
Apr.	15	For my ½ your Joint Shipment to London . . .	$1600.		
May	18	" Your ½ my acct. sales of Joint Shipment ⅌ "Vixen"	4093.05	5693	05
		Balance due P. D. **Due by equation 1st Jan. last.** *		1745	28
		E. E., NEW YORK, 30th June, 1867.			

NOTE.—For clearness and brevity there is no better mode of stating a short account than this. The subtraction of the credits from the debits is made to show the balance. When the balance is against you, the form has to be a little varied, as you see by Hay's account following.—See page 103.

(Form III.)   WILLIAM HAY, Esq.,

IN ACCT. CURRENT WITH P. DUFF, Dr.

1867.					
Mar.	2	For your **half** Walker's Invoice of Rice Bot. on joint acct. .		600	
	16	" Carter's protested **note endorsed by you** . . .		300	
Apr.	15	" Your **half joint shipment to Liverpool** ⅌ "Erie" . .		1799	
May	4	" **Your half Finlay & Co.'s Invoice of Pork Bot. on joint acct.**		2500	
June	30	" **Balance carried to your credit in new acct.** . . .		10813	12
				16012	12

Crs.

1867.					
Feb.	12	For your Invoice of Table Linen .		1500	
Mar.	1	" Cash on acct. of purchases on joint speculation .		2500	
		" My half your Invoice of Wines sent me for sale on joint acct. .		450	
	5	" Your half my acct. sales of goods sold on joint acct. .		1400	
Apr.	5	" Your Invoice of Pork .		2000	
	15	" Amt. advanced by you in joint shipment ⅌ "Erie" .		1065	
June	1	" Your half net proceeds of joint shipment to Boston .		3129	
	28	" Your half returns of joint shipment to Liverpool .		2160	
		" Your ¼ **dividend net** profits of Ship Roscoe .		1808	12
				16012	12
	30	By Balance due Mr. Hay brought down . .		10813	12
		E. E., NEW YORK, 30th June, 1867.			

* This is ascertained by what we call a COMPOUND EQUATION. As we do not see the rule in any of our arithmetics, we subjoin it.

RULE.—Find the equated time of each side of the account by a simple Equation—note 2, p. 68. Then multiply the lesser side by the time that intervenes between these two equations, and divide the product by the balance of the account; the quotient is the time to count back or forward. If the balance is on the side of the latest equation, COUNT FORWARD from that date; but if it be on the side of the earliest equation, COUNT BACK from that date.

Let us illustrate the rule by Taylor & Co.'s account as above stated—refer to the Day-Book for the time when each amount falls due. We find by simple equation that the Dr. side falls due April 6th, and the Cr. side May 5th. The time between these equations is 29 days and the lesser side of the account is $5693. × 29 days = 165,098 ÷ $1745 (the balance) = 95 days. Now the balance being on the side of the earliest equation—April 6th, we must COUNT BACK from that date 95 days, which brings us to the 1st January, the day upon which this balance is due.

116

MERCANTILE FORMS.

FORM IV.—See Note 1, p. 82.

SALES OF MERCHANDISE sold by order and for account of R. Morris, Esq., London.

1867. Feb.						
Feb.	5	Sold for Cash to J. Lorillard—				
		1 pipe, 120 galls., Port Wine . . . . @ $3.				360
	9	Sold to William Park at 4 months—				
		5 pipes, 600 galls., Port Wine . . . . u 3.50				2100
		Sold for Cash to W. Bryant & Co.—				
		3 pipes, 360 galls., Port Wine, . . . u 3.				1080
	18	Sold R. Banks for Cash—				
		2 pipes, 240 galls., Port Wine . . . . u 3.50				840
Mar.	12	For net proceeds of 10 pipes Port Wine sold in New Orleans, Rec'd Barclay & Co.'s acceptance at 60 days				
		from date for . . . . . . 4500.				
		Taken to my acct. the remaining 9 pipes, 1080 galls., at				
		market price @ 60 days . . . @ $3. 3240.				7740
						12120
		———— CHARGES. ————				
1867. Feb.						
Feb.	1	Paid Duties 2222.22				
		u Freight and Primage 167.78				
	5	u For Gauging 1.50				
		u Cartage and Cooperage 3.50				
	12	u Cartage, Freight, and Insurance of 10 pipes shipped				
		to New Orleans . . . . . 28.				
	20	u R. Banks, for overgauged Wine . . . . 21.				
Mar.	12	Storage 3.50				
		Advertising 14.50				
		Commission and Guarantee 5 per cent. on $12120. . 606.				3068
		Net proceeds due in Cash 2d May				9052

E. E. NEW YORK, }
March 12, 1867. }   P. DUFF.

---

1. The Account Sales is always drawn from the Commission Sales Book; or, if that book is not kept, from the Day Book. No entry whatever ought to appear in the account but what relates to the sales; and nothing should appear in the charges but the expenses attending the Sales.—See Note 3, p. 68.
2. The rule for equating the time is given on page 68. Or the student may, if he prefers them, work by those given in his Arithmetic; but I would recommend him to practise upon the one he intends to use until he can operate with dexterity and accuracy.
3. When you make out an Account Sales, with part of the consignment unsold, give a concise statement of the goods unsold at the foot of the account.—See Note 4, p. 68.

Form V.—See Note 4, p. 90.

ACCOUNT SALES of **40** Bales Brussels Carpeting, sold for the joint account of P. Duff of New York, R. Morris of London, and J. Taylor & Co. of New Orleans, each one-third.

1867. May	13	Sold to Warden & Bell—		
		120 pieces, 4250 yds. . . . . @ $2.		8500
	18	Net proceeds of 55 pieces sold at Austin & Co.'s Auction . .		3560
		Taken to my own account the remaining 55 pieces, 1907 yds. @ $2.		3814
				15874
		CHARGES.		
1867. Apr.	20	Paid Duties to the Custom-house . . .	3000.	
		" Freight and Primage per "Vixen" . . .	150.	
		" Insurance against fire	33.	
		" Cartage and labor	2.	
May	18	Storage $3, Advertising $10	13.	
		Commission 2½ per cent. on $15874 . . .	396.85	3594 85
		Net proceeds		12279 15
		Of which my ⅓ is 4093.05		
		" R. Morris' do. at his credit due this day . 4093.05		
		" J. Taylor & Co. do. do. . 4093.05		
		$12279.15		
		E. E. New York, } May 18, 1867. } P. Duff.		

Form VI.—A Foreign Bill of Exchange.—See Note 6, p. 76.

Exchange for £1000 Sterling.   New York, February 25, 1867.

Sixty days after sight of this our first Exchange (second and third not paid), pay to the order of Peter Duff One Thousand Pounds Sterling, for value received, and place the same to account as per advice from

To Robert Morris, Esq., }   Yours, respectfully,
    Merchant, London. }   Baker & Fox.

Form VII.—An Inland Bill, or Draft.—See Note 2, p. 70.

$1000.₁₀₀⁰⁰   New Orleans, December 10, 1866.

Ten days after sight, pay to the order of Messrs. Ryan & Dale One Thousand Dollars, value received, for account of,

To Mr. Peter Duff. }   Yours, respectfully,
    Merchant, New York. }   John Taylor & Co.

Form VIII.—An Order.—See Jan. **24**, p. 72.

$500.₁₀₀⁰⁰   New York, January 24, 1867.

Pay to the order of Messrs. Warden & Bell Five Hundred Dollars, for value received, for   Yours, respectfully,

To James Walker, Esq., }   P. Duff.
    Merchant, New York. }

Form IX.—An Order for Merchandise.—See Note 3, p. **70**.

$108.₁₀₀⁰⁰   New York, January 15, 1867.

Pay to the order of Mr. **Henry Pryor** One Hundred and Eight Dollars, in Merchandise out of your store, for **account of**

To Mr. Peter Duff, }   James Carter.
    Merchant, New York, }

FORM X.—A PROMISSORY NOTE.—See Note 4, p. 72.

$1515.$\frac{75}{100}$.   NEW YORK, January 30, 1867.

SIXTY DAYS after date, for value received, I promise to pay to the order of Mr. Peter Duff FIFTEEN HUNDRED AND FIFTEEN DOLLARS, $\frac{75}{100}$.

WILLIAM HAY.

Extensive houses now generally arrange such transactions with an acceptance. The following is the form:

FORM XI.—AN ACCEPTANCE FOR THE ABOVE TRANSACTION.

$1515.$\frac{75}{100}$.   NEW YORK, January 30, 1867.

SIXTY DAYS after date, for value received, please pay to my order FIFTEEN HUNDRED AND FIFTEEN DOLLARS, $\frac{75}{100}$.

To WILLIAM HAY, Esq.   P. DUFF.
   Merchant, New York.

With the left side up, Hay writes across the face, in red ink, "Accepted."

WM. HAY.

This form will be found convenient for making payable at a particular place—say Philadelphia. The drawer then says "pay to my order in Philadelphia." The acceptor must name the place where he will have funds to take it up—thus, he writes across the face. "At the Girard Bank." WM. HAY.

To negotiate this acceptance, the drawer has to endorse it himself, it being payable to his own order.

FORM XII.—A JOINT PROMISSORY NOTE.

$500.$\frac{00}{100}$.   NEW YORK, January 30, 1867.

On demand, for value received, we or either of us, promise to pay to the order of Mr. Peter Duff, FIVE HUNDRED DOLLARS.

WM. HAY,
JAMES CARTER.

FORM XIII.—A RECEIPT IN FULL.—Note 4, p. 70.

NEW YORK, January 16, 1867. Received from James Carter FIVE HUNDRED AND SIXTY DOLLARS in full.

$560.$\frac{00}{100}$.   P. DUFF.

FORM XIV.—A RECEIPT FOR MONEY ON ACCOUNT.—Note 2, p. 84.

$800.   Received from Peter Duff, EIGHT HUNDRED DOLLARS, on account.
NEW YORK, March 31, 1867.   R. LENOX.

FORM XV.—A RECEIPT FOR AN ENDORSEMENT UPON A NOTE.—Feb. 12, p. 74.

$2000.$\frac{00}{100}$.   Received from Mr. Thomas Edwards, TWO THOUSAND DOLLARS, which is endorsed upon his note.
NEW YORK, February 12, 1867.   P. DUFF.

FORM XVI.—A RECEIPT FOR A PROMISSORY NOTE.—January 18, p. 72.

$600.   Received from Mr. James Carter, his note at twenty days for SIX HUNDRED DOLLARS, which, when paid, will be in full to date.
NEW YORK, January 18, 1867.   P. DUFF.

FORM XVII.—AN ENDORSED NOTE.—Feb. 9, p. 74.

$2100.$\frac{00}{100}$.   NEW YORK, February 9, 1867.

Four months after date, for value received, I promise to pay to the order of Messrs. Warden & Bell, TWO THOUSAND ONE HUNDRED DOLLARS.

WM. PARK.

☞ Endorsed notes are always drawn payable to the endorser, not to the holder.

SET II.—MERCANTILE FORMS.

FORM XVIII.—A LETTER OF INTRODUCTION.

NEW YORK, May 30, 1867

Dear Sir,

      I have the pleasure of introducing to you the bearer, my much esteemed friend, William Hay, Esq., Merchant of this city. While in London he wishes to confer with you upon some business, the nature of which he will himself explain to you.

Recommending Mr. Hay to your usual kind attention, I remain,

Dear Sir,

To ROBERT MORRIS, Esq., }	Yours, Respectfully,
Merchant, London. }	P. DUFF.

FORM XIX.—A LETTER OF CREDIT.

NEW ORLEANS, March 30, 1867.

Dear Sir,

      If the bearer, Mr. James Draper, desires to make any purchases of merchandise of you on credit, you may consider us responsible to you for the payment of the same, to any amount not exceeding ONE THOUSAND DOLLARS. In the event of his failing to make his payments according to agreement, we require you to give us timely notice of the same. We are,

Dear Sir,

To MR. PETER DUFF, }	Yours, Respectfully,
Merchant, New York. }	JOHN TAYLOR & Co.

FORM XX.—A LETTER WITH AN ACCOUNT.—See Form I., p. 115.

NEW YORK, June 30, 1867.

Dear Sir,

      Inclosed I hand you your account current balanced by $5676.59, in my favor due this day; to which, if you find it correct, please make your books conform. I am without any of your favors to reply to, but remain,

Dear Sir,

To R. MORRIS, Esq., }	Yours, Respectfully,
Merchant, London. }	P. DUFF.

FORM XXI.—A LETTER OF ADVICE.—See Note 5, p. 84, and Note 1, p. 86.

NEW YORK, April 10, 1867.

Gentlemen,

      I have to inform you that I have this day paid your bill of $1200, on Sidney Wood & Co., which was protested for non-payment. Your bill of $600 on the same parties, has also made its appearance, and the drawees having apprised me of their inability to give protection to your signature, I have accepted for your honor and will take care of it at maturity.

Bill paid $1200. Expenses $4. Commission ½ per ct., $6. Due this day $1210.

Bill accepted *supra protest* $600. Protest $1. Commission $3. Due 23d inst., $604 which amounts please place to credit of,

Gentlemen,

To Messrs. JOHN TAYLOR & Co., }	Yours, Respectfully,
Merchants, New Orleans. }	P. DUFF

FORM XXII.—A LETTER OF ADVICE.—See Note 4, p. 76.

LONDON, December 24, 1866.

Dear Sir,

      In my respects of the 18th instant, I inclosed you an invoice and bill of lading of a consignment of 30 Pipes Port Wine shipped per "Herald," which sailed on the 19th.

I have now to advise you that I have this day valued upon you at 10 days on account of the same for $2500 in favor of Robert Banks, which please honor for account of

To Mr. P. DUFF, }	Yours, Respectfully,
Merchant, New York. }	R. MORRIS.

DUFF'S BOOK-KEEPING.

PART II.

DUFF'S BOOK-KEEPING.

PART II.

EXEMPLIFYING PARTNERSHIP BOOKS

Upon two different methods, for greatly abbreviating and simplifying the usual process of DOUBLE ENTRY BOOK-KEEPING. Adapted to the most limited retail, or to the most extended wholesale business; with the whole of the auxiliaries, with part, or without any of them. Illustrating a new method of

PROVING THE LEDGER:*

By means of which, NO ENTRY ONCE MADE UPON THE DAY BOOK OR ANY OF THE AUXILIARIES CAN AFTERWARDS BE OMITTED AT ANY STAGE OF ITS PASSAGE TO THE LEDGER WITHOUT CERTAIN DETECTION. Embracing also an exemplification of the

PRIVATE LEDGER,

By means of which the results of the business can only be known to the partners.

Practical directions for transferring the contents of THE OLD LEDGER TO THE NEW ONE, illustrating the formation of a

NEW FIRM BY THE INTRODUCTION OF A NEW PARTNER.

Also, particular directions for conducting partnership books during settlement, after dissolution.

MAKING OUT PARTNERSHIP BALANCE SHEETS.

RATES OF COMMISSION AND STORAGE established by the Chambers of Commerce of the cities of

NEW YORK and PHILADELPHIA, with various additional matters of important information for men of business.

---

* We do not present the six-columned Day Book or Journal as original. Our method of proving the Books is applicable to any form of Day Book or Journal.

PRELIMINARY REMARKS.

1. WE now propose to supply what other authors have omitted—an arrangement of the DOUBLE ENTRY principle, practically adapted to retail business,—a method divested of the cumbrous machinery of Auxiliaries, the dilatory intervention of the Journal, and, above all, the voluminous masses of writing created by the common mode of keeping and posting the Cash and Merchandise accounts.

2. Though the following method is conducted strictly under the first fundamental rule of Double Entry—equal debits and credits—it will be readily seen that a great saving of books, writing, posting and checking is effected, with increased security against error, with the full benefit of all the information obtained by the ordinary Double Entry process, and with the convenience of having your personal accounts daily posted up and ready for settlement at a minute's notice. Let us state its advantages over the common process more distinctly.

1st.—Dispensing with all books but the Day Book and Ledger.
2d.—Writing in the cash and merchandise accounts in the Ledger reduced to about ONE LINE FOR ONE HUNDRED.
3d.—Checking the cash and merchandise posting, reduced in the same proportion.
4th.—A yearly saving of forty or fifty folios of the Ledger.
5th.—Increased security against error, as no entry once entered upon the Day Book can be omitted in posting without detection.—See Note 1, p. 135.
6th.—Daily posting of the personal accounts, thereby having them always ready for settlement.

3. These are considerations which entitle this method to the particular attention of all retailers. And though, in ordinary retail business, the Day Book and Ledger are the only books absolutely required, we shall show hereafter, that as the business increases this arrangement will not be disturbed by the introduction of any one, or all the auxiliaries in use. It is therefore not only adapted to the most minute retail business, but to the most extensive operations of commerce.

4. No person should attempt to learn the science by commencing here. If he is unacquainted with its principles, he must first acquire them by the course of instruction in the preceding part of this work. Afterwards the form of these books, although somewhat complicated in appearance, can be understood and practised with ease. Indeed, after the Day Book Entry is once correctly made, the subsequent steps partake much of the simplicity of Single Entry. But, for obvious reasons, no one should attempt to apply it to business until he has gone through a course of exercises.

5. The following Day Book is ruled with six columns; the debits, as usual, always occupying the left, and the credits those on the right. The column next the writing on the left and that on the right, as you perceive by the post marks, are the only ones that are posted in detail. The cash and merchandise amounts, both debits and credits, are forwarded from page to page until the 30th March—p. 128. From there they are posted in one sum, affixing to it the post mark as usual.

In making the Day Book Entry, care must be taken to extend all cash and merchandise entries into their own columns. And those who are very expert in addition, and who desire to keep their work free from erasures, should foot and prove the addition first upon a waste sheet of paper, taking care afterwards to keep each set of figures under its own column.

6. In making an entry, the same form of expression is used as upon a common Journal. In entering an invoice of sale, the particulars are first short-extended, like Evans's or Butler's entries on the next page.

7. Observe, the Cash and Merchandise accounts can be posted monthly or yearly, as may suit your convenience, recollecting that every time these accounts are posted, it makes a period in the amounts brought forward on the Day Book, and the new period commences with the heads of the columns empty.—See Note 1, p. 128.

DRS.   NEW YORK, January 2, 1867.   CRS.   1

Mdse.	Cash.		L.F.		L.F.	Cash.	Mdse
4000				Cash, Dr. to Sundries,			
				To P. Duff, received on account of capital,	1	2500	
				" W. Gordon,	1	1500	
3380				Mdse., Dr. to Sundries,			
				To T. P. Cope & Sons, for Invoice,	1	2500	
				" Wm. Hay, for Invoice,	1	800	
				" Cash, paid freight,		80	
				5.			
				Sundries To Cash,		1605 50	
		1 50	3	Expense account paid laborers.			
		1200	1	T. P. Cope & Sons, remitted them.			
		400	1	Wm. Hay, remitted him.			
		4	3	Exchange account, paid Premium on drafts.			
		9 50	2	Robert Martin (270 Bowery), To Mdse.,			9 50
				1 pair fine Boots, ... $6.			
				Repairing two pair do. . . . 1.			
				1 pair Ladies' Boots 2.50			
		4 50	2	James Carter, To Mdse.,			4 50
				1 pair Boys' Shoes, . . . $1.75			
				Footing 1 pair Boots, ... 2.75			
		271 25	2	Robert Evans (Buffalo), To Mdse.,			271
				12 pair Boots, at $8. $96.			
				24 " " Light, " 6. 144.			
				24 " Boys' Shoes, " 1.25 30.			
				Packing case and cartage, 1.25			
				10.			
		5	1	P. Duff, To Cash on account,		5	
		∅	Pt. 206	James Moore (Pine St.), To Mdse., 1 pr. Boots,"		∅	
		337 25	2	Robert Butler (Albany), To Mdse.,		337 25	
				48 pair Ladies' Boots, at $2. . $96.			
				60 " Men's do. " 3. . 180.			
				60 " Boy's do. " 1. . 60.			
				Box and cartage, . . . 1.25			
	954			Cash To Mdse. for sales to date,			954
				20.			
		10	1	W. Gordon, To Cash on account,		10	
		4	2	J. Carter, To Mdse., for 2 pair Shoes, . . $2.			4
3380	4954	2247		Amounts forwarded, ...	7300	1700 50	1580 50
		4954		Cash, ...	1700 50		
		3380		Merchandise	1580 50		
Paid	1700 50	10581		Proof	10581		
Bal.	3253 50						

1. Pencil the cash paid under the amount received, and you can see the balance as often as you desire.—See Note 1, p. 128.

* Entries that are collected before posting, are marked so in the folio column, and the pen is run lightly through the figures on both sides. Omit these figures in the addition, and dispose of the cash as if received for a ready money sale.

Mdse.	Cash.		L.F.		L.F.		Cash.	Mdse.
3380	4954	2247		Bro't forward, . .		7300	1700 50	1580 50
		50	2	R. Martin (270 Bowery), To Mdse., rep'g Boots,				50
				31.				
		6	1	P. Duff, To Mdse. for 1 pr. fine Boots,				6
		2 50	1	W. Gordon, To Mdse. for 1 pr. Ladies' Boots,				2 50
				Feb. 1.				
74				² Mdse. To Sundries,				
				To Cash paid Journeymen to date,			24	
				" J. Day, foreman's wages to date,	3	50		
		45	3	James Day, To Sundries,				
				To Cash, paid him on account,			20	
				" Mdse., a Black Dress Coat,				25
				5.				
		3 20	3	Expense acct. to Cash pd. for Coal $3, post. 20,			3 20	
				Sundries To Cash,			706 50	
		500	1	T. P. Cope & Sons, remitted draft.				
		200	1	Wm. Hay, do. do.				
		6 50	3	Exchange acct., paid Prem. on the above drafts.				
				10.				
				Sundries To Mdse.,				47
		12	3	J. Day, pd. his order to W. Price.				
		35	2	R. Martin, do. to James Reed.				
16				Mdse., Dr. to Cash pd. Journeymen,			16	
				15.				
630				Mdse. To Cash, pd. Davis's Auction Bill,			630	
		25	3	J. Day, Dr. to R. Martin.	2	25		
				For our order on R. Martin.				
		45	2	A. Bell To Mdse., for 1 full Circle Cloak,				45
				20.				
60				Mdse., Dr. to Edward Pryor,	3	60		
				For his Invoice of Trimmings,				
	200			Cash To E. Pryor, rec'd in loan,	3	200		
		2 50	2	A. Bell To Mdse., repaired Coat and Vest,				2 50
		16	3	E. Pryor To Mdse., 2 pr. Blk Cassim. Pants at $8.				16
		3146 20		³ Amounts forwarded, ...			7635	
		5154		Cash, ...			8100 20	
		4160		Merchandise			1725	
		12460 20		Proof			12460 20	

1. After the books are open we discontinue the useless, though universal, practice of continually repeating the place of business at the head of every page.
2. Mdse. is Dr. for the expense of manufacturing, although it is more proper to carry rents, clerks' wages, and the expense of selling it, to the Expense account.
3. To save writing we may, hereafter, set the footings of the Cash and Merchandise columns, at once into the proof column.

Mdse.	Cash.	L.F.		L.F.	Cash.	Mdse.
4160	5154	3146 20	Bro't forward, . . .	7635	3166 20	1725
			"			
26			Mdse. To Cash, pd. Journeymen,		36	
			"			
50			Mdse. To J. Day, wages to date as foreman,	3	50	
			Mar. 1.			
		200	3	[1] E. Pryor To Cash, pd. loan of 20th ult.		200	
			"			
			Sundries To Mdse.,			84
		48	1	P. Duff, for 6 yds Black Cloth, at $8.			
		36	1	W. Gordon, 16 yds. Fig'd Satin, 1.50 24.			
			1 doz. Black Cravats, 12.			
			10.			
	250		Cash To R. Evans, rec'd by mail,	2	250	
			"			
			Sundries To Mdse.,			51
		45	2	R. Evans, 1 ps., 36 yds., Satin, at $1.25			
		6	3	E. Pryor, pd. his order to A. Wood.			
			"			
			Sundries To Mdse.,			48
		5	2	A. Bell, 1 fine Hat.			
		43	3	Samuel Gaynor, 4 yds. B. Blk. Cloth, at $10. 40.			
			1 " Cassimere, 3.			
			20.			
		800	1	[2] T. P. Cope & Sons To Cash,		800	
			Pd. their draft at sight for Bal. of account.			
			"			
	300		Cash, Dr. To Robert Butler, rec'd per mail,	2	300	
			"			
		40	3	Edward Pryor To Andrew Bell,	2	40	
			for our order on the latter.			
			"			
		48	3	[3] S. Gaynor To Mdse., paid his order			48
			to H. Wallace,			
			25.			
534			Mdse. To Sundries,			
			To T. P. Cope & Sons, for Invoice of Cloths,	1	504	
			" Cash, paid freight on same,		30	
			30.			
	650		Cash To Mdse.,			650
			For Cash sales to date.			
		4417 20	Amounts forwarded, ...	8779		
		6354	Cash, ...	4166 20		
		4780	Merchandise	2606		
		15551 20	Proof	15551 20		

1. We wish our readers to observe, that though want of
room compels us generally to write only the initials
of the Christian names of persons, in business we
direct these to be written in full; confusion and
trouble are frequently occasioned by the contrary
practice. Legal titles should also always be chosen:
"Commercial Advertiser" or "Evening Express"
are not the proper titles for accounts in our books.
2. Recollect Note 1, Carter's accr., p. 105.
3. Recollect Rule IX., p. 40.

Mdse.	Cash.		L.F.		L.F.	Cash.	Mdse.
4780	6354	4417 20		Bro't forward, . .	8779	4166 20	2606
		60	3	Expenses To Cash, paid store rent to date,		60	
50				Merchandise To James Day, for foreman's wages to date.	3	50	
				31.			
		45	2	James Carter, Dr. to Cash on account,		45	
		90	3	Expense account To James Carter, for 3 months' salary to date,	2	90	
		20	4	Profit & Loss To Cash, for a counterfeit $20 note,		20	
	37 25			Cash To Robert Butler, Received in full per mail.	2	37 25	
		4632 20		Total amount to date		8956 25	
		6391 25	1	Cash	1	4291 20	
		4830	1	Merchandise	1	2606	
		15853 45		Proof		15853 45	

Merchandise on hand per Inventory at date is $3217.50.—See Invoice Book, p. 137.

1. To find the balance of cash in hand, after a period of the Day Book is posted, you must add, with your pencil, the balance of the posted part of the cash account on the Ledger to the footing of the debit column of that account on this book; then deduct the amount of the credit column, and you have the balance in hand, as in note 1, p. 23.

2. Care must be taken to extend the cash and merchandise entries into their own columns. Each entry should be carefully examined before adding up.

3. This form of Day Book will be found applicable to almost any kind of business, the Cash columns being always required as they are here. Those which we use for Merchandise may be used for any title that will represent the person's principal business; the Medical and Legal professions can use it for their Practice; Manufacturers would use it for their Factory, Hotels would use it for their Expenses, &c.

4. Every business has an account from which its principal income is derived. This and the cash account must always create a great number of entries, and any mode of posting these entries in accumulated amounts, must materially diminish the amount of writing in the Ledger. No method has yet been tried which accomplishes this object with so much simplicity and accuracy as those explained in this and the following set. I am aware that some do it, or attempt to do it, by the page, by the week, and by the month, by means of what is called a "collecting sheet." But, on account of its great impediment to checking, and still greater difficulty in detecting errors, this mode of posting can never be recommended.

PARTNERSHIP BOOKS.

THE LEDGER.

INTRODUCTORY REMARKS.

1. The following Ledger is opened, conducted, and closed upon the same principles as those already explained. I have made one or two slight deviations from the common course, which the book-keeper may or may not adopt, as he pleases. In order to conflict as little as possible with the established process of teaching, I retained the prepositions To and By in the Double Entry Ledgers in the first part of this work; but as I consider them of no more use than the old practice of filling up the cent column with unmeaning ciphers, I have dropped them in both Ledgers in this part of the work.

2. In the next place, I have in some instances briefly detailed the Day-Book entries on the Ledger. I am aware that some ridicule all attempts at entering details of any kind of business upon the Ledger, and many persons are impressed with the idea, that it is contrary to the rules of accounts to do so. But retailers will be perfectly safe in giving what I suggest a trial. It is as easy to write 1 ℔ tea, a hat, a coat, or a pair of boots, at a man's account, as merchandise. The book-keeper's experience will soon enable him to judge how far it will be for his convenience to carry out this method of posting, recollecting that it is only recommended to retailers.

3. While teaching the principles of the science, dividing the Profit & Loss account into Expense, Exchange, Interest, &c., renders the subject more complex and tends to retard rather than facilitate the student's progress. For this reason none of these accounts were introduced in any of the preceding sets: but we have given an exemplification of each in this and the following set, with the necessary directions for closing. We may also observe, that these accounts ought always to be kept in every business that creates any considerable number of entries for them. Note 4, p. 24.

4. I have opened the Ledger with a cash capital of $4000, placing $2500 at the credit of Duff, and $1500 at the credit of Gordon. The business closes with a gain, which is divided and carried to the credit of each partner in *proportion to his capital.*

5. It may be proper to observe here, that the rules of accounts have nothing to do with regulating the division of profits or losses; that is altogether a matter of private agreement. In our next Ledger will be found an illustration of the equal division of profits; and on page 181, various modes of adjusting the difference of capital by interest: our students shall have an ample variety of illustrations.

6. After closing this Ledger we have transferred the contents to a new set. This was done for the purpose of giving another practical elucidation of that process, and also to get an opportunity of exemplifying the application of our method of proving the books to an entire set. We think it proper to give this explanation here, because many persons imagine that every new partner who is introduced into a firm, makes it necessary to have a new set of books. This is not necessary, provided the old books have been regularly kept. It is, however, generally necessary to take an inventory of the property on hand and to make out a Balance sheet. The new partner's name is then introduced, with a credit for whatever he brings in, and a debit for what the firm may assume for him. The old partners' accounts are closed and their respective shares in the business at that period brought down.

7. A suspended list ought always to be opened upon these occasions for such debts as the old partners have any doubt of collecting.—See Suspended List, p. 134.—Of course they must make good to the new firm all old debts for which they credit themselves: and if many of these debts should afterwards prove wholly or partially irrecoverable, the adjustment of the matter has always to take place after the lapse of considerable time,—perhaps several years: it then becomes an awkward and very troublesome operation. In all such cases it is better, at the commencement, for the old partners to carry no debts to their credit but such as they are absolutely certain of collecting. Leave all the others behind upon the suspended list, and make new dividends of them, between themselves, as collected.—See Duff and Gordon's Account, page 169.

I   129

ON CLOSING A PARTNERSHIP LEDGER.

1. THE principles of opening, closing, transferring, and re-opening books have been already so carefully explained in the first part of this work, that it is to be hoped nothing need now be repeated that has been there explained.

2. The only new features in the process now before us are the dividends of gain or loss, the partners' accounts, and the suspended list; the management of all the other accounts is in every respect the same as in individual business.

3. The manner of finding the net gain or loss, is the same as we have previously explained: the division of it, and the operation of closing the account, can be best explained at the account itself—p. 134.

4. In closing the personal accounts, omit the partners' accounts, and leave them open until the last: they, like the stock account in individual business, being always affected, as you perceive by referring to them, by the closing entries of Profit & Loss, and must, therefore, be left open to receive their entries of gain or loss when that account is closed, which cannot be done until it receives all its transfers from the other accounts. Therefore, the partners' accounts, Profit & Loss and Balance, must be remaining open after all others are closed: these are then closed—first, Profit & Loss into the partners' accounts, then the partners' into Balance: then, if all be correct, Balance will be exactly closed by these last transfers from the partners' accounts. The accountant should always first make the closing entries of these last accounts in pencil, to be certain that the Balance will close by the last entries. For although this trial may have come out all correct, errors or omissions may have got into the work that he has done since, which will compel him to scratch and disfigure these, the most conspicuous accounts in his Ledger.

5. It may be proper to remark, that though both our partners' accounts here close To Balance, when a partner draws out more than his share of the gain and the amount he has paid in, his acct. closes By Balance. When all the partners' accounts close in this way, then the firm is insolvent. In short, after partners have received their transfer from Profit & Loss, their accounts then close in every respect like those of other persons.—See Notes, Balance account, p. 35.*

6. We have already alluded to the use of the Suspended List, and have now only to state, that it is opened for the purpose of exhibiting a list of all such accounts as we think we cannot safely make a dividend upon: the partners must themselves mark these for the book-keeper. The amount of such accounts must be known in order to enter the Profit & Loss account, for the Ledger will not, of course, balance without disposing of these accounts either in Profit & Loss or Balance: besides, the practical merchant or mechanic will find this companion to the Balance sheet a useful monitor every time it is made out.

7. The book-keeper can often materially shorten the balance sheet by sending round, before making it out, and paying off all trifling balances against him, and, at the same time, by collecting all balances of this kind. From inattention to what I here suggest, I have seen balance sheets made out with fifty or sixty accounts of trifling sums upon them, nearly all of which would have been paid if called for.

NOTE.—We think it unnecessary to annex an index to this Ledger: we give one to the next—page 164.

* If a partner is taken into the firm without capital, his account will open without a credit, and will remain so until the business places a profit at his credit.

Dr.	P.					DUFF.	Cr.		1

<table>
<tr><td>1867.
Jan. 10</td><td>Cash,</td><td></td><td>1</td><td>5</td><td>1867.
Jan. 2</td><td>Cash,</td><td></td><td>1</td><td>2500</td></tr>
<tr><td>31</td><td>1 pr. Fine Boots,</td><td></td><td>2</td><td>6</td><td>Mar. 31</td><td>Profit & Loss,</td><td>2943.47
49.
2694.47</td><td>f. 4</td><td>443 47</td></tr>
<tr><td>Mar. 1</td><td>6 yds. Blk. Cloth @ $8.</td><td></td><td>3</td><td>48</td><td></td><td></td><td></td><td></td><td></td></tr>
<tr><td>31</td><td>Balance,</td><td>59.</td><td>f. 4</td><td>2884 47</td><td></td><td></td><td></td><td></td><td></td></tr>
<tr><td></td><td></td><td></td><td></td><td>2943 47</td><td></td><td></td><td></td><td></td><td>2943 47</td></tr>
</table>

1. Credit each partner for what he pays in, and for his share of the net gain, and debit him for what he draws out, and for his share of the net loss. Close To or By Balance.—Notes 4 and 5, p. 130.

2. When a partner leaves home, taking money with him to lay out for the business, he should leave a memorandum of the amount with the cashier, who can count this paper as money until the partner sends him a statement of the outlay: then the final entry is made. The practice of encumbering a partner's account with such transactions can never be recommended.

	W.						GORDON.		

<table>
<tr><td>1867.
Jan. 20</td><td>Cash,</td><td></td><td>1</td><td>10</td><td>1867.
Jan. 2</td><td>Cash,</td><td></td><td>1</td><td>1500</td></tr>
<tr><td>31</td><td>1 pr. Ladies' Boots,</td><td></td><td>2</td><td>2 50</td><td>Mar. 31</td><td>Profit & Loss,</td><td>1766.08
48.50
1717.58</td><td>f. 4</td><td>266 08</td></tr>
<tr><td>Mar. 2</td><td>16 yds. F. Satin @ 1.50</td><td></td><td>3</td><td>24</td><td></td><td></td><td></td><td></td><td></td></tr>
<tr><td></td><td>1 doz. Cravats,</td><td>48.50</td><td></td><td>12</td><td></td><td></td><td></td><td></td><td></td></tr>
<tr><td>31</td><td>Balance,</td><td></td><td>f. 4</td><td>1717 58</td><td></td><td></td><td></td><td></td><td></td></tr>
<tr><td></td><td></td><td></td><td></td><td>1766 08</td><td></td><td></td><td></td><td></td><td>1766 08</td></tr>
</table>

	T. P.	(Philadelphia)				COPE & SONS.		

<table>
<tr><td>1867.
Jan. 5</td><td>Cash,</td><td>1</td><td>1200</td><td>1867.
Jan. 2</td><td>Mdse. ⅌ Invoice,</td><td>1</td><td>2500</td></tr>
<tr><td>Feb. 5</td><td>"</td><td>2</td><td>500</td><td></td><td></td><td></td><td></td></tr>
<tr><td>Mar. 20</td><td>"</td><td>3</td><td>800</td><td></td><td></td><td></td><td></td></tr>
<tr><td></td><td></td><td></td><td>2500</td><td></td><td></td><td></td><td>2500</td></tr>
<tr><td>31</td><td>Balance</td><td>f. 4</td><td>504</td><td>Mar. 25</td><td>Mdse. ⅌ Invoice,</td><td>3</td><td>504</td></tr>
</table>

	WILLIAM					HAY.		

<table>
<tr><td>1867.
Jan. 5</td><td>Cash,</td><td></td><td>1</td><td>400</td><td>1867.
Jan. 2</td><td>Mdse.,</td><td>800.
600.
200.</td><td>1</td><td>800</td></tr>
<tr><td>Feb. 5</td><td>"</td><td>600</td><td>2</td><td>200</td><td></td><td></td><td></td><td></td><td></td></tr>
<tr><td>Mar. 31</td><td>Balance,</td><td></td><td>f. 4</td><td>200</td><td></td><td></td><td></td><td></td><td></td></tr>
<tr><td></td><td></td><td></td><td></td><td>800</td><td></td><td></td><td></td><td></td><td>800</td></tr>
</table>

	CASH					ACCOUNT.		

<table>
<tr><td>1867.
Mar. 31</td><td>Sundries to date,</td><td>6391.25
4291.20
2100.05</td><td>4</td><td>6391 25</td><td>1867.
Mar. 31</td><td>Sundries to date,</td><td>4</td><td>4291 20</td></tr>
<tr><td></td><td></td><td></td><td></td><td></td><td>"</td><td>Balance,</td><td>f. 4</td><td>2100 05</td></tr>
<tr><td></td><td></td><td></td><td></td><td>6391 25</td><td></td><td></td><td></td><td>6391 25</td></tr>
</table>

	MERCHANDISE					ACCOUNT.		

<table>
<tr><td>1867.
Mar. 31</td><td>Sundries to date,</td><td></td><td>4</td><td>4830</td><td>1867.
Mar. 31</td><td>Sundries to date,</td><td></td><td>4</td><td>2606</td></tr>
<tr><td>"</td><td>Profit & Loss,</td><td>f. 4</td><td></td><td>993 50</td><td>"</td><td>Balance,</td><td>5823.50
4830.
993.50</td><td>f. 4</td><td>3217 50</td></tr>
<tr><td></td><td></td><td></td><td></td><td>5823 50</td><td></td><td></td><td></td><td></td><td>5823 50</td></tr>
</table>

1867.						1867.					
Jan.	5	1 pr. Fine Boots,	1	6		Feb.	15	Our order to J. Day,	2	25	
		Repairing 2 pr. do.		1		Mar.	31	Suspended List,	f. 4	20	
		1 pr. Ladies' Boots,		2	50						
	20	Repairing Boots,	2		50						
Feb.	10	Pd. order to J. Reed		35							
				45						45	
May	23	Bal. bro't down,		20		May	23	Pd. Duff, Gordon & Co.		20	

Note 7, p. 129, and 6, p. 130.
1. The above account remained closed until Martin paid the amount to the new firm. It was then re-opened to record the payment: this must always be done in such cases.

2. If the business of the new firm had re-opened in these books, it would then have been necessary to re-open the suspended accounts with a Day Book Entry, making them Dr. To Duff & Gordon: then credit them for the payment.

      JAMES   (Clerk)   **CARTER.**

1867.						1867.					
Jan.	5	Shoes 1.75, Boots footed 2.75,	1	4	50	Mar.	31	3 mos. sal'y to date,	4	90	
	20	2 pr. Pumps, @ $2,		4							
Mar.	31	Cash, 53.50	4	45							
		Balance, f.	4	36	50						
				90						90	

      ROBERT   (Buffalo)   **EVANS.**

1867.						1867.					
Jan.	5	Mdse. @ Invoice,	1	271	25	Mar.	10	Cash by mail,	3	250	
Mar.	10	36 yds. col'd Satin 1.25	3	45			31	Suspended List, f.	4	66	25
				316	25					316	25
May	31	Bal. bro't down,		66	25	May	31	Pd. Duff, Gordon & Co.		25	
						June	10	"		41	25
				66	25					66	25

See Martin's account above, and Note 2, Suspended List, p. 134.

      ROBERT   (Albany)   **BUTLER.**

1867.						1867.					
Jan.	10	Mdse. @ Invoice,	1	337	25	Mar.	20	Cash @ mail,	3	300	
							31	" "	4	37	25
				337	25					337	25

      ANDREW   **BELL.**

1867.						1867.					
Feb.	15	1 full circle cloak,	2	45		Mar.	20	Our order to E. Pryor,	3	40	
	20	Coat and vest repaired,		2	50		31	Profit & Loss, f.	4	12	50
Mar.	10	1 Beaver Hat,	3	5							
				52	50					52	50

Considering this a bad debt, we close it into Profit & Loss.

Dr.		JAMES		(Foreman)		DAY.		Cr.	**3**
1867.					1867.				
Feb.	1	Cash,	2	20	Feb.	1	Mdse. wages to date,	2	50
		Black Dress Coat,		25		28	" "	3	50
	10	Pd. order to W. Price,	2	12	Mar.	30	" " 150.	4	50
	15	Our order on R. Mar-					68.		
		tin, 87.		25					
Mar.	31	Balance, fol.	4	68					
				150					150

EXPENSE ACCOUNT.

1867.					1867.				
Jan.	5	Cash,	1	1 50	Mar.	31	Profit & Loss, fol.	4	154 70
Feb.	5	"	2	3 20					
Mar.	30	" Store Rent,	4	60					
	31	J. Carter, salary, 154.70		90					
				154 70					154 70

EXCHANGE ACCOUNT.

1867.					1867.				
Jan.	5	Cash,	1	4	Mar.	31	Profit & Loss, fol.	4	10 50
Feb.	5	10.50	2	6 50					
				10 50					10 50

1. This and the preceding account are branches of Profit & Loss, and are always closed into it.—Note 4, p. 24, and Note 3, p. 129. The student can never be at any loss in conducting them, they being of the same nature as Profit & Loss, and are therefore always debited when you lose, and credited when you gain by them.

EDWARD PRYOR.

1867.					1867.				
Feb.	20	2 pr. Blk. Pants, @ $8.	2	16	Feb.	20	Mdse. ⅌ Invoice,	2	60
Mar.	1	Cash Loan 20th ult.,	3×	200			Cash Loan, 200.		200
	10	Mdse. pd. order to Wood		6	Mar.	31	Balance, fol.	4×	2
	20	Our order on A. Bell 262.		40					
		2.		262					262

This method of entering loans dispenses with the Borrow & Loan account.

SAMUEL GAYNOR.

1867.					1867.				
Mar.	10	4 yds. best Blk. Cloth,	3	40	Mar.	31	Balance, fol.	4	91
		1 " Cassimere,		3					
	20	Paid order to H. Wal-							
		lace, 91.		48					
				91					91

133

1867.					1867.					
Mar. 31	Cash counterfeit money	4	20		Mar. 31	Mdse.,	fol.	1	993	50
	Andrew Bell, fol.	2	12 50							
	Expense acct.,	3	154 70			993.50				
	Exchange acct.,		10 50			283.96.				
	Suspended acct., 283.95	4	86 25			Gain, 709.55				
	P. Duff's net gain,	1	443 47							
	W Gordon ″		266 08							
			993 50						993	50

Read **Note** 4, p. 130.
1. The marginal pencil figures on each side show how the net gain **is found: Then,**

      Duff's Capital was   2500.
      Gordon's   1500.
      ———
      4000 : 709.55 :: 2500 : 443.47, Duff's share of the gain.
    Then, 4000 : 709.55 :: 1500   266.08, Gordon's do.   do.

2. When each partner's share of the gain, thus found, is placed to the debit of this account, it must exactly close it.

BALANCE   ACCOUNT.

1867.					1867.					
Mar. 31	Cash,	fol. 1	2100	05	Mar. 31	T. P. Cope & Sons, fol.	1	504		
	Mdse.,	1	3217	50		Wm. Hay,		200		
	E. Pryor,	3	2			James Carter,	2	36	50	
	S. Gaynor,		91			James Day, 108.50	3	68		
	5410.55					P. Duff, for net capital,	1	2884	47	
						W. Gordon, ″	1	1717	58	
			5410	55				5410	55	

See Balance accounts, pp. 17 and 35.
1. This account is made up from the Ledger, in all respects as in individual business; and the difference between the amount of the effects, and the debits owing by the firm, is the net joint capital. The proportion of that capital which belongs to each partner, can only be known from his account. When each partner's balance is transferred, it must, as you see above, close this account: neither more nor less.
2. If any of the partners overdraw their capital, then, of course, the balance they owe the firm, like a balance due from any other individual, is part of the effects and comes to the Dr. side of this account.

SUSPENDED   LIST.

1867.					1867.					
Mar. 31	Robert Martin,	fol.	2	20	Mar. 31	Profit & Loss,	fol.	4	86	25
	Robert Evans,			66 25						
				86 25					86	25

See Note 7, p. 129, and Note 6, p. 128.
1. This account, as you perceive above, is closed into Profit & Loss. It will be seen by these accounts—p. 132—that when a payment is received upon it, the account must be re-opened by bringing the suspended balance down.
2. I wish the learner to observe that when the business is transferred to new books, as in this case, there is no occasion for closing the suspended accounts. Find the balances as directed—Note 3, p. 113—and transfer them to the list and leave the accounts standing open until paid. But I have closed them, because, by so doing, it is easier to convey the idea of what was done with the balances, and more particularly when and how they were settled after the Ledger was closed, and all other accounts transferred.
3. After what has been stated in Note 3, p. 113, it will be seen that it is never necessary to **close an** account for the mere purpose of finding its balance to make up **any sheet or list.**

		fol.	
P. Duff	. . . . .	fol.	1
W. Gordon .	. . .		
T. P. Cope & Sons	. . . .		
W. Hay	. . . . .		
Cash	. . . . . .		
Mdse. .	. . . . . .		
Robert Martin .	. . . . .	2	
Jas. Carter .	. . . . .		
R. Evans .	. . . . .		
Robt. Butler	. . . . .		
Andrew Bell	. . . . .		
James Day .	. . . . .	3	
Expense Account	. . . .		
Exchange Account	. . . . .		
Edward Pryor	. . . . .		
Samuel Gaynor	. . . . .		
Profit & Loss	. . . . .	4	

1. The above Proof or Trial sheet must embrace all amounts that have been posted since the last balance—closed accounts as well as open ones. See Cope & Sons' account above. By this means we have not only proof by equal debits and credits, but we have the sum total of the postings to the Ledger agreeing in amount with the sum total of the Day-Book transactions. Compare the above with the Day-Book footings, p. 128. This is the strongest and most conclusive proof that our Day-Book is completely posted. If one dollar or one cent be omitted, it is evident that this Trial must fall just that amount SHORT of the Day-Book footing. On the contrary, if any entry by any means gets twice posted, the Trial will certainly show it by footing up just the amount of the error MORE than the Day-Book.

2. In our next set our students will find an illustration of the monthly trial, also a full explanation of the mode of detecting and correcting errors.

3. If the business had continued in this Ledger, you must recollect, that in re-opening, the amounts composing the old Balance account do not pass through the Day-Book, for this reason, when you take your next trial, it will foot just the amount of this Balance account more than the Day-Book. Therefore at each succeeding trial after the first, until the re-opening entries are passed again through the Day-Book, deduct the amount of the previous Balance from the footing of the trial sheet, and the remainder must agree with the footing of the Day-Book as above.

SET II.—PART II.

OPENING WITH A TRANSFER OF THE CONTENTS OF THE LAST LEDGER.—EXHIBITING
ALSO THE FORMATION OF A NEW FIRM BY THE ADMISSION OF A NEW PARTNER.—
ILLUSTRATING THE USE OF ALL THE AUXILIARIES IN THE NEW PROCESS FOR
DETECTING ERRORS AND

PROVING THE LEDGER.

1. We have shown in the last set our method of proving the Books, applied to the Day-Book and Ledger only. That set, as already stated, is only intended for a retail business. As the business extends, the Auxiliaries and the Journal become necessary. I may however remark, that the Journal would seldom be required in any ordinary business, if all persons about the establishment were instructed in keeping a Day-Book upon this principle. Where this is not done, a common Day-Book must be kept, from whence the book-keeper journalizes the entries.

2. Our purpose is now to show, that our method of detecting errors and proving the books, is applicable with the use of as few or as many of the Auxiliaries as the book-keeper may consider it necessary to keep.

3. By a slight alteration in the form of the Invoice Book, and adding up and forwarding the amounts from page to page, it will be seen that this book, the merchandise debit column in the Journal, and the debit side of the merchandise account in the Ledger, will correct each other; and by attending to the footings of this book and the Journal, an error cannot pass unobserved for a single page. It is to be observed, however, that all entries affecting the debit side of the merchandise account, must originate upon this book.

4. The next question that presents itself is, how are invoices of consignments to be disposed of? We exemplify two entries of this kind: one on April 30, p. 137, and one on June 4, p. 138. By these entries it will be seen that all such invoices, and invoices on account of ourselves and others in company, can be entered upon this book, without disturbing the entries of our own invoices, the amounts of which are extended into the right-hand column to be footed and forwarded as before directed.

5. By a similar arrangement it will be seen that we have made our Sales Book, the Merchandise credit column in the Journal, and the credit side of the merchandise account in the Ledger, agree with each other.

By the common mode of keeping the Cash Book, its balance and that of the cash account in the Ledger must agree, otherwise there must be error in one or the other—perhaps in both. This, however, furnishes no clue to where the error exists. From our arrangement of this Book in connection with the cash columns in the Journal, it will be seen that you can always in a few minutes point out the very page and generally the side of the Book upon which the error exists.

6. The Bill Books both control their representatives in the Ledger upon the principles explained in Note 4, p. 48. The Commission Sales Book governs the Consignment Sales acct. in the Ledger in a similar manner. And the same harmony is maintained between the Check Book and the Bank Account.

7. The following Invoice Book opens with an inventory of the Merchandise brought into the new firm by the old partners, as will be seen by the Journal; this Merchandise is carried to their credit. The Day-Book and Cash-Book show their other effects.

136

							MDSE. DR.	
	6 pieces, 112½, 115½, 116, 112, 118, 117 = 691 yds. Ingrain							
	Carpeting				@ $1.	691		
	4	*n*	Blk. Broadcloth, 20½, 21½, 20½, 19½ = 82 yds.		10.	820		
	2	*n*	Blk. Gros de Naples, 60, 60 = 120 yds.		1.	120		
	12	*n*	Blk. Bombazine		15.	180		
D. B. 1.	20	*n*	Colored Florence	1510 yds.	. 30 cts.	453		
	20	*n*	Blk. Crape de Paris		5.	100		
	4	*n*	Black Satin Vestings	120 yds.	2.	240		
	2	*n*	Green Broad Cloth	41 yds.	6.	246		
	100	*n*	Prints		3.	300		
	20	*n*	Furniture		3.25	65		
	1	*n*	do.			2	50	3217	50

10.

BOSTON, April 6th, 1867.

D. B. 1	MESSRS. DUFF, GORDON & CO.							
	Bo't of WM. HAY.							
D. G.	500 ps. Merrimac Prints			@ $3.	1500		
& Co.	200 *n* Furniture			4.	800		
	80 *n* Rolled Jaconets			1.25	100		
	60 *n* *n* *n*			1.50	90		
	Packing cases				4	40	2494	40
	Paid Cash, Freight, and Cartage						11	60

n

NEW YORK, April 10th, 1867.

D B. 1.	MESSRS. DUFF, GORDON & CO.					
	Bo't of A. STUART & CO.					
	1 ps. Super Wool Black Cloth	22½ @ $8.	180		
	1 *n* Double Mill'd Cassimere	24 1.50	36	216

20.

D. B. 1.	MESSRS. DUFF, GORDON & CO.				
	Bo't of A. STUART & CO.				
	1 ps., 60 yds., Blk. Gros de Naples	@ 75 cts.	45	
	1 *n* 60 *n* *n* Bombazine	50	30	75

30.

Invoice of 40 pieces Brussels Carpeting, consigned to DUFF, GORDON & Co., for sale by order and for account of A. Stuart & Co.

No. 4.	10 ps., 360 yds.			@ $1.	360
n 6.	10 *n* 360 *n*			1.25	450
n 8.	10 *n* 360 *n*	Ingrain		1.50	540
n 10.	10 *n* 360 *n*	do.		2.	720
	NEW YORK, April 30th, 1867.				2070

May 1.

D B. 2.	MESSRS. DUFF, GORDON & CO.					
	Bo't of EDWARD PRYOR.					
	4 yds. Black Silk Velvet	@ $4.	16		
	6 *n* Fine Black Broadcloth	@ $8.	48	64	
	Forwarded				6078	50

	Bro't forward		6078	50

MESSRS. DUFF, GORDON & Co.

D. B.2.   Bo't of SAMUEL GAYNOR.

| 4 ps., 240 yds., Black Gros de Naples | @ $1. | 240 | |
| 1 ps. Green Crape | | 25 | 265 |

NEW YORK, May 1st, 1867.

23.

PHILADELPHIA, May 10th, 1867.

MESSRS. DUFF, GORDON & Co.

D. B.3.   Bo't of T. P. COPE & SONS.

| 500 bbls. Superfine Flour | @ $4. | 2000 | |
| 50 " Herring | 6. | 300 | 2300 |

June 4.

INVOICE of Broadcloths, consigned to DUFF, GORDON & Co.,
F. H.   for sale by order and for account of Francis Hardman

6 ps. Super Blue, 19?, 20?, 21, 19, 18, 22 = 120 yds., @ $8.	960	
7 " Wool Black, 17, 23, 18, 22, 19, 21, 20 = 140 " @ 9.	1260	
Packing case	2	

BOSTON, June 1st, 1867

2222

D. B.4. Taken to our account @ 3 months, 3 pieces A. Stuart & Co.'s
Carpeting, viz. 2 pieces 72 yds. @ $1.50, and 1 piece 36
yds. @ $2. 180

MESSRS. DUFF, GORDON & Co.

D. B.4.   Bo't of S. HENRY & Co.

12 Cashmere Shawls	@ $50.	600	
12 " "	30.	360	
12 " "	10.	120	
12 " Lamb's Wool Plaid do.	3.	36	1116

Rec'd Payment,
NEW YORK, June 4th, 1867.   S. HENRY & Co.

10.

DUFF, GORDON & Co.

D. B.5.   Bo't of WM. HAY.

| 24 pr. Super Bath Blankets | @ $7. | | 168 |

DUFF, GORDON & Co.

D. B.5.   Bo't of THOMAS FREEMAN.

| 12 pr. Super 10-4 Rose Blankets | @ $6. | | 72 |

20.

DUFF, GORDON & Co.

D. B.5.   Bo't of JAMES HAVEN.

| 14 pieces Satin Ribbon | @ $2. | | 28 |

DUFF, GORDON & Co.

D. B.5.   Bo't of A. STUART & Co.

| 500 ps. Merrimac Prints | @ $2. | | 1000 |

Rec'd payment By note @ 3 months,
NEW YORK, June 20th, 1867.   A. STUART & Co.

| June 30, Total purchases to date | | 11207 | 50 |

4 ps., 320 yds., Ingrain Carpeting	.	.	.	@ $1.	320
700 " Merrimac Prints	.	.	.	4.	2800
400 barrels S. F. Flour	.	.	.	4.	1600
300 ps. Furniture Prints	.	.	.	4.	1200
400 " " "	.	.	.	2.	800
10 Cashmere Shawls	.	.	.	50.	500
8 "	.	.	.	30.	240
50 barrels Herring	.	.	.	6.	300
10 ps. 200 yds., Broadcloth	.	.	.	3.	600
4 " 230 " Blk. Gros de Naples	.	.	.	1.	230
6 " 360 " Fancy "	.	.	.	1.	360
4 " 82 " Broadcloth .	.	.	.	10.	820
6 " Crape de Paris	.	.	.	5.	30
			Enter'd Ledger 2.		9800

CONCLUDING REMARKS.

1. It is not necessary to pass the Inventory of goods on hand through the books, unless at the transfer to new books, although there are no objections to doing so in the common mode of keeping books; but upon this plan, for the reasons named in note 3, p. 135, it would cause some trouble with the next trial sheet.

2. In a business where the invoices are so long, that copying them entire becomes inconvenient, an abstract of them will be found sufficient for this book; but we must again remind our student that he must see this book made complete. Every entry affecting the debit side of his merchandise account must originate here; but when this is done, this book becomes a direct and perfect check upon the Dr. side of the merchandise account in the Ledger. Nothing so completely establishes the correctness of this part of the book-keeper's work as the agreement of this book with its representative in the Ledger; and this is done on any day or at any hour you choose to compare its footing with those of the Journal: you are not obliged to wait until the time of making out the trial sheet.—Compare the footing of the last page with that of the debit merchandise column on the Journal, p. 161.

3. On the other hand, as the Invoice Book is usually kept, it affords no protection whatever against error in the Ledger. It is, indeed, of no practical use, except as a memorandum of the prices of the goods.

4. When this book is kept in this form, the work of posting can be shortened by another process. Post all the personal accounts direct from here to the Ledger, post marking them as usual; and at last post the merchandise debit from the end of the month or the end of the quarter, as may be decided upon, inserting the post mark on the same line with the sum. We shall show hereafter—p. 142—that the Sales Book can be posted in the same way, and thus do away with the merchandise columns in the Journal.

5. This is perhaps the shortest and simplest of all methods of posting; but there is not the same security against errors, nor the same facility in detecting them, that we have in the other arrangement. besides, there are some kinds of business to which it will not be applicable, whereas the arrangement we have given is applicable to any kind of business whatever.

THE SALES BOOK.

THE object for keeping this book is to avoid entering long invoices of sales upon the Day Book. It is generally ruled with one set of money columns; but for our purpose two sets are required. By means of these two sets of columns, it will be seen that all entries, usually made on a Sales Book, can be made upon this, in the common form, and with very little trouble, All amounts affecting the Merchandise account are separated, footed, and forwarded like the credit Merchandise column on the Journal; while all the particulars of the invoice of the sale are stated and exhibited in the inner column, as usual. It is so simple that any further explanation seems unnecessary. The first entry on April 30, and the last one on May 23, exemplify the management of entries when only a part of the amount is to go to the credit of merchandise.

NEW **YORK**, Saturday, April 10, 1867.

	Sold Robert Butler (Buffalo), @ 3 mos.,					
	50 pieces Merrimac Prints . . . . $4.	200				
D. B. 1.	10 " Rolled Jaconets . . . 2.	20				
	1 " 22¹ Fine Wool Black Broadcloth . . 10.	225				
	30 " Furniture Prints . . . 5.	150				
	Packing case	1	50		596	50
	"					
D. B. 1.	Edward Pryor to Mdse. for 2 yds. fine Brown Cloth @ $8.				16	
	"					
	Sold Richard Howe for Cash					
	70 pieces Prints . . . $4.	280				
D. B. 1.	5 " Furniture . . . .5.	25				
	Packing box . . .		75		305	75
	Tues. 20.					
D. B. 2.	¹ Paid E. Pryor's order to J. Burk in Mdse. .				45	
	"					
D. B. 2.	² Sold Samuel Gaynor on his order favor of C. Rhodes,					
	1 piece 20 yds. Super Black Cloth . . @ 11.	220				
	1 " 118 yds. Ingrain Carpet 1.50	177			397	
	"					
D. B. 2.	Sold James Camp for Cash,					
	2 pieces 19²,20²=40 yds. Super Blue Broadcloth @ 11.	440				
	1 " 60 yds. Black Gros de Nap. . 1.	60				
	10 pair Bath Blankets . 12.	120				
	60 pieces English Prints . 5.	300				
		920				
	5 per cent. for Cash .	46			874	
	Friday 30					
D. B. 2.	Sold Joel Post for Cash,					
	24 yds. Purple Silk Velvet . . @ 4.50, $108.					
	30 " Crimson and Gold Fringe . 1 30.	138			138	
	4 ps. 144 yds. A. Stewart & Co.'s Carpets 2.50	3C0				
		498				
	Merchandise forward .				2372	25

1. There is no necessity to specify the articles you have sold in payment for this order. Your possession of it is evidence of your having paid it.
2. When you furnish merchandise upon an open order—that is, an order permitting the bearer to draw any amount he desires—it is necessary to specify what you sell upon it, and to furnish the drawer of the order with a bill.

	Bro't forward	.				2372	25
D. B. 2.	Sold P. Duff on account,						
	4 yds. best Black Cloth .	@ $8.	32				
	1 yd. Black Silk Velvet . .	.	5			37	
D. B. 2.	Sold C. Spencer on his note @ 20 days,						
	40 ps. Merrimac Prints . . .	@ $3.	120				
	10 " Furniture .	" 4.	40				
	1 " 20? Black Cloth .	" 6.	123				
	Packing case . .	. .	1	50		284	50
D. B. 2.	Sold W. Gordon on account,						
	16 yds. Fig'd Gros de Naples .	@ $1.25	20				
	1 Silk Cravat .	. .	1	50		21	50
D. B. 2.	Sold James Carter on account,						
	1 pr. Black Silk Gloves		1	25			
	12 yds. Linen . . .	@ 75c.	9			10	25
D. B. 2.	Sold Robert Banks on account,						
	1 yd. Fancy Velvet, $1.50. 2? Fancy Cassimere, @ $2.					6	50
D. B. 3.	Received Cash for sales of Mdse. this day .					160	

Monday, 23.

	Invoice of Mdse. shipped by the Brig "Tribune," Truck,					
	Master, by order and for account and risk of Messrs.					
D. B. 3.	T. P. Cope & Sons, Philadelphia.					
	40 bbls. No. 1 Mackerel . .	@ $6.	240			
	300 boxes Smoked Herring .	1.	300		540	
	———— CHARGES. ————		540			
	Commission 5 per cent. on $540 . .	$27.				
	Cash paid for cooperage, cartage, &c. .	12.	39			
	E. E. NEW YORK, May 23, 1867.		579			

Tuesday, 31.

D. B 4.	Sold William Evans, payable in 10 days,				
	4 ps. Furniture Prints . . .	@ $3.	12		
	2 " " "	" 4.	8	20	
D. B. 4.	Sold J. Reed, payable next week,				
	1 ps. Super Black Cloth . . .	22?, @ $8.		182	
D. B. 4.	Sold Joel Post, payable in 10 days,				
	2 yds. Super Blue Broadcloth . .	@ $9.		18	
D. B. 3.	Received Cash for sales 23d, $180. 31st, $86 . .			266	
D. B 4.	Sold R. Butler wrappers for a bale A. Stuart & Co.'s Carpet			1	50
	Merchandise forwarded . . .			3919	50

	Bro't forward	.		3919	50
D. B. 4.	Sold James Reed on account,				
	1 ps., 36 yds., Brussels Carpet	. .	@ $2.25	81	
	1 Silk Shawl	. .	.	15	96
	"				
D. B. 4.	Sold Wm. Hay on account 1 Cashmere Shawl .		. .		60
	"				
D. B. 4.	Sold Robert Parker, payable 1st July—				
	1 Cashmere Shawl . . .				60
	"				
D. B. 4.	Sold George Draper, on his note,				
	6 Cashmere Shawls . . .	. @ $55.		330	
	6 " " .	" 30.		180	
	6 Silk " . . .	. " 20.		120	630
	10.				
D. B. 5.	Sold R. Banks on account,				
	6 pr. 10-4 Super Bath Blankets .	. @ $10.		60	
	6 " 10-4 " Rose "	. . " 8.		48	108
	"				
D. B. 5.	Sold Edward Pryor on account,				
	3 pr. 10-4 Super Bath Blankets .	. @ $10.		30	
	3 " 10-4 " Rose "	. " 8.		24	
	1 ps., 21? yds., Blk. Broadcloth .	. " 6.		129	183
	20.				
D. B. 5.	Sold William Garden for Cash deposited,				
	500 ps. Merrimac Prints . .	@ $2.50		1250	
	Total sales to date	. .		6306	50

·CONCLUDING REMARKS.

1. Compare the above footing with that of the credit merchandise column in the Journal, p. 161, and every person at all acquainted with the subject must be convinced that there cannot be a more conclusive evidence of the correctness of this part of the work.

2. When the Sales Book is kept in this form it admits of being posted, as we have directed at the Invoice Book, note 4, p. 139; post the personal accounts as usual, and the merchandise in one sum from the foot of the account above.

3. If no Commission Sales Book is kept, the sales on consignment can be short extended as in first entry Apr. 30, p. 140.

4. It is scarcely necessary to observe that the way the Sales Book is generally kept, it affords no means whatever of proving its contents to be all transferred or posted; and there is the strongest reason to believe that errors, deeply affecting the interest of the proprietors, frequently pass for ever undiscovered in this book.

5. A few years ago a Western merchant called at the office of an extensive wholesale dealer in Philadelphia to pay his account. On referring to the Ledger it was found balanced. Upon the merchant representing that he had a subsequent invoice from them, the Sales Book was searched, and an invoice of about $1300 found marked off that book as if journalized, but no entry appeared upon the Journal. Now, in this case, it is evident that the discovery of this omission was purely accidental, and it is equally certain, that, by our plan, it would have been undoubtedly discovered before we had journalized another page.

COMMISSION SALES BOOK.

1. We give here another exemplification of this book, for the purpose of illustrating a different mode of conducting the account in the Ledger. The management of this book itself is not essentially different from the former one, p. 65.

2. It is credited for all the sales, and debited for all charges, and for the net proceeds, when you pay it over or carry it to the credit of the owner; when it must be closed as you perceive Hardman's account is below.

3. You will perceive that there is not a separate account on the Ledger for each consignment account, as in our former set. Here we carry every one's sales and charges to one account. When you render account, and settle the sales, you do it upon this book, taking care that all the entries you make here are carried to the commission sales account on the Ledger.

4. The work is proved by comparing the total debits and credits of all the accounts on this book, with the total footings of the Commission Sales account on the Ledger.

Dr.   **Cr.**

Sales of Merchandise by order and for account of A. Stuart & Co.

1861.						
Apr. 30	Paid Cash for Freight Cartage and Labor	24		1 50		25 50

1861.				
Apr. 30	Sold Joel Post for Cash,		360	360
May 4	ps. 144 yds. best Brussels Carpet @ $2.50			
May 31	Sold R. Butler @ 2 mos., due July 31,			
	5 ps. 180 yds. Brussels Carpet .	82,	216	
	4 " 144 "	1.50	108	576
June 4	Taken to our acct. @ 3 mos., due Sept. 4,			
	2 ps. 72 yds. Brussels Carpet @ $1.50		108	
	1 " 36 "	2.	72	180

Sales of Merchandise by order and for account of Francis Hardman.

1861.						
June 4	Paid Cash Freight and Cartage	12		7 36		7 48
" "	Duties					
June 10	Commiss'n on Total Sales 2740 @ 5 per ct.	137		1855		1992
	Cash paid F. Hardman in full for n. p.					2740

1861.				
June 4	Sold to Jennings & Co. for Cash,			
	6 ps. Super Blue Broadcloth, viz.:			
	1 " " " "	19?		
	1 " " " "	20?		
	1 " " " "	21		
	1 " " " "	19		
	1 " " " "	18		
	1 " " " "	22 120 @ $10		1200
June 10	Sold M'Kenzie & Abbott for Cash,			
	3 ps. S.W. Blk. Cloth, 17,23,18—58			
	4 " " " 22,19,21,20—82 140,$11		1540	2740

1 Dr.   **C A S H**

1867							
Apr.	1	Sundries	Balance ⅌ old Ledger, fol. 4.		2100	05	
		P. Duff (S. A.)	Rec'd balance of his capital		115	53	
		P. Duff	Rec'd on acct.		500		
		W. Gordon (S. A.)	Rec'd balance due on his capital		1282	42	
		J. Carter (S. A.)	Rec'd on acct of his capital		2000		
	10	Merchandise	Rec'd from Howe		305	75	
		R. Butler	Rec'd on acct.		100		
	20	Merchandise	Rec'd of Camp		874		
	30	Commission Sales	Rec'd for Stuart's carpets		360		
		Merchandise	Rec'd of J. Post		138		
					7775	75	7775 75
			Balance in hand bro't down		48	15	
May	1	S. Gaynor	Rec'd on acct.		50		
		Merchandise	Rec'd for sales this day		160		
	23	B. Receivable	Rec'd for Spencer's Note		284	50	
		Merchandise	Rec'd for sales this day		180		
		Duff & Gordon	Rec'd Martin's acct. Ledger A. p. 2		20		
	31	Merchandise	Rec'd for Sales this day		86		
		S. Gaynor	Rec'd on acct.		20		
		Duff & Gordon	Rec'd of R. Evans, Ledger A. p. 2		25		825 50
					873	65	
			Balance in hand bro't down		9	65	
June	4	Joel Post	Rec'd in full		18		
		James Reed	Rec'd on acct.		100		
		Commission Sales	Rec'd of Jennings for cloths		1200		
	10	R. Butler	Rec'd ⅌ mail		100		
		Commission Sales	Rec'd of McKenzie for cloths		1540		
		Duff & Gordon	Rec'd of R. Evans in full		41	25	
	20	Profit & Loss	Rec'd gain on auction purchase		150		3149 25
			Total amt. received to date				11750 50

1. In business the Cash Book ought generally to be balanced every night; never at longer periods than a week. For obvious reasons, we could not, in a work like this, introduce a sufficient number of entries to do so: we have, therefore, only balanced it monthly.

2. The manner of making the entries upon this book, is in all respects the same as note 9, p. 53. The right hand column is used for carrying forward the sums total of all money received and paid, thereby enabling us to keep a constant check upon the Journal.—Compare the footings above, June 30, with those of the Journal, p. 161. And it will facilitate the detection of error to balance this book when the Journal is footed at the bottom of any page, where you can compare the cash columns together.

3. Observe, this Cash Book is always balanced in the inner columns, until the period of

144

ACCOUNT.

Cr. 1

1867.							
Apr.	1	City Bank	Paid in deposit	5800			
		Store Expenses	Pd. for fuel	3			
		James Day	Pd. him on acct.	8			
	10	Mdse.	Pd. freight of W. Hay's Invoice	11	60		
		R. Banks	Pd. him on acct. of store expenses	20			
		P. Duff	Pd. him on acct.	30			
	20	B. Receivable	Pd. R. Parker net proceeds of note	979	50		
	30	Commission Sales	Pd. cartage, &c., on Stuart's Carpets	1	50		
		" "	Pd. freight on " "	24			
		P. Duff	Pd. him on acct.	60			
		W. Gordon	Pd. him	25			
		James Carter	Pd. him	15			
		City Bank	Pd. in deposit	750		7727	60
			Balance in hand carried down	48	15		
				7775	75		
May	1	R. Banks	Pd. him on acct.	30			
		Expense acct.	Pd. a quarter's rent	60			
		James Day	Pd. him on acct.	12			
		W. Gordon	" "	10			
		P. Duff	" "	5			
	23	T. P. Cope & Sons	Pd. Charges ⅌ "Tribune"	12			
		James Day	Pd. him ten dollars, JAMES DAY*	10			
		W. Gordon	Pd. him on acct.	40			
	31	Profit & Loss	For counterfeit money	20			
		E. Pryor	Pd. him on loan	200			
		R. Banks	Pd. him on acct.	10			
		W. Gordon	" "	5			
		City Bank	Pd. in deposit	450		864	
			Balance in hand carried down	9	65		
				873	65		
June	4	James Day	Pd. him on acct	5			
		Commission Sales	Duty, &c., on Hardman's goods	748			
		City Bank	In deposit	100			
	10	" "	"	100			
		Commission Sales	Pd. F. Hardman in full, net proceeds	1855			
		James Day	In full	13			
	20	R. Banks	On acct.	90			
		James Haven	In full	28		2939	
			Total payments to date			11530	60
			Balance in hand carried down			219	90
						11750	50

posting the Cash from the Journal; it is then closed in the outer column; but the balance is brought down or forward in the inner column. The balance brought down must not be extended as money received again. This was done before the last balance. It must, however, be added in in striking the balance.

4. As in the Ledger, we have dropped the useless appendages of TO and BY in this book.

5. By having a folio column next the date or the money column the entries may all be posted direct from this book to the Ledger, and the sum total of money received and paid is posted in one sum from the bottom, as from the Journal.

* Day's signature—See Note 7, page 76.

K

145

CHECK BOOK.

1. In this form we follow our favorite theory of making this book prove the correctness of its representative in the Ledger. Our column of deposits, and that of checks, is preserved unbroken, and carried forward from page to page, corresponding with the debit and credit side of the Bank account in the Ledger—compare and see p. 168—until we get our Bank pass-book balanced; then we balance both our Check Book and Bank account in the Ledger, bringing the balances down as usual. The detection of errors in this form is so simple, and so speedy, that I cannot think it necessary to offer any directions.

2. I must insist, however, upon your drawing and numbering all your checks upon your own book. Any deviation from this practice will, sooner or later, give trouble.

Date.	Depo-sit.		Date.	To whom paid.	No.	Check.		
1867. Apr.	1	5800	1867.				No. 1. NEW YORK, Apr. 20, 1867.	
	30	750					THE CASHIER OF THE CITY BANK, NEW YORK, pay to *myself, or bearer,* Seven *Hundred and three* Dollars $\frac{00}{100}$.	
May	1	400	Apr. 20	for 2 notes	1	703 65		
	13	91					$703.$\frac{00}{100}$.	P. DUFF.
7041. 2703.65 4337.35			May 23	W. Hay	2	2000		
				2703.65				
				Bal.		4337 35		
		7041				7041		
Bro't down		4337 35						
May	31	450	May 31	Cope & Son	3	500		
		400						
June	4	200						
		100	31	W. Hay	4	200		
	10	491 95						
		100						
7329.30 3051.20 4278.10	20	1250	June 4	Stuart's n'e	5	291		
			4	S. Henry	6	1060 20		
			4	Cope & Son	7	1000	No. . NEW YORK, . 186 .	
				3051.20			THE CASHIER OF THE CITY BANK, NEW YORK,	
				Bal.		4278 10	pay to or bearer Dollars $\frac{}{100}$.	
		7329 30				7329 30	$ $\frac{}{100}$	
Bro't down		4278 10						

3. When a deposit is made it must be entered in your pass-book, at the time it is made; all writing in this book must be done by the bank officers. The New York city banks collect notes and bills in the city, free of charge; but, if protested for non-payment, the owner must pay the expense of it.

4. Three days' grace are allowed upon all notes, for which discount is also taken: thus, a note having 60 days to run, 63 days' discount is deducted.—See note 2, p. 45.—In some of the States they charge 64 days' interest in such cases, charging interest both for the day of date and day of payment.

5. You can at any time show the balance in the margin with your pencil, as is shown by the small marginal figures above; but the deposit and check columns must be carried forward unbroken until your pass-book is balanced.

6. To prevent fraud, when dealing with strangers, checks are sometimes made payable to order: the bank will not then pay them until the holder endorses them and identifies himself the person named in the check.

EXPENSE BOOK.

1. This book is kept for the purpose of enabling **the** Book-keeper to avoid passing all minute items of expense separately through the books. One **of** the junior clerks, say R. Banks, is paid a sum **of** money sufficient to defray the expenses for a few weeks. The Book-keeper debits Banks, and credits his Cash account for this money when placed in Banks' hands. The Cash account is, by this means, kept free from derangement, and Banks should **be** provided with a separate drawer to keep this money in; and as he pays it out for expenses he must enter a precise statement of all the items upon this book, adding it up and carrying forward the amount to the end of the month, or to the time when it is proposed to enter the amount in the books. After examining the amounts and additions, the Book-keeper may make Expense Dr. to Banks, at the same time balancing this book as below.—See Day-Book, note 3, p. 155. Afterwards this book re-commences in all respects as before, Banks receiving an additional sum from the Cashier when the amount in his hands is expended.

2. If it be preferred, however, when the amount is paid into Banks' hands, the Book-keeper may make Expense Account Dr. To Cash at once, without passing it into Banks' account. The amount is then placed on the Cr. side of this book, and the details of expenditure on the Dr. side, in all respects as before, until the money is expended, when the book should be balanced, and re-commence anew as before. Either of these methods will greatly abridge the expense account in any business.

1867.					1867.		
Apr.	10	For Cash paid postages		70	June 30 By amount to R. Banks Cr.		45
	12	" cartage of goods		30			
		" coach-hire		50			
		" laborers		50			
	14	" 2 rms. wrapping-paper	2	50			
		" 4℔ twine	1				
	15	" for mending desk-stool		50			
		" ream letter-paper	2	50			
		" postage to N. Orleans		50			
		" cartage of goods	3	50			
	20	" Box rent at Post Office	5				
		" printing 500 cards	6				
	25	" painting a new sign	8				
	30	" blank book		50			
		" wafers		20			
		" sealing-wax		50			
May	1	" 6 mos. sub. Tribune	3				
		" 1 year " Sun	3				
		" Taxes	4				
	5	" postage for R. Butler		10			
		" " W. Hay		20			
	10	" laborers		50			
	15	" omnibus		10			
	23	" advertising	1				
June	5	" postages		10			
	10	" wafers		10			
	20	" ink, sand, &c.		22			
				45			

BILLS RECEIVABLE.

DATE	No.	DRAWER'S NAME	IN WHOSE FAVOR	ON WHAT ACCOUNT	TIME TO RUN	1	2	3	4	5	6	7	8	9	10	11	12	AMOUNT	WHEN	AND HOW DISPOSED OF	AMOUNT
1867.																			1867.		
Apr. 10	1	S. Gaynor	Ourselves	Bal. of acct.	30 days					13								91	May 13	Rec'd in Cash	91
20	2	R. Parker	"	Money lent	4 months								23					1000	June 20	Carried down	1000
May 1	3	C. Spencer	"	Merchandise	20 days						24							284 50	May 23	Rec'd in Cash	284 50
4	4	R. Butler	"	Bal. of acct.	3 months							4						496 50	June 10	Disct. City B'k	496 50
June 4	5	C. Draper	"	Merchandise	3 "													630	June 30	Carried down	630
																		2302			2302
Apr. 20	2	R. Parker	Ourselves	Money lent	4 months								23	7				1000			
June 4	5	G. Draper	"	Merchandise	3 "									7				630			

1. I must take this opportunity of directing attention to a prevailing, but surely a very improper practice, that of writing, in ink, memorandums of date, name, &c., on the back of notes or acceptances. The back of a note ought certainly not to be defaced in this manner any more than the face of it. The utmost liberty that ought to be taken in this way, is to write the holder's private number upon it; but even this ought not to be done by any party until he actually becomes the holder. When a banker refuses to discount a note, he ought to return it as good as he receives it, and not with an indelible memorandum of its rejection, which must afterwards damage it more or less in the market. Pencil marks would, in all such cases, answer for private memorandums, and would not be liable to the objections just named.

BILLS PAYABLE.

WHEN ACCEPTED	No.	DRAWER'S NAME	IN WHOSE FAVOR	ON WHAT ACCOUNT	TIME TO RUN	1	2	3	4	5	6	7	8	9	10	11	12	AMOUNT	WHEN	AND HOW PAID	AMOUNT
1867.																			1867.		
Apr. 10	1	Wm. Hay	On ourselves	Bal. of acct.	10 ds. sight				23									200	Apr. 20	Paid by check	200

THE DAY BOOK.—SET II., PART II.

INTRODUCTORY REMARKS.

1. This set opens with the formation of a new firm, by the admission of James Carter as a partner. It will be seen that the contents of the old Ledger form the opening entries of these Books.—Compare Balance account, p. 134, with the first entry in the following Day Book, also with the first entry in the Invoice Book, p. 137, and the first debit entry Cash Book, p. 144. It is arranged that each partner shall contribute $3000 capital; the two old members bring in the effects of their former business as so much of their capital, the new firm at the same time assuming their liabilities.

2. The usual manner of opening and conducting partners' accounts is to credit each for what capital he pays in at the time the books are opened and for each succeeding payment afterwards. I would, however, recommend that two accounts be opened with each partner, a PRIVATE ACCOUNT and a STOCK ACCOUNT.—See the partners' private accounts, p. 165, and their stock accounts, p. 173. The stock account to be credited for the whole amount of capital *to be paid in.* The private accounts are to be debited for any amount that is deficient of the stock, and for what they withdraw from the firm, and credited for what they pay in of the deficient stock, and for what they may temporarily pay over their capital.— See Duff's and Carter's accounts, p. 165.

3. By this arrangement, the stock account of each partner remains undisturbed until the time of closing the books, and if any adjustment of interest has to take place it will be upon the private account.

4. All judicious practical merchants are aware of the importance of avoiding all needless exposure of their affairs. This, in some establishments, is unavoidable where the partners' accounts and the results of the business are all exhibited on the public Ledger. In order to avoid this inconvenience I have, in this set, exemplified the PRIVATE LEDGER.

5. Keeping this book entails no additional trouble upon the book-keeper; there are no entries to make in it, except at the opening and closing of the Books. It opens—see p. 173—with nothing but the partners' stock accounts; the Profit & Loss, Balance and Suspended list are opened at the time of closing. By referring to these accounts—p. 174—it will be seen that the results of the business can only be known to those who have access to this book; it is impossible to find out any thing about it from the public Ledger alone.

6. In business it will also be advisable to place the opening entry of the business upon a PRIVATE JOURNAL, from whence it is posted direct to the Ledger without appearing upon the public Journal. This will create no impediment to our system of proof, for the book-keeper has only to obtain the footing of this private Journal, and add it to that of the public Day Book and Journal, and the amount must agree with that of the Trial Sheet. It is deemed unnecessary to give an exemplification of this private Journal here. It stands connected with the public Journal upon the same principle as the private Ledger does with the public one. Indeed the readiest way to comprehend them is to consider the two books as one.

7. The following Day Book is made up partly of original entries and partly by transfers from the old Ledger and the Auxiliaries. I shall show hereafter that the Journal may be composed direct from the Auxiliaries, without passing the entries through the Day Book. but for reasons before given—p. 62—I do not consider it advisable to attempt that process. until after the student is entirely master of the whole subject. The mode of procedure in transferring the Auxiliaries to the Day Book is not, however, unlike that of journalizing them; it forms a useful preparatory exercise for that operation.

SET II.—DOUBLE ENTRY BOOK-KEEPING.

1. It does not matter which of your Auxiliaries you transfer first: we shall commence with the Invoice Book, p. 137. We commence on the 10th April (the previous entry being already transferred in the opening entry), and transfer the two entries under that date to the Day Book—compare and see. Then turn to the Sales Book, p. 140, and do the same with three entries we find under that date, taking care to mark them off these books; but not until they are actually entered in the Day Book—Note 4, p. 142; next, look into the Commission Sales Book, but it contains no entries on this day. Go on to the Cash Book—p. 144—and you find two debits and three credits; pass them into the Day Book and mark them off as directed—Note 7, p. 53. The entries of the Check Book are generally made on the Day Book when they occur. The contents of the Expense Book are not usually transferred until the end of the quarter or the end of the month, as may be directed. Bills Receivable—p. 148—has one transfer, and Bills Payable two upon this date. After they are transferred mark them off as directed in the Cash Book. This completes the transfer of that day's business from the Auxiliaries: you now re-commence and go over them all in the same way again for the next day's business, and so on until the contents are all transferred. Observe, you cannot transfer several dates from any one book in one entry, because this throws the dates in confusion in the Ledger.

2. Our Day Book is footed and forwarded from page to page, and if all journalized correctly, must always exactly agree with that book. We generally only pencil the footings of the Day Book in practice: and you ought to bring forward these footings as fast as you journalize, in order to get the earliest notice of error if it gets in. You may foot your Day Book column any where on the page, when you desire to find the amount corresponding with the foot of the page on the Journal.

3. In making compound entries upon this Day Book, you must guard against the practice of extending both debits and credits, as many persons do. For instance, in the first entry on the opposite page, if we had full extended the $5410.55 a second time, it would have caused a disagreement between the Day Book and Journal at once, of that amount.

4. In order to have our books all agree in amount, it is necessary that all entries relative to the balancing of accounts at the time of settlement should originate upon this book.—See first entry, May 10, p. 153.

5. We have dropped the useless practice of perpetually writing the name of our place of business at the head of every page of our Day Book and Journal. It is proper and perhaps necessary to do so on the first page of any book, but the repetition of it afterwards is entirely useless. But it will often be found useful to insert the day of the week with the day of the month.

6. I would advise the student not to be in too much haste to write these exercises, but first take a survey of the operations recorded by tracing them from one book to another up to the Ledger: thus mentally examining the whole subject before he attempts the mechanical execution of it.—See Note 4, p. 27.

7. I need hardly observe that if the preceding Sales Book be dispensed with then full particulars of every sale must appear upon the Day Book.

150

P. Duff, W. Gordon, and J. Carter have this day entered into partnership;
it is agreed that each partner shall furnish a capital of   .   3000.
Duff and Gordon bring in as a part of their capital, the effects of their late
firm, and the new firm assumes their liabilities ℔ their Balance acct.
Ledger A. fol. 4, viz. :

[1] Cash in hand .	℔ Ledger A. fol. 1.	2100.05	
Merchandise .	1.	3217.50	
Edward Pryor owes .	3.	2.	
S. Gaynor .	3.	91.	5410 55
Balances due to			
T. P. Cope & Sons .	Ledger A. fol. 1.	504.	
Wm. Hay .	1.	200.	
James Carter .	2.	36.50	
James Day .	3.	68.	
P. Duff for his net capital	1.	2884.47	
W. Gordon do. do. .	1.	1717.58	
		5410.55	

"

Rec'd the following sums in cash ℔ Cash Book 1.

From P. Duff for Balance due on his capital .	115.53	
" do. on his private account .	500.	
" W. Gordon for Balance due on his capital .	1282.42	
" James Carter on account of his capital .	2000.	3897 95

"

Paid the following sums ℔ C. B. 1.

To the City Bank in deposit .	5800.	
For Fuel .	3.	
To James Day on account .	8.	5811

"

[2] James Carter's ½ joint capital is   .   .   . $3000.
Balance due him by Duff and Gordon as above is 36.50.
Cash received as above   .   .   .   2000.   2036.50

Balance due on his capital to debit of his private account . .		963 50

Saturday, 10.

Bought Mdse. of Wm. Hay @ 3 mos. ℔ Invoice Book 1. .	2494.40	
Paid cash for freight of same . . .	11.60	2506

"

Bought of A. Stuart & Co., at 30 days, Mdse. ℔ Invoice Book, p. 1. .	216

"

Sold R. Butler on account, @ 3 months,

Mdse. ℔ Sales Book, p. 1. .	596.50	
Sold E. Pryor on acct. Mdse. ℔ S. B. 1. .	16.	
Sold R. Howe for cash do. do. .	305.75	918 25

"

Received cash of R. Butler on acct. .	100

"

Paid cash to R. Banks on acct. of Expenses . . .	20.	
" do. to P. Duff on account . . .	30.	50
	Forward	19873 25

1. This entry embraces both sides of the Balance account in the last Ledger.—See p. 134. **The pupil**
  will insert the pages of his own Ledger—not ours.
2. As the journalizing proceeds, mark the entries off the Day Book as directed.—Note 7, p. 28. The
  pages of the Journal are not necessary the dates are always a sufficient reference.
3. See Note 2, p. 149.

2

Bro't over	19873	25
Received Samuel Gaynor's note No. 1, @ 30 days, for bal. of acct.	91	
Acc'd Wm. Hay's draft No. 1 on us, @ 10 days, for bal. due him 1st inst.	200	
Acc'd T. P. Cope & Sons' draft No. 2 on us, @ 10 days, for bal. due them	504	
Gave James Day our order on E. Pryor, payable in Merchandise, for	20	

Tuesday, 20.

Paid our acceptance No. 1 to Wm. Hay, due 23d inst., $200, less disct. 10 cts.		$199.90	
do. do. No. 2 to T. P. Cope, due 23d inst., $504, less disct. 25 cts.		503.75	
Paid by check on City Bank		703.65	
Amount of discount is		.35	704
Paid E. Pryor's order in favor of J. Burk in Mdse. from store			45
Paid S. Gaynor's order in favor of C. Rhodes in Mdse. from store			397
Cash to Mdse. received for sale to J. Camp			874
Mdse., Dr. to A. Stuart & Co. for Invoice of Silks, &c.			75
Discounted for R. Parker his note No. 2, @ 4 mos., for $1000.			
Paid him in cash, net proceeds		979.50	
4 3/10 months' discount is		20.50	1000

Friday, 30.

Paid cash freight and cartage of A. Stuart & Co.'s goods		25.50	
" P. Duff on acct.		60.	
" Wm. Gordon		25.	
" James Carter		15.	
" the City Bank in deposit		750.	875	50
Received cash for sale of A. Stuart & Co.'s goods, C. S. B. 1.		360	
" " Mdse. @ S. B. 1.		138.	498

Saturday, May 1.

' Rec'd on account of our James Carter, cash deposited in City Bank,			
Net proceeds of his Bill on Gibson, Bright & Co.		$300.	
Interest due him on Hall's mortgage		100.	400
Bought Mdse. of Edward Pryor, I. B. 1.		64.	
do. of Sam'l Gaynor, do. 2.		265.	329
Sold Mdse. @ Sales Book 2. To P. Duff on account		37.	
To C. Spenser on his note No. 3 @ 20 days		284.50	
" W. Gordon on account		21.50	
" James Carter on account		10.25	
" Robert Banks		6.50	359	75
' Rec'd of R. Butler his note, No. 4, @ 3 mos., to close acct.			496	50
Forward			26742	

1. The firm have no entry to make with Gibson, Bright & Co.; though this bill was drawn by Carter, one of our partners, it was on his own private account. We credit him for the money received for the Bill, and also for the interest collected on Hall's mortgage.
2. The number of a note must always accompany it, to enable us to post it as directed, note 1, p. 167.

Bro't forward		26742
Gave our note, No. 3, to A. Stuart & Co., to close acct., for . . .		291
"		
Received Cash on acct. from S. Gaynor, C. B. 1. . . .	50.	
" " for sales this day	160.	210
"		
Paid Cash to R. Banks on acct., C. B. 1.	30.	
" " a quarter's rent of store	60.	
" " to James Day on acct.	12.	
" " to W. Gordon *"*	10.	
" " to P. Duff *"*	5.	117

Monday, 10.

[1] Rendered James Day his account; balance due him is . . .	28
"	
[1] Rendered Samuel Gaynor his account; balance due us is . .	82

Thursday, 13.

Received Cash, paid the City Bank in deposit, for S. Gaynor's note No. 1	91

Monday, 23.

Gave Wm. Hay our check on the City Bank on acct. for	2000
"	
Bought Mdse. of T. P. Cope & Sons on acct., L. B. 2. . . .	2300
"	
Shipped by the Brig "Tribune," by order and for account of T. P. Cope & Sons,	

Mdse. *⅊* Sales Book 2.	540.	
Paid charges in cash	12.	
Commission on $540, @ 5 per ct.	27.	579

"			
Received Cash for Spencer's Note No. 3. . . .	284.50		
" " from R. Martin for an old debt due Duff & Gordon	20.		
" " for sales of Mdse. this day . . .	180.	484	50
"			
Paid Cash to James Day on account	10.		
" " to W. Gordon *"*	40.	50	

Tuesday, 31.

Balance in deposit in the City Bank this day on settlement . . .	4337	35
"		
Received Cash this day for sales	86.	
" " of S. Gaynor on account	20.	
" " of R. Evans for Duff & Gordon . .	25.	131
"		
Paid Cash to Edward Pryor in loan	200.	
" " Lost by counterfeit money	20.	
" " to R. Banks on acct.	10.	
" " W. Gordon	5.	
" " City Bank in deposit	450.	685

Forward	38127	85

1. In order to preserve that harmony between the books, upon which our method of proof is founded, no entry must appear upon the Ledger (except the closing entries at the general balance) without originating upon the Day Book or some of the auxiliaries. When we settle with an individual we enter the balance as above, and pass it through the Journal.—Notes 1 and 2, p. 156.

	Bro't over	. .	38127	85

Sold W. Evans on acct. Mdsc. ⅌ Sales Book 2 .   20.
James Reed on acct.   *   * 2 .   182.
Joel Post   *   * 2 .   18.   220

*

Sold Robert Butler (Erie) on acct. Stuart & Co.'s goods, C. S. B. 1   576.
of our Mdsc., S. B. 2   1.50   577 50

*

Gave T. P. Cope & Sons our check on City Bank on acct. .   500
Gave W. Hay   *   *   * .   200

*

[1] Received cash on acct. of James Carter, deposited in City Bank.
For Cutler, French & Co.'s Note . . . . . 250.
From Stay & Hall on acct. 150.   400

Saturday, June 4.

Take to our acct. 3 ps. A. Stuart & Co.'s Carpet, I. B. 2 . .   180

*

Bo't Mdsc. of S. Henry & Co., I. B. 2, @ 5 ⅌ ct. disct. for Cash $1116.
Net amount paid by check on City Bank . . . 1060.20
Discount 55.80   1116

*

Paid by check on City Bank our Note, No. 3, in favor of A. Stuart & Co.   291

*

J. Reed's private acct. is Dr. for transfer from "Sundry Drs. acct." . .   182

*

[2] Received Cash, deposited, of E. Pryor for our loan of 31st ulto. . .   200

*

Sold Merchandise, S. B. 3, to James Reed on acct. . . . 96.
*   * to Wm. Hay   *   * . . . 60.
*   * to Robert Parker * * . . . 60.
*   * to Geo. Draper on Note No. 5, @ 3 mos.   630.   846

*

Received Cash of Joel Post in full . . . . 18.
*   * of James Reed on acct. . . . 100.
*   * of Jennings & Co. for sale of Hardman's goods   1200.   1318

*

Paid Cash to James Day on acct. . . . . . 5.
*   * to City Bank in deposit . . . . . 100.
*   * to freight and duty on Hardman's cloths, . . 748.   853

*

Settled with T. P. Cope & Sons.
Gave them our check on the City Bank for .   1000.
Our Note, No. 4, at 30 days to close acct. . . 221.   1221

Forward, . .   46232 35

---

1. Here, as at Note 1, p. 152, the firm has collected money for their partner, Carter. It is almost unnecessary to say, that we have no entry to make about Cutler, French & Co.'s Note, nor about Stay & Hall's account, though we name them on the Day Book. We credit Carter for the amount collected; and he keeps his own private account with these parties.
2. We do not pass this cash into the Cash account because we sent it immediately to the Bank. The Bank account by this means materially diminishes the cash transactions, and renders that acct. easier to keep.—Note 1, Pryor's acct., p. 133.

	Brot. Forward	.	.		**46232**	**35**
Bot. of William Hay on account Mdse. I. B. 2	.	.	.	168.		
Bot. of Thomas Freeman on account do.	2	.	.	.	72.	**240**	

"

Sold R. Banks on account Mdse. S. B. 3	.	.	.	108.		
do. E. Pryor do.	3	.	.	.	183.	**291**

"

Discounted at City Bank R. Butler's Note No. 4. for $496.50				
Net proceeds at our Cr. in deposit	491.95			
55 days' Discount	4.55	**496**	**50**	

"

Received Cash on account of R. Butler by mail . .	100.		
Rec'd do of McKenzie & Abbot for sale of Hardman's			
goods, C. S. B. 1	1540.		
Rec'd do. of R. Evans, for Duff & Gordon . .	41.25	**1681**	**25**

"

[1] We close sales of Hardman's cloths. Total sales C. S. B. 1, is $2740.			
Our commission on the same 5 ⅌ ct., is	137.		
Net proceeds paid F. Hardman in cash, is . . .	1855.	**1992**	

"

Paid cash deposit in the City Bank	100.	
Paid James Day cash in full	13.	**113**

Monday, 20.

Bot. Mdse. of James Haven on account I. B. 2 . .	28.		
Bot. Mdse. of A. Stuart & Co. on our Note, No. 5, @ 3 mos.	1000.	**1028**	

"

[2] Sold Mdse. to W. Garden for cash deposited	**1250**

"

Bot. at auction 10 cases Irish linen, amounting to $1500. Sold them again	
at the auction room for 10 ⅌ ct. advance. Rec'd the advance in cash.	**150**

"

Paid cash to R. Banks on account	90.	
Paid cash to James Haven in full	28.	**118**

Thursday, 30.

[3] Cash paid Expenses Apr. 1st to date by R. Banks ⅌ Expense		
Book 1	45.	
R. Banks' salary as clerk 1st April to date is . . .	300.	**345**
	[4] Total transactions to date . .	**53937**	**10**

1. See Note **3**, p. 143. Where you will see how this account is closed upon the Sales Book. There is no separate account opened for it upon the Ledger.
2. For the reasons given in Note 2, last page, this cash never appears in the cash account.
3. Refer to Notes 1 and 2, p. 147. You perceive Banks must here be credited for his salary and also for what he has paid out for the store by the Expense Book.
4. Compare this amount with the footing of the Journal, p. 161. This affords indisputable proof of the Day-Book being entirely Journalized. To every practical merchant the importance of this test between these books, must be at once apparent; for there is no step in the process of book-keeping, where omissions are more likely to take place, and where they are less looked for than between this book and the Journal. The major part of Book-keepers direct all attention to the Ledger: and they will sometimes search for weeks to find out a trifle that prevents their trial from coming out correct, while they perhaps never spend an hour in comparing their Day-Book and Journal. And after all, their trial of the Ledger proves nothing, even when it comes out correct, except that the Ledger agrees with itself. If it does not prove it to agree with any one other book, while our trial proves it to agree with the whole of them.—Note 4, p. 142.

REMARKS ON THE JOURNAL.

The following Journal is, in form, similar to that of the Day-Book, p. 125.

The columns on the left of the writing contain the debits and those on the right the credits. The columns next the writing on each side are the only ones posted in detail: the two others representing cash and merchandise, are footed and forwarded from page to page to the end of the month, or the end of the year, as may be desired, and from there posted in one sum into the Ledger, and the post mark affixed as usual.—See posting of our cash and merchandise accts. from the foot of page 161

In the Journal in the first part of this work, an entry was made for every receipt and payment of cash, and for every purchase and sale of merchandise. Here you will find several collected together—see second and third Day-Book entries, April 1st,—and the student will perceive that there are several other entries that might be incorporated in one, for instance, the first and second entries on the 10th April, are both merchandise debits, and might, therefore, have been journalized in one entry; but I thought it better to leave something to the student's own discretion in the matter.

Before footing your Journal, always go over the entries again to see that all the amounts are extended into the proper column. Then foot them first upon waste paper, which ought to be ruled to the pattern of the Journal, otherwise you are sometimes liable, after the additions are correctly made, to transpose the figures, and place them in the columns to which they do not belong.

As you foot and forward the Journal, the Day-Book ought to be kept up also in order to get the earliest intimation of error, if it gets in. The Day-Book is generally only footed in pencil, and you can do it anywhere on the page where you wish to obtain the amount that ought to correspond with the Journal.

In posting the Journal to the Ledger you make use of the same phraseology as upon the Double Entry Ledger in the first part of this work. In our last Ledger, which is intended principally for a retail business, we, to some extent, particularized the Day-Book entries: that principle of posting, however, can hardly ever be carried to any extent in a wholesale business. Indeed it will rarely ever be necessary, because bills or invoices almost always accompany the sale.

As your posting is completed, you should always go over the work again and check it as directed—Note 2, p. 32. No one can expect to keep his books free from errors without this precaution.

These books are specially adapted to daily posting, and if my young readers are disposed to profit by my experience in this matter, they will never allow their books to fall behind for a single day, if they can possibly avoid it. In some kinds of business, keeping the books up is almost indispensable for successful and efficient management. There are a great many book-keepers who have got it into their heads, that posting books once a week, or once a month, is sufficient. There is a method of journalizing and posting all accounts only once a month, upon which I shall have some observations to make hereafter: but I now repeat that my advice to all book-keepers is, to keep their books in such a manner that when called upon for an account, they have only to open the Ledger and find the whole account before them, ready for settlement. Those who will give this mode of posting six months' trial, will not be easily persuaded to change it.

Mdse.	Cash.		L.F.		L.F.		Cash.	Mdse.
				Sundries To Sundries, $5416.55.				
	2100 05			¹ Cash . . . . . Ledg. A, fol. 1				
3217 50				Mdse. . . . . . . " 1				
		2	3	Edward Pryor . . . . " 3				
		91	1	Samuel Gaynor . . . . " 3				
				To T. P. Cope & Sons . . " 1	2	504		
				" William Hay . . . " 1	2	200		
				" James Carter's Stock acct. " 2	1	36 50		
				" James Day . . . " 3	3	68		
				" P. Duff's Stock acct. . " 1	1	2984 47		
				" W. Gordon's Stock acct. . " 1	1	1717 58		
				"				
	2897 95			Cash To Sundries,				
				To P. Duff's Stock acct. . . . 1		115 53		
				" P. Duff 1		500		
				" W. Gordon's Stock acct. . . . 1		1282 42		
				" James Carter's Stock acct. . . . 1		2000		
				"				
				Sundries To Cash			5811	
		5800	4	² City Bank				
		3	4	Expense account.				
		8	3	James Day.				
				"				
		963 50	1	James Carter, Dr.				
				To James Carter's Stock acct. . . . 1		963 50		
				10.				
2506				Mdse. To Sundries,				
				To Wm. Hay 2		2494 40		
				" Cash			11 60	
				"				
216				Mdse., Dr. to A. Stuart & Co. 2		216		
				"				
				Sundries To Mdse., ...				918 25
		596 50	5	R. Butler.				
		16	3	Edward Pryor.				
	305 75			Cash.				
				"				
	100			Cash To R. Butler, ... 5		100		
				"				
				Sundries To Cash			50	
		20	5	R. Banks.				
		50	1	P. Duff.				
5939 50	6403 75	7530		Amounts forward		13082 30	5572 60	913 25
		6403 75		Cash		5372 60		
		5939 50		Merchandise		918 25		
		19873 25		Proof		19873 25		

1. In opening new books, always give a direct reference to the old Ledger for the transfers.
2. We now open an account with the Bank, and debit it for all deposits, and credit it for all checks we draw. —Notes 1 to 7, p. 146.
Post mark each entry with the Ledger page, on the same side and on the same line with the sum. Some write their post marks in red, but I can see no practical utility in doing so; and it keeps you handling two pens, while it is desirable to confine your whole attention to matters of greater importance.

Mdse.	Cash.		L.F.		L.F.		Cash.	Mdse.
5039 50	6403 75	7530		Bro't forward,		13082 40	5872 00	918 23
		91	3	Bills Receivable, No. 1, To S. Gaynor to close,	1	91		
				1 Sundries To Bills Payable,				
		200	2	Wm. Hay for No. 1	3	200		
		504	2	T. P. Cope & Sons for No. 2	3	504		
		20	3	James Day To E. Pryor	3	20		
				20.				
		704	3	1 Bills Payable To Sundries,				
				To City Bank, No. 1, $200, and No. 2, $504,	4	703 65		
				" Interest acct.	4	35		
				Sundries To Mdse.				442
		45	3	Edward Pryor.				
		397	1	S. Gaynor.				
	874			Cash To Mdse.				874
75				Mdse. To A. Stuart & Co.	2	75		
		1000	3	Bills Receivable, No. 2, To Sundries,				979 50
				To Cash				
				" Interest acct.	4	20 50		
				30.				
				Sundries To Cash				875 50
		25 50	5	Commission Sales.				
		60	1	P. Duff.				
		25	1	Wm. Gordon.				
		15	1	Carter.				
		750	4	City Bank.				
	498			Cash To Sundries,				
				To Commission Sales	5	360		
				" Mdse.				138
25156.75*						25156.75		
				May 1.				
		400	4	City Bank to James Carter	1	400		
329				Mdse. To Sundries,				
				To E. Pryor	3	64		
				" S. Gaynor.	1	265		
				Sundries To Mdse.				359 75
		37	1	P. Duff.				
		284 50	3	Bills Receivable, No. 3.				
		21 50	1	W. Gordon.				
		10 25	1	James Carter.				
		6 50	5	Robert Banks.				
		496 50	3	Bills Receivable, No. 4, To R. Butler to close acct.	5	496 50		
12622 75				Amounts forwarded,		16282 40		
7775 75				Cash,		7727 60		
6343 50				Merchandise		2732		
26742				2 Proof		26742		

1. Each note being posted separately, it becomes necessary to particularize them by number on the Journal.—See Bill acct., p. 167.

2. Compare the total footings here with those of the Day Book, p. 152.

* These figures are given to assist the learner in making out the trial sheet—p. 172.

Mdse.	Cash.	L.f.		L.f.	Cash.	Mdse.
6343 50	7775 75	12622 75	Bro't forward, . . .		16282 40	7727 60	2732
		291	2	A. Stuart & Co. To B. Payable No. 3 to close acct.	3	291	
	210			Cash To Sundries,			
				To S. Gaynor	1	50	
				" Mdse. received for Sales			160
				Sundries To Cash		117	
		30	5	R. Banks.			
		60	4	Expense account.			
		12	3	James Day.			
		10	1	W. Gordon.			
		5	1	P. Duff.			
				10.			
		28	3	¹ James Day's old acct. Dr. to his new acct.	3	28	
		82	1	² Samuel Gaynor's new acct. Dr. to his old acct.	1	82	
				13.			
		91	4	City Bank To Bills Receivable No. 1 . . .	3	91	
				23.			
		2000	2	³ William Hay To City Bank.	4	2000	
2300				Mdse. To T. P. Cope & Sons	2	2300	
		579	2	T. P. Cope & Sons To Sundries,			540
				To Mdse.			
				" Cash		12	
				" Commission	6	27	
	484 50			Cash To Sundries,			
				To Bills Receivable No. 3 . . .	3	284 50	
				" Duff & Gordon	5	20	
				" Mdse.			180
				Sundries To Cash		50	
		10	3	James Day.			
		40	1	Wm. Gordon.			
				31.			
		4337 35	4	⁴ City Bank new acct. To old acct. . . .	4	4337 35	
	131			Cash To Sundries,			86
				To Mdse.			
				" S. Gaynor	1	20	
				" Duff & Gordon	5	25	
				Sundries To Cash		685	
		200	3	⁵ E. Pryor (in loan).			
		20	4	Profit & Loss.			
		10	5	Robert Banks.			
		5	1	W. Gordon.			
		450	4	City Bank.			
	20883 10			Amounts forwarded, ...		25838 25	
	8601 25			Cash, ...		8591 60	
	8643 50			Merchandise		3698	
	38127 85			Proof		38127 85	

1. Here you first post the debit and balance Day's account; then post the credit in the new account.
2. Here you must first post the credit and balance Gaynor's acct.; then post the debit in the new acct.
3. Hay is made Dr. to the Bank for the check; no entry is required in the Cash Book.
4. You must now also balance your Check Book.—See p. 146.
5. See Note 1, p. 133.

Mdse.	Cash		L.F.		L.F.		Cash	Mdse.
2 643 50	8001 25	20883 10		Bro't forward, . . .		25835 25	8591 60	3608
				"				
				Sundries To Mdse.				220
		20	6	1 W. Evans (S. D. acct.).				
		182	6	James Reed (S. D. acct.).				
		18	6	Joel Post (S. D. acct.).				
				"				
		577 50	5	Robert Butler To Sundries,				
				To Commission Sales	5	576		
				" Mdse.				1 50
				"				
				Sundries To City Bank . . .	4	700		
		530	2	T. P. Cope & Sons.				
		200	2	Wm. Hay.				
				"				
		400	4	City Bank To James Carter	1	400		
				14868.60 14868.60				
				June 4.				
180				Mdse. To Commission Sales.	5	180		
				"				
1116				Mdse. To Sundries,				
				To City Bank	4	1060 20		
				" Interest	4	55 80		
				"				
		291	3	Bills Payable No. 3, To City Bank . . .	4	291		
				"				
		182	6	James Reed To Sundry Drs. acct. . . .	6	182		
				"				
		200	4	City Bank To E. Pryor for Loan of 31st ultimo,	3	200		
				"				
				Sundries To Mdse., ...				848
		96	6	James Reed.				
		60	2	Wm. Hay.				
		60	6	Robert Parker (S. D. acct.).				
		620	3	Bills Receivable, No. 5.				
				"				
	1318			Cash To Sundries,				
				To Joel Post in full	6	18		
				" James Reed	6	100		
				" Commission Sales	5	1200		
				"				
				Sundries To Cash			853	
		5	3	James Day.				
		100	4	City Bank.				
		748	5	Commission Sales.				
				"				
		1221	2	T. P. Cope & Sons To Sundries to close acct.				
				To City Bank	4	1000		
				" Bills Payable, No. 4	3	221		
	26373 60			Amounts forwarded		32022 25		
	9919 25			Cash		9444 60		
	9939 50			Merchandise		4765 50		
	46232 35			2 Proof		46232 35		

1. These letters indicate SUNDRY DEBTORS account.—See
p. 170. We place these marks here as a guide to
learners, but no such marks are required in business, because the book-keeper determines for himself, when he is posting, whether he will open an
account for the individual or place his name with
the amount on the Sundry Drs. account.
2. See Day Book, footing p. 154.

Mdse.	Cash.		L.F.		L.F.		Cash.	Mdse.
9939 50	9919 25	26373 60		Bro't forward,		32022 25	9444 60	4765 50
240				Mdse. To Sundries,				
				To Wm. Hay	2	168		
				" 1 Thomas Freeman (S. C. acct.)	6	72		
				Sundries To Mdse. . . .				291
		108	5	R. Banks.				
		183	3	E. Pryor.				
				Sundries To Bills Receivable No. 4 . .	3	496 50		
		491 95	4	City Bank.				
		4 55	4	Interest.				
	1681 25			Cash To Sundries,				
				To R. Butler	5	100		
				" Commission Sales . .	5	1540		
				" Duff & Gordon . . .	5	41 25		
		1992	5	Commission Sales To Sundries,				
				To Commission . . .	6	137		
				" Cash			1855	
				Sundries To Cash			113	
		100	4	City Bank.				
		13	3	James Day in full.				
				20.				
1028				Mdse. To Sundries,				
				To James Haven (S. C. acct.) . .	6	28		
				" Bills Payable No. 5 . . .	3	1000		
		1250	4	City Bank To Mdse.				1250
	150			Cash To Profit & Loss	4	150		
				Sundries To Cash . . .			118	
		90	5	Robert Banks.				
		28	6	James Haven in full.				
				30.				
		345	4	Expense account To R. Banks . . .	5	345		
				13951.75　　　　　　13911.75				
	30279 10			Total Amounts to date.		36100		
	11750 50		2	" 2 Cash	2	11530 60		
	11207 50		2	" Merchandise . . .	2	6306 50		
	53937 10			3 Proof		53937 10		

1. This indicates SUNDRY CREDITORS' account.—See Note 1, last page, and p. 170.
2. This makes our first Journal period. From here the total amounts of the cash and merchandise debits and credits are posted into the Ledger.—See p. 166.
3. Compare this amount with our Day Book footing, p. 155, also with the trial sheet, p. 171.

CONCLUDING REMARKS UPON THE JOURNAL.

1. The mode of journalizing the last Day Book, it is presumed, will be sufficiently understood by the examples. We shall now endeavor to explain verbally the manner of composing the Journal from the Auxiliaries, without passing the entries through the Day Book, as we have here done. When the nature of the business will admit of this, it will considerably lessen the amount of writing.

2. It is to be observed, however, that in a business which frequently creates compound entries, journalizing in this way will meet with many awkward impediments; for instance, the first Day Book entry of this set, cannot be explicitly stated without embracing the first merchandise entry on the Invoice Book, and the first debit entry on the Cash Book. The only way of getting over this obstacle in journalizing the auxiliaries, is to let such entries pass into the Day Book and begin a new period—that is, commence immediately after these entries bringing forward and journalizing. We will now endeavor to explain the process of

JOURNALIZING FROM THE AUXILIARIES.

3. When this is done, the Day Book will contain a much smaller number of entries; for, if you adopt this method of journalizing, you must keep the entries belonging to each auxiliary upon itself. They must not appear upon the Day Book (except in such cases as above stated); if they do, they will certainly lead to confusion.

4. Although it does not matter which book we journalize first, yet it is better to adopt some regular course: say we begin with the Day Book, and journalize all the entries under the present date. Then make Cash Dr. to Sundries for all entries on the Dr. side of the Cash Book, and Sundries Dr. to Cash for all entries on the Cr. side. Merchandise is Dr. to Sundries for all entries under the same date on the Invoice Book; and Sundries Dr. to Merchandise for all entries on the Sales Book. Mark the entries off the Cash Book as directed Note 7, p. 53, and off the Sales and Invoice Book, as directed for the Day Book, Note 7, p. 28. Bills Receivable, Bills Payable, and Commission Sales Book, are each journalized in their turn in the same way, and marked off as directed with the Cash Book.

5. You next take each book in the same order, and journalize the following day's business as before; and so on, until you have all brought up; observing that the footings of the Invoice, Sales and Cash Book, agree with their representatives in the Journal as you proceed.

6. This process of journalizing does not disturb our mode of proof. The footing of the Auxiliaries, and that of the Day Book, have only to be added together to agree with the Journal.

7. Some journalize a whole month of the Cash Book in one entry, and then do the same with the Sales Book, preserving the order of the dates in the margin of the Journal; but this method produces such a confusion of dates in the Ledger, that it can never be recommended.

We have now to explain the SECOND MODE of abbreviation, viz.:

POSTING ALL THE PRIMARY BOOKS DIRECT TO THE LEDGER.

8. When the nature of the business admits of it, this plan of posting effects the greatest reduction in writing that perhaps can be made in Book-keeping. But it is subjected to the same impediments from compound entries, that we have just noticed, Note 2, and which can only be got over in the same way. We have already explained the manner of posting the Invoice and Sales Book, p. 139 and 142. When it is intended to post the Cash Book in this manner, a folio column will be required either next the money columns or next the date columns, in which you will insert the folio of the Ledger, as you proceed with the posting. The footings of these three books are summarily posted at the end of the month or the end of the quarter as from the Journal.

9. The Bill Books and the Commission Sales Book, may be posted, both sides, by the same process; but I would recommend their passing into the Day Book.

10. The Day Book should have the entries all made in Journal form, when it is intended to post it in this way. I am now alluding to the common form of Day Book.

11. Our proof is obtained by adding together the footings of the Cash, Invoice, Sales, and Day Book. The amount must agree with the amount of the Ledger trial, as on p. 171.

ON MONTHLY JOURNALIZING.

1. The object of this method is to condense, not only the cash and merchandise, but all the accounts in the Ledger, into one line each in the month. Many persons are strongly prejudiced in favor of this plan of journalizing, on account of the abridgment it makes in the accounts in the Ledger: in some kinds of business it will no doubt work tolerably well; but where the book-keeper is frequently called upon to make up statements of accounts, and to effect settlements, in a business of any magnitude, there must ever be this insuperable objection to it:—the books can never be kept up. You cannot commence the journalizing of the month's business until the month has expired, and before you can journalize and post this month, a considerable part of the next must have elapsed; in a word, the nature of the process will never permit you to get your books up to the date of settlement. Even the strongest advocates of this method admit the force of this objection, and can offer no advantage to counterbalance it, but the abridgment of the accounts in the Ledger. I must, however, name other objections to the process, viz. the chances of errors and omissions in journalizing; the risk of making errors in drawing off accounts current, and making settlements without having your books posted; the correctness of which can only be determined when the accounts are posted; then, the time required in searching up the Day Book entries for the Journal, is certainly at least equal to the time required for writing them. Consequently, in less time than any person could possibly journalize a month's business in this way, by our plan of posting our first Day Book, we should have it all posted up into the Ledger. The author once kept a set of books upon this plan; these remarks are, therefore, dictated by experience.

2 Some directions will now be required on the

DETECTION AND CORRECTION OF ERRORS.

If your trial does not agree with the footings of the Journal, compare the footings of your Cash Debits and Credits with those in that book: also, those of the Merchandise account; then the Bill Books and the Bill accounts. Get a trial from the Commission Sales Book to compare with its representative in the Ledger, compare the footings of the Check Book with the Bank account; and if you have posted direct from the Invoice, Sales and Cash Book, these books must be compared with their representatives in the Ledger. If all these books and the Ledger agree, the error must be in some of the personal accounts or some account not represented by any of the above books, and must be, between the Journal and the Ledger, in the Ledger or in the trial itself. Taking the Day Book and Journal as the best authority, we ascertain the difference between them and the Ledger trial. Sometimes we find one side agreeing with the Journal: in this case our attention is confined to one side of the Ledger only. In all cases it is proper to know the amount of error; for if there be but one, knowing the amount of it, sometimes readily leads to its discovery. When the error is found, if it cannot be corrected as directed, page 98, the correcting entry must originate upon the Day Book or some other primary Book.

3. When an error occurs in the Journal by extending into the wrong column, if you have footed and forwarded the amounts before discovering it, at your next footing *add* the amount to the column to which it belongs, and *subtract* it from that into which it was erroneously extended.—Read Note 2, p. 98.

Errors in any of the primary books are corrected as directed, Notes 10 and 11, page 98, and Note 2, p. 125.

4. We will now endeavor to give our readers some useful directions

IN RULING BOOKS OF ACCOUNTS.

In ordering books, always provide the binder with an exact pattern of the size of paper and ruling. Never choose books of any kind that will keep you constantly cramped for space to write upon. Many persons use Day Books and Cash Books made of cap paper "folded long," and are forever trying to cram their entries upon a line, very often leaving them half finished in the attempt.

In the next place, never throw away unnecessary space in margins and date columns

Five-tenths of an inch is ample space for the month, and three-tenths for the date and cent columns. The width of the dollar column depends on the magnitude of the business; but the figures in this column ought not to be crowded. Five-tenths of an inch is a good space for four figures, and six figures ought to have seven-tenths. Three-tenths faint ruling is a good size for common Day Books, Journals, &c.; but Ledgers and the six-column Day Book or Journal may be somewhat narrower.

Mechanics and retailers, proposing to post their Ledgers as suggested, Note 2, p. 129, will find it useful to have the debit writing space, ruled one-fourth or one-third wider than the credit space. In small Ledgers it is better to bind the index in the book; in large ones it is more convenient to have it bound separate. In either case, direct the binder to "throw over" the first leaf of the index, and commence lettering on the third page. This enables the book-keeper to place the upper letter upon each leaf on the left page, and the lower one on the right, thus giving each letter a full page throughout the index.

In the six-column Day Book or Journal, it will be well to have the dividing lines between the cash and sundries column, on both sides, black or some dark color; it will also be useful to order a red footing line across the bottom of the page, the fourth line from the bottom.

Before concluding this subject, I will take leave to offer a suggestion upon the construction of

BOOK-CASES.

In vaults and safes, the book-cases are almost universally constructed for setting all the books on end, leaving the whole weight of the paper, by this means, hanging and straining upon the binding, and not unfrequently breaking it. It will take no more space to contain the books upon horizontal fixtures than in perpendicular ones, and it is obvious that all large books are less liable to injury in the one position than the other.

INDEX TO LEDGER B.

1867.						1867.					
Apr.	10	Cash,		1	30		Apr.	1	Cash,	1	500	
	30	"		2	60		June	30	Duff & Gordon, fol.	5	53	91
May	1	Mdse.			37							
		Cash,	122.	3	5					421.91		
June	30	Balance,	fol.	2	421	91						
					553	91						
											553	91
							June	30	Balance bro't down,		421	91

Read Notes 2 and 3, p. 149.
1. This and the two following accounts are the partners' private accounts; they are debited for all sums withdrawn and credited for any sums paid in over the capital. The credits of June 30 at this and Gordon's account are their dividends of debts collected for the old firm.

1867.						1867.					
Apr.	30	Cash,		2	25		June	30	Duff & Gordon, fol.	5	32	34
May	1	Mdse.			21	50			Balance,	2	69	16
		Cash,		3	10							
	23	"	101.50		40							
	31	"	32.34		5							
			69.16		101	50					101	50
June	30	Balance bro't down,			69	16						

1867.						1867.					
Apr	1	J. Carter's Stock acct.,		1	963	50	May	1	City Bank,	2	400	
	30	Cash,		2	15			31	"	800.	4	400	
May	1	Mdse.,	988.75 / 800.	2	10	25	June	30	Balance, fol.	2	188	75
			188.75		988	75					988	75
June	30	Balance bro't down,			188	75						

1. The first debit entry above, is what this partner was deficient in his capital when the books were opened.—Refer to his stock account, p. 178.
2. The two credits are payments on account of this deficiency. If interest is to be charged, a Day Book entry will be made of it, and it will be brought to this account, not to his stock account.

1867.						1867.					
Apr.	1	Amt. ꝑ Ledger A, fol.	3	×	91		Apr.	10	Bills Receivable,	2	×	91
	20	Mdse.		2	397		May	1	Mdse.,			265
									Cash,	3		50
								10	Balance debit in n/a.,			82
					488							488
May	10	Balance on settlement,			82			31	Cash,	3		20
							June	30	Balance, fol.	2		62
					82							82
June	30	Balance bro't down,			62							

Refer to Note 2, Warden & Bell's account, p. 165.
1. Where a settled account is comprised in a single line, it is sufficient to mark the entries on each side as above, and omit them in the next account current. But the author has witnessed so much confusion and trouble in accounts from inattention to closing them at the time of settlement, that he again requests the student's attention to Note 1, Wood's account, p. 15, Note, p. 20, Notes 5 and 6, p. 23, Note 4, p. 70, and Note 1, Carter's account, p. 165.

1867.						1867.					
June	30	Sundries to date,	11750.50 11530.60 219.90	5	11750 50	June	30	Sundries to date,		5	11530 60
								Balance,	f. 2		219 90
					11750 50						11750 50
Jun	30	Balance bro't down,			219 90						

MERCHANDISE   ACCOUNT.

1867.						1867.					
June	30	Sundries to date,		5	11207 50	June	30	Sundries to date,		5	6306 50
		Private Ledger,	f. 2		6306 50			Private Ledger,	f. 2		11207 50
					17514						17514

1. Post the new business to this account as before. When closing the Ledger, transfer again with a double balance as above.

T. P.   (Philadelphia)   COPE & SONS.

1867.						1867.					
Apr.	10	Bills Payable,		2	x 504	Apr.	1	Sundries ⅌ Ledg. A, f.	1	x 504	
May	23	Sundries,		3	579	May	23	Mdse.,		3	2300
	31	City Bank,		4	500						
June	4	Sundries,			1221						
					2804						2804

2. This account affords another illustration of what is alluded to in Note 1, Gaynor's account, p. 165. In business this mark is made upon the double red line, and so small as not to disfigure the account.

WILLIAM   (Boston)   HAY.

1867.						1867.					
Apr.	10	Bills Payable,		2	x 200	Apr.	1	Sundries Ledg. A,	f. 1	x 200	
May	23	City Bank,		3	2000		10	Mdse.,			2494 40
	31	" "		4	200	June	10	"	2862.40 2460. 402.40	5	168
June	4	Mdse.,	2460.		60						
	30	Balance,	fol. 2		402 40						
					2862 40						2862 40
						June	30	Balance bro't down,			402 40

A.   STUART & CO.

1867.					1867.					
May	1	Bills Payable,	3	291	Apr.	10	Mdse.,	1	216	
						20	"	2	75	
				291					291	

1867.						1867.						
Apr.	1	Cash,		1	8		Apr.	1	Sundries, Ledg. A,	f.	3	68
	10	E. Pryor,		2	20							
May	1	Cash,		3	12							
	10	New acct.,			28							
					68							68
May	23	Cash,		3	10		May	10	Old acct.,		3	28
June	4	"		4	5							
	10	"		5	13							
					28							28

1. The last debit entry before the first balance above, and the first credit after it, are in one Journal entry, the first one posted *before* the account is balanced, and the last one *after* it.—Note 1, p. 150, and Note 1, p. 152.

EDWARD   (25 John Street)   PRYOR.

1867.						1867.						
Apr.	1	Amt. Ledg. A,	f.	3	2		Apr.	10	James Day,		2	20
	10	Mdse.,		1	16		May	1	Mdse.,			64
	20	"		2	45		June	4	City Bank, Loan of			
May	31	Cash in Loan,		3	200				31st ult.,	284.	4	200
June	10	Mdse.,	446. 284.	5	183			30	Balance	f.	2	162
			162.		446							446
June	30	Bal. bro't down,			162							

1. The above loan on May 31st, is passed through account as directed at Pryor's acct., p. 133.

BILLS   RECEIVABLE.

1867.							1867.						
Apr.	10	S. Gaynor,	No. 1,	2	91		May	13	City Bank,	No. 1,	3	91	
	20	Sundries,	2,	2	1000		June	30	Carried down,	2,		1000	
May	1	Mdse.,	3,		284	50	May	23	Cash,	3,	3	284	50
		R. Butler,	4,		496	50	June	10	Sundries,	4,	5	496	50
June	4	Mdse.,	5,	4	630			30	Carried down,	5,		630	
					2502							2502	
June	30	Bro't down,	No. 2,		1000								
		" "	5,		630								

BILLS   PAYABLE.

1867.						1867.						
Apr.	20	Sundries,	No. 1,	2	200		Apr.	10	W. Hay,	No. 1,	2	200
		"	2,		504				Cope & Sons,	2,		504
June	4	City Bank,	3,	4	291		May	1	Stuart & Co.,	3,	3	291
	30	Carried down,	4,		221		June	4	Cope & Sons,	4,	4	221
		" "	5,		1000			20	Mdse.,	5,	5	1000
					2216							2216
							June	30	Bro't down,	No. 4,		221
									" "	5,		1000

1. Referring our readers to the copious directions for the management of these accounts, pp. 33, 34, 52, 103, and 104, we have now only to explain the peculiarity in the mode of posting adopted above. The notes are all posted separately, accompanied with their respective numbers, and the counter-post, with its number, must be always kept upon the same line with the first entry, leaving blanks opposite all **notes** in hand in the Bills Receivable account, and opposite all unpaid notes in the Bills Payable account.

2. **In** closing, the blanks must be all filled in red, and the same notes, with their numbers, recapitulated in new account. This method of posting these accounts will contribute much to their correctness, and, in some cases, renders the Bill Book unnecessary.

4 Dr.   **CITY**   **BANK.**   **Cr.**

1867.						1867.					
Apr.	1	Cash,	1	5800		Apr.	20	Bills Payable,	2	703	65
	30	"	2	750		May	23	Wm. Hay,	3	2000	
May	1	J. Carter,		400			31	Balance to n/a,		4337	35
	13	Bills Receivable,	3	91							
				7041						7041	
	31	Bal. bro't down,		4337	35	May	31	Sundries,	4	700	
		Cash,	3	450		June	4	Mdse.,		1060	20
		James Carter,	4	400				Bills Payable,		291	
June	4	E. Pryor,		200				Cope & Sons,	1051.20	1000	
		Cash,		100			30	Balance,	f. 2	4278	10
	10	Bills Receivable,	5	491	95						
		Cash,		100							
	20	Mdse., 7329.20 / 3051.20 / 4278.10		1250							
				7329	30					7329	30
June	30	Bal. bro't down,		4278	10						

See Note 2, p. 157, and Note 1, Day's account, p. 167.
Every house doing a business of any magnitude, should keep a Bank account. It simplifies and shortens the Cash account, and diminishes the trouble and chances of error in making payments.

     PROFIT   **&**   **LOSS.**

1867.						1867.					
May	31	Cash,	3	20		June	20	Cash,	5	150	
June	30	Pr. & Loss, Pr. Ledg. f.	2	130							
				150						150	

1. This account is continued in this Ledger until the time of closing, when its balance is transferred to the Profit & Loss in the Private Ledger.—See the above balance in Profit & Loss account, p. 174.

     EXPENSE   **ACCOUNT.**

1867.					1867.					
Apr.	1	Cash,	1	3	June	30	Private Ledger,	f. 2	408	
May	1	"	3	60						
June	30	R. Banks,	5	345						
				408					408	

     INTEREST   **ACCOUNT.**

1867.						1867.					
June	10	Bills Receivable,	5	4	55	Apr.	20	Bills Payable,	2		35
	30	Pr. & Loss Pr. Ledg. f.	2	72	10			Bills Receivable,		20	50
						June	4	Mdse., 76.65	4	55	80
				76	65					76	65

1. This, and the Expense account, are both closed into the Profit & Loss account in the Private Ledger, p. 174.

Dr.   **COMMISSION SALES.**   **Cr.**   **5**

1867.					1867.				
Apr.	30	Cash,	2	25 50	Apr.	30	Cash,	2	360
June	4	"	4	748	May	31	Robert Butler,	4	576
	10	Sundries, 2765.50	5	1992	June	4	Mdse.,		180
	30	Balance, f.	2	3856			Cash,		1200
						10	" 3856.	5	1540
						30	Balance, f.	2	2765 50
				6621 50					6621 50

| June | 30 | Bal. bro't down, | | 2765 50 | June | 30 | Bal. bro't down, | | 3856 |

See Notes 1 to 4, p. 143.
1. This account represents all our commission business. All the accounts are kept and settled on the Commission Sales Book.
2. We have closed this account by *Double Balance*, for the purpose of practically exemplifying that operation, though this mode of balancing was not required here, or, indeed anywhere, except when transferring an account from one Ledger to another, which you wish to leave closed on the old book, and to re-open on the new one with the whole amount of each side brought forward. You will perceive that the above operation will effect that purpose.—See Morris' Sales, p. 107.

ROBERT   (Clerk)   BANKS.

1867.					1867.				
Apr.	10	Cash,	1	20	June	30	Expense acct., 345. 264.50	5	345
May	1	Mdse.,	2	6 50			80.50		
		Cash,	3	30					
	31	"		10					
June	10	Mdse.,	5	108					
	20	Cash, 264.50		90					
	30	Balance, f.	2	80 50					
				345					345
					June	30	Bal. bro't down,		80 50

ROBERT   (Albany)   BUTLER.

1867.					1867.				
Apr.	10	Mdse.,	1	596 50	Apr.	10	Cash,	1	100
					May	1	Bills Receivable,	2	496 50
				596 50					596 50
May	31	Sundries,	4	577 50	June	10	Cash,	5	100
						30	Suspended List, f.	2	477 50
				577 50					577 50

DUFF   &   GORDON.

1867.					1867.				
June	30	P. Duff, fol.	1	53 91	May	23	Cash,	3	20
		W Gordon	1	32 34		31	"		25
					June	10	" 86.25	5	41 25
				86 25					86 25

1. This account is credited for all collections made of **Duff & Gordon's** old debts, and **if any thing** is lost upon any of the accounts from which they credited themselves **in the** new firm, this account will be **debited for** the amount. Of the above collections they make a dividend in the same *proportion as they divided the gain when they* closed their books.—See Profit & Loss account, p. 134.

169

1867.					1867.					
May	31	W. Evans,	4	20	June	30	W. Evans, car. down,			20
		Jas. Reed,		182		4	Jas. Reed's acct.,		4	182
		Joel Post,		18			Cash of Joel Post, 200.			18
June	4	Robert Parker, 20. 200. 80.		60		30	R. Parker, car. down,			60
				280						280
June	30	W. Evans, bro't down,		20						
		R. Parker, "		60						

1. In every business there are frequently small sales and unsettled balances due from persons with whom we expect to have no farther dealings. The simplest and easiest way to keep account of such transactions is under a SUNDRY DRS. head. Enter the name, sum, date, &c., as above, taking care to index each individual's name, as you perceive we have done—refer to the index, and see.
2. When payment is made, it comes through the books as far as the Journal, as though the party had an open account. By the index, the name is found on this account, post it like Joel Post's entry, 4th June, above, on the same line opposite the debit, and it settles the transaction.
3. You must recollect, however, that you cannot make more than one debit and one credit to each individual. If the transactions exceed this, you must re-page the party's name in the index, and transfer, through the Day Book, the amount from this account to his private account, as we have done above with J. Reed.

SUNDRY   CREDITORS.

1867.					1867.					
June	30	T. Freeman car. down,		72	June	10	Due T. Freeman,		5	72
	20	Cash paid J. Haven,	5	28		20	" Jas. Haven, 100. 72.			28
				100						100
					June	30	Due T. Freeman, bro't down,			72

1. This account is managed in all respects like the last one, except that the entries first appear at the credit side.
2. When a purchase is made of a party with whom you have not an account, and intend to pay it in a short time, let the transactions, as those in the last account, come through the books as far as the Journal, in the usual way, then post the name, amount, &c., to this account, recollecting to index the name. When payment is made, it must be always placed on the Dr. side, on the same line with the credit, as with Haven's entry above.
3. These two accounts close by filling up the vacant spaces in red, as above, recapitulating all the names and amounts in the new account.

JAMES   REED.

1867.					1867.					
June	4	Sundry Drs. acct.,	4	182	June	4	Cash,		4	100
		Mdse., 278. 100. 175.		96		30	Suspended List, f.	2	178
				278						278

1. This account was first commenced under the SUNDRY DRS. head, but finding he was going to deal farther with us, we re-indexed his name, and opened a private account with him. This will frequently occur in business, but, as the name is already in the index, the trouble is trifling compared with the old-fashioned plan of keeping a petty Ledger for such accounts.

COMMISSION   ACCOUNT.

1867.					1867.					
June	30	Profit & Loss, f.	2	164	May	23	Cope & Sons,		3	27
					June	10	Commission Sales, 164.		5	137
				164						164

P. Duff .	fo!	1
W. Gordon		
James Carter .		
S. Gaynor .		
"		
Cash .		2
Merchandise .		
T. P. Cope & Sons		
Wm. Hay .		
A. Stuart & Co. .		
James Day .		8
"		
Edward Pryor		
Bills Receivable .		
Bills Payable .		
City Bank .		4
" .		
Profit & Loss		
Expense Account .		
Interest Account		
Commission Sales		5
Robert Banks		
Robert Butler		
"		
Duff & Gordon		
Sundry Debtors		6
Sundry Creditors		
James Reed		
Commission		
Private Ledger		

1. By comparing these footings with those of the Day-Book and Journal, and finding them to agree, we have direct and indisputable evidence that no omissions can have occurred either in journalizing or posting. Whereas the common Trial Balance affords no security against any errors but such as disturb its equilibrium. And it is well known that omissions deeply affecting the interest of the Merchant frequently take place between his Sales Book, or his Day-Book and his Journal, which the method we are now introducing affords the means, and the ONLY MEANS, of detecting with certainty.—Note 4, p. 142.

2. There are so many obvious advantages in taking a MONTHLY TRIAL, that it is strongly recommended in business. On the next page, I have given a form, by which, when the titles are once written, the amounts only require to be afterwards inserted until the end of the year.

AN IMPROVED FORM OF MONTHLY TRIAL SHEET FOR 1867.

Accounts.	Fol.	Dbs. APRIL.	Crs.	Dbs. MAY.	Crs.	Das. JUNE.	Crs.
P. Duff,	1	90	500	42			
W. Gordon,		25		76 50			
James Carter,		978 50		10 25	800		
Samuel Gaynor,		488	91	82	417		
Cash,	2	7775 75	7727 60	825 50	864	3149 25	2939
Merchandise,		6014 50	2372 25	2629	1547 25	2564	2387
T. P. Cope & Sons,		504	504	1079	2300	1221	
Wm. Hay,		200	2694 40	2200		60	168
A. Stuart & Co.			291	291			
James Day,	3	28	68	50	28	18	
Edward Pryor,		63	20	200	64	183	200
Bills Receivable,		1091		781	375 50	630	496 50
Bills Payable,		704	704		291	291	1221
City Bank,	4	6550	703 65	5678 35	7037 35	2141 95	2351 20
Expense Account,		3		60		345	
Interest Account,			20 85			4 55	55 80
Commission Sales,	5	25 50	360		576	2740	2920
Robert Banks,		20		46 50		198	345
R. Butler,		596 50	100	577 50	496 50		100
Private Ledger,	1		9000				
APRIL		25156 75	25156 75				
Profit & Loss,	4			20			150
Duff & Gordon,	5				45		41 25
Sundry Debtors,	6			220		60	200
Commission,					27		137
MAY				14868 60	14868 60		
Sundry Creditors,	6					28	100
James Reed,						278	100
JUNE						13911 75	13911 75

1. The above form of monthly trial will require medium or royal paper, ruled with six debit and credit columns on each page. This will enable the book-keeper to take his trial in about half the usual time, inasmuch as the titles once written serve for the whole year.
2. As our Journal is not posted in monthly periods, you cannot find the cash and merchandise amounts for the above trial from the Ledger, but you can procure them from the Sales, Invoice, and Cash Books; and I have given the monthly totals in small figures in the margin of the Journal, so that you can see when your trial agrees with that book.
3. Before making out each month of this sheet, go over the Ledger, carefully adding up the month's business, inserting it in pencil in the margin of each account: from these marginal figures the trial is filled up.
4. To facilitate this operation, the author originally had his Ledger ruled with two sets of money columns on each side, so that every account could have each month's business extended in monthly sections, like our Cash Book. But some of his mercantile friends expressing a strong dislike to this manner of ruling the Ledger, he has been induced, in deference to their opinion, to abandon it, although his own opinion of its practical utility remains unchanged.
5. Want of time is the greatest objection to the monthly trial, but it is believed, that if a proper estimate is made of the time usually required for correcting books at the end of the year, the advantage will often be in favor of the monthly trial, which gives timely notice of the existence of error, and but a short space of business to examine in order to find it.
6. In conclusion we may also name another advantage of the monthly trial. When it always comes out correct, there is not any necessity of ever making out a Balance Account. Dividends can be safely made upon the Profit & Loss Account, after closing into it all accounts representing gain or loss. Indeed, this may be done in any case where there is satisfactory evidence of the entire correctness of the books; but, as all experienced accountants know, in the ordinary mode of keeping books, the Balance Account affords the only satisfactory evidence of this. When a dividend is made, and a net capital exhibited in the Stock or Partners' Accounts, the Balance Account must at the same time be shown, as evidence of the existence of effects to represent that capital.

THE PRIVATE LEDGER.

1. The object of this book having been explained, Note 4, p. 149, we have now only to observe, that, although it is, in business practice, always a separate book, it must be dealt with as though it formed part of the other Ledger. After the accounts are opened, no public business can require any reference to it. Indeed, no reference is ever required to it, except at the time of closing the books or taking the trial. The sum of its footings must appear upon the trial as you see on p. 171. At the time of closing, the transfers are all made from the public Ledger to Profit & Loss, Suspended List, and Balance, as if these accounts were opened in the same book. If the dividend is made without making out a balance account, as suggested in Note 6, p. 172, the course to be followed with the other accounts in this book will still be the same as it now is.

Dr.	P.		(Stock Acct.)	DUFF.		Cr.	1
			1867.				
			Apr. 1	Sundries, Ledg. A, f. 1	2884	47	
				Cash, 1000. 1	115	53	
			June 30	Profit & Loss, f. 2	1400	53	
				Net Capital at date,	4400	53	

	W.		(Stock Acct.)	GORDON.			
			1867.				
			Apr. 1	Sundries, Ledg. A, f. 1	1717	58	
				Cash, 1000. 1	1282	42	
			June 30	Profit & Loss, f. 2	1400	53	
				Net Capital at date,	4400	53	

	JAMES		(Stock Acct.)	CARTER.			
			1867.				
			Apr. 1	Sundries, Ledg. A, f. 2	36	50	
				Cash, 1	2000		
				J. Carter's Pr. acct. 1000. 1	963	50	
			June 30	Profit & Loss, f. 2	1400	54	
				Net Capital at date,	4400	54	

1. We have, above, carried the whole amount of each partner's dividend to his credit in Stock account, but our attentive student no doubt recollects what we stated, Note 5, p. 129, and he will therefore readily understand, that the partners may order various other dispositions of their dividends; for instance, they may agree to carry a certain percentage on their capital to the credit of their private accounts to cover sums that they have withdrawn, and allow the remainder to pass to the credit of their Stock accounts to increase their capital. They may think proper to order the whole amount to the credit of their private accounts, or draw the cash for it as soon as the amount is known, as in banks and joint stock companies.

2   Dr.   **MDSE.**   **ACCT.**   Cr.

1867.					1867.				
June 30	From Public Ledg., f.	2	11207	50	June 30	From Public Ledg f.	2	6306	50
	Profit & Loss,	2	4899			Balance,	2	9800	
			16106	50				16106	50
	Balance,		9800						

1. The balance will always be brought down upon this Ledger. Every time the Ledger is balanced, **the total postings to the** account on the Public Ledger are transferred by double balance as above.

          PROFIT   **&**   **LOSS.**

1867.					1867.				
June 30	Expense, Public L. f.	4	408		June 30	Pr. & Loss, Pub. L., f.	4	130	
	Suspended List, 1083.50	2	655	50		Merchandise,	2	4899	
	P. Duff, ⅓ n/g.	1	1400	53		Interest,	4	72	10
	W. Gordon, ⅓ "	1	1400	53		Commission, 5265.10 1063.30	6	164	
	J. Carter, ⅓ "	1	1400	54		3) 4201.60 1400.53			
			5265	10				5265	10

See Notes 4 and 5, p. 130, and Note 1, p. 173.
The above gain is carried to the partners' stock accounts.

        BALANCE   **ACCOUNT.**

1867.					1867.				
June 30	W. Gordon, fol.	1	69	16	June 30	P. Duff, fol.	1	421	91
	James Carter,		188	75		Wm. Hay,	2	402	40
	Samuel Gaynor,		62			Bills Payable,	3	1221	
	Cash,	2	219	90		Commission Sales,	5	3856	
	Mdse.,		9800			R. Banks,		80	50
	Edward Pryor,	3	162			Sundry Crs.,	6	72	
	Bills Receivable,		1630			P. Duff, n. c.,	1	4400	53
	City Bank,	4	4278	10		W. Gordon, n. c.,		4400	53
	Commission Sales,	5	2765	50		James Carter, n. c.,		4400	54
	Sundry Drs., 19235.41	6	80						
			19235	41				19235	41

        SUSPENDED   **ACCOUNTS.**

1867.					1867.				
June 30	Robert Butler, f.	5	477	50	June 30	Profit & Loss, fol.	2	655	50
	James Reed, 655.50	6	178						
			655	50				655	50

See Notes 1 to 3 Suspended List, p. 134.
1. We have only to remark further, that if these accounts have been closed, you will allow them to remain so, until you receive a payment upon them. When this takes place the account is to be re-opened with a debit for the suspended balance; but this cannot be done upon the face of the Ledger. Profit & Loss having been debited for the amount at the last balance, must now be credited for it upon the Day Book, making the individuals' Dr. To Profit & Loss for balance per Suspended List. It may, perhaps, be asked, why not carry such payments to the credit of Profit & Loss, without re-opening these accounts? This will not do, because these individuals' accounts must record the payments they have made upon them.

BALANCE SHEET, DUFF, GORDON & CO. JUNE 30, 1867.

EFFECTS.

1867. June 30.	f.		
Balance due on W. Gordon's account	1	69	16
do. do. J. Carter's do.		188	75
do. do. Saml. Gaynor's do.		62	
Cash in hand	2	219	50
Merchandise in hand per Inventory		9800	
Balance due on K. Pryor's account		162	
Bills Receivable in hand	3	1680	
Balance of deposit in City Bank	4	478	10
Advances on consignments	5	2765	50
Sundry debtors	6	80	
		19255	41

LIABILITIES.

1867. June 30.	f.			
Balance due P. Duff on private account	1		421	91
do. due Wm. Hay	2		402	40
do. on notes in circulation	3		1221	40
Amount of sales on consignment	5		3866	
Balance due R. Banks on account	6		80	50
Sundry creditors			72	
P. Duff's paid up capital		$3000.		
Dividend now carried to his credit		1400.53	4400	53
W. Gordon's paid up capital		3000.		
Dividend now carried to his credit		1400.53	4400	53
Jas. Carter, for his paid up capital		3000.		
Dividend now carried to his credit		1400.54	4400	54
			19255	41

ABSTRACT OF DUFF, GORDON & CO.'S

1867. June 30.	f.		
Incidental expenditures to date	4	20	
Amount of expense account		408	50
Doubtful debts		655	50
⅓ gain to Duff's credit, P. bal. sheet	$1400.53		
do. to Gordon's do.	1400.53		
do. to Carter's do. do.	1400.54		
Net gain on 3 months' business		4201	60
		5285	10

PROFIT & LOSS ACCOUNT, JUNE 30, 1867.

1867. June 30.	f.		
Incidental gains to date	4	160	
Gain on merchandise account		4809	10
Gain on Interest account		72	
Gain on commission account		164	
		5285	10

Merchants will recognize in the above balance sheet a perfectly practical form, by which a detailed and most comprehensive view can be given, of any kind or any extent of business, in a form that can be understood by any person. Business men will find it a useful substitute for those fancy balance sheets, which, on account of the difficulty in applying them, never have been, and probably never will be, generally adopted in business practice.

ON PARTNERSHIP SETTLEMENTS.

DIRECTIONS FOR CONDUCTING THE BOOKS AFTER THE DISSOLUTION OF THE FIRM, AND RECORDING THE TRANSACTIONS FOR EFFECTING THE SETTLEMENT AND FINAL CLOSURE OF THEM.

WHEN a concern is dissolved, the books being generally left in the hands of one or more of the firm for the purpose of settling up, each of the partners should be provided with a Balance Sheet, similar to that on the preceding page. From this Balance Sheet each retiring partner makes the proper Journal entry in his own books. If the remaining partners continue the business in their own name, unless they have bought out the interest of the retired partners, they should make no use of any of its books to record transactions relating to their own business.

To those who understand the preceding set of books, the following Exercises will fully explain the subject. The student should write out his own answers before he consults those in our Key.

EXERCISES ON WINDING UP PARTNERSHIP BOOKS.

1. On the 30th June, the day on which the preceding books were balanced, suppose that Gordon and Carter retire from the firm, and leave the books in the hands of Duff for settlement: what entry will each retiring partner make in his own private books in conformity with the Balance Sheet of the late firm, supposing they had no previous entry in their private books of their investment in the firm?

2. What entry will Duff make in his books?

3. The Bank Deposit, Cash in hand, and Bills Receivable, being available property, what entry will Duff make of the same in his books on receipt of them?

4. What entry will he make for the same in the books of the firm?

5. What entry for the Merchandise in hand and debts due the firm?

6. What entry in his own books when he makes a payment of $1000 in cash to Gordon, one of the retired partners, on account of his Stock?

7. What entry for the same transaction in the books of the firm?

8. What will be Gordon's entry when he receives the money?

9. What will be Duff's entry, in his own books, when he sells Merchandise belonging to the firm for cash, $2000?

10. What entry in the books of the firm for this sale?

11. What entry in the firm's books if he sell James Carter, one of the retired partners, $3000 worth of Merchandise, on account of the balance due him by the firm?

12. What entry for this sale in Duff's private books?

13. What entry will Carter make in his books for the same?

14. What entry in his own books, when Duff collects cash due the firm; say the amount of S. Gaynor's account?

15. How will the same be entered in the books of the firm?

16. What entry in his own books when he pays, cash, a debt due by the firm; say the balance due Robert Banks?

17. What entry for the same in the books of the firm?

18. When the merchandise belonging to the firm is all disposed of, how is the account to be closed upon the books of the firm?

19. If any of the personal accounts due the firm are wholly or partially lost, what entry in the books of the firm at the final settlement?

20. When any of the suspended accounts, say Robert Butler's, is collected in cash, what entry in the books of the firm?

21. When the effects of the firm are all made available, how is the Profit & Loss account to be finally closed on their books?

22. How will the partners' accounts be finally closed on the books of the firm?

23. What entry will each partner make on his own books to close the account with the firm, after the effects are all paid over?

THE foregoing exercises illustrate the course to be pursued when a firm is dissolved with a view to dividing the effects only as they are collected and made available. But it will always be found more convenient and advantageous for all parties, if the retiring partners agree upon a stipulated allowance for bad debts, expense of collecting, &c. In this case, the books and all the effects of the firm become the property of the remaining partners, and they continue the business in the same books as before the dissolution; at the same time becoming liable to the retired partners, in the terms agreed upon, for the balances they have accepted for their interest in the house.

24. Suppose Gordon and Carter retire, and Duff takes the effects, books, and the whole business into his own hands, assuming all the liabilities of the firm, as also the balances due the retiring partners, less five per ct. off their last dividend, to cover bad debts, what entry will he make upon the books of this discount?

25. What entry will Carter and Gordon make upon their books to show the transaction?

After this, Duff debits them as he pays them off, in cash, merchandise, &c.; they at the same time making conforming entries in their books.

In the above exercises, we have made no allusion to the open consignment accounts. In every house doing a commission business there must always be a number of consignments on hand, partly sold at the time of closing the books. When a balance sheet is made up, either for the purpose of admitting a new partner, or settling with a retiring one, it is obvious that the commission upon these sales, as far as they are effected, must be taken into account; and to do so, the commission, so far earned, must be carried to the credit of the commission account. In doing so, some other account must be debited for the same amount: now, the question is, what is the proper account to debit? It would be manifestly improper to debit the sales account without rendering the owner a statement, and it is by no means proper nor desirable to render him an account, unless he calls for it, until the sales are completed.

The commission thus earned, being part of the effects of the parties who have thus far conducted the sales, their Balance account must be debited for it. To make Balance account Dr. to Commission, is a peculiar and somewhat anomalous entry; and it will, perhaps, be asked, what effects have we got to represent it? To this we reply, that the entry represents our claim against this person's sales; and this claim is of the same nature as that against Pryor, or any other individual. The only difference is, that we do not, just now, for the reasons above named, place the amount to the debit of the sales.

Now, it must be recollected, that the Commission account closes *By Balance* and to Profit & Loss; and, like all other balance-closing entries, this one must be brought down into new account; and when the account afterwards receives its credit for the commission on the sales, when completed, the effect of this debit entry, so brought down, will be to extinguish its amount out of the credits of the account at the next dividend, thus preventing a new dividend of that portion of the commission accounted for in the old account.

When dividends are made as we have suggested, note 6, p. 172, without making up a Balance account, then our Day Book entry will be, Commission new account, Dr. To old account. After posting the credit entry, close the account into Profit & Loss; and, after the closing lines are drawn, post the debit entry.

It is to be observed that, in business, the entries we are now considering will often have to embrace the commission upon a large number of different accounts. A Day Book entry, specifying all the particulars, will, therefore, always be required in form something like the following:—

BALANCE ACCOUNT DR. TO COMMISSION.

For commission 5 per ct. on A. B.'s sales effected to date, $500. . . $25.
" " 2¼ " on C. D.'s " " " 2000. . . 50.
" " 5 " on E. F.'s " " " 3400. . . 170. $245.

It may be proper to remark, that this adjustment of the commission due upon the sales thus far effected makes no change in the disposition of the balance of the account. The differences between the sales and the charges must appear in the balance sheet, as usual.

M

I may also observe, that I am now treating the subject of Partnership Settlements for professional readers only; persons not well versed in the science of accounts will not, therefore, find it intelligible until they make themselves acquainted with the principles of the art, as explained in the preceding part of this work. The experienced book-keeper will, however, no doubt, perceive that this mode of adjusting the commission effects all that is necessary for making and recording a dividend, without disturbing a figure in the consignment accounts—avoiding the awkward expedient of either making a partial charge of commission in the account, or rendering a statement of it, before the sales are completed.

Such of our readers as understand the application of this principle to the Consignment accounts, will readily perceive that it may be, at any time, conveniently applied under similar circumstances, to the Interest or Profit & Loss account, or any of its branches.

In consequence of the unexpected retiring of a partner, between the periods of annual or semi-annual settlement of the books, a balance sheet and settlement may require to be made with the retiring partner, when it would be extremely inconvenient and irregular to present your accounts to your mercantile neighbors and correspondents for settlement. In extensive houses, where interest is allowed and charged on book accounts, there will be many accounts upon which interest will be running, some in favor of the house, and some against it. We now propose to show by a short *pro forma* statement, with what ease and simplicity interest upon any number of accounts, notes, bonds, &c., may be adjusted in a partnership settlement without disturbing or disfiguring the accounts. It must be recollected, that such statements must be always made upon the Day Book, with full particulars for future reference, if required. The form will be something like the following:—

BALANCE DR. TO INTEREST ACCOUNT.

For balance of interest due us on Cox & Martin's account to date,	$68.		
" " on G. Haven's "	122.		
" " on Henry Noble's "	140.		
" " on John Manly's note . . .	60.	390.	
Less balance of interest due G. W. Smith on account . .	70.		
" " Martin Rowley on bond . .	40.	110.	
Balance to credit of interest .		280.	

This entry is posted to the Balance and Interest accounts, as directed with the Commission account last page. But no entry is now made at the accounts of any of the above parties for these amounts of interest. Their accounts are carried on without interruption until the next period of settlement, when they will have an entry for the interest for the whole period, as if no adjustment of this kind had now taken place between the partners; and though the interest account will then get credit for the whole amount computed upon the accounts, the balance entry, now brought down from the old account, will extinguish that amount of it, leaving only what will have accrued after the present settlement for a new dividend.

Our attentive reader, no doubt, already perceives that this principle may be applied to any account which we do not wish to disturb at the time of settling or balancing the books. For instance: the 1st Co. Sales or Ship Roscoe and owners, p. 109, may be dealt with in the same way, by making Balance Dr. to Profit & Loss for our share of the gain to date. Then Profit & Loss would re-open as before stated, and the ship's account would remain undisturbed until the time of making the dividend.

ON PARTNERSHIP SETTLEMENTS.

ON KEEPING PARTNERSHIP BOOKS WITH A STOCK ACCOUNT.

THOUGH the author considers the manner of keeping Partnership Books exemplified in the preceding sets, the best adapted for general business in private co-partnership, yet in some large firms, particularly manufacturing establishments, where there are a number of silent partners, it will be found more convenient to place the whole capital at the credit of a STOCK ACCOUNT, as is done in Banks and other Joint-Stock Companies. In this case, the amount of capital invested by each partner is shown by receipts or other private documents. All the partners' transactions with the concern are recorded precisely as they are at the partners' private accounts in the preceding Ledger; and the opening Journal entry will be the same in all the debits and credits, with the exception of the $3000 carried to the credit of each partner's stock account. This will appear in one sum ($9000) at the credit of the Stock Account; and no separate stock account will be opened for each partner. Take, for illustration, the first, second, and fourth entries of our Journal, p. 157, and embrace them in one entry, viz.:

```
SUNDRIES TO SUNDRIES   . $10272.
   Cash          .    .    .    .    .  $5998.
   Merchandise   .         .     3217.50
   E. Pryor      .    .    .    .    .    2.
   S. Gaynor     .    .    .    .    .    91.
   James Carter  .    .    .    .    .   963.50
        To T. P. Cope & Sons .    .    .    .    .   504.
         " William Hay   .    .    .    .    .   200.
         " James Day     .    .    .    .    .    68.
         " P. Duff   .   .    .    .    .    .   500.
         " Stock      .    .    .    .    .    .  9000.
```

Carrying the whole capital to the credit of the Stock account, as if it were an individual business.

As we have before remarked, the disposition of the Profits is altogether a matter of private agreement. If it be agreed to carry the whole profit to Stock, to increase the capital, the Profit & Loss will close thus—see p. 174.

```
PROFIT & LOSS TO STOCK for net gain   .    .   $4201.60
```

If it be arranged that the profits are to be divided:

```
PROFIT & LOSS TO SUNDRIES    .    . $4201.60
   To P. Duff for his ⅓ net gain .    .    .    .   1400.53
    " W. Gordon    "     .    .    .   1400.53
    " J. Carter    "     .    .    .   1400.54
```

Or, if they agree to divide, say 10 per cent. upon their capital, and allow the surplus to increase the stock—10 per cent. on $9000 is 900.

```
PROFIT & LOSS TO SUNDRIES        $4201.60
   To P. Duff for his 10 per cent. dividend .    .   300.
    " W. Gordon       "       .    .   300.
    " J. Carter       "       .    .   300.
    " Stock for surplus profits  .    .    .   3301.60
```

At the time of dissolution, or any other time, if desired, the stock may be closed into the partners' accounts, thus:

```
STOCK TO SUNDRIES, to close account   . $13201.60
   To P. Duff for his ⅓ capital  .    .    .    .   4400.53
    " W. Gordon     "     .    .    .    .   4400.53
    " J. Carter     "     .    .    .    .   4400.54
```

The partners' accounts will then show what is due them by the firm, or what they have to refund, if any of them have overdrawn.

179

ON ADJUSTING INTEREST ON PARTNERS' ACCOUNTS.

THE author left the exemplification of this matter out of his Partnership Books, believing that he could give a more comprehensive explanation of it in a separate section, than upon a Day-Book.

Many book-keepers cast interest upon each partner's capital, and, after deducting from this, interest on the sums withdrawn, carry the balance to each respective partner's credit, and to the debit of the Interest account. Although the results arising out of this disposition of the interest will all come out perfectly correct, yet it gives such a distorted appearance to the Interest account, that we think the following adjustment will be preferred by all good accountants. It will be observed that the interest is adjusted between the partners' accounts without disturbing the Interest account, which should embrace nothing but the interest of business transacted with the firm.

Suppose Hay & Gordon, partners, to share equally in the gain or loss, and the interest upon Gordon's capital to be . . . . $240.

 Less interest on sums withdrawn . . . . 80.   Balance 160.

 Interest upon Hay's capital . . . . . . 150.
 Less interest on sums withdrawn . . . . . 50.   Balance 100.

   Balance of interest in favor of Gordon . . . . 60.

Here we cancel the $100 interest due to Hay, and allow it to extinguish that amount out of the $160 due to Gordon. Then, by a little reflection, the reader will perceive, that if he credits Gordon for the remaining $60, and debits the Interest account, Gordon will himself have afterwards to pay, out of his share of the profits, one-half of this $60, and Hay the other half: then, if we make

   Hay Dr. To Gordon for half balance of Interest, $30.

the result will be correct. It will leave both partners' accounts in the same position as if they had been credited for their respective balances of interest above stated.

When there are more than two partners a different operation is required. The following rule will serve for any number :—

RULE.—Add together the balances of interest due to each partner : divide the sum by the number of partners ; the quotient is the average, or amount, of interest that would be due to each partner, provided they were equally interested. Therefore, the balances ABOVE the average must be placed to the credit of their respective owners, and those BELOW it must appear at the debit of their owners. The sum of the differences above, and that of the differences below, the average, will always equal each other, as will be seen by the following illustration :—

Suppose the bal. of Interest due Duff $650 — 394. Bal. for Duff's Cr. 256.
   "   " Gordon 490 — 394. "   Gordon Cr. 96. Total Crs. 352.
   "   " Hay   250.
   "   " Banks 186.
   Number of partners . . 4)1576.
        394 — 186. Bal. for Banks' Debit 208.
    And . . 394 — 250. "   Hay's " 144. Total Drs. 352.

The Journal entry will be,
    Sundries To Sundries $352.
   Banks, for balance of interest on his capital $208.
   Hay, for   "   .   "   "   .   144.
    To Duff, for balance of interest due him on his capital . . 256.
    " Gordon, for "   "   "   . 96.

ON PARTNERSHIP SETTLEMENTS.

THE principle just applied to the settlement of partners' interest, will often be found useful in arranging other matters in partnership settlements. We have known an expert accountant not a little perplexed to settle a matter similar to the following.

George Draper, William Stone, James Best, and Charles Hill, having lately dissolved their firm, sold off all their effects, divided the proceeds, and find their accounts standing as follows :—

There is a balance due to Draper of $460, to Stone, $270, to Best, $184, to Hill, $430. Their shares in the business were each one-fourth, their books were kept by Single Entry, and there are no farther effects to divide. Required the settlement of the matter between the partners.

```
Balance due Draper is  .   $460 — 336 = 124.
       "     Stone, is  .    270.
       "     Best, is   .    184.
       "     Hill, is   .    430 — 336 =  94.  218.

Number of partners,       4)1344
Each partner's loss,   .    336 — 270 =  66
                            336 — 184 = 152.  218.
```

Now, it appears that the whole loss was $1344, which, when borne equally by the four partners, will leave a balance due to each of $336, and those who have drawn out so far as to reduce their balances *below* this, must refund the difference to those whose balances *exceed* this amount. It will be better understood in a Journal entry.

```
Sundries To Sundries, $218.
George Draper,  .    .    .    .    .    .    $124.
Charles Hill,   .    .    .    .    .    .      94.
    To Wm. Stone, .   .    .    .    .    .           66.
     " J. Best,  .   .    .    .    .    .          152.
```

When the above sums are paid over by Stone & Best, and received by Draper & Hill, the above Journal Entry will be made, and when the amounts are posted, they will leave the balances due to each partner equal, viz.: $336, the amount of each partner's loss.

Before concluding the subject of partnership settlements it will be proper to direct the reader's attention to settlements upon investments of part of the joint capital of the firm, in which it is arranged that the profits or losses are to be divided in different proportions from those of their general business: for instance, suppose Hay, Wood & Banks, equal partners in business, purchase the Union Cotton Factory for $16000, paying one-fourth in cash, and giving the notes of the firm for the balance, $12000. Wood & Banks decline owning more than one-fourth each of the mill, whereupon Hay takes the other half. It is agreed that the gain or loss by the factory shall be divided in these proportions. Required the Journal entry for opening the account.

```
Sundries To Sundries.
Hay,  .    .    .    .    .    .    .    .    .   $8000
Wood,  .    .    .    .    .    .    .    .    .    4000.
Banks,  .    .    .    .    .    .    .    .    .    4000.
    To Bills Payable,  .    .    .    .    .    .          12000.
     " Cash,  .    .    .    .    .    .    .    .           4000.
```

The receipts and expenditures of the mill will be kept under the head of, Union Mill and owners, and dividends made of the gain or loss, as with Ship Roscoe and owners, page 97. But the cost of purchase can be placed to no other accounts than those of the owners while they own it in proportions different from their business.

181

CONCLUDING REMARKS UPON SET II.

We have already demonstrated the advantages of this mode of arranging and conducting books. We have practically exemplified its efficacy in preventing error, and the facilities it affords for detecting it when it occurs. We have shown that no entry once made upon the Day Book, or any of the primary books, can afterwards be omitted, in its passage through the books, without detection. While the common Double Entry Trial Sheet proves nothing, but that Ledger agrees with itself; if what is posted into it is posted correctly the trial will say, all is right, no matter how much you may leave behind in the primary books. Our trial requires the Ledger to agree with all the other books, thereby affording a security against error, which we believe has never yet been introduced into practice.

It will be proper to point out the advantage that will be derived from even a partial adoption of this method. Persons who do not choose to adopt and apply it to its full extent, may introduce a single book at a time, and keep it upon this principle in connection with the common Double Entry books, and derive all the advantages we have pointed out, as far as that book is concerned, without disturbing either their other books or their business. Take our Cash Book, for instance, p. 144, and you will find nothing in it to prevent its being kept in connection with any kind of books whatever. It admits of being balanced like any other ·Cash Book, at any time that it suits your convenience, the outer columns being always forwarded, unbroken by the balances, to correspond with their representatives in the Ledger, and as soon as an error gets into one book or the other, a disagreement between the amount of these columns is the immediate consequence. You see at once which side it is upon, and then have only to ascertain where this disagreement commences, and you find the error immediately.

But with the old form of Cash Book, although you perceive by its disagreeing *in balance*, with that of the account in the Ledger, it affords not the slightest clue to where, or upon which side, the error exists. You have no means of finding it, but by beginning at the time the account was last balanced on the Ledger, and comparing every entry on both sides.

The same remarks apply to our Bill Books. The clearness and simplicity of these accounts, when conducted upon this method, must be apparent to all. We have spent days in correcting a Bill account, where the number of entries was not over one hundred, but where the notes on one side were frequently posted in collected amounts, and on the other, broken up and posted in partial payments, endorsed upon the notes. We have no fear of any bookkeeper, who has had a task of this kind to perform, readily appreciating the value of our plan of keeping these books and accounts.

Those who keep a Sales Book can derive the same advantages from it in connection with common books as we do. It will check the credit side of the merchandise account, and if they choose, they can post the merchandise from it, in accumulated amounts, as we have recommended, p. 142. The same remarks apply to the Invoice Book if properly kept. And there is nothing to prevent any one from footing and forwarding the amount of their Day Book to check the Journal. Our form of Check Book may be introduced in any business, with all the advantages we have pointed out in correcting the Bank account. In a word, the introduction of our method requires no upsetting of the established principles of conducting accounts, in any establishment. It can be introduced by piecemeal—one book at a time until its practical working is fairly tested.

KEY,

CONTAINING THE ANSWERS OF SUCH EXERCISES AS ARE NOT GIVEN IN THE PRECEDING WORK.

ANSWERS TO THE QUESTIONS FOR EXAMINATION ON BALANCING THE INTRODUCTORY SET

PAGE 36.

ANS. 1.—The Stock and Balance accounts show the net capital $2980.
　　　　At the second balance it is . . . . 28500.
　2.—The Profit & Loss account shows a loss of . . 20.
　　　　In the second balance, a gain of . . . 520.
　3.—My whole gain was $260.; my whole loss was $280.
　　　　In the second balance, the whole gain was $673.75; the whole loss, $153.75.
　4.—I gained $170. on the first, and $600. on the second balance.
　5.—$1700. on the first, and (the balance brought down included) $4600. in the second balance.
　6.—$1870. in the first, and $2200. in the second balance.
　7.—None in the first balance; in the second, $3000.
　8.—$3080. in the first, and $7300. in the second balance.
　9.—$500. in the first, and $3000. in the second balance.
　10.—$300. in the first, and the same in the second balance.
　11.—The Cr. side of Balance account shows it to be $900. in the first, and $2800. in the second balance.
　12.—The Dr. side of Balance account shows the first $3880.; the second, 31,300.
　13.—The Cr. side of Stock shows it to be $3000. in the first, and $2980. in the second balance.
　14.—Solution given for first Balance, is 71\frac{24}{25}$.
　15.—　do.　　　do.　　is 10 per cent.

PROOF SHEET FOR LEDGER B, June 30, 1867.

		DRS.	CRS.
Stock . . . . f.	1		
Merchandise			
Bills Receivable	3		
William Hay			
Bills Payable	4		
House in Broadway			
Robert Morris	5		
Ship Hudson	6		
Profit & Loss			
Shipment to Liverpool	7		
J. Taylor & Co.	8		
Commission			
Estate A. Lenox	10		
House in Cedar Street			
City Bank Stock			
C. Lenox			
R. Lenox			
Cash	12		
C. Hartwell			

DUFF'S BOOK-KEEPING.

ANSWERS TO THE EXAMINATION ON PAGE 36,

ANS. 1.—Stock and Balance show it to be $61,544.50.

2.—Profit & Loss account shows it to be $28,044.50.

3.—Total gains, $31,599.30. Total expenses and losses, $3554.80.

4.—I gained $13,743.12.

5.—Total purchases were $50,830.10.

6.—Total sales, $46,445.

7.—Amount on hand, per Inventory, is $18,128.22.

8.—Cash account shows it to be $8891.

9.—Bills Receivable account shows it to be $8680.

10.—Bills Payable account shows it to be $6927.22.

11.—The Balance account shows it $46,750.34.

12.—The Balance shows it $108,294.84.

13.—The Stock shows it $31,300.

14.—Allowing 156 business days between the 1st January and 30th June,— the average daily sales would be $297.72

15.—The total purchases were 50,830.10
The amount on hand is 18,128.22

Leaving the cost of the part sold . . . $32,701.88

Then, 32,701.88 : 13,743.12 :: 100 : 42 per cent. average gain, nearly.

The teacher should now require the learner to give, upon a slate or sheet of paper, the opening Journal entry of the contents of this Ledger, supposing it was required to transfer the same to a new set of books. It would be:

SUNDRIES TO STOCK				$108,294.84
Merchandise	fol.	1	$18,128.22	
Bills Receivable . . .	"	3	8,680.	
House in Broadway . . .	"	4	15,000.	
R. Morris	"	5	5,676.59	
Ship Hudson	"	6	16,000.	
Shipment to Liverpool . .	"	7	8,000.	
John Taylor & Co. . . .	"	8	1,745.28	
House 49 Cedar Street . .	"	10	12,000.	
City Bank Stock . . .	"	"	10,000.	
Charlotte Lenox . . .	"	"	500.	
Robert Lenox	"	"	800.	
Cash	"	12	8,891.	
C. Hartwell	"	"	2,863.75	
STOCK TO SUNDRIES			$46,750.34	
To William Hay . .	fol.	3	.	$10,813.12
" Bills Payable . .	"	4	.	6,927.22
" Estate of A. Lenox .	"	10	.	29,010.

He should also be directed to make the same entry upon the principle explained in Note 1, p. 70, viz.—

SUNDRIES TO SUNDRIES, $108,294.84.

Inserting the debits of the Balance account for one side of the entry, and the credits for the other side. This form of the opening entry of books makes only one entry for the Stock account—the net capital, and is to be preferred to the common method of making two entries.

KEY.

ANSWERS TO THE EXERCISES ON PAGE 176.

1. Duff, Gordon & Co., the late firm, **Dr.** to stock for the balance due them on the firm's books.
2. The same as the other partners.
3. Sundries, Dr. to Duff, Gordon **& Co.**
   Cash, for the money in hand.
   City Bank, for balance transferred.
   Bills Receivable, for amount of Notes in hand.
4. Duff, Dr. to Sundries.
   To City Bank, to close account.
   " Cash,   do.   do.
   " Bills Receivable,   do.
5. No **entry** until converted into available funds.
6. Duff, **Gordon** & Co., Dr. to Cash $1000.
7. Gordon, **Dr.** to Duff   .   .   .   1000.
8. Cash, Dr. **to** the late firm   .   .   1000.
9. Cash, Dr. **to** Duff, Gordon & Co.   2000.
10. Duff, Dr. **to** Merchandise   2000.
11. Carter, Dr. to Merchandise   .   3000.
12. No entry, he having given the firm no credit for the Merchandise.
13. Merchandise, Dr. to Duff, Gordon & Co.   **$3000.**
14. Cash, Dr. to Duff, Gordon & Co.   .   .   62.
15. Duff, Dr. to S. Gaynor, to close account   .   62.
16. The firm, Dr. to Cash, paid R. Banks in **full**   80.50
17. Banks, Dr. to Duff, to close **account**   .   .   80.50
18. The same as if the firm still existed, To or By Profit & Loss.
19. Profit & Loss, Dr. to the individual, for the amount lost.
20. Re-open the **account** as directed, Suspended List, p. 174; then, Duff, Dr. to Butler, for the amount **received.**
21. In the usual way, **To or By** the partners' accounts.
22. When Duff pays over **each partner the balance due him, it will** close both their accounts and his.
23. They will close their accounts To **or By Profit & Loss.**
24. Sundries, Dr. to Profit & Loss .   .   .   .   140.05.
    J. Carter, for 5 ⅌ cent. discount on $1400.53 $70.02
    W. Gordon,   do.   do.   .   .   70.03
25. Duff, Dr. to Stock, for balance due on account, less discount allowed.

REMARK.—By a careful comparison of the above **answers** with the questions, p. 176, and the amounts in the balance sheet, it will be seen, that although the firm no longer exists, each partner **must** keep his account with it, and it **keeps** account with them until finally settled up. **The** books **of** an old firm **must** record **the** whole settlement of its affairs, as completely as if it still existed.

The retiring partners can **never** debit the remaining ones for their claim against **the** firm. The remaining partners **are not** accountable any faster than the effects are converted into available funds. **To carry such** entries into private account would inevitably lead to the greatest confusion.

It **is at all** times advisable, where **the amount** can be **agreed** upon, **for the** parties to agree to an allowance for bad debts, &c., **and one** party to sell **out, and the other to** buy, as exemplified in questions 24 and 25. The business then goes on without interruption.

When this arrangement cannot be effected, the new firm **has no other** course to follow, **than that laid** down upon page 176. **And if** it has dealings **on its own** account with the retired partners, the greatest care **must** be taken to distinguish **between** payments made on private account, and on account of **the** late firm, otherwise the accounts of the new and old firm may **become** involved in inextricable confusion.

MANUFACTURERS' FORMS.

TIME AND WAGES REGISTER OF THE PITTSBURGH NOVELTY WORKS.

1867.	JANUARY 1.				JANUARY 8.		
Name.	Quantity.		Rate.	Amount.	Quantity.	Rate.	Amount.
Patrick Birch	6 doz.	Locks.	$4.	24			
John Brown	5½ "	"	5.	27 50			
Robert Hammer	4 "	"	6.	24			
Levi Wall	3½ "	"	7.	24 50			
Joel Black	2½ "	"	8.	20			
Wm. End	15 "	Latches.	1.50	22 50			
Charles Dunn	12 "	"	1.75	21			
Joseph Castle	10 "	"	2.	20			
John Cross	25 "	Hooks.	.50	12 50			
George McCoy	30 "	"	.40	12			
Forward				208			

The above form is designed for paying the men by the piece, in weekly payments. We have extended the first week's wages upon the first page. In business, the above $208 is brought forward into the head of the "amount" column upon the next page, and so continued from page to page until the whole list of workmen (often several hundred) is complete. On pay-day the whole list is extended as above. The men assembled, the pay-clerk calls the names in their order upon the Register, hands each the amount due him, and checks it upon the left money column, thus √.

From the foot of the last page of the Register, the weekly amount total is transferred and marked "entered Cash Book."

This book should be made of paper large enough to contain four weeks' business. It will save writing to continue the ruling over two pages. The names will not then have to be re-written until the weekly spaces are all filled. If a workman is discharged, it is noted opposite his name, and his remaining weekly spaces remain blank.

186

TIME AND WAGES REGISTER OF THE PITTSBURGH UNION FOUNDRY,

For Two Weeks, ending Saturday, January 12, 1867.

NAMES.	M.	Tu.	W.	Th.	Fr.	S.	M.	Tu.	W.	Th.	Fr.	S.	Extra Time.	Whole Time.	Rate per Week.	Amount.	Paid.	Due.	Remarks.
John Mills	1	1	1	1	1	1	1	½	½	1	½	½		11	12	22	22	7	
Joel Post	1	1	1	1	1	1	1	1	1	½	¼	¼		10	15	25	25	8	
Frank Hart	1	1	1	1	1	1	1				1	1		9	18	27	20		
Hiram Hardy	1	1	1	1	1	1	1	1	1	1	1	1	4	16	18	48	40		
John Frost	1	1	1	1	1	1	1	1	1	1	1	1	3	15	12	30	30		
Neil Gow	1	1	1	1	1	1	1	1	1	1	1	1	1	13	12	26	26		
James McKee	1	1	1	1	1	1	1	1	1	1	1	1		12	12	24	24		
William Park	1	1	1	1	1	1	1	1	1	1	1	1		12	12	24	24		
G. W. Silk	1	1	1	1	1	1	1	1	1	1	1	1		12	18	36	30	6	
James Tanner	1	1	1	1	1	1	1	1	1	1	1	1		12	15	30	30		
Patrick Wade	1	1	1	1	1	1	1	1	1	1	1	1		12	12	24	24		
Ent'd Cash Book																	295		

If the men are paid weekly, only six day-columns are necessary. When paid every second week, the above form will enable the foreman to register every man's time accurately. Men who work extra time have it recorded in that column. If one page will not contain all the names, continue the list as directed in the last form, forwarding the "paid column" to the end of the list, where it is marked, as above, "Entered in Cash Book." The men are paid as directed in the last form, and usually paid in full; but if any desire part of their wages to stand over till the next pay-day, the balance is extended into the "due column," to be added to their earnings on the next register.

By having a large book, one space for names will serve for four weeks; the ruling for the third and fourth week to extend upon the opposite page.

The foregoing forms will guide the book-keeper in projecting forms for registering time and wages for any manufacturing establishment; for payment by the day, week, or month, by piece, or by weight, as the nature of the business may require.

187

FORM OF A RECEIVING AND
RECEIVED.

Date.		Marks and Articles.	Received from.	Consigned to.	Weights.		Charges paid.	
1867. Jan.	2	C. D. 14 Bales	Penna. R. R.	C. Day, Cincinnati	700,	70	369	72
					460,	970		
					466,	671		
					221,	970		
					447,	100		
					801,	1200		
					740,	1427		
						9243		
	10	W. Wade, 170 B. Flour	P. F. W. & C. R. R.	W. Wade, N. Y.			85	
Feb.	1	R. O., 2 Hhds.	S. B. Velocity	R. Owens, Philada.				
Mar.	10	W. & Co. 10 Hhds. Hams	S. B. Dart	Webb & Co., N. Y.				
	20	B. & Co., 200 B. Flour	S. B. Peru	Beck & Co., N. Y.			50	
Apr.	1	J. P. 9 Bales	Penna. R. R.	J. Pope, St. Louis, Mo.	400,	740	102	60
					300,	860		
					660,	610		
					430,	920		
					210,			
						5130.		
	10	W. H. 300 B. Oil	S. B. Diadem	Pike & Co., Baltimore			75	

The above form will be found suitable to almost all kinds of Receiving and Forwarding business. It will be seen that the column for "weights" is left blank when the freight is charged by the package; and the money column, "charges paid," is only used when we have to pay charges to the carrier from whom we receive the articles.

The amounts of commission and charges are entered in the Cash Book and Journal, out of the column "commission and charges," when the amount is marked off thus, √. Sometimes we collect both commission and charges of the conveyance by which we forward, inserting the amount in their bill of lading, to collect of the consignee when they deliver the freight. If we have an account with the consignee, we can debit his account for the amount. Suppose this to be the case with the first entry above, our Journal entry will be

C. Day, Dr. to Sundries . . . $415.94
To Cash, paid charges to Penna. R. R. on 14 bales   369.72
   # Commission, forwarding same p. S. B. Herald   46.22.

FORWARDING REGISTER.

FORWARDED.

Date.		Conveyance.	Articles and Weights.	Consigned to.	Comm.		Comm. & Charges.	
1867. Jan.	4	Steamer Herald	14 Bales 9243 cwt.	C. Day, Cincinnati	46	22	415	91
Feb.	15	Penna. R. R.	170 Bbls. Flour	W. Wade, New York	8	50	93	50
	16	" "	2 Hhds. Tobacco	R. Owens, Philada.	2		2	
Mar.	20	" "	10 Hhds. Hams	Webb & Co., N. York	10		10	
	21	" "	200 B. Flour	Beck & Co., N. York	10		60	
Apr.	4	S. B. Dart	9 Bales	J. Pope, St. Louis	25	65	128	25
	11	Penna. R. R.	300 Bbls. Crude Oil	Pike & Co., Baltimore	30		105	

Or, if our arrangements require us to charge the boat or company by which we forward, take the second entry:

Penna. R. R. Co, Dr. to Sundries . . . $93.50
To Cash paid P. F. W. & C. R. R. on 170 Bbls. Flour   85.
" Commission, forwarding same . . . . 8.50.

If we collect of the conveyance, we debit cash for the amounts so collected. Credits as above.

In extensive business, this book must be paged and the consignees' names indexed. The index will be of the common form, and lettered in the beginning of the book.

189

RATES OF STORAGE

ALLOWED BY THE CHAMBER OF COMMERCE OF PHILADELPHIA WHEN NO SPECIAL AGREEMENT IS MADE, OR NOTIFICATION GIVEN.—CHARGEABLE PER MONTH.

	Ground Floor Cents.	Cellars or lofts. Cents.
Almonds, per bale	10	8
Ashes, per bbl.	7	6
Bale Rope, per 100 lbs	2	1½
Barilla, per ton	30	25
Bark, Quercitron, per hhd.	30	25
Bottles, per gross	8	6
Burr Stones	½	⅜
Butter, per keg	1½	1
Candles, per box 25 lbs	¾	½
〃 Sperm, per box	1	¾
Cassia, per box	5	4
〃 per 100 lb mats	12½	10
Champagne, in baskets, per doz.	1½	1¼
Cheese, per 100 lbs	2	1½
Coal, in shed or yard, ¼ per bushel.		
Cocoa, per 100 lbs	2	1½
Codfish, per drum	12½	10
〃 loose, per 100 lbs	1½	1
Coffee, per hhd.	20	15
〃 in 100 lb bags	1½	1
Copper sheathing, per case	12½	10
〃 rods, per 100 lbs	12½	10
Cordage, per 100 lbs	2	1½
Corks, per bale	12	10
Cotton, per square bale	12½	10
〃 per round bale	15	12
Duck, per pack, 2 bolts	1½	1
Dyewoods, Braziletto and Nicaragua, per ton	50	37½
〃 other kinds, per ton	25	20
Earthen and glass ware, per hhd.	20	15
Figs, per drum	¼	⅛
Fish, per barrel	5	4
Flax, per 100 lbs	2½	2
Flax seed, per tierce	9	7
Flour, and other clean barrels	3	2
Ginger, per 100 lbs	2½	2
Grain and seed, in bulk, per bushel	¾	½
Hams, per hhd.	15	11
Hay, per bale	12½	10
Hemp, loose, per ton	75	62½
〃 in bales, per 100 lbs	2	1½
Hides, each	1	¾
Hoops, in yard or wharf, 15 c. per 1000.		
Hops, per bale	10	8
Horns, per 1000	50	37½
Indigo, per seroon	6	5
〃 per case,	12	10
Iron, bloom, or pigs, per 1000 lbs	8	6
〃 bars	10	8
〃 hollow ware	20	15
Lard, per keg	1½	1
Lead, in pigs, per 1000 lbs	7	5
〃 in sheets,	10	8
〃 in oil or dry	15	11
Leather, per side	½	⅜
Lemons, per box	2	1½
Lumber, in yard, per 1000 feet 12½ c.		
Madder, per hhd.	25	20
Molasses, per hhd.	25	20
〃 per tierce	18	14
〃 per barrel	6	5
Nails, per 1000 lbs	15	10
Naval stores, per barrel	6	4
Oil in casks, per 100 gallons	20	15
Oil in baskets, per dozen	¾	⅝
Pepper and Pimento, per 100 lbs	1½	1
Plaster, not under cover, 10 c. pr ton.		
Provisions, per bbl.	6	4
Quicksilver, per flask	1½	1
Raisins, per keg	1½	1
〃 per box	½	⅜
Rice, per tierce	12	10
Salt, per bushel	¾	½
Saltpetre, per bag	1½	1¼
Segars, per 1000	1	1
Steel, per 1000 lbs	10	8
Staves, in yard or wharf. for pipes, per 1000, 25 c.		
Sugar, per hhd.	25	20
Sugar, per bbl.	5	4
〃 per box, under 500 lbs	6	4½
〃 other packages 100 lbs	1½	1¼
Tea, per chest	4	3
Tin, block, per 1000 lbs	10	8
〃 sheet, per box	½	⅜
Tobacco, Ohio & Maryland, p. hhd.	25	20
〃 other kinds	30	22
〃 manufactured, per keg	3	2
〃 per seroon	4	3
Wines and Liquors, per cask of		
〃 130 to 150 gallons	30	25
〃 less than 130 gallons	25	20
〃 not over 63 〃	12½	10
〃 not over 35 〃	6	5
〃 not over 20 〃	5	4
〃 per dozen bottles	1	¾

All merchandise taken on storage pays for one month, and it is chargeable with another month if it remains one day after this time. The owners of the goods pay all charges for storing, tiering reasonably high, and for delivering.

RATES OF COMMISSION

ESTABLISHED BY THE CHAMBER OF COMMERCE OF THE CITY OF PHILADELPHIA,
WHEN NO SPECIAL AGREEMENT EXISTS,

ON INLAND AND FOREIGN BUSINESS.

PER CT.

MERCHANDISE, for selling, *on the total amount* (Foreign) . . . 5

" (Domestic) 2½

for purchasing and shipping, or accepting bills for purchases, *on cost and charges* 2½

for receiving and forwarding, *on the value* ½

on responsibilities incurred for same . 2½

VESSELS, for purchasing or selling, on *the gross amount* . . 2½

for chartering to proceed to another port or for procuring freight . 2½

for collecting freight or general average, *on the amount collected* . 2¼

paying for repairs, outfits, or disbursements, *on the total amount* . . 2½

MARINE INSURANCE, for effecting, when the premium does not exceed 10 ₽ ct., *on the amount covered* . . ½

if the premium exceed 10 ₽ ct., *on the amount of premium* . . . 5

settling and collecting losses without litigation, *on the amount collected* . 2½

FIRE INSURANCE, for effecting, *on the amount of premium* . . . 5

for adjusting and collecting losses, *on the amount collected* . . . 1

PER CT.

INLAND AND FOREIGN BILLS OF EXCHANGE, endorsing or drawing and negotiating, in every case, *on the proceeds* 2½

for purchasing without endorsing, *on cost and charges* . . . ½

for selling, *on the net proceeds* . . ½

for collecting, *on the amount collected* ½

for paying over, *on the amount paid* . ½

for remitting, *on the amount remitted* ½

SPECIE AND BANK NOTES, DRAFTS AND PUBLIC STOCKS, for selling, *on the proceeds* . . . . . ½

for purchasing, *on cost and charges* . ½

PUBLIC STOCK, for collecting dividends, on the amount collected . . ½

Advancing money, or for accepting bills, *in all cases on the amount advanced or accepted* . . . 2½

COLLECTING claims on insolvent estates or litigated or disputed accounts, *on the amount recovered* . . . 5

RECEIVING AND PAYING all moneys from which no other commission is rec'd 1

Receiving " . . . . ½

Paying " . . . . ½

Guarantee, in every case . . . 2¼

All consignments of merchandise withdrawn or re-shipped are subject to full commission to the extent of all advances and responsibilities incurred, and to half commission on the current value of remainder.

For selling merchandise previously consigned to another house, but withdrawn from them, when no responsibilities are incurred, only half commission is to be charged upon the current value, such value to be determined in all cases by the certificates of two competent merchants or brokers.

Bills remitted for collection under protest for non-acceptance or non-payment are subject to half commission only.

The above commissions are exclusive of storage, brokerage, guarantee, and all other expenses incurred.

Unless he order Insurance, the risk of loss by fire, robbery, and all other unavoidable risk, is with the owner of the consignment, ordinary care being taken by the consignee to secure it.

RATES OF COMMISSION

ESTABLISHED BY THE CHAMBER OF COMMERCE OF THE CITY OF NEW YORK,
WHEN NO SPECIAL AGREEMENT EXISTS TO THE CONTRARY.

[Extracted from the Minutes, Vol. II., pp. 29 and 30.]

FOR INLAND BUSINESS.

	PER CT.
MERCHANDISE, for buying, selling, shipping, or accepting for purchases without funds in hand to cover the same	2½
STOCKS, for buying or selling	1
SPECIE, " "	½
BILLS OF EXCHANGE, selling without endorsement	½
BANK NOTES, or Drafts, uncurrent, for selling	½
BILLS OF EXCHANGE, endorsing and selling	2½
VESSELS, purchasing or selling	2½
chartering, to take in cargo at other ports	2½
procuring freight	2½
collecting freight	2½
outfits, repairs, and disbursements	2½
collecting general average	2½

	PER CT.
REMITTANCES in Bills, in every case	½
RECEIVING AND FORWARDING goods, on the value of the same	½
when the same is entered for duty or debenture	1
COLLECTING dividends on stocks	½
COLLECTING BILLS, and paying over the amount	1
RECEIVING AND PAYING money upon which no other commission has been received	1
COLLECTING AND SETTLING Insurance losses	2½
MARINE INSURANCE, for effecting, in every case where the premium does not exceed 10 ℔ ct., *on the amt. covered*	½
when the premium exceeds 10 ℔ cent., *on the amount of premium*	5

FOR FOREIGN BUSINESS.

	PER CT.
MERCHANDISE, for selling	5
for buying and shipping with funds in hand, *on the total amount of cost and charges*	2½
STOCKS, for purchasing or selling	1
SPECIE, " "	½
BILLS, DRAWING or ENDORSING, in every case	2½
VESSELS, purchasing or selling	2½
for procuring freight	5
collecting freight on general average	2½
repairs, outfits, or disbursements, with funds in hand	2½
MARINE INSURANCE, for effecting, in every case where the premium does not exceed 10 ℔ cent., *on the amount covered*	½

	PER CT.
MARINE INSURANCE, for effecting, in every case where the premium exceeds 10 ℔ cent., *on the amount of premium*	5
DIVIDENDS ON STOCK, for collecting	½
LITIGATED OR DELAYED ACCOUNTS, collecting	5
INSURANCE LOSSES, adjusting and collecting	2½
RECEIVING AND PAYING MONEY upon which no other comm. is charged	1
REMITTANCES IN BILLS, in every case	½
LANDING and re-shipping Merchandise from vessels in distress, *on the value*	2½
RECEIVING AND FORWARDING Merchandise entered at the Custom-House, *on the value*	1
on all responsibilities incurred for the same	2½

The above commissions are without guarantee of debts for sales on time, brokerage, storage, and all other charges incurred. In the absence of instructions for insurance, the risk of loss by fire is always borne by the proprietor, as also the risk of loss by theft, robbery, or any other unavoidable accident, provided ordinary care be taken for the security of the property. Bills remitted for collection and returned under protest for non-acceptance, or non-payment, are subject to the same commission as when duly honored. All consignments of merchandise withdrawn or re-shipped are subject to full commission, to the extent of the advances or responsibilities incurred, and to half commission on the balance of value.

RATES OF STORAGE

CHARGEABLE MONTHLY, ESTABLISHED BY THE CHAMBER OF COMMERCE OF THE
CITY OF NEW YORK, WHEN NO PRIVATE AGREEMENT EXISTS.

[Extracted from the Minutes, Vol. II., p. 31 to 34.]

	CENTS.		CENTS.
Almonds in packages, per cwt.	6	Liquors, in puncheons of 120 galls., per	
Alum in bags or casks, per ton	40	puncheon	30
Ashes, pot or pearl, per bbl.	8	Liquors, in quarter casks	6½
Beef do.	6	do. in pipes 120 gallons	30
Bottles, quart, in crates or hampers, per		do. bottled in casks or boxes, per	
gross	8	dozen	1½
Bark, Quercitron, in casks, per ton	60	Leather, per side	1
Bagging, in bales or loose, per piece	3	Lard, in 60 lb firkins	2
Butter, in firkins of 60 lb, per firkin	2	Lead, in sheets or pigs, per ton	20
Cocoa, in bags or casks, per cwt.	2½	do. ground in oil or dry, per ton	40
Chocolate, in 50 lb boxes, per box	2	Molasses, in 110 gallon hhds.	30
Candles, in 50 to 60 lb boxes, per box	2	Other casks in proportion to their size.	
Coffee, in casks, per cwt.	2½	Nails, in casks, per cwt.	2
do. in bags, per cwt.	2	Oil, in 110 gallon casks or hhds.	30
Copperas, in casks, per ton	40	do. in 30 flask chests, per chest	4
Copper, in pigs, do.	20	do. in baskets, per dozen bottles	1½
do. in sheets or bolts, do.	30	Paints, in kegs or casks, per ton	40
do. braziers' bottoms, do.	75	Pork, per barrel	6
Cordage	50	Pepper, in bags, per cwt.	2½
Cassia, in boxes or bags, per cwt.	10	Pimento, in casks or bags, per cwt.	2½
Cotton, American, in square bales 300 lbs	12½	Rice, in tierces, per tierce	12
do. do. round bales	16	do. in half tierces, per half tierce	8
do. E. I., in bales, per 300 lbs	9	Rags, in bales, per cwt.	6
Cheese, in boxes or loose, per cwt.	3	Raisins, Malaga, in casks	3
Duck, heavy, per bolt	1½	do. in boxes	1
do. Ravens, or Russia sheeting, per		do. other packages, per cwt.	2
piece	¾	Saltpetre, in bags, per cwt.	2
Dry goods, in bales or boxes, per 40		do. in casks, per cwt.	2½
cubic feet	40	Salt, in kegs or bulk, per bushel	1
Earthenware, in crates of 25 to 30 ft.	15	Shot, in casks, per ton	37½
do. in hhds. of 40 to 50 ft.	30	Soap, in 50 or 60 lb boxes, per box	2
Fish, pickled, per bbl.	6	Steel, in bars or bundles, per ton	30
do. dry, in boxes or casks, per cwt.	4	do. in boxes or tubs, per ton	40
do. in bulk, per cwt.	2½	Sugar, in boxes or bags, per cwt.	2
Figs, in frails or drums, per cwt.	2½	do. in casks, per cwt.	2½
Flax, per ton	60	do. refined in p'kges or casks, per cwt.	3
Flax seed or other articles, in casks of		Tallow, in casks or other packages, do.	2
7 bushels	10	Tea, Bohea, in whole chests, per chest	15
Flour, or other dry articles, per barrel	4	do. in half chests	8
Grain, in bulk, per bushel	1	do. green or black, in qr. chests	4½
Ginger, in bags, per cwt.	2	do. other size boxes in proportion.	
Glass, window, in 50 feet boxes	1½	Tin, block, per ton	20
Hemp, per ton	75	do. in the usual sized boxes, per box	1½
Hides, dried or salted, per hide	1½	Tobacco, in hhds., per hhd.	37½
Hardware, in casks or cases, per 40 feet		do. in bales or seroons, per cwt.	4
cubic	40	do. manufactured, in 100 lb kegs	2
Indigo, in boxes or seroons	4	Woods for dyeing, under cover, per ton	50
Iron, in bar or bolts, per ton	20	do. in yards, per ton	25
do. in hoops, sheets, or nail rods, per ton	30	Whiting, in hhds., per ton	37½

On articles rating by weight, it is understood to be gross weight; and on liquors, oils, &c., the rate always refers to the whole capacity of the casks, whether they are full or not. The expense of putting the goods in store, stowing away, and turning out of store, to be borne by the proprietor of the goods. All goods stored are subject to one month's storage; if taken out within fifteen days after the expiration of the month, to pay half a month's storage; if after fifteen days, a whole month charged.

THE QUANTITY OF GOODS TAKEN FOR A TON IN FREIGHTING VESSELS.

EXTRACT FROM THE BY-LAWS OF THE CHAMBER OF COMMERCE OF THE CITY OF NEW YORK.

Resolved, That when vessels are freighted by the ton, and no special agreement is made between the owner of the vessel and the freighter of the goods, respecting the proportion of tonnage, which each particular article shall be computed at, the following regulations shall be the standard of computation.

That the articles, the bulk of which shall compose a ton, to equal a ton of the heavy materials, shall be in weight as follows:

1568 lbs of Coffee in casks.
1830 lbs of Coffee in bags.
1120 lbs of Cocoa in casks.
1307 lbs of Cocoa in bags.
 952 lbs of Pimento in casks.
1110 lbs of Pimento in bags.
   8 barrels Flour, 196 lbs each.
   6 do.   Beef, Pork, Tallow, Pickled Fish, Pitch, Tar, and Turpentine.
  20 cwt. Pig and Bar Iron, Pot Ashes, Sugar, Logwood, and all heavy Dyewoods, Rice, Honey, Copper Ore, and all other heavy goods.
  16 cwt. Coffee, Cocoa, and Dried Fish in bulk.
  12 cwt. Dried Codfish, in casks of all sizes.
   6 cwt. Ship Bread, in casks.
   7 cwt.   do.   in bags.
   8 cwt.   do.   in bulk.
 200 gallons Wine measure (on the full capacity of the cask) of Oil, Wine, Brandy, and all other Liquors.
  22 bushels of Grain, Peas, or Beans, in casks.
  36   "   "   "   in bulk.
  36   "   European Salt, in bulk.
  31   "   Salt from the West Indies.
  29   "   Sea Coal.
  40 feet (cubic) of Mahogany, Square Timber, Oak Timber, Oak Plank, Pine, and other Boards, Beaver, Furs, Peltry, Beeswax, Cotton, Wool, and Bale Goods of all kinds.
   1 hhd. of Tobacco.
  10 cwt. Dried Hides.
   8 cwt. China Raw Silk.
  10 cwt. Net Bohea Tea.
   8 cwt. Green Teas.

DUFF'S BOOK-KEEPING.

PART III.

DUFF'S BOOK-KEEPING.

PART III.

COMMERCIAL CALCULATIONS,

COMPREHENDING ABBREVIATED METHODS OF PRACTICAL COMPUTATION, SETTLEMENT
OF ACCOUNTS, &c. NOT FOUND IN COMMON ARITHMETICS.

ADDITION.

Young accountants, though good arithmeticians, often experience difficulty in adding up long columns of figures with certainty. Such persons will find the following method useful:

Set down upon waste paper the sum of each column under each other, adding downwards for proof, and if found correct, point off the right hand figures, carrying the left to the next column, thus:

4796.27	4.1
9832.39	3.7
325.41	1.9
9800.99	2.4
4723.78	3.5
70.87	29

Mark off the two upper places in the column of amounts, for cents. Read the figures marked off at the right upwards—29549.71, the total product. Any persevering student can in a few weeks attain a high degree of proficiency and accuracy in addition by writing out long columns of figures upon slips of paper, say sixty or seventy figures in length, and practice adding them for half an hour, daily. By this means of regular daily exercise, the student can ultimately attain such a facility of addition as to enable him to add several columns of figures at once. Take the above four columns of dollars, and carrying 3 from the cents makes the first amount read 73; 73 and 4723 are 4796; 4796 and 9800 are 14596, and so on to the head of the column. The student must practice first upon short columns, such as will require but little carrying. As he uses longer columns, carrying becomes unavoidable, but the eye soon becomes accustomed to the reading process in figures as well as letters. It only requires time and application to acquire it in either.

PROFIT AND LOSS.

Under this head we shall confine ourselves to exercises upon the rule for determining the per centage gain or loss upon a merchandise account. See pp. 33 and 36.

EXAMPLE 1. Purchases of merchandise for $11400.25. Sales effected in seventy-three days, $9400.84. On hand, $3400.84. Required the total gain, the average daily sales, the average gain per cent. and the average daily profits.

ANSWER.
Total gain	. . . . . .	$1401.43.
Average daily sales	. . . .	128.78, nearly.
Average gain per cent.	. . . .	17½, nearly.
Average daily profits	. . . .	19.19+.

EX. 2. Suppose the purchases $12405. Sales effected in 150 days, $7609. On hand, $6800. Required the total gain, the average gain per cent. the average daily sales, and the average daily gains.

ANS. Total gain, $2004. Average gain per cent. $35.$\frac{845}{1121}$. Average daily sales, $50.72⅔. Average daily profits, $13.36.

Ex. 3. Purchased, $8000. Sold in 90 days, $5000. Amount on hand, $4000. Required the daily average sales, the daily average profits, the total gain, and the gain per cent.

ANS. Total gain, $1000. Daily sales, $55.55⅗. Daily profits, $11.11¼, and 25 per cent. gain.

Ex. 4. Purchased, $4226. Sold in 60 days, $1585. Remaining on hand, $3202. Required the daily average sales, the total gain, the daily gain, and the gain per cent.

ANS. Total gain, $561. Daily gain, $9.35. Daily sales, $26.416. Average gain, 54$\frac{33}{41}$ per cent.

Ex. 5. Purchases, $6895. Sold in 36 days, $4011. On hand, $2223. Required the total gain or loss, the daily sales, the daily gain or loss, and the gain or loss per cent.

ANS. Total loss, $661. Daily sales, $111.41⅔. Daily loss, $18.36¼, and 14 + per cent. loss.

The same rule gives the per centage gain or loss upon any amount of sales.

Ex. 6. Bought candles at 13 cents and sold them at 16 cents. Required the gain per cent. ANS. 23$\frac{1}{13}$ per cent.

Ex. 7. Bought sugar at 5½ cents ℔ lb and sold it at 7½ cents. Required the gain per cent. ANS. 36$\frac{4}{11}$ per cent.

Ex. 8. Bought molasses at 25 cents ℔ gal. and sold it for 23¾ cents. Required the loss per cent. ANS. 5 per cent.

Ex. 9. Bought cloth at $2.62½ and sold it at $3.10. Required the gain per cent. ANS. 18$\frac{2}{21}$ per cent.

Ex. 10. Sold merchandise at 10 per cent. advance on the first cost, from which I deduct 5 per cent. from the face of the invoice for prompt payment. Required the per centage gain. ANS. 4½ per cent.

Ex. 11. Sold merchandise at 30 per cent. advance; from the face of the invoice deducted 20 per cent. Required the net per centage gain. ANS. 4 per cent.

Ex. 12. Sold merchandise at 50 per cent. advance on the prime cost. Allowed the retailer 40 per cent. discount on the face of the invoice. What is my net per centage, gain or loss? ANS. 10 per cent. loss.

Ex. 13. A manufacturer sold his productions by retail at 25 per cent. advance on the cost of production. He gave up the retail business, and agreed to furnish retailers at 20 per cent. discount upon his retail prices. Required his net per centage gain. ANS. Nothing.

NOTE.—The effect of discounts in such cases as the above is often overlooked by the inexperienced. The results of these examples show the practical importance of understanding the matter.

TO FIND COMMISSION AND BROKERAGE.

RULE.—For 1 per cent. point off two places, and for 10 per cent. point off one place, to the right of the given sum. Take aliquot parts for the intermediate rates.

Ex. 1.	Required ¼	per cent.	brokerage on	$1268.	Ans. $3.17.
Ex. 2.	〃 ½	〃	〃	1842.	Ans. 9.21.
Ex. 3.	〃 ¾	〃	〃	850.	Ans. 6.375.
Ex. 4.	〃 1	〃	.	899.	Ans. 8.99.
Ex. 5.	〃 1¼	〃	commission on	1668.88.	Ans. 20.861.
Ex. 6.	〃 2½	〃	〃	248.44.	Ans. 6.211.
Ex. 7.	〃 5	〃	〃	1499.90.	Ans. 74.995.
Ex. 8.	〃 7½	〃	〃	664.40.	Ans. 49.83.
Ex. 9.	〃 10	〃	〃	779.49.	Ans. 77.949

Ex. 10. Received $5000 to invest in a bill on New Orleans, which I purchase at par. Required the amount of the bill, and also my brokerage, which is ½ per cent. on the bill.
Ans. Bill, $4975.124. Brokerage, $24.876.

Ex. 11. Received $3000 to invest in a bill, which I procure at 2 per cent. discount Required the amount of the bill, also my brokerage, which is ½ per cent. on the face of the bill. *Ans. Bill, $3045.68+. Brokerage, $15.23, nearly.

Ex. 12. Net proceeds of J. Taylor & Co.'s sales, $2639. They desire the amount invested in a bill on New Orleans, and remitted them. Bills are 1 per cent. premium. My brokerage is ½ per cent. on the investment. Required the amount of the bill.
Ans. $2600.

Ex. 13. Remitted my correspondent in Mobile, $6000, to be invested in cotton. His commission is 5 per cent. on the investment. Required the amount of the invoice and his commission. Ans. Invoice, $5714.29. Commission, $285.71.

Ex. 14. Received from G. Page, $9000, to be invested in hops. My commission for purchasing is 2½ per cent. on the investment. Required the amount of my invoice and my commission. Ans. Invoice, $8780.49. Commission, $219.51.

ON INTEREST.

The legal rate of interest in Pennsylvania, New Jersey, Delaware, Maryland, Virginia, North Carolina, Tennessee, Kentucky, Ohio, Indiana, Illinois, Missouri, Arkansas, District of Columbia, and on all debts due the United States, is 6 per cent.

In New York, Michigan, Wisconsin, Iowa, and South Carolina, it is 7 per cent.

In Georgia, Alabama, Mississippi, Texas, and Florida, it is 8 per cent.

In Louisiana it is 5 per cent.

In England and France, 5 per cent.

In Canada, Nova Scotia, and Ireland, it is 6 per cent.

When the rate of interest is above or below 6 per cent., first find the interest at 6 per cent., then add or subtract the difference, viz.: For 5 per cent. deduct ⅙, for 7 per cent. add ⅙, and for 8 per cent. add ⅓ of the interest found at 6 per cent.

TO FIND THE INTEREST AT SIX PER CENT. FOR MONTHS.

RULE I.—Remove the decimal point two places to the left in the principal, then multiply by half the number of months. The product is the interest required.

TO FIND THE INTEREST FOR DAYS.

RULE II.*—For 60 days, point off two places in the principal, and it becomes the interest. For 6 days, point off three places, and the principal becomes the interest. For 5, 10, 15, 20, 25, 30, &c. days, take aliquot parts of the interest found as above for 60 days. For other numbers, multiply the interest found as above for 6 days by $\frac{1}{6}$ the given number of days. The product is the answer.

	EXAMPLE 1.	Required the interest of $448.12 for	1 month.						ANS.	$2.24†
″	2.	″	″	229.70	″	2 mos.			″	2.297
″	3.	″	″	664.40	″	3 ″			″	9.966
″	4.	″	″	712.60	″	4 ″			″	14.25†
″	5.	″	″	964.30	″	5 ″			″	24.107†
″	6.	″	″	667.60	″	6 ″			″	20.028
″	7.	″	″	1267.70	″	7 ″			″	44.369†
″	8.	″	″	1461.12	″	8 ″			″	58.444†
″	9.	″	″	48.48	″	9 ″			″	2.181†
″	10.	″	″	194.14	″	10 ″			″	9.707
″	11.	″	″	3344.20	″	11 ″			″	183.931
″	12.	″	″	1616.60	″	12 ″			″	96.996
″	13.	″	″	1718.80	″	16 ″			″	137.504
″	14.	″	″	2120.40	″	2 years and 1 mo.			″	265.05
″	15.	″	″	412.12	″	2 ″	3 ″		″	55.636†
″	16.	″	″	1886.18	″	2 ″	9 ″		″	311.219†
″	17.	″	″	1854.54	″	3 ″	8 ″		″	407.998†
″	18.	″	″	1794.92	″	4 ″	5 ″		″	475.653†
″	19.	″	″	1763.30	″	4 ″	8 ″		″	493.724
″	20.	″	″	2788.80	″	4 ″	10 ″		″	808.752
″	21.	″	″	5.	″	60 days.			″	.05
″	22.	″	″	7.	″	6 ″			″	.007
″	23.	″	″	180.48	″	5 ″			″	.15†
″	24.	″	″	234.60	″	10 ″			″	.391
″	25.	″	″	363.24	″	11 ″			″	.665†
″	26.	″	″	1216.40	″	15 ″			″	3.041
″	27.	″	″	1800.90	″	20 ″			″	6.303
″	28.	″	″	2412.64	″	22 ″			″	8.846†
″	29.	″	″	1518.90	″	25 ″			″	6.328†
″	30.	″	″	1920.60	″	30 ″			″	9.603
″	31.	″	″	1266.48	″	33 ″			″	6.965†
″	32.	″	″	2424.66	″	35 ″			″	14.143†
″	33.	″	″	1098.48	″	40 ″			″	7.323†
″	34.	″	″	726.24	″	44 ″			″	5.325†
″	35.	″	″	960.48	″	50 ″			″	8.004
″	36.	″	″	1566.96	″	63 ″			″	16.453†
″	37.	″	″	1399.97	″	66 ″			″	15.399†
″	38.	″	″	1224.12	″	1 ″			″	.204†
″	39.	″	″	369.18	″	2 ″			″	.123†
″	40.	″	″	96.84	″	7 ″			″	.112†
″	41.	″	″	636.69	″	8 ″			″	.848†
″	42.	″	″	224.42	″	12 ″			″	.448†
″	43.	″	″	846.60	″	13 ″			″	1.834†

* This Rule, though admitted to be slightly inaccurate, has been sustained by judicial decisions, and it is almost universally used by merchants in this country. It is based on the supposition of the year being divided into twelve equal months of 30 days each—360 days. It therefore gives the interest $\frac{5}{365} = \frac{1}{73}$ part too much.

ON COMMERCIAL CALCULATIONS.—PART III.

EXAMPLE 44.	Required the interest of	$960.84 for	17 days.	ANS.	$2.722+
" 45.	"	" 1236.18	" 19 "	"	3.914+
" 46.	"	" 1122.22	" 27 "	"	5.049+
" 47.	"	" 1860.48	" 29 "	"	8.992+
" 48.	"	" 246.24	" 37 "	"	1.518+
" 49.	"	" 321.21	" 39 "	"	2.087+
" 50.	"	" 9666.	" 40 "	"	64.44

Ex. 51. A note is dated January 27, 1853, @ 60 days. Required the unexpired time, February 27. ANS. 32 days.

Ex. 52. A note dated March 30, @ 90 days. Required the unexpired time, May 23. ANS. 39 days.

Ex. 53. A note dated 31st March, @ 3 months. Required the unexpired time on the 1st June. ANS. 32 days.

Ex. 54. A note dated October 31, 1852, @ 4 months. Required the unexpired time, February 1, 1853. ANS. 30 days.

Ex. 55. A note for $1368.72, dated 10th September, 1852, having 12 months to run, is discounted on the 21st October. Required the interest on the unexpired time.

OPERATION.

	Year.	Month.	Day.
Due .	1853 . .	9 . .	13
	1852 . .	10 . .	21
		10 . .	23 unexpired time.*

ANS. Interest on the same, $73.682+.

Ex. 56. A note for $360, dated May 31, @ 6 months, is discounted September 14. Required the unexpired time and interest for that time. ANS. Time, 80 days. Interest, $4.80.

Ex. 57. A note for $960.96, dated 30th June, @ 90 days, is discounted September 9. Required the unexpired time and the discount. ANS. Unexpired time, 22 days. Discount, $3.523+.

It now remains to notice what is called Partial Payments—where notes or bonds are paid by installments. There are two rules for computing the interest in such cases.

I. THE MERCANTILE RULE.—Find the amount of the principal at the date of settlement; then find the amount of each payment to the same date; subtract the sum of these amounts from the amount of the principal. The remainder is the balance due.

This is the principle upon which Morris' Account Current is settled. (Page 114.)

II. THE LEGAL RULE.—Compute the interest on the principal to the time of the first payment, or such payments as, taken together, exceed the interest then due. From the amount of the principal and interest subtract the payment. The remainder is the new principal. Proceed in the same manner with all subsequent payments.

The Courts of the United States and most of the State Courts have adopted this rule. No person of ordinary attainments in Arithmetic will have any difficulty in applying either of these rules. Our object in introducing them here is to show the widely different results that will often arise from their application. The following transaction, which recently came into our hands for settlement, will serve to show it:

* See note on page 200.

Bond for $900 on interest at 6 per cent. commencing May 8, 1838, was settled Sept. 8. 1852. Payments as follows, viz:

1st payment,	May	8, 1839	. . . .	$168.
2d "	June	4, 1839	. .	86.
3d "	Jan.	9, 1840	. .	50.
4th "	June 10, 1840		. . .	104.
5th "	Jan. 15, 1841		. . .	28.
6th "	May 25, 1841		. . .	50.
7th "	June 12, 1841		. .	6.
8th "	July .2, 1841		. . .	5.
9th "	Aug. 19, 1841		. . .	20.
10th "	Sep. 1, 1841		. . .	20.
11th "	Nov. 1, 1841		. . .	15.
12th "	Dec. 7, 1841		. . .	10.
13th "	Feb. 16, 1842		. . .	10.
14th "	. Sept. 24, 1842		. . .	19.
15th "	Oct. 27, 1845		. . .	80.50.
16th "	July 6, 1846		. . .	25.
17th "	Oct. 14, 1846		. .	50.
18th "	Mar. 20, 1847		. .	25.
19th "	Mar. 2, 1848		. .	40.
20th "	May 4, 1848		. .	20.
21st "	July 4, 1848		. .	35.
22d "	Sep. 30, 1848		. .	43.50.
23d "	Apr. 15, 1849		. .	58.
24th "	Mar. 1, 1850		. .	48.
25th "	Sep. 7, 1852		. .	9.

Upon computing the interest on the above transaction by the Mercantile Rule it leaves a balance due on the mortgage of $88.07. By the Legal Rule we find the balance $266.37, making a difference in the settlement of this $900 mortgage of $178.30. It must be admitted, however, that the annual rests usually made by merchants in settling accounts would have made a difference in favor of the creditor; but as these rests were not made at the proper time we could not go back into the account and make them afterwards. It is to be observed, however, that the Legal Rule, in this and all similar cases, gives the creditor compound interest in its most exacting form, as every time the debtor makes a payment the interest is compounded against him. I could have adduced many other examples to show, in the most striking manner, the difference resulting from these different methods of computing interest —to show that the difference is always increased in an accelerated ratio as the payments are multiplied or the time prolonged. In the case of *Clancerty* vs. *Latouche*, 1 *Ball & Beat.* 420, the difference resulting from the different methods of computing interest was about £24000 sterling. It may be asked what remedy is to be proposed in the confusion and uncertainty that exists in the law relating to this matter? We answer, None. It is only proposed to make all concerned aware of the difference resulting from the two methods, and leave the parties interested to govern their transactions accordingly. If I mistake not, the law allows the debtor, when paying money to a person to whom he is indebted on two accounts, to appropriate the payment to the discharge of whichsoever account he pleases— the one which is the most burthensome to him, the one which bears interest—provided he makes his election at the time of payment. If he does not do so, the creditor can make his election, and will, of course, apply the payment to discharge the interest first, and the surplus to paying the principal. If neither party makes an election, I believe the law will do it for them, and will apply the payments to discharge that debt which bears hardest upon the debtor.

It will be seen that the debtor on the above mortgage made eight payments upon it in one year, and the creditor, availing himself of the Legal Rule at the time of settlement, compounded the interest against him eight times in that year. Nothing but ignorance of the consequences would permit any debtor to make payments in such a manner. What I have now stated will, it is to be hoped, make the matter fully understood.

ADJUSTMENT OF INTEREST, GAIN, LOSS, &c.

For Rule see page 180.

EXAMPLE 1. Kay's paid up capital for 12 months is   .. $12000.
      He drew out for 6 months . . . . $600.
      Long's paid up capital for one year was . $14000.
      He drew out for 5 months . . . . $800.

Required the Journal entry for adjusting the interest between the partners without passing it into the interest account.

ANSWER. Kay Dr. .   . . . $59.
      To Long .   . . . $59. .

Ex. 2. C. paid in $8000 for 1 year and drew out $400 for 9 months.
      D. paid in $16000 for 1 year and drew out $800 for 3 mos. and $400 for 8 mos
      E. paid in $14000 for 1 year and drew out $11000 for 4 months.
      F. paid in $11000 for 1 year and drew out nothing.

Required the Journal entry for adjusting the interest between the parties.

ANS. Sundries, Dr. to D. $263.50
      C. $206.50
      E. 48.50
      F. 8.50

The same rule will adjust lost time between mechanics who are in partnership.

Ex. 3. Three mechanics, X., Y., & Z, equal partners in their business, with the understanding that each is to be charged with $1.50 per day for all lost time. At the time of settlement it was found that X. had lost 24 days, Y. 6 days, and Z. 32 days. Required the Journal entry for adjusting the matter between them.

ANS. Sundries To Y. . . . . $22.
      X. . . . . $ 5.   .
.   Z. . . . . 17.

Ex. 4. N. is ⅖, O. ⅔, P. ¼, and Q. ⅔, proprietors in the business. N. lost 24, O. 48, and P. 6 days. Q. lost no time. Each was chargeable with $1.50 per day for lost time. Required the Journal entry for adjusting the matter.

ANS. O. To Sundries $42.75
      " N. 87.87
      " P. 5.63
      " Q. 29.25

Ex. 5. R., S., T., & U. dissolved partnership, and divided all their effects, when it was found that the following balances were due to each, viz.:

R. . . . $760.   T. . . . . $582.
S. . . . 470.   U. . . . , 680.

The books were kept by single entry. The partners are equal in gain or loss. Required the Journal entry that will be made when the sums are paid and received for final settlement.

ANS. Sundries To Sundries . $194.
      R. . . . . . . $137.
      U. . . . . . . 57.
      To S. . . . $153.
      " T. . . . 41.

Ex. 6. V., W., & X. dissolved partnership, and after dividing all their effects there was a balance due V. of $940; due W. $90. X. was indebted $140. The firm owes a note of $268

DUFF'S BOOK-KEEPING.

The partners are equal in gain or loss. Required the sums to be paid and received among the partners, which will leave them all to share equally in the loss, and take up their note. ANS. V. receives $554. W. pays $296. X. pays $526.

Journal entry when the money is paid and received:

Sundries To Sundries, $822.
Bills Payable, for note taken up . . . $268.
V. for amount paid him . . . . 554.
To W., for amount refunded . . . $296.
" X. " " . . . 526.

Ex. 7. G. is ⅖, H. is ⅓, I. ⅓, and J. ¼, partners in business. After dissolution and division of all their effects, their accounts stood as follows:—Balance due G. is $28, H. $84, I. is indebted to the firm $44, and J.'s account is balanced. Required the Journal entry that will be made in the books of the firm, when the amounts are paid and received, for the final settlement between the partners.

ANS. Sundries To Sundries, $78.
G. $2.50
H. 75.50
To I. . . . $61.
" J. . . . . 17.

Ex. 8. K., L., M., and N. partners in business, kept their books by single entry, and after dissolution and division of all their effects, they find their accounts standing as follows upon their books, viz.:—There is a balance due K. of $280; due L. $840; M. is indebted to the firm $440, N.'s account stands balanced. K.'s original capital was $3400; L.'s, $1200; M.'s, $2220; and N.'s, $2180. The profit or loss was to be divided in proportion to the original paid up capital. Required the Journal entry that will be made in the books of the firm, when the amounts are paid and received, to effect the final settlement between the partners.

ANS. Sundries To Sundries, $772.44
K. for amt. received . . $23.11
L. " " . . 749.33
To M. for amt. paid in . . $607.73
" N. " " . 164.71

Ex. 9. C. Rush, R. Lyell, and F. Fish, partners in business, kept their books for several years by single entry. They finally closed them, made a dividend of the profits, and re-opened them by double entry, which necessarily exhibited each partner's net capital at this date. Some time afterwards, Rush furnished their book-keeper with an account of $840, which he had withdrawn for his own use from the firm, previous to the closing of the old books, and which he had kept a private account of without entering it to his account in the books of the firm. Rush and Lyell were each ¼ and Fish ½ gain or loss in the business. Required the Journal entry to settle the above $840 between them on their new books.

ANS. Rush To Sundries, $630.
To Fish . . . . $420.
" Lyell . . . . 210.

Ex. 10. On July 1, 1853, W. Wood retires from the firm of Hay & Wood. Their Balance Sheet is made out for settlement. We find their Profit & Loss Account Dr. $1280, Cr. $2450, and their Commission Account is credited $3400, in addition to which it is entitled to 5 per cent. commission on sales effected on the following consignments, which are only partly sold, viz.:—On R. Cargo's sales, which is Dr for charges posted, $400, and Cr. for sales effected, $7800; due by average May 1, 1853. M. Loder's sales is Dr. for charges posted, $300, Cr for sales effected, $9400, due by average September 1, 1853.

Required the Ledger specification exhibiting the disposition of the above consignments, with the commission and interest on the same in the partners' Balance sheet. (See Directions, page 177.)

204

Then suppose Hay continues the business in his own name and completes the sales of Cargo's goods—total sales, $9800. He also completes Loder's sales—$10,400. The charges posted are, in both cases, as above stated. Under the Ledger specification already made, exhibit Hay's Commission Account, re-opened and credited for the commission on the final settlement of the consignments.

Ans. The firm will owe Hay $70.10 int.

The student will write out the Ledger specification.

BUYING AND SELLING STOCKS, &c.

Ex. 1. Required the value of Hudson River Railroad Stock, which makes a dividend of 8% per annum, payable semi-annually, money being worth 6 per cent. per annum, payable semi-annually.

Solution.—6 : 100 : 8 :: $133⅓. Ans. That is, $100 of stock is worth $133⅓, or 33⅓ per cent. advance.

Ex. 2. What is the value of the Citizens' Bank Stock, which has made a dividend of 5 per cent. per annum? Money worth 6 per cent. Ans. 16⅔ per cent. discount.

Ex. 3. Bought $500 in Exchange Bank Stock, which divides 9 per cent. dividend per annum. Money being worth 6 per cent. interest. I am to pay the amount in Tennessee money which is at 3 per cent. discount. Required the amount of Tennessee money it will take to pay for the stock. Ans. $773.20, nearly.

Ex. 4. Sold $2000 of City Bank Stock, which divides 7½ per cent. per annum. Received in part payment $1000 of Winchester Railroad Stock, which divides 4½ per cent. per annum. Money worth 6 per cent. interest. Required the balance I am to receive in money. Ans. $1750.

Ex. 5. London Bridge Stock is said to divide 2 per cent. per annum. Money in England being worth 5% interest. Required the value of this stock. Ans. 60% discount.

DOMESTIC AND FOREIGN EXCHANGES.

Ex. 1. Bought a bill on Boston, for $780, at 1% premium. What must I pay for it? Ans. $787.80.

Ex. 2. Bought a bill on New Orleans, for $1680, at ¾ per cent. discount. What must I pay for it? Ans. $1667.40.

Ex. 3. Sold my bill on St. Louis, for $1840, for 1½% discount. Required the amount I shall receive. Ans. $1812.40.

Ex. 4. Sold my bill on London, for £450 sterling, for 8 per cent. premium. Required the amount.* Ans. $2160.

Ex. 5. Bought a bill on London, for £1266 15s.† at 9½% premium. What shall I have to pay for it? Ans. $6164.85.

Ex. 6. I owe Holderness & Chilton, of Liverpool, $7218, net proceeds of sales of merchandise effected for them, which I am to remit them in a Bill of Exchange on London for such amount as will close the transaction, less ¼ per cent. on the face of the bill, for my

---

* Rule.—To change sterling money into Federal currency, multiply by 4⁴⁄₉. To change Federa. currency into sterling, divide by 4⁴⁄₉.

† If there be shillings and pence, change them into the decimal of a pound, and multiply as before.

commission for investing. **Bills on London are 8 per cent. premium.** Required the amount of the bill, in sterling, to be remitted. ANS. £1500 5s. 6†d.

Ex. 7. A., of Pittsburgh, sent articles to the World's Fair, in London, which were afterwards sold by B., of London, on A.'s account—net proceeds, £1266 15s. sterling. B. was instructed to invest this amount in Bills on New York, and remit to A., which was accordingly done. B. charged ¼ per cent. brokerage, on the face of the bills, for investing, and purchased the bills at 7 per cent. discount. Required the amount of the bill A. must receive in Federal currency to close the transaction. ANS. $6037.53, nearly.

We confine our illustrations of Foreign Exchange to Great Britain, because a knowledge of it is necessary to understanding the accounts in this system of Book-keeping. But to treat of Exchange upon all foreign countries would require space which we can appropriate to matters of greater interest to the majority of our patrons.

INDIRECT EXCHANGE

Effects a remittance through one distant place to another. It is sometimes termed the

ARBITRATION OF EXCHANGE.

Ex. 1. I wish to remit George Wildes & Co., of London, £3600 sterling. Exchange on London, in New York, is 10 per cent. premium. Exchange on London can be obtained at Halifax, Nova Scotia, for 9 per cent. premium. New York Bills on Halifax are ¼ per cent. discount. If I remit a draft to Halifax, and pay my agent ½ per cent. for investing it in Bills on London, what will I gain over the direct Exchange?

SOLUTION.

£3600 sterling = $16000 @ 10% prem. = cost of the direct Exchange . . $17,600.00
Halifax Bill on London, @ 9% + ½% for investing . . $17,520.00
¼% discount for New York on Halifax 43.80
Cost of the indirect Exchange 17,476.20
Gain $123.80

Ex. 2. I have to remit £6300 to London. New York Bills on London are 10¼ per cent. premium. New York on St. John, New Brunswick, ¾ per cent. discount. St. John on London is 9¼ per cent. premium. If I pay my agent in St. John ½ per cent. for investing, what will I gain by the indirect Exchange? ANS. $370.48.

INSURANCE.

INSURANCE is a security given by underwriters or insurance companies to the owners of ships, houses, or other property, to indemnify them in case of loss by fire or shipwreck.

The premium is always a percentage on the value insured. The written and printed document held by the party insured as evidence of the contract of indemnity is called the POLICY.

Ex. 1. If I get my house insured for $4500, at 1¼ per cent. premium, what shall I pay as premium? ANS. $56.25.

ON COMMERCIAL CALCULATIONS.—PART III.

Ex. 2. Insured my ship, the Chieftain, for $65000, to Canton and back, for 4¼ per cent. premium. What will it amount to? Ans. $2762.50.

Ex. 3. Insured the ship Ironwood, for $48000, at 2½ %, and gave my note for the premium. Before the note was paid the ship was lost, and the insurers paid the loss. Required the amount I received, taking up my note as part payment. Ans. $46800.

Ex. 4. Insured the ship Roscoe, (which was worth $47500,) for $45000 at 2 per cent. policy, $1, to Liverpool and back to New York. Freight out was $12500. Expenses at Liverpool, $4500. The ship was lost on her return. The insurance company has paid the insurance. Required each owner's share of the net proceeds of the vessel. W. Hay is ⅓, myself ⅓, and C. Hartwell ⅔.

Ans. My share, $13024.75. Hay's, $13024.75. Hartwell's, $26049.50.

Ex. 5. I wish to insure merchandise on board the ship Chieftain, for San Francisco. Amount of invoice, $12447; cost of policy, $1; premium is 2 per cent. Required the premium, and the sum upon which we insure to cover the premium and policy. (See Note 3, page 84.) Ans. Amount to cover, $12702.04. Premium, $254.04.

SIMPLE EQUATIONS.

RULE.—See page 68.

Ex. 1. Received from John Fowler, for sale on commission, 900 bbls. flour, upon which paid freight and charges, $14. After charges, storage, 6¼ cts. ℔ bbl. Laborers' wages, for storing and hoisting out, $2.50. Commission for selling, 2½ %. Sales effected as follows, viz.

May 1,	40 bbls.	@ $4.50,	for cash;
" 19,	60 "	@ 4.75,	on acct. @ 30 days;
June 2,	150 "	@ 4.80,	on note, @ 60 "
" 2,	50 "	@ 4.50,	for cash;
" 11,	500 "	@ 4.75,	on note, @ 90 days;
" 21,	50 "	@ 4.80,	" @ 30 "
" 30,	50 "	@ 4.50,	for cash.

Required the account sales showing the net proceeds, and when due.
Ans. Net proceeds, $4071. Due, August 13th.

Ex. 2. Received from Lyon, Haven & Co. for sale on consignment, 150 bbls. mackerel and 40 bbls. salmon, upon which paid freight and cartage, $190. Labor in storing, $1.70. Commission on the sales, 5 per cent. Sales effected as follows, viz:

June 7,	40 bbls. mackerel,	@ $12.50,	on acct. @ 3 mos.
" 19,	10 " salmon,	@ 18.75,	on note, @ 30 days;
July 1,	5 " "	@ 18.00,	for cash;
" 17,	100 " mackerel,	@ 12.75,	on note, @ 60 days;
" 29,	16 " salmon,	@ 18.75,	on acct. @ 30 days.

State the account sales, showing the net proceeds, when due by equation, and the balance of goods on hand.
Ans. Net proceeds, $2043.175. Due, September 5.

Ex. 3. Received from George Carver, for sale on his account, 80 tons Iron. Freight and charges paid, $74. Commission for selling, 5 per cent. which was sold as follows :*

---

* The sales being all at 6 months, we may equate between the days of sale.

207

May 20, Sold at 6 months, on acct. 12 tons, @ $65.
" 31,   "   "   "   8 " @ 66.
June 20,   "   "   "   15 " @ 65.
" 30,   "   "   "   18 " @ 64.
July 11,*   "   "   "   5 " @ 66.
" 11,   "   "   "   4 " @ 65.
" 11,   "   "   "   8 " @ 65.
" 19,   "   "   "   4 " @ 66.

We are to pay Carver the net proceeds in a note payable 6 months after date. Required the amount of it, and the day on which it must be dated. Also, the account sales, showing the amount on hand.

ANS. Date of note, for $4494.55, June 22. On hand, 6 tons.

EX. 4. Sold John Taylor & Co. :

April 30, Invoice of Merchandise, @ 4 months, $620.49
May 1,   "   "   @ 6   "   730.50
" 30,   "   "   @ 30 days   480.80
July 1,   "   "   @ 60   "   560.95
" 11,   "   "   @ 60   "   330.40
" 11,   "   "   @ 4 months, 500.00

Required the day upon which the above account will fall due, by average.
ANS. September 16.

EX. 5. Received of Charles Page, for sale on his account, 30 hhds. N. O. sugar, upon which paid freight, $60; cartage, $7.50; storage $9. Commission and guarantee, 5 per cent. Sales effected as follows :

Aug. 1, Sold, on note @ 60 days, 4 hhds. 4660 lbs. less 10 per cent. tare, 5½ cts.
" 30, "   "   @ 3 mos. 6 " 5880 "   "   "   " 5½ "
" 30, " for cash,   3 " 3390 "   "   "   " 5¼ "
" 30, " on acct. @ 60 days, 7 " 6990 "   "   "   " 5¼ "
Sep. 16, " for cash,   4 " 4830 "   "   "   " 5¼ "
" 30, " on note, @ 3 mos. 6 " 5960 "   "   "   " 5¼ "

Required the account sales, exhibiting the net proceeds and the day when the same is due, by average.   ANS. Net proceeds, $1424.78. Due, November 1.

STORAGE EQUATIONS.

Equation is applied to the storage of property by the following

RULE.—Multiply the number of packages by the number of days that they have been in store. Divide the product by 30; the quotient is the number of packages subject to one month's storage.‡

EX. 1. I have stored 1500 bbls. flour for 4 days. Required the number of bbls. subject to one month's storage.

Solution.—1500 × 4 days = 6000 ÷ 30 = 200 bbls. ANS.
Proof.—1500 : 200 : : 30 : 4.

* This and the two following sales may be added together and make but one product.
‡ NOTE.—Where a number of packages are received and delivered at different dates, proceed as in Compound Fellowship.

Ex. 2. May 1, Received 200 bbls. flour.   May 10, Sold 150 bbls.
        " 16,   "   300 "   "   " 18, "   30 " "
        June 1, "   400 "   "   June 10, " 550 "
        July 13, "   500 "   "   July 30, " 660 "
        Aug. 20, "   700 "   "   Aug. 30, " 700 "

Required the number of bbls. subject to one month's storage on August 31.

                                                    Ans. 1269 bbls

Ex. 3. Received the following consignments from J. L. Starr & Co., viz.:

Sept. 1, Received 15 hhds. sugar.   Sept. 20, Sold 12 hhds. sugar.
  "   12,   "   80 bbls. molasses.   Oct. 1, "   40 bbls. molasses.
  "   30,   "   30 hhds. tobacco.   Nov. 1, "   43 hhds. sugar.
Oct. 6,   "   40 "   sugar.   " 10, "   60 bbls. molasses.
  "   20,   "   50 bbls. molasses.   Dec. 1, "   65 hhds. tobacco.
Nov. 30,   "   40 hhds. tobacco.

Required the number of hhds. and bbls. subject, each, to one month's storage, Dec. 1.
                Ans. 48 hhds. sugar. 160 bbls. molasses. 63 hhds. tobacco.

COMPOUND EQUATIONS.

For Rule, see note on page 116.

Ex. 1. May 1, 1866, received of R. Morris, London, 40 bales carpet. Paid freight and other charges in cash, $1600. Sold the carpets the same day, on note at 6 mos. for $6000. Commission and guarantee, 5%. Required the day on which R. Morris' net proceeds are due in cash.   Ans. January 11, 1867.

Ex. 2. Received, May 30, of C. Hartwell, of Boston, 50 cases Lowell prints. Paid freight and charges in cash, $120. June 2, accepted his draft on me at 30 days' sight for $2000. On the same day sold the 50 cases prints, on note at 4 mos. for $5400. Commission and guarantee, 5%. Storage, $10. Required the day on which the balance of the net proceeds will be due in cash.   Ans. Balance, $3000. Due, Dec. 5, 1866.

Ex. 3. July 2, 1866, sold R. Manly an invoice of dry goods, amounting to $2800, on account, at 4 mos. On the same day I bought of him an invoice of flour, at 30 days, for $1800. I am to have his note at 4 mos. for the balance. Required the day on which this note must be dated so that neither party will lose interest.
           Ans. Note for $1000. Balance will bear date December 15, 1866.

Ex. 4. Our account with Robert Carver is as follows:

1867. Jan. 1. Sold him goods on account, at 3 months .   . $600.00
         " 27.   "   "   "   "   "   .   .   550.50
       Feb. 20.   "   "   "   "   "   . .   .   449.80
       Mar. 12.   "   "   "   "   "   .   .   500.49
       Apr. 1   "   "   "   "   "   .   .   400.21
                                   Crs.
1867. Jan. 16. Received cash on account .   .   . $250.00
       Feb. 10.   "   "   " 300.00
       Mar. 4.   "   his order on John Doe, at 10 days   350.00
       Apr. 1.   "   cash on account .   .   .   200.00

Required the day on which the balance of the account will fall due by average.
                                                    Ans. July 14.

Ex. 5. Find the day on which the balance of William Hay's account (page 116) will fall due.   Ans. May 16.

Ex. 6. Our account with George Draper stands as follows, viz.:

July	1.	Sold him merchandise, at 4 mos.	. . . . $1600
"	10.	Paid his order in cash	80
"	30.	Merchandise at 60 days	600
Aug.	2.	" " 3 mos.	850
"	19.	Paid his order in cash	100
Sept.	30.	Merchandise at 30 days	300
Oct.	1.	" " 60 "	450
July	30.	Credit for his note at 4 mos. . . . $1680
Aug.	31.	" " 90 days . .	1450
Oct.	1.	" " 30 " . . .	400
"	30.	" cash in full . . .	450

Required the interest due to us or by us on the above account by equation.

ANS. Dr. equation, Oct. 26. Cr Nov. 29. Interest due us, Oct. 30, $20.33.

COMPUTING FREIGHT.

Marine freights are computed by the ton of 2240 lbs for all articles occupying less than forty cubic feet to the ton.

RULE.—Multiply the given number of tons by the rate; the product is the freight.

Ex. 1. Required the freight of 131 tons 15 cwt. of Iron, at $2.50 per ton.
ANS. $329.38

Ex. 2. Required the freight of 71 tons 5 cwt. of Copper, at $2.40 per ton.
ANS. $171.

In the Western River Navigation freight is computed by the net 100 lbs.

RULE.—Multiply the given number of pounds by the rate, and divide the product by 100; the quotient is the freight.

Ex. 3. Required the freight of 47491 lbs, at 15 cents per 100 lbs.
ANS. $71.24, nearly.

Ex. 4. Required the freight of 61221 lbs, at 37½ cents per 100 lbs.
ANS. $229.58, nearly.

Ex. 5. Required the freight of 31121 lbs, at 18¾ cents per 100 lbs.
ANS. $58.35+.

Ex. 6. Required the freight of 40411 lbs, at 12½ cents per 100 lbs.
ANS. $50.51+.

The same Rule applies in computing the price of Scantling, Boards, &c.

Ex. 7. Required the amount of 1721 feet of Scantling, at $1.37½ per 100 feet.
ANS. $23.66+

Ex. 8. Required the amount of 118372 feet of Boards, at $11.25 per M.
ANS. $1331.69

Ex. 9. Required the amount of 70112 feet of Flooring, at $21 per M.
ANS. $1472.35+.

Ex. 10. Required the amount of 1129 feet of Oak Scantling, at $3.12½ per C.
ANS. $35.28+.

GENERAL AVERAGE.

When damage or loss is incurred by any part of the vessel or cargo, for the benefit of all concerned, all who profited by the safety of the vessel or cargo must contribute to the relief of those whose property was thus sacrificed. This contribution is called General Average.

Such sacrifices cannot be made without consultation of the officers and crew, and must be absolutely necessary for the safety of the vessel, otherwise General Average will not take place.

Particular Average means a partial loss of the ship or cargo, by the dangers of the sea, fire, or other unavoidable accident. This loss must be borne by the owners of the property, or their insurers.

The vessel and goods injured, saved or lost, are valued at what they would have brought in cash at the port of destination.

It is customary, in calculations of General Average, to allow only two-thirds of the cost of replacing vessels' masts or furniture, the new articles being worth one-third more than the old. The rule for finding the General Average is similar to that of Fellowship.

RULE.—As the sum of the values of the contributory articles is to the total loss, so is 100 to the per centage loss.

Ex. 1. Suppose the Ship Hudson, on her passage from Liverpool to New York, to have sustained the following damages, viz.:

Cost of replacing masts, rigging, and cables, cut away	$3000	
Less ⅓, extra value for being new	1000	$2000
Cost of one anchor, which was lost		800
15 pipes of wine, thrown overboard		3000
Towing into harbor		200
General average loss		$6000

Contributory interests, viz.:

Ship Hudson, valued at			$16000
Cargo			42000
Freight		$4000	
Less portage bill		2000	2000
			$60000

As 60000 :: 6000 : 100 :: 10 per cent.

So that the ship's owners must contribute	$1600
Owners or insurers of the cargo	4200
Owners or insurers of the freight	200
	$6000

Ex. 2. The ship Roscoe, on her voyage from New Orleans to New York, was thrown upon her beam ends and obliged to cut away her masts, when she righted, but sprung a leak, in consequence of which the following property was thrown overboard to lighten the vessel, which was ultimately towed into New York:

20 hhds. Sugar, belonging to R. Dyer			$1600
30 " " " W. Kane			1800
Damage done to G. Halis' goods			1600
Freight of goods thrown overboard			120
Cost of new cables, masts, sails, and rigging		$3600	
Less ⅓, for newness		1200	2400
Towing the ship into port			80
			$7600

Contributory interests, viz. :

R. Dyer's goods, thrown overboard	.	$1600
W. Kane's " "	.	1800
Value of W. Hay's goods, less freight and charges	.	4200
" G. Page's " " " "		5950
" R. Manly's " " " "	.	12650
" G. Halis' " " " "		14800

" the ship	$20000	
Deduct for damages	3600	
		16400
Value of the freight	$6800	
Less seamen's wages	3400	
		3400
		$60800

Required the per centage that each party must lose of his interest in the ship, cargo, and freight..

ANS. 12½ per cent.

We have above given the rule for General Average, with illustrations to explain its application, which any good arithmetician will readily understand. But it is to be observed, that to understand in all cases what will constitute a General Average loss, and what interests are to contribute to it, requires an intimate knowledge of the Law of Insurance. For instance, it has been decided that the damage sustained by a merchant vessel and cargo, in fighting and beating off a privateer, is not a subject for General Average. Also, the removal of a quantity of perishable fruit while the vessel was in a port of refuge for the purpose of repairs, which removal increased an incipient decay, and caused an entire loss of the fruit; this was also decided to be no matter for General Average. In fact, it is said by an eminent writer upon law to be "the most intricate and perplexing in the whole Law of Insurance." The subject will be found judiciously treated in the American editions of "Smith's Mercantile Law," and "Abbott upon Shipping."

ON OPENING BOOKS BY DOUBLE ENTRY.

Ex. 1. I open my books with cash in hand, $100. Deposit in the City Bank, $4900. R. Gain's note for $4000; interest due on the same, $200. I own house and lot on Water Street, worth $30000, upon which I owe $10000 on bond, with $500 interest due on the same. H. Stubbs owes me on account, $700. I owe R. Ryan on account, $1500. Required the Journal entry for opening my books.

Ex. 2. Commenced business with cash in hand, $250. Deposit in Exchange Bank, $7000. Eighty shares Hudson River Rail Road Stock, $100 per share, with 25 per cent. paid upon it. Forty shares City Bank Stock, $50 per share, in full. One hundred shares Central Rail Road Stock, $100 per share, with 60 per cent. paid upon it. Required the opening Journal entry.

Ex. 3. Jacob Ring pays in cash, $2100. Aaron Budd, $1990. They are to do business under the firm of Ring & Budd. Required the Journal entry for opening their books.

Ex. 4. J Park and P. Buchan, partners in business. Park pays in cash, $1000; merchandise, $1100. Buchan pays in cash, $1000; merchandise, $890; notes due him, $100. Required the Journal entry for opening their books.

212

Ex. 5. Rowen & Cox commence business with the following capital, viz. : ·
    J. Rowen pays in cash, $2000; merchandise, $500; notes due him, $400. Wm Tell owes him, on account, $100. Rowen owes debts which the firm assumes, viz. : On his notes, $300; to Wm. Yates, on account, $400.
    B. Cox pays in cash, $1800; merchandise, $800; notes due him, $600. J. Pond owes him, on account, $300. Cox owes debts which the firm assumes, viz. : On his notes, $700; to Geo. Oates, on account, $500.
    Required the Journal entry for opening their books.

Ex 6. Dean & Brady commence business as follows :
    R. Dean pays in cash, $1400; notes due him, $1200; interest due on these notes, $130; merchandise, $600. Sands & Turner owe him, on account, $200. The firm assumes the following debts owing by Dean, viz. : On his notes, $500; to Fulton & Gowan, $200.
    D. Brady pays in cash, $1200; notes due him, $1500; interest due on these notes, $160. The firm assumes notes owing by Brady, $980.
    Required the Journal entry for opening their books.

Ex. 7. D. Mills is the owner of a Factory, which, together with other effects belonging to his business, constitutes a net capital of $40000, which is at the credit of his Stock Account in a regular set of double entry books. Without closing his books or exhibiting any inventory of his property, he agrees to admit J. Roy and B. Gates as equal partners, on their paying into the firm as capital $20000 each, and paying him a bonus of $10000 each, also, in cash; which was to constitute all three partners equal in property, and equal in gain or loss. Required the Journal entry for introducing the new partners and their capital into the old books.

Ex. 8. Suppose Mills' capital to be $60000, at the credit of his Stock Account. Roy and Gates agree to come in as ⅓ partners in the business by paying in, as capital, $30000 each, in cash, and also to pay Mills a bonus of $5000 each, in cash. Required the Journal entry to introduce the new partners' names into the books. Mills to be ½, and Roy and Gates each ¼ in property and ⅓ gain or loss.

When a firm establishes branches of its business at distant points, these branches are debited and credited in all respects like strangers, and the branches do the same with each other and with the head of the firm.

EXERCISES IN CLOSING THE LEDGER.

Ex. 1.

Stock	is Dr. $1200		Cr. $2800		
Merchandise	"	3470	"	2400, on hand, $1250	
Profit & Loss	"	850	"	1650	
Bills Receivable	"	2700	"	1800	
Bills Payable	"	240	"	1200	
W. Horn	"	180	"	270	
D. Camp	"	1900	"	420	

Write out a Ledger specification of the above, open a Balance Account, and close the whole of the accounts.

Ex. 2.

Stock	is Dr. $1800		Cr. $2200		
Merchandise	"	7500	"	4600, on hand, $3500	
Profit & Loss	"	2150	"	250	
Bills Receivable	"	980	"	880	
Bills Payable	"	200	"	6600	
R. Irons	"	750	"	150	
John Doe	"	1600	"	300	

Write out the Ledger statement, open the Balance Account, and close the books.

Ex. 3.

Stock	is Dr.	$750		Cr.	$4800
Profit & Loss	"	1220		"	1880
Interest	"	150		"	450
Expense	"	1410		"	110
Storage	"	750		"	1250
Commission	"	——		"	600
Balance	"	9890		"	5080

Write out the Ledger statement and make the final closing entries.

Ex. 4. John Doe and Richard Roe, partners in business, are balancing their books, which they find standing at the final closing as follows:

J. Doe's account is Dr.		$420		Cr.	$3800
R. Roe's	"	60		"	3600
Profit & Loss	"	700		"	4900
Balance	"	17320		"	6200

The partners are equal in gain or loss. Required the final closing of the Ledger.

Ex. 5. S. Boon and R. Simmons find their books standing as follows:

S. Boon's acct. is Dr.		$1230		Cr.	$2700
R. Simmons'	"	1050		"	1300
Profit & Loss	"	6600		"	900
Balance	"	9220		"	13200

S. Boon is $\frac{2}{3}$ and R. Simmons $\frac{1}{3}$ gain or loss. Required the final closing of the Ledger.

PARTNERSHIP SETTLEMENTS BY SINGLE ENTRY:

In single entry Book-keeping, where no Profit & Loss Account is kept, the gain or loss is determined as directed on page 18.

Ex. 1. A. paid into firm $600, and drew out $180. B. paid in $300, and drew out $120. The undivided effects amount to $450. A. is $\frac{2}{3}$ and B. $\frac{1}{3}$ gain or loss. Required the division of the $450 between them.

Ex. 2. C. paid in $2400, drew out $750.
  D.   "   2100,   "   1100.
  E.   "   2000,   "   120.

Each partner's share in the gain or loss is equal. At the date of dissolution they are owing debts, $2750, and have cash, notes, merchandise, and other effects, $8660. Required the balance due each partner. ANS. Due C. $2110; D. $1460; E. $2340.

Ex. 3. A. paid in $700, drew out $150.
  B.   "   800,   "   290.
  C.   "   500,   "   400.

At the time of their dissolution their cash, merchandise, and other effects amount to $1848, and they owe $950. The partners share equally in the gain or loss. Required the balance due each. ANS. Due A. $462.67; B. $422.67; C. $12.66.

Ex. 4. F. pays in $3200, draws out $650.
  G.   "   1624,   "   500.
  H.   "   1500,   "   1450.

F. is to be $\frac{1}{2}$ gain or loss, and G. and H. each $\frac{1}{4}$. G. and H. retire from the business. The cash and merchandise on hand is $3800. Outstanding debts due the firm $2850, upon which it is agreed to allow 10 per cent. discount for bad debts. The firm owes, on notes and book debts, $3400. Required the sums F. will have to pay G. and H. on retiring—F. to become the owner of all the effects of the firm and assuming all their liabilities, as above stated. ANS. F. pays G. $934.25, and H. pays F. $139.75.

Ex. 5. A. was ⅔ and B. ⅓ gain or loss, and at the time of dissolution B. agrees to take the whole stock of cash, merchandise, and other effects of the firm, for $3010.79—A. retiring from the business. By their accounts it appeared that A. had drawn out $592.82, and paid in $1146.78; B. had drawn out $103.27, and paid in $504.92. No interest was to be charged on either side. Required the sum B. must pay A. on retiring.
ANS. $1924.68.

FOR RECTIFYING DERANGED DOUBLE ENTRY BOOKS.

RULE.—Close all the impersonal accounts into Profit & Loss; then place the amount of each side of the Profit & Loss in the list of Effects and Liabilities, carrying back to the Profit & Loss the difference between the Effects and Liabilities. Close the Profit & Loss into the partners' accounts in all respects as in double entry. This transforms the single entry Ledger into a double entry one. (See pp. 7, 18, and 19.)

Ex. 6. N. paid in $2460, drew out $975.
     O.   *   2660,   *   420.
     P.   *   2800,   *   1100.
At the time of dissolution they owe $4500, and have cash, merchandise, and other effects, $8840. They also have an expense account open which is debited for $1260. Required the balance due each partner, exhibiting the expense account closed, each partner sharing equally in the gain or loss.
ANS. Due N. $1123.34.   Due O. $1878.33.   Due P. $1338.33.

Ex. 7. Q. paid in $2560, drew out $1075.
     R.   *   2770,   *   520.
     S.   *   2890,   *   200.
At the time of settlement the firm owes $4450, and have cash, merchandise, and other effects, $8780. Their expense account is debited for $1480. Profit & Loss is Dr. $640, and Cr. $1400. Commission account is credited for $1850. The partners are equal in gain or loss. Required the balance due each, and exhibit the impersonal accounts all closed.
ANS. Due Q. $786.67.   Due R. $1551.67.   Due S. $1991.66.

If there be property accounts open, close them By Balance for the value on hand, and bring the balance down, and carry the gain or loss to the Profit & Loss account. Then proceed as directed in the above Rule.

Ex. 8. N., O., and P., partners in business, paid into the concern as follows:

     N. paid in $2464, and drew out $985.
     O.   *   2665,   *   424.
     P.   *   2880,   *   1110.

At the time of dissolution they owe $4595. They have merchandise on hand valued at $4400; cash, $1840; notes and book debts due them, $2218. Their expense account is debited for $1286. Their merchandise account is debited for $40050, and credited for $39500. Their Profit & Loss account is debited for $1665, and credited for $1580. Each partner shares equally in the gain or loss. Required the balance due each at the time of dissolution. ANS. Balance due N. $936.67   Due O. $1698.67.   Due P. $1227.66.

Ex. 9. R. and S., partners in business, desire to make a dividend of their gain or loss
They find their books standing as follows:

R.'s account is	Dr.	$6600	Cr.	$15000
S.'s "	"	950	"	12000
Merchandise	"	24000	"	12500 on hand, $11000
Cash	"	13000	"	9500
Bills Receivable	"	16500	"	7500
Bills Payable	"	4800	"	8300
Profit & Loss	"	700	"	2700
Commission			"	2200
Interest	"	880	"	1400
R. Roy	"	2200		
C. Page			"	800

Required the Ledger Specification of the book, exhibiting the balance sheet and each
partner's capital.

Ans. R.'s capital, $9375. S.'s capital, $12025. Each partner's gain, $975

When the capital is paid in at different times, and it is agreed that profit or loss is to be
divided in proportion to the time it is invested, the gain or loss is found by the preceding
rules, and divided by the following

RULE.—Multiply each partner's capital by the time it was employed; then add all the
products together and say, as the sum of these products is to each partner's product, so is
the whole gain to each partner's share of it.

Ex. 10. K., L., and M., partners in business, commencing 1st January, 1866.

Jan.	1,	K. paid in	. . .	$1200
March	1,	" "	. . . .	900
June	1,	" "	. . . . .	1100
Aug.	1,	" drew out	. . . .	800
Jan.	1,	L. paid in	. . . .	1100
May	1,	" "	. . .	1400
Oct.	1,	" drew out	. . .	200
Jan.	1,	M. paid in	. . .	1800
		" drew out nothing		

At the time of dissolution, 31st December, 1866, the firm has cash and merchandise in
hand, $5500; notes and book debts, $4500. They owe $3200. The gain or loss is to be
divided in proportion to the amount of capital paid in by each partner, and for the time it
was in the business. Required the balance due each partner.

Ans. K.'s gain, $112.14. Balance due him, $2512.14.
L.'s " 98.48. " " 2398.48.
M.'s " 89.38. " " 1889.38.

Ex. 11. N., O., and P. partners in business, commencing January 1, 1867.

Jan.	1,	N. pays in	. . . .	$600
March	1,	" "	. . .	800
July	1,	" draws out	. . .	. 200
Sept.	1,	" pays in	. . .	600
Jan.	1,	O. "	. . . .	700
May	1,	" "	. . . .	400
June	1,	" draws out	. l. . .	. 200
Aug.	1,	" pays in	. . .	1200
Jan.	1,	P. "	. . . .	. 1000
Oct.	1,	" "	. . . .	600

ON COMMERCIAL CALCULATIONS.—PART III.

At the date of settlement, December 31, 1867, the firm has cash and other effects in hand, $7500, and are owing debts to the amount of $3400. Required the division of the gain or loss, in proportion to the amount and time each partner's capital was invested, and the net balance due each partner.

Ans. N.'s net loss, $494.83.   Balance due him, $1305.17.
       O.'s   "   488.79.   "   "   1611.21.
       P.'s   "   416.38.   "   "   1183.62.

Ex. 12.   X. and Y. partners in business, commencing 1st January, 1867.

Jan.   1,   X. paid in $9000
May   1,   "   "   2400
June   1,   " drew out   1800
Sep.   1,   "   "   2000
Oct.   1,   " paid in   800
Jan.   1,   Y   "   3000
March 1,   " drew out   1600
May   1,   "   "   1200
June   1,   " paid in   1500
Oct.   1,   "   "   8000

At the time of settlement, on the 31st of December, 1867, their merchandise account was Dr. $32000; Cr. $27000. Balance of merchandise on hand, per inventory, $10500. Cash on hand, $4900. Bills Receivable, $12400. R. Draper owes on account, $2450. They owe on their notes, $1890. They owe G. Roe on account, $840. Their Profit & Loss account is Dr. $866; Cr. $1520. Expense account is Dr. $2420. Commission account is Cr. $2760. Interest is Dr. $480; Cr. $950. The gain or loss is to be divided in proportion to each partner's capital, and in proportion to the time it was invested. Required each partner's share of the gain or loss, the net balance due each, and a Ledger specification exhibiting the closing of all the accounts and the balance sheet.

Ans. X.'s share net gain, $6671.73.   Net balance due him, $15071.73.
      Y.'s   "   "   2748.27   "   "   12448.27.

Ex. 13.   J. Boyd and W. Page, partners in business, dividing the gain or loss equally. Page retires from the firm. Their books are kept by single entry; and the partner's accounts stood as follows:—J. Boyd is Dr. for sums withdrawn, $6200; Cr. for sums paid in, $8100. W. Page is Dr. for sums withdrawn, $5100, and Cr. for sums paid in, $7800. Their effects consist of

Cash which Page takes to his account   .   .   .   .   . $4400.
Bills Receivable which he also takes to acct.   .   .   .   .   3700.
Mdse. on hand which Boyd takes to his acct.   .   .   .   .   5600.
Book debts which he also takes to acct.   .   .   .   .   6300.
They owe on notes, which Boyd assumes   .   .   .   .   2200.
They owe Book debts, which he assumes   .   .   .   .   1100.

Required which partner is indebted to the other, and what amount?

Ex. 14.   A. became embarrassed, and failed in business. His effects were sold off at auction, and the net proceeds, $7770, paid over by the auctioneer to the assignee. A. was indebted as follows, viz:

To B. on notes and book account   .   . $4800
  " C. on account   5600
  " D.   "   3600

Each creditor is to receive in proportion to the amount of his claim. The assignee's commission is 5 per cent. on the amount paid over to the creditors. Required the amount to be received by each.   Ans. B. receives $2537.14.
                                                    C.   "   2960.
                                                    D.   "   1902.86.

ON THE SETTLEMENT OF ACCOUNTS.

Referring to our directions for making out accounts, (page 114,) we have only to observe that, under the date of the semi-annual settlement, spare space is usually left in the Day-Book to insert entries of all omissions that are discovered upon exchanging accounts current. These omissions are entered and posted up under date of the last day of the last month's business embraced in the account for the semi-annual settlement; but the payment must appear under the date upon which it takes place. To enter or post it under a back date would derange the cash account.

In those cases in which we expect to receive the balance of the account rendered before any new transactions take place, it is unnecessary to balance the account on the Ledger until we can post up the payment and close the account. But if new transactions take place between the parties before the payment of the balance of the old account is made, it will generally be found more convenient to balance the old account in the Ledger, and bring down the balance into new account, in which an entry of the payment will appear when made. Those who prefer excluding this old balance and its payment from the next account current, can star out the entries on the Ledger, as seen in the following specification, and leave the amounts out of the new account current. Loans of money, and other transient matters, may be left out of the account current by the same means. (See Pryor's account, page 167.)

Dr.						R. CARVER.			Cr.		
1867.						1867.					
Jan.	17	To Merchandise	7	416	40	Feb.	4	By Cash	15	416	40
Feb.	1	" "	14	4200	20		28	" Bills Receivable	19	4000	
Mar.	10	" "	20	780	80	Mar.	8	" Merchandise	20	918	80
June	28	" Sundries	27	1160		June	30	Bal. to new acct.		1222	20
				6557	40					6557	40
June	30	To Bal. ¼ acct. ren'd		1222	20	July	1	By Merchandise		730	
July	7	" Merchandise	30	480			17	" Cash on old acct.	34×	800	
Aug.	4	" Order to F. Oaks	39	79	74		20	" My order per }	33	140	
Sep.	30	" " to R. Rankin	46	130	40			Ryan & Co. }			
Oct.	21	" Merchandise	56	494	70	Aug.	1	" Cash in full for }	38×	422	20
Dec.	7	" Order to Winters	69	73	30			old acct. }			
	30	" Merchandise	84	360	60						

In business a note is generally taken for such a balance as the above, and the account is immediately closed.

Between houses keeping interest accounts with each other, unless the balance of the account is paid, with a note or money, on presentment, it and the other payments will appear in the next account.

On page 146 will be found a practical exemplification of the Check Book, kept in such a manner as to check both sides of the Bank account in the Ledger. We shall now add some additional directions for settling with your banker.

When you get your Pass Book balanced, if it contains any charges for discounts, commissions, or any entries not in your books, enter them both on your Check Book and Day-Book. If all your checks have not been returned, enter the numbers and amounts, in red ink, on the

ON COMMERCIAL CALCULATIONS.—PART III.

Dr. side of your Check Book and Ledger, **and if** all your work is right, **the** balance in deposit will close the account. Close **the** account, and bring down the balance **on the** Check Book and Ledger in the usual manner, and bring down the outstanding checks **in the same** manner on the Cr. side. To make the matter clearly understood, we subjoin a specification **of** it on a Check Book:

DATE.		AMOUNTS DEPOSITED.			DATE.		NAME.	No.	AMOUNT.		CHECKS.
1867.					1867.						
June	30	Bro. forw'd	4248	10	June	30	Checks out,		1100	40	
July	5	Deposited	800		July	2	R. Hill,	174	900		
	12	"	1300			5	W. Wood,	175	600		
August	1	"	400		Aug.	2	R. Cox,	176	1100	60	
	19	"	1140		Sept.	9	B. Ray,	177	970		
Sept.	1	"	660	90		13	W. Boon,	178	1430		
	4	"	340	40	Sept.	30	Balance,		5095	80	
	7	"	521	24							
	24	"	216	16							
Out, 175		$600.									
177		970.	1570								
			11196	80					11196	80	
Sept.	30	Balance	5095	80	Sept.	30	Checks out,		1570		

You will understand that the above $5095.80 represents the balance made by the banker on your Pass Book; but he made that balance before two of your checks (Nos. 175 and 177) were presented; consequently your books will not show the same balance until the amount of these checks is counterentered. This should be done in red in the old, and black in the new account.

I feel confident that no business man will try this form of Check Book, and not prefer it to the old practice of entering Checks and Deposits all in one column.

Young accountants will find the advantage of having their Pass Books frequently balanced. In a business of any magnitude it should be done monthly—never at longer periods than three months.

EXERCISES IN INVOICES.

See Forms, page 59.

Ex. 1. Sold Draper, **Son & Co.** July 6, 1867 : 1 piece superfine Black Broadcloth, No. 427, 19^2 yds. @ $3.62½. 1 end, 10^2 yds. Green do. No. 401, @ $3.62½. 1 end Blue do. No. 644, 10 yds. @ $3.62½. 2 pieces Black do. Nos. 4202 and 4203, 18 and 18^2 yds. @ $3.31½. 4 ends Vesting, 6^2, 8^2, 9^1, and 7^1 yds. @ $2.50. 2 pieces do. 14 and 16 yds. @ $3. Required the invoice, exhibiting the correct amount.   Ans. $434.66.

Ex. 2. Sold King, Wood & Co., July 10, 1867, 12 doz. Black Silk Hose, @ $10. 9 doz. Ladies' best Black Kid Gloves, @ $7.62½. 4 doz. Men's do. @ $9.87½. 2 doz. do. out sizes, @ $11.50. 6 doz. Men's fancy **colored** do. @ $9.75. 8 doz. Children's do. @ $4.62½. 6 doz. do. Thread, @ $2. 12 doz. Men's fancy Silk Half Hose, @ $3.75. 6 doz. do. Black Ribbed, @ $4. Required **the invoice,** exhibiting the correct amount. Ans. $427.63.

219

Ex. 3. Sold George Gains & Co. July 30, 1867 : 10 doz. Lyell's Shovels, @ $7.75. 15 doz. Bowman's Spades, @ $10.75. 5 doz. do. Cast steel, @ $12.50. 5 boxes Derby Scythe Stones, @ $3.50. 20 doz. Grass Scythes, @ $11.50. 12 doz. Corn do. @ $13.50. 3 Mouse-hole Anvils, 120, 230, and 330 lbs. @ 12 cts. ℔ lb. ¾ Birmingham Anvils, 100, 150, and 250 lbs. @ 8 cts. ℔ lb. Required the invoice and correct amount. ANS. $832.35.

Ex. 4. Sold Richard Carver & Son, July 31, 1867.

At 5% discount*—55 Patent Balances, @ $10. 30 doz. Patent Coffee Mills, @ $5. 20 doz. Lippincott's Axes, at $10. 25 doz. do. Hatchets, @ $4. 30 doz. do. @ $3.75.

At 10% discount—30 Roland's 6-feet Mill Saws, @ $3.75. 25 do. 6½-feet Cross-cut Saws, @ $3.75. 4 doz. Hand Saws, @ $7.50. 6 doz. do. @ $9. 4 doz. do. @ $6.50.

The following are net—10 gross Gilt Vest Buttons, of each No. 479, @ $1; 566, @ 1.20; 667, @ $1.30; 494, @ $1.40; 993, @ $1.50; 337, @ $1.60. 2 doz. Rodgers' Penknives, of each No. 4200, @ $7; 4900, @ $8; 4300, @ $9; 4400, @ 9.50. 12 doz. best balance-handled Ivory Table Knives and Forks, @ $10.50 Required the invoice and amount.
ANS. $1614.49.

Ex. 5. Sold David Chesman & Co. 4 hhds. Sugar, each 1146, 1104, 1107, and 1003 lbs gross, tare 10%, @ 5 cts. 16 boxes Mould Candles, 56 lbs each, @ 10½ cts.; boxes 25 cts. each. 30 boxes Bloom Raisins, @ $3. 40 doz. Corn Brooms, @ $2. 2 chests, 84 lbs each, Y. H. Tea, @ 68 cts. 6 half chests do. 240 lbs, @ 65 cts. Required the invoice and amount. ANS. $734.52.

Ex. 6. Sold Mason & Sands : 6 Detached Lever Silver Watches, @ $12. 8 do. @ $15. 5 do. Gold do. @ $40. 5 Duplex Lever Gold do. @ $65. 6 do. do. @ $75. 1½ doz. Gold Spectacles, @ $60 per doz. ½ doz. do. @ $75 per doz. 3 doz. Silver do. @ $10. 2 doz. do. @ $15. 1 doz. Eight-day Clocks, $65. ¼ doz. Church Clocks, @ $80. Required the invoice. ANS. $1439.50

EXAMINATION ON

SETTLING CONSIGNMENTS AND JOINT ACCOUNTS.

See Questions 25 and 26, page 41.

Ex. 1. William Mount's sales are completed. Total sales, $3420. Charges posted, $780. After charges, viz.: Commission and guarantee, 5%. Storage, $20. Required the Journal entry to close the sales on the Ledger, supposing the net proceeds to be carried to Mount's credit.

Ex. 2. G. Glen's sales are effected to amount of $14040. Charges posted, $1729. After charges, viz.: Commission and guarantee, 5%. Storage, $56. Required the Journal entry for closing the sales, supposing we pay over the net proceeds at the same time in cash.

Ex. 3. Effected sales for David Carman, $4660. Charges posted, $4440. After charges are, Commission, 5 per cent.; Storage, $36. Required the Journal entry to close the sales.

Ex. 4. Effected sales of Michael May's goods, $9840. Charges posted, $9910. After charges, Commission and guarantee, 5 per cent.; Storage, $45. Required the Journal entry to close the sales.

Ex. 5. Completed sales of merchandise on joint account with Wm. Hay, each one-half. Our first cost was $2400. Total sales, $6400. Charges posted, $800. After charges, Commission and guarantee, 5 per cent. Storage, $18. Required the Journal entry to close the sales, carrying Hay's net proceeds to his account.

Ex. 6. Completed sales of merchandise on joint account with Wm. Hay, each one-half. Our half, first cost, $6000. Total sales, $12600. Charges posted, $490. After charges,

---

* Short-extend each discount, and from the marginal addition subtract the discount, full-extending the net amounts. Less than five mills count nothing in the extensions; five mills and upward count another cent.

ON COMMERCIAL CALCULATIONS.—PART III.

Commission and guarantee, 5 per cent. Storage, $66. Required the Journal entry for closing the sales; carrying Hay's net proceeds to his credit.

Ex. 7. Suppose the above total sales to be $6000. Our half, first cost, the same, ($6000). No charges are made. Required the Journal entry to settle the transaction, supposing we give Hay our note at 60 days for his share of the net proceeds.

Ex. 8. Suppose our half, first cost, and the total sales to be equal, as in the last problem —$6000 each—and the after charges, Storage, $30; Commission and guarantee, 5 per cent. Required the Journal entry to close the sales, supposing Hay's net proceeds to be paid him in cash.

Ex. 9. Suppose our half, first cost, $9000. Total sales, only $8000. Commission and guarantee, 5 per cent. Storage, $28. Required the Journal entry to close the account, supposing we give Hay an order on James Carter for his share of the net proceeds.

Ex. 10. Our half, first cost, was $11500. Charges posted, $500. Total sales, $18000. After charges, Storage, $84; Commission and guarantee, 5 per cent. The inventory of the joint property unsold is $8000.* Required the Journal entry to close the account, supposing Hay's ½ net proceeds to be carried to his account.

Ex. 11. Suppose our half, first cost, $10500. Charges posted, $560. Total sales, $15000. After charges, Commission and guarantee, 5 per cent.; Storage, $48. Property on hand, $6200. Required the Journal entry for closing the account, paying over Hay his half net proceeds in cash.

Ex. 12. Our half, first cost, was $14800. Charges posted, $150. Total sales, $7800. Joint property on hand, $13200. After charges, viz.: Storage, $64; Commission and guarantee, 5 per cent. Required the Journal entry to close the account, supposing it to include our note to Hay for his half net proceeds.

Ex. 13. Our half, first cost, was $9000. Charges posted, $8800. Commission, 5 per cent. Storage, $24. Total sales, $4400. Joint property unsold, $2200. Required the Journal entry to close the account and carry Hay's share of the deficiency to his account.

EXERCISES IN DISCOUNTING BUSINESS PAPER.

Ex. 1. Received Hall Smith's note for $1200, dated August 31, 1867, at 6 months, endorsed by James Betts. Discounted the same December 27. Required the note, the unexpired time, and discount.

Ex. 2. Received J. W. Frost's note for $900, dated October 28, 1867, at 4 months, endorsed by W. Summer. Discounted December 13. Required the note, unexpired time, and discount.

Ex. 3. Received A. T. Howden's note for $1800, dated October 31, 1867, at 4 months, endorsed by D. Bowers. Discounted November 30. Required the note, the unexpired time, and discount.

Ex. 4. Received J. Warden's note for $1266, dated March 31, 1867, at three months, endorsed by I. N. Forner. Discounted May 31. Required the unexpired time, and discount.

Ex. 5. Received R. Manly's note for $624, dated March 30, 1867, at 3 months, endorsed by J. Carter. Discounted May 1. Required the note, the unexpired time, and discount.

Ex. 6. Received W. S. Haven's note for $1566, in my favor, dated April 30, 1867, at ninety days. Discounted June 26. Required the note, the unexpired time, and discount.

Ex. 7. Received Hay & Wood's note, in my favor, for $1824, dated August 30, 1867, at ninety days. Discounted September 30. Required the note, unexpired time, and discount.

Ex. 8. Received H. Winslow's note, in my favor, for $966, dated December 30, 1867, at ninety days. Discounted February 28. Required the note, the unexpired time, and discount.

---

* See Note 4, 1st Co. Sales, page 109.

Ex. 9. A JUDGMENT NOTE.—(January 10, p. 70.)

$3000.⁰⁰   NEW YORK, January 10, 1867.

    Thirty days after date, for value received, I promise to pay to the order of P. Duff, THREE THOUSAND DOLLARS, and in case of non-payment at maturity I hereby authorize any attorney in any court in the United States or elsewhere, to enter up judgment upon the same, without stay of execution or benefit of any exemption law, with costs and five per cent. attorney's fees for collecting.

                                THOMAS EDWARDS.

NOTE.—If the holder wishes to enter judgment on receipt of this note, leave out the clause, "and in case of non-payment at maturity."

FINAL EXAMINATION.

1. What is the fundamental rule in Double Entry Book-Keeping? (See note 1, page 26.)
2. What constitutes the distinction between Single and Double Entry? (Note 1, Bills Payable account, p. 17.)
3. How is the capital disposed of in opening books by Single Entry, in an individual business? (Note 1, p. 7.)
4. How in Double Entry? (Notes 1 and 2, Stock acct. p. 33.)
5. How is the capital disposed of in opening Partnership Books by Single Entry? (Note 2, p. 7.)
6. How in Double Entry? (Note 1, Duff's acct. p. 131.)
7. Is there any difference in the rule for conducting personal accounts in Single and Double Entry? (Notes 3 and 4, p. 7, and 3 and 4, p. 26.)
8. Is there any difference in recording Orders, Drafts, &c.? (Note 5, p. 7, and Rule 9, p. 40.)
9. What is the use of the Cash-Book? (Note 1, p. 9, and note 1, p. 53.)
10. Where are all cash transactions generally first entered? (Note 6, p. 53.)
11. What is done with the Cash-Book entries as they are transferred to the Day-Book or Journal? (Note 7, p. 53.)
12. How do we ascertain the balance of money in hand? (Note 4, p. 53.)
13. How are the Ledger titles for money received and paid exhibited? (N. 10 and 11, p. 53.)
14. How are entries made on the Day-Book? (Note 5, p. 24.)
15. What is meant by posting a Day-Book or Journal? (Note 7, p. 24.)
16. What is the first thing to be done after the Day-Book or Journal is posted? (Note 4, p. 14, and note 2, p. 32.)
17. How do the partners' accounts close after the Profit & Loss is closed into them? (Note 2, Duff's account, p. 15, and note 4, p. 130.)
18. What does the final closing entry of the partners' account represent? (Note 1, Gordon's acct. p. 15; note 1, Balance acct. p. 134.)
19. What will it represent if he draws out more than he has in the firm? (Note 2, Balance acct. p. 134.)
20. When an acct. has filled up its space, how is it continued to a new page? (Note 2, Wood's acct. p. 15, and note 1, p. 102.)
21. How does an account re-open on the same page? (Note 2, Hay's acct. p. 16, and note 2, p. 113.)
22. Upon which side of an account is the final closing entry made? (Sect. 1, p. 18.)
23. Why note the transfers on the face of the Ledger folio? (Note 6, p. 18, and note 5 Stock acct. p. 33.)
24. What are the objections to making original entries affecting the personal accounts on the Ledger, without a Day-Book entry? (Note 7, p. 18, and note 3, p. 25.)
25. What is the general rule for finding the gain or loss in Single Entry Book-Keeping? (Sect. 4, p. 18.
26. How is it found in Double Entry? (Note 4, Profit & Loss acct. p. 35.)

FINAL EXAMINATION.—PART III.

27. What balances are brought down in re-opening Single Entry books? (Note 1, p. 19.)
28. What is meant by closing an account? (Note 6, p. 23.)
29. Why not carry Expense, Commission, and Exchange directly to Profit & Loss, and avoid opening these accounts? (Note 4, p. 24, and note 3, p. 129.)
30. What is meant by checking? (Note 2, p. 32.)
31. What is the use of the Journal? (6, p. 25.)
32. How may this book be dispensed with? (6, p. 25, and 5, p. 91.)
33. What other title would better express the nature of the Stock account? (Note 1, p. 26.)
34. Why drop the ciphers in the cent column? (Note 8, p. 27.)
35. How do we show how far the Day-Book is Journalized? (7, p. 29.)
36. How do we show how far the Journal is posted into the Ledger? (6, p. 29.)
37. What is to be done when the Journal is posted? (Note 2, p. 32.)
38. What must be done before attempting to close the Ledger? (Note 3, p. 32.)
39. What is the use of the Trial Sheet? (Note 1, p. 36.)
40. All closing entries for the Balance account are written red, while Profit & Loss, and all others, are black. Why is this distinction? (Note 6, Stock acct. p. 33, and note 7, Merchandise acct. p. 33.)
41. What composes the Dr. and Cr. sides of Stock? (Notes 1 and 2, Stock acct. p. 33.)
42. What composes the Dr. and Cr. sides of Merchandise? (Notes 1 and 2, Mdse. acct. p. 33.)
43. How does this account close if all the property be sold? (Note 3, Mdse. acct. p. 33, and Rule 2, p. 99.)
44. How does it close if part of the property remain in hand? (Note 5, Mdse. acct. p. 33, and Rule 2, p. 99.)
45. What is an Inventory, and where is it entered? (1st entry, pp. 59, 61, 137, and 139.)
46. What composes the Dr. and Cr. sides of Bills Receivable account? (Note 1, Bills Rec. acct. p. 33.)
47. What does the difference between the two sides represent?
48. How does this account always close?
49. What do the Dr. and Cr. sides of the Cash account represent? (Cash acct. p. 34.)
50. What does the difference between the two sides represent?
51. How does this account always close?
52. What does the difference between the sides of Bills Payable represent? (Bills Payable acct. p. 34.)
53. How does this account always close?
54. If the Dr. side be $4000, and the Cr. side $6000, what does the difference represent?
55. How do all personal accounts close? (Hay's acct. note 2, p. 34.)
56. How do property accounts close if all or part of the property be on hand? (Case 2, Rule 2, p. 99.)
57. What do the Dr. and Cr. sides of Profit & Loss exhibit? (Profit & Loss acct. p. 35.)
58. What accounts close into it? (Note 2, Profit & Loss, p. 35; Note 1, Bell's acct. p. 132; Exchange acct. p. 133.)
59. When is this account closed, and into what account or accounts does it close? (Note 3, Profit & Loss, p. 33; Sect. 4, p. 130; Note 2, Profit & Loss, p. 134.)
60. What is Expense account Dr. for, and how does it close? (Note 1, Exchange acct. p. 133.)
61. What is the Exchange account Dr. and Cr. for, and how does it close? (Note 1, Exch. acct. p. 133.)
62. What is the Interest account Dr. and Cr. for, and how does it close? (Note, Interest acct. p. 168.)
63. What is the Suspended List debited for, and how does it close? (Note 6, p. 130; Note 7, p. 129; Note 1, p. 134.)
64. What is to be done when a suspended account is paid? (Note 1, Martin's acct. p. 132.)
65. What do the Dr. and Cr. sides of Balance account represent? (Balance, p. 35.)
66. If the Dr. side be $15000, and the Cr. side $10000, what does the difference represent? (Note 4, Balance acct. p. 35.)
67. If the Drs. be $8000, and Crs. $12000, what does the difference represent? (Note 3, Balance acct. p. 35.)

223

68. What precaution is necessary in closing this account? (Balance acct. p. 35, and note 4, p. 130.)
69. Where should this account be made? (Sect. 1, p. 19.)
70. What is meant by re-opening a Ledger? (Note 1, p. 113.)
71. Suppose there be not sufficient space under the old account to re-open? (Note 1, p. 113.)
72. How are the daily average sales ascertained for any given time? (Note 14, p. 36.)
73. How is the average gain per cent. ascertained upon sales of Merchandise when all is sold? (Note 15, p. 36.)
74. How if part of the Merchandise remain on hand?
75. What entry is made of an invoice of a consignment received? (Note 21, p. 41.)
76. What is the rule for keeping account of consignments received? (Rule 10, p. 41.)
77. When the property is sold, how do we find the net proceeds? (Note 25, p. 41.)
78. If the owner of this consignment draw on you on account of these sales, what account do you debit for his draft? (Note 29, p. 41.)
79. How do you keep account of property which you consign to others for sale on your own account? (Rule 11, p. 41.)
80. If you draw on the consignee on account of a consignment? (Note 31, p. 41.)
81. What are Joint Accounts? (Note 1, p. 42.)
82. What title does the manager of a joint speculation give the account in his books? (Note 4, p. 42.)
83. What title do the silent partners use in their books? (Note 9, p. 42.)
84. What is the general rule for conducting joint accounts as manager? (Rule 12, p. 43.)
85. How do the other partners keep an account of their investments in the speculation? (Note 1, 2d Co. Shipment to London, p. 111, and note 9, p. 42.)
86. How does the manager find the net proceeds when all the property is sold? (Note 1, p. 43.)
87. How if part of the property remains on hand? (Note 4, 1st Co. Sales, p. 109.)
88. How does the manager find his net gain or loss? (Note 13, p. 43, and note 3, p. 80.)
89. What is the rule for determining the maturity of an acceptance or note having its running time in days? (Note 1, p. 45.)
90. When the running time is months? (Note 3, p. 45.)
91. When will one day's advance in the date of a note give three or four days' advance in the time of payment? (Note 1, p. 46.)
92. When will one day's advance in the date give two days' advance in the maturity? (Note 2, p. 46.)
93. Upon what occasions may three or four notes, dated on different days, having the same running time in months, all become due on the same day? (Note 1, p. 47.)
94. When will two notes, dated on different days, having the same running time in months, become due on the same day? (Note 2, p. 47.)
95. What ought to be done with notes which remain in hand over due? (Note 4, p. 52.)
96. How do we enter a note on the Bill Book when received? (Note 1, p. 49.)
97. How when passed away? (Note 2, p. 49.)
98. What is the use of the Invoice Book? (Note 1, p. 58.)
99. Where is the first entry of an Invoice? (Note 3, p. 58.)
100. What particulars of an Invoice is required in the Day Book? (Note 3, p. 58.)
101. What is the use of the Sales Book? (Note 1, p. 62.)
102. When this book is not kept, where are the particulars of the sales entered? (N. 3, p. 62.)
103. How is the Commission Sales Book kept? (Note 1, p. 65.)
104. What composes its Dr. and Cr. sides? (Notes 2 and 3, p. 65.)
105. Where do the entries pass from this book? (Sect. 3, p. 66.)
106. How is the net proceeds found, and how is it disposed of when found? (N. 2, p. 66.)
107. How do you enter a re-consignment on the Commission Sales Book? (Entry Feb. 12, Commission Sales Book, p. 67.)
108. Repeat the rule for equating time on account of sales. (Rule, p. 68.)
109. Repeat the rule for the Compound Equation. (Rule, p. 116.)
110. Where do we obtain the materials for opening a new set of books in continuation of old ones? (Note 1, p. 69.)

FINAL EXAMINATION.—PART III.

111. How can a new set of books be opened from old ones without passing the contents through the Day Book and Journal? (Sect. 3. p. 19.)
112. What is the general rule for correcting errors in the Ledger? (Notes 2 and 5, p. 98.)
113. What is the general rule for correcting errors in the Journal? (Notes 10 and 2, p. 98.)
114. How are errors corrected in the Day Book? (Notes 11 and 2, p. 98.)
115. What precaution is necessary in indexing accounts? (Note 1. p. 100.)
116. Where do we obtain the particulars for an account current? (Note 3, p. 114.)
117. Where do we obtain the particulars for an account of sales? (Note 1, p. 117.)
118. How are the Cash and Merchandise accounts posted from the six-column Day-Book or Journal? (Note 7, p. 124, and note 2, p. 161.)
119. How can the Merchandise Drs. be posted direct from the Invoice Book? (N. 4, p. 139.)
120. How may the Merchandise Crs. be posted from the Sales Book? (Note 2, p. 142.)
121. What is the use of the Private Ledger? (Note 1, p. 173.)
122. What accounts are kept in it? (Pages 173 and 174.)
123. What is the rule for settling interest on partners' capital? (Page 180.)
124. What is the rule for casting 1 and 10 per cent. commission? (Rule, p. 199.)
125. How are the intermediate rates found?
126. What is the rule for finding interest at 6 per cent. for months? (Rule, p. 199.)
127. What is the shortest rule for finding it for 60 days? (Rule, p. 200.)
128. What for 6 days?
129. What if the rate be over or under 6 per cent.?
130. What is the mercantile rule for settling interest on running accounts? (Rule, p. 201.)
131. What rule is adopted in the United States Courts? (Rule, p. 201.)
132. What is the rule for working storage equations? (Rule, p. 208.)
133. What is the rule for ascertaining general average? (Rule, p. 211.)
134. Repeat the rule for dividing profits in proportion to time and amount of capital. (Rule, p. 216.)

DUFF'S BOOK-KEEPING.

PART IV.

JOINT STOCK ACCOUNTS,

ILLUSTRATED IN A COMPLETE SET OF

NATIONAL BANK BOOKS:

AND ONE SET OF

RAILROAD BOOKS.

TO WHICH IS ADDED A FULL SET OF

PRIVATE BANKER'S BOOKS.

INTRODUCTORY REMARKS.

In the following set of National Bank Books, we present all the practical details of the first six months' business, from the preliminary proceedings of the originators of the company, down to the declaration of the first dividend. The exercises are such as will guide the accountant in opening, conducting, and closing Joint Stock Books of any kind.

We have given explanatory notes wherever we deemed them necessary for the learner's information; but for the rules and principles of the science he must refer to the early part of the work, where he will find them minutely explained, and where every one ought to commence the study of it.

In the transactions recorded in Foreign Bills of Exchange we have to acknowledge our obligations to Messrs. JAMES G. KING & SONS, Bankers of New York, for valuable information promptly and courteously afforded us in matters upon which we could obtain no information from other Banks, as but few Joint Stock Banks in New York do any direct business with foreign countries.

We have arranged the forms of the following set for posting by three different methods, viz. :—

FIRST.—By Journalizing the contents of the General Cash Book.

SECOND.—By constructing the General Cash Book so as to admit of direct posting from it to the Ledger.

THIRD.—We have arranged the Ledger Titles upon the Receiving and Paying Teller's Cash Books in such form as to admit of direct daily posting from those books to the Ledger without the intervention of either a Journal or General Cash Book, introducing the greatest abridgment that the process will admit of.

For obvious reasons, we have made no entries of the present premiums upon Gold.

228

MINUTE BOOK.

CITY NATIONAL BANK.

DECEMBER, 1866.

1. This book is a journal of the preliminary proceedings of the Company. We have not continued it after the general business of the Bank commenced. After that date there is but little to record but the date and names of the members present at each meeting. The book is usually in the charge of the Cashier.

MINUTES OF THE BOARD OF DIRECTORS OF
THE CITY NATIONAL BANK.

FIRST MEETING.

The provisional Board met at the office of John Ward, Esq., December 16th, 1866.

PRESENT.

John Ward,	Wm. B. Archer,
James Harper,	Wm. Hay,
Wm. Major,	J. C. Baker.

Mr. Ward, the acting President, stated that Article V. of the Articles of Association directs us to call a meeting of the Stockholders for the purpose of electing three additional Directors, to complete the Board, within ten days of the date when the subscription to the Capital Stock was completed. As all the stock has been subscribed, he would offer the following resolution :—

Resolved, That the subscribers to the Capital Stock of the City National Bank be notified that an election of three Directors, to complete this Board, will be held at this office on the 20th day of December, 1866, between the hours of 12 M. and 4 P.M.

Adjourned to meet on December 20th.   CHAS. P. DUFF,
                                                                    Acting Cashier.

MINUTES OF SECOND MEETING.

Office of John Ward, Esq., Thursday, December 20th, 1866.

PRESENT.

John Ward,	Wm. B. Archer,
J. C. Baker,	James Harper,
Wm. Hay,	Wm. Major.

Mr. Ward, acting President, laid before the meeting the following report of the inspectors of elections.

The undersigned, inspectors of the election of Directors for the City National Bank, hereby certify that the following statement is the true and correct number of votes given for the three Directors elected this day at the office of John Ward, Esq., by the Stockholders of the said Bank, to complete the Board of Directors for the same for the year 1867 :—

> Thomas Mitchell, 4400 votes.
> Robert Lenox,   4391 "
> Robert Banks,   3998 "
>
>   R. C. Root,
>   Richard Irvin, } Inspectors of Election.
>   Thos. B. Smith,

Sworn before me this 20th day of December, 1866.

                                        Thos. Archer, Alderman.

Mr. Harper then offered the following resolution, which was adopted :—

RESOLVED, That Thomas Mitchell, Robert Lenox, and Robert Banks, are duly elected members of this Board, and the acting Cashier is hereby directed to notify the said parties of their election.

Mr. Hay then proposed the following resolution, which was adopted :—

RESOLVED, That the Board adjourns to meet at this office on Monday, December 24th, 1866, at 2 P.M., for the purpose of electing a President and Cashier.

Adjourned.

CHAS. P. DUFF,

ACTING CASHIER.

MINUTES OF THE THIRD MEETING.

At the office of John Ward, Esq., Monday, December 24th, 1866.

PRESENT.

JOHN WARD,	WM. B. ARCHER,
JAMES HARPER,	WM. HAY,
WM. MAJOR,	J. C. BAKER,
THOMAS MITCHELL,	ROBERT LENOX,

ROBERT BANKS.

Mr. Ward stated that the Board had met for the purpose of electing Bank Officers for the year 1867. For the office of President of the Board he understood there were but two candidates, Mr. Archer and himself. He declined saying any thing of his own qualifications; but of his friend Mr. Archer, he felt it his duty to say that his long, successful, and honorable career among us as a merchant eminently fitted him for this responsible office.

Mr. Hay arose and stated that he fully agreed with Mr. Ward in his high opinion of his friend Mr. Archer; but he thought the members of the Board would agree with him in the opinion that both the candidates were eminently fitted for the office.

Mr. Lenox then moved that the Board proceed with the election. And for this purpose he nominated, as Judges, Robert Banks and Thomas Mitchell, who were accepted.

The Directors voted, as usual, by ballot, and the Judges reported

For John Ward, five votes.   For Wm. B. Archer, four votes.

Mr. Banks then announced to the Board that Mr. John Ward was duly elected President of the City National Bank for the year 1867.

The Board next proceeded to elect the Cashier.

Mr. Harper nominated Mr. Chas. P. Duff.

Mr. Lenox nominated Mr. Wm. Draper.

Upon the ballot Mr. Duff received six votes; Mr. Draper received three votes.

Whereupon Mr. Banks announced that Mr. Chas. P. Duff was duly elected Cashier of the City National Bank.

The President suggested the appointment of a committee of three to procure a suitable building for the Bank.

Mr. Ward nominated Mr. **Archer.**

Mr. Harper nominated **Mr. Hay.**

Mr. Lenox nominated **Mr. Banks.**

When the following resolution was read and adopted :—

RESOLVED, That Messrs. W. B. Archer, Wm. Hay, and Robert Banks, are hereby appointed a **committee** to procure a suitable building for a Bank, and report upon the same **at the next** meeting of the Board.

The President next recommended the **appointment of a** committee to draft By-Laws **to define the** duties and regulate **the powers of the Officers and Directors**

Mr. Major nominated Mr. **J. C. Baker.**

Mr. Mitchell nominated Mr. Robert Lenox.

Mr. Hay nominated Mr. Jas. Harper.

Whereupon the following **resolution was read** and adopted :—

RESOLVED, That **Messrs. J. C. Baker,** Robert Lenox, and James Harper, are hereby **appointed a committee to draft By-Laws for the** government of the Officers and Directors **of this Association.**

The **meeting adjourned to meet on Monday,** December 31st, 1866.

CHAS. P. DUFF,

CASHIER.

MINUTES OF THE FOURTH MEETING.

At the office of John Ward, Esq., Monday, December **31st, 1866.**

PRESENT.

THE PRESIDENT,

WM. B. ARCHER,	J. C. BAKER,
JAMES HARPER,	THOS. MITCHELL,
WM. HAY,	ROBERT LENOX,
WM. MAJOR,	ROBERT BANKS.

After reading the minutes of the last meeting, Mr. Archer, chairman of the Committee on Bank Building, reported, That, not being able to find a building that they can recommend for purchasing, the **committee** advise the Board to lease the premises No. 41 Wall Street, recently occupied as a Banking House by Messrs. Greenwood, Cox & Co. Immediate possession can be obtained at a rent of $4000 per annum, **and** the committee are of the opinion that $1400 will cover all expenses necessary **to** prepare the building for our business.

Mr. Mitchell then offered the following resolution, which was adopted :—

RESOLVED, That **the President** is hereby authorized to lease the premises No. **41** Wall Street, for a **term of five years from the** first day of January, 1867, for **the** use of this Association, and to contract for such repairs and improvements upon the same as he may deem necessary **to** fit them for our Bank, and that the expenses of all such repairs and improvements, **together** with the rents of the said premises, during the said lease, be paid out of the funds of the Bank.

Mr. **Lenox** proposed the following, which was also adopted :—

NATIONAL BANK ACCOUNTS.

RESOLVED, That the Cashier is authorized to purchase the necessary furniture, books, stationery, and such other articles as he and the President shall deem necessary to prepare the Bank for business.

The President then stated that about $300,000 of the Capital Stock had been paid in. Would it not be proper to invest a part of this amount in United States Bonds?

Whereupon Mr. Harper moved the following resolution:—

RESOLVED, That the President is hereby authorized to invest in United States Bonds such amount of the funds of this Association, now in hand, as he may deem expedient. Adopted.

Mr. Banks then proposed the following resolution, which was also adopted:—

RESOLVED, That the third instalment of 50 per cent. of the Capital Stock of this Association shall be due and payable on the 10th day of January next ensuing, and that the Cashier notify the subscribers of the same.

Mr. J. C. Baker, from the Committee on By-Laws, presented their report, which was read, adopted, and ordered to be engrossed in a suitable book for reference by the Directors and Officers.

Mr. Banks stated that the repairs of the Banking rooms could no doubt be so far completed as to admit of holding their next meeting in them; Therefore,

RESOLVED, That the Board shall meet at their Bank, No. 41 Wall Street, on the 5th day of January next, at 12 M., for the purpose of appointing clerks, &c. Passed.

Adjourned.

CHAS. P. DUFF,
CASHIER.

MINUTES OF THE FIFTH MEETING.

At the City National Bank, Saturday, January 5th, 1867.

PRESENT.

THE PRESIDENT,

WM. B. ARCHER,	J. C. BAKER,
JAMES HARPER,	THOMAS MITCHELL,
WM. HAY,	ROBERT LENOX,
WM. MAJOR,	ROBERT BANKS.

The minutes of last meeting were read.

The President stated that he had leased the premises in which we are now met, for the use of the Bank, for five years from the 1st instant, for the annual rent of $4000, and that he had contracted with B. Carpenter & Co. for the necessary repairs and alterations for $1400. He also stated that he had invested $200,000 of the Bank funds in United States Five-Twenty Bonds, bearing interest at 6 per cent., which he had deposited with the Comptroller of the Currency of the United States, at Washington, as security for the issues of the Bank, as required by the "National Currency Act," which now authorizes us to commence business, which he would recommend the Board to announce at an early day; Therefore,

233

RESOLVED, That the Cashier give public notice that the City National Bank will be open for business on the 10th inst.

Mr. Archer moved that the Board now consider the appointment of General Book-keeper, Teller, &c. There were a number of applicants for each office, but he hoped the Board would deem it their duty to allow no consideration to influence these appointments but that of capability

After considering the credentials of the different applicants, the following appointments were agreed upon:—

For General Book-keeper, W. J. Parker.

For First Teller, (Paying,) J. J. Jones.

For Second Teller, (Receiving,) Geo. Dexter.

For Messenger, Simon Parry.

The Cashier was directed to apprize the parties of their appointment, and to request them to execute the necessary bonds, with sureties, to lodge with the President on or before the 10th instant.

These appointments were deemed sufficient for the business of the Bank at its commencement. Others are left until increased business requires them.

Adjourned to meet 10th instant.

CHAS. P. DUFF,
CASHIER.

MINUTES OF THE SIXTH MEETING.

At the City National Bank, Thursday, January 10th, 1867.

PRESENT.

THE PRESIDENT,

WM. B. ARCHER,	J. C. BAKER,
JAMES HARPER,	THOMAS MITCHELL,
WM. HAY,	ROBERT LENOX,
WM. MAJOR,	ROBERT BANKS.

The minutes of the last meeting were read.

The President stated that the officers appointed at the last meeting had executed and lodged with him the necessary bonds, with sureties, and had entered upon their duties; and the Comptroller of the Currency having authorized us to commence business, the Bank was accordingly opened this morning.

The Offering Book was then laid before the Board, and such notes as were approved were passed.

Adjourned.

CHAS. P. DUFF,
CASHIER.

BY-LAWS OF THE CITY NATIONAL BANK,

ADOPTED DECEMBER 31, 1866.

ARTICLE I.—The Bank shall be open for general business every weekday from 10 A.M till 3 P.M., except holidays and such days as the Government appoint as public fast-days. And the Board of Directors shall meet for the transaction of their regular business every weekday from 12 M. to 1 P.M.

ARTICLE II.—The President, when present, shall preside at all the meetings of the Board. In case of his absence, a majority of the members present shall elect a President pro tem. And at all meetings of the Board the President or Cashier, with four Directors, shall constitute a quorum for the transaction of business.

ARTICLE III.—There shall be a standing committee of Two, called the Examining Committee, who shall inspect the assets of the Bank, compare them with the books, and make quarterly reports of the same to the Board. These committees are elected as follows. The President nominates a member of the Board. If this member is approved, he nominates a second, who, if approved, in turn nominates a third: the yeas and nays being taken on each nomination.

ARTICLE IV.—A book of minutes shall be kept of the meetings of the Board, recording
The names of each member present,
The resolutions adopted,
And other general business of the Board.

ARTICLE V.—The President, on entering upon his duties, must subscribe to the following oath:—"I, the undersigned, do solemnly swear (or affirm) that I will truly and faithfully administer and discharge all the duties, trusts, and obligations devolving upon me as President elect of the City National Bank of New York, and deliver the same to the custody of my successor."

ARTICLE VI.—The Cashier and Clerks employed by the Board must give such bonds and sureties, for the faithful performance of their several duties, as shall be satisfactory to the Board; these bonds to remain in the custody of the President.

ARTICLE VII.—All business transactions of the Board, the votes and opinions of members, the business of the customers of the Bank, with the state of their accounts, shall be held in the strictest confidence, and never disclosed out of the Bank, unless required in a court of justice.

ARTICLE VIII.—The Cashier shall be required to lay before the Board, at their meetings, all such statements of the affairs of the Bank as they require, in reference to
Its Liabilities and Assets.

The Liabilities as principals and **endorsers of** customers.
Discounted Notes **on** hand.
Discounted **Notes under protest.**
Overdrafts **of Depositors.**
Notes **of** the **Bank in** circulation.
Deposits **on hand.**
Specie on hand.
To register all notes put in circulation.
To check the Tellers' Books and balances.
To report promptly all delinquencies **connected with the Bank.**

ARTICLE IX.—The Cashier shall pay all the expenses of the Bank, and report the same to the Board monthly.

ARTICLE X.—In granting loans to individuals on collateral security, the vote of the members present shall decide the acceptance or rejection of the application. If there be a tie, the President may give the casting vote. When he deems the security unexceptionable, the President may discount business-paper between the meetings of the Board, to an amount not exceeding $10,000 ; and he may purchase Foreign Bills of Exchange of undoubted security, to an amount not exceeding $50,000; but he must report all such transactions to the Directors at their next meeting. No note or draft will be accepted for discount for less than $100, and none for collection for less than $50.

ARTICLE XI.—The Board may at any time reconsider any question or resolution before it, unless the motion to reconsider be negatived by the President.

ARTICLE XII.—When any Director shall cease to own, in his own right, Ten Shares of the Capital Stock of the Bank, he shall vacate his seat at the Board, and a majority of the remaining Directors shall elect his successor.

ARTICLE XIII.—No Teller, Clerk, or Book-keeper shall be allowed to keep an account of deposit with the Bank.

ARTICLE XIV.—The following salaries shall be paid the officers and employees of the Bank for the year 1867, payable quarterly, viz.:—

To the President.............................$2000 per annum.
To the Cashier................................ 1800 "
To the General Book-keeper.............. 1500 "
To the Receiving Teller.................... 1000 "
To the Paying Teller........................ 1000 "
To the Messenger .... 600 "
$7,900

ARTICLE XV.—The foregoing By-Laws may be amended by a vote of two-thirds of the entire Board, upon one week's previous notice of the motion.

Adopted, by resolution of the Board of Directors, December 31, 1866.

ARTICLES OF ASSOCIATION.

CITY NATIONAL BANK.

1866.

237

ARTICLES OF ASSOCIATION OF THE
CITY NATIONAL BANK OF NEW YORK.

Know all men by these presents, that we who have hereunto subscribed our names and set our seals do hereby associate ourselves for the purpose of conducting the business of Banking, under the Act of Congress of the United States to provide for a National Currency, secured by pledge of United States Stocks, approved June 3d, 1864. And we hereby bind ourselves, our heirs, administrators, and assigns, to comply with all the regulations and obligations of the following articles, hereby solemnly ratifying and confirming the same as our Articles of Association.

ARTICLE I.—Our Association shall be called the CITY NATIONAL BANK, and shall be situated in the City of New York, with a Capital Stock of Six Hundred Thousand Dollars, divided into Six Thousand Shares of One Hundred Dollars each, agreeably to Section 12 of said Act of Congress.

ARTICLE II.—The first instalment of THIRTY DOLLARS on each share of the above-named Capital Stock shall be due and payable within five days after signing these articles, and the second instalment of TWENTY DOLLARS shall be due and payable within twenty days after subscribing to these articles. The dates of payment for the balance of the Capital Stock to be named by the Board of Directors, to be chosen as hereinafter prescribed, for the direction and management of our Bank. All instalments shall be payable in lawful money of the United States, or such funds as are readily convertible into the same.

ARTICLE III.—The powers and privileges conferred upon our Association by the aforesaid Act of Congress, authorize us to delegate the management of our business to Nine Directors, of whom a majority shall constitute a quorum, who are further authorized to appoint a President, Cashier, and Clerks, and to determine their salaries and their duties; and also to enact and adopt such By-Laws, not at variance with the aforesaid Act of Congress, or with any of these Articles, as they shall deem necessary for the regulation of the business of the Bank.

ARTICLE IV.—The Board of Directors shall be composed exclusively of citizens of the United States; and, agreeably to Section 9 of the aforesaid Act, no person shall be eligible to a seat in the Board who does not hold in his own name at least Ten Shares of the Capital Stock; and we hereby nominate and appoint the following parties as a Provisional Board of Directors, leaving the remaining three seats to be filled by the election of the Stockholders:—

JOHN WARD,	WM. B. ARCHER,
JAMES HARPER,	WM. HAY,
WM. MAJOR,	J. C. BAKER.

. And we further appoint the said JOHN WARD President pro tem., and CHAS. P. DUFF Cashier pro tem.

ARTICLE V.—An election to complete the Board of Directors shall be called by our said President pro tem. within ten days after the subscription to our Capital Stock is completed; and there shall be an annual election of Directors for our Association held in the City of New York on the first Monday in January; ten days' previous notice of said election to be published in two of the city daily papers. Each Stockholder shall be entitled to one vote on each share of stock held by him.

ARTICLE VI.—At their first meeting, or as soon after as practicable, the Directors shall elect by ballot one of their number as President of this Association, who shall be, and who is hereby, acknowledged as the official head of this Association; who, when present, shall preside at all meetings of the Board, and who is hereby authorized and empowered, with the consent of the said Board, to purchase and convey all such Real Estate as it may be lawful for this Company to hold; to buy, sell, and transfer stocks, bonds, and mortgages, or other property or evidences of debt, held as security or belonging to this Company, and to receive all rents, dividends, and incomes arising from the same; to invest the funds of the Company in United States Bonds, and to deposit the same with the Comptroller of the United States Currency, in the City of Washington, as security for the notes put in circulation by this Bank, and to sign all its notes so put in circulation; to sue and be sued for values claimed by or of this Company; to grant and sign Powers of Attorney for special purposes; and to perform all other acts consistent with these Articles of Association, and the aforesaid Act of Congress, that may be beneficial to this Association. And in case of the unavoidable absence of the President, the Board of Directors are hereby empowered to elect a President pro tem., who is authorized to perform all the aforesaid duties until the President can resume his office, or until a new President is elected.

ARTICLE VII.—The Directors shall appoint the Cashier, who shall keep the minutes of the meetings of the Board, countersign and register all notes issued, examine the books of the Tellers' accounts, and conduct the business of the Bank agreeably to the instructions of the Board, furnishing them at all times with such information as they may require.

ARTICLE VIII.—The Board of Directors shall require the Cashier, Tellers, and all other employees, before entering on their duties, to give bonds, with sureties satisfactory to the President, for the faithful discharge of all trusts and duties required of them.

ARTICLE IX.—The Board of Directors are authorized to appoint, from time to time, committees composed of their own body, and to empower them to transact special matters of business, and to revoke such appointments at pleasure. They are also authorized to appoint three of the Stockholders to serve as Inspectors and Judges to conduct the annual elections of Directors. But no Director can be eligible to the office of judge of elections. And we

hereby nominate and appoint R. C. ROOT, RICHARD IRVIN, and THOS. B
SMITH inspectors of our first election of Directors.

ARTICLE X.—The Cashier pro tem. shall grant receipts to the subscribers of the
Capital Stock for each instalment as paid in, such receipts to be countersigned
by the President pro tem. No Certificate of Stock shall be granted to any
subscriber until the whole amount of the subscription is paid in.

ARTICLE XI.—All Certificates of Stock shall be signed by the Cashier and the
President, and all transfers of stock shall invest the new holders with all the
rights and privileges, interests and obligations, conferred by these Articles; and
each subscriber to these Articles, in consideration of the number of shares set
aside for him or her, hereby holds himself or herself bound by these Articles
for the full amount of such shares of Capital Stock as are written opposite his
or her name, hereby binding themselves to make punctual payment of all
instalments due on the same by these Articles, or by subsequent orders of the
Board of Directors, and to pay six per cent. interest upon any instalments
that may remain overdue; and when any instalment is withheld for sixty
days, the Directors are hereby empowered and authorized to transfer, forfeit,
and sell for the benefit of this Association such share or shares, with all payments made on the same, agreeably to Section 15 of the aforesaid Act of
Congress, and to erase the name or names representing the same from the
books of the Company.

ARTICLE XII.—The Directors are authorized to pay all expenses of this Association out of the funds of the same. And for the general information of the
Stockholders, they shall make out and submit to their inspection semi-annual
statements of the Assets, Liabilities, Expenditures, and Profits, verified by the
Cashier and President; and the Directors shall declare and pay the Stockholders such dividends as they may deem proper out of the net profits of the
Company.

ARTICLE XIII.—This Association shall commence business in the month of
January in the year of our Lord One Thousand Eight Hundred and Sixty-
Seven, and shall have succession by the name designated in these Articles for
twenty years, agreeably to Section 8 of the aforesaid Act of Congress, unless
sooner dissolved by the act of the Shareholders.

ARTICLE XIV.—The Directors of this Association may at any time propose
amendments to these Articles, upon giving thirty days' notice, with a copy of
the proposed amendments, to each Stockholder; and upon the representatives
of two-thirds of the Capital Stock signing their written consent to the same,
then the said amendments shall become as binding on the Company as the
Articles above written and now adopted.

NATIONAL BANK ACCOUNTS.

We, the undersigned, subscribe to the foregoing Articles of Association of the CITY NATIONAL BANK OF NEW YORK, and for the Capital Stock of the same set opposite our names and seals at the date of subscription.

DATE.		NUMBER OF SHARES.	SHARES.	SIGNATURE AND SEAL.	RESIDENCE.
1866. Dec.	1	I subscribe for Five Hundred Shares,	500	John Ward, . . . Seal,	New York.
		I subscribe for Five Hundred Shares,	500	Jas. Harper, . . Seal,	New York.
		I subscribe for One Hundred Shares,	100	James W. Cox, . . . Seal,	New York.
		I subscribe for One Hundred Shares,	100	J. C. Baker, . . . Seal,	Jersey City.
		I subscribe for One Hundred Shares,	100	Wm. H. Duff, . . . Seal,	Pittsburgh, Pa.
		I subscribe for Two Hundred Shares,	200	Wm. Hay, . . . Seal,	Brooklyn.
		We subscribe for Three Hundred Shares	300	Barclay, Hope & Co., Seal,	New York.
	5	I subscribe for Fifty Shares, . . .	50	Harriet Lenox, . Seal,	New York.
		I subscribe for One Hundred Shares,	100	Robert Lenox, . . Seal,	New York.
		I subscribe for Two Thousand Shares,	2000	W. B. Archer, . . Seal,	New York.
		I subscribe for One Hundred Shares,	100	R. C. Root, ... Seal,	New York.
	10	I subscribe for One Hundred Shares,	100	P. Duff, ... Seal,	Pittsburgh, Pa.
		I subscribe for Twenty Shares, . .	20	Wm. Draper, . . Seal,	Buffalo, N. Y.
		I subscribe for Thirty Shares, . . .	30	James R. Compton, Seal,	Lockport, N. Y.
		I subscribe for One Hundred Shares,	100	Samuel Warren, Seal,	Brooklyn.
		I subscribe for Six Hundred Shares,	600	Robert Banks, Seal,	Jersey City.
		We subscribe for One Hundred Shares,	100	Richard Irvin & Co., Seal,	New York.
		I subscribe for Five Hundred Shares,	500	Thos. Mitchell, . . Seal,	New York.
		I subscribe for One Hundred Shares,	100	Thos. B. Smith, . . Seal,	New York.
		I subscribe for One Hundred Shares,	100	James Harper, . . Seal,	New York.
		I subscribe for Three Hundred Shares,	300	Wm. Major, . . . Seal,	Brooklyn.
			6000		

In witness to the foregoing subscriptions and signatures, we, the undersigned, hereunto set our hands and seals, in the City of New York, this tenth day of December, A.D. 1866.

JOHN WARD, President pro tem.   Seal.

CHAS. P. DUFF, Cashier pro tem.   Seal.

Q

241

INSTALMENT No. 1.

Subscribers to the Capital Stock of the CITY NATIONAL BANK. Thirty Dollars per share due December 1st to 15th, 1866. Agreeably to Articles of Association, Article II.

WHEN DUE.	WHEN REC'D.	SUBSCRIBERS' NAMES.	SHARES.	INSTALMENT.	INT.	AMOUNT REC'D.	
1866. Dec. 6	1866. Dec. 1	Barclay, Hope & Co., . .	300	9000		9000	
6	5	John Ward, ...	500	15000		15000	
6	5	James Harper, ...	500	15000		15000	
6	5	Jas. W. Cox, ...	100	3000		3000	
6	5	J. C. Baker, ...	100	3000		3000	
6	6	Wm. H. Duff, . . .	100	3000		3000	
6	9	Wm. Hay, ...	200	6000	3	6003	
10	10	Harriet Lenox, . . .	50	1500		1500	
10	10	Robert Lenox, ...	100	3000		3000	
10	10	Wm. B. Archer, . . .	2000	60000		60000	
10	10	R. C. Root, ...	100	3000		3000	
15	15	P. Duff, ...	100	3000		3000	
15	15	Wm. Draper, . . .	20	600		600	
15	15	Jas. R. Compton, . .	30	900		900	
15	15	Samuel Warren, .	100	3000		3000	
15	15	Robert Banks, . . .	600	18000		18000	
15	15	Richard Irvin & Co., .	100	3000		3000	
15	15	Thos. Mitchell, . . .	500	15000		15000	
15	18	Thos. B. Smith.	100	3000	1 50	3001 50	
15	18	James Harper, . . .	100	3000	1 50	3001 50	
15	18	Wm. Major, ...	300	9000	4 50	9004 50	
			6000	180000	10 50		
		Interest, . . .		10 50			
				180010 50		180010 50	
		Dec. 1 Ent'd Cash Book 1		9000			
		5 " " " 1		36000			
		6 " " " 1		3000			
		9 " " " 1		6000			
		10 " " " 1		67500			
		15 " " " 1		43500			
		18 " " " 1		15000			
		" " " 1		10 50			
				180010 50			

INSTALMENT No. 2.

Subscribers to the Capital Stock of the CITY NATIONAL BANK. Twenty Dollars per share due December 21st to 31st, 1866. Agreeably to Articles of Association, Article II.

WHEN DUE.	WHEN REC'D		SUBSCRIBERS' NAMES.	SHARES.	INSTALMENT.	INT.	AMOUNT REC'D.
1866. Dec. 21	1866. Dec.	19	John Ward, .	500	10000		10000
21		19	James Harper, . .	500	10000		10000
21		19	Jas. W. Cox, ...	100	2000		2000
21		21	J. C. Baker, ...	100	2000		2000
21		21	Wm. H. Duff, ...	100	2000		2000
21		21	Wm. Hay, ...	200	4000		4000
21		27	Barclay, Hope & Co., .	300	6000	6	6006
25		25	Harriet Lenox, . . .	50	1000		1000
25		25	Robert Lenox, . . .	100	2000		2000
25		28	Wm. B. Archer, . .	2000	40000	20	40020
25		25	R. C. Root, ...	100	2000		2000
30		28	P. Duff, ...	100	2000		2000
30		28	Wm. Draper, .	20	400		400
30		28	Jas. R. Compton, . .	30	600		600
30		30	Samuel Warren, . .	100	2000		2000
30		31	Robert Banks, . . .	600	12000	2	12002
30		30	Richard Irvin & Co., .	100	2000		2000
30		30	Thomas Mitchell, . .	500	10000		10000
30		30	Thos. B. Smith, . .	100	2000		2000
30		30	James Harper, . . .	100	2000		2000
30		30	Wm. Major, ...	300	6000		6000
				6000	120000	28	
			Interest,		28		
					120028		120028
			Dec. 19 Ent'd Cash Book 1		22000		
			21 " " " 1		8000		
			25 " " " 1		5000		
			27 " " " 1		6000		
			28 " " " 1		43000		
			30 " " " 1		24000		
			31 " " " 1		12000		
			• " " " 1		28		
					120028		

INSTALMENT No. 3.

Subscribers to the Capital Stock of the CITY NATIONAL BANK. Fifty Dollars per share due January 10th, 1867. Agreeably to resolution of the Board of Directors, passed December 31st, 1866.

When Due.		When Rec'd.		Subscribers' Names.	Shares.	Instalment.	Int.	Amount Rec'd.
1867. Jan.	10	1867. Jan.	9	John Ward, ...	500	25000		25000
	10		9	James Harper, . . .	600	30000		30000
	10		9	Jas. W. Cox, ...	100	5000		5000
	10		9	J. C. Baker, ...	100	5000		5000
	10		9	W. H. Duff, ...	100	5000		5000
	10		9	Wm. Hay, ...	200	10000		10000
	10		9	Barclay, Hope & Co., . .	300	15000		15000
	10		9	Harriet Lenox, ...	50	2500		2500
	10		9	Robert Lenox, ...	100	5000		5000
	10		10	Wm. B. Archer, . . .	2000	100000		100000
	10		10	R. C. Root, ...	100	5000		5000
	10		10	P. Duff, ...	100	5000		5000
	10		10	Wm. Draper, ...	20	1000		1000
	10		10	Jas. R. Compton,. . .	30	1500		1500
	10		10	Samuel Warren, . . .	100	5000		5000
	10		10	Robert Banks, . . .	600	30000		30000
	10		10	Richard Irvin & Co., . .	100	5000		5000
	10		10	Thomas Mitchell, . .	500	25000		25000
	10		10	Thomas B. Smith, . . .	100	5000		5000
	10		10	Wm. Major, ...	300	15000		15000
					6000	300000		300000
				Jan. 9 Ent'd Cash Book 1		102500		
				10 " " " 1		197500		
						300000		

244

Instalment Scrip

Instalment Scrip No. 1.

Dated Dec. 5, 1866.

City National Bank.

500 Shares of $100 each.

$15,000.

First Instalment, 30 per cent.

Received Receipt for same,

James Harper.

(No. 1.) Instalment Scrip No. 1.

$15,000.

Stamp.

Received of James Harper, Wm. H. Duff, Thousand Dollars, being Thirty Dollars for share and the First instalment on Five Hundred Shares of the

CAPITAL STOCK OF THE CITY NATIONAL BANK.

The said shares received and set apart for him or his assigns, on condition that he at any forfeit this letter of subscription.

In Witness Whereof, We herewith subscribe our names, in the City of New York, this 6th day of December, One Thousand Eight Hundred and Thirty-Six.

Chas. D. Duff, CASHIER.   John Wead, PRESIDENT.

City National Bank of New York.

500 Shares,
OF $100 each.

Stock Certificate

City National Bank

No. 5.   Stock Certificate   No. 5.

Stock Certificate No. 5.

Issued to Wm. H. Duff.

For 100 Shares.

Dated Jan. 9, 1867.

Received this Certificate,
Wm. H. Duff.

Stamp.

CAPITAL STOCK.
$600,000.

CITY NATIONAL BANK OF NEW YORK.

We hereby certify that William H. Duff is entitled to One Hundred Shares, of One Hundred Dollars each, in the Capital Stock of the City National Bank, transferable only on the Books of the said Bank by him or his lawful attorney, on surrender of this Certificate.

In Witness Whereof, We have hereunto affixed our signatures, in the City of New York, this 9th day of January, in the year of our Lord One Thousand Eight Hundred and Sixty-Seven.

Chas. D. Duff, CASHIER.   John Wead, PRESIDENT.

NUMBER OF SHARES
6,000,
OF $100 Each.

---

1. The book of Instalment Scrip exhibits the numbers and particulars of the Instalment receipts.
2. When the stock is all paid in, these receipts are exchanged for Certificate of Stock at the terms following:
3. When the Stock is transferred, the old Certificate is given up, and a new one issued.

245

THE TRANSFER BOOK.

The Stockholder fills up and signs the order for transferring the whole or part of his Stock. Post-mark in the left column

10 Shares.

New York, March 16th, 1867.

For value received, I hereby assign and transfer to George R. Duncan all my right, title, and interest in Ten Shares of the Capital Stock of the City National Bank, standing in my name on the Books of the said Bank.

WITNESS:
Chas. P. Duff.

James R. Compton.

L.F.	March 16th, 1867.
	FROM
✓	James R. Compton.
	TO
✓	George R. Duncan.
✓	10 Shares of $100 each. $1000
	No. of Certificates.
	CANCELLED. ISSUED.

20 Shares.

New York, April 15th, 1867.

For value received, I hereby assign and transfer to George R. Duncan all my right, title, and interest in Twenty Shares of the Capital Stock of the City National Bank, standing in my name on the Books of the said Bank.

WITNESS:
Chas. P. Duff.

William Draper.

L.F.	April 15th, 1867.
	FROM
✓	William Draper.
	TO
✓	George R. Duncan.
✓	20 Shares of $100 each. $2000
	No. of Certificates.
	CANCELLED. ISSUED.

NOTE.—When Stock is transferred by an attorney, his authority to do so must be lodged with the Bank. (See form p. 252.)

CITY NATIONAL BANK,

GENERAL CASH-BOOK,

1867.

1. All receipts and payments preceding the commencement of general business are first recorded in this book. Afterwards it is made up from the Receiving and Paying Tellers' Cash Books. In a large business it ought to be journalized and balanced daily, and its balance must agree with the balance of money in the vault, and in the Tellers' hands, consisting of

Notes of other Banks,
Checks on other Banks,
Treasury Notes,
Specie, and
Our own Notes in hand, used as money.

2. In our Private Banker's accounts, we shall exhibit this book posted direct to the General Ledger, which may be done in any banking business. But we think the Journal will make this set more easily understood by the student. When it is to be posted direct to the Ledger, the form of our Private Banker's book is preferable. See p. 352.

1866. Dec.					
Dec.	1	Capital Stock	Received on First Instalment	9000	
	5	" "	" " "	36000	
	6	" "	" " "	3000	
	9	" "	" " "	6000	
	10	" "	" " "	67500	
	15	" "	" " "	43500	
	18	" "	" " "	15000	
		Discount and Interest	" on past due Instalments	10	50
	19	Capital Stock	" Second Instalment	22000	
	21	" "	" " "	8000	
	25	" "	" " "	5000	
	27	" "	" " "	6000	
	28	" "	" " "	43000	
	30	" "	" " "	24000	
	31	" "	" " "	12000	
1867. Jan.		Discount and Interest	" on past due Instalments	28	
Jan.	9	Capital Stock	" Third Instalment	102500	
	10	" "	" " "	197500	
				600038	50
			Balance bro't down	399238	50
Jan.	10	Depositors	Per Receiving Teller's C. B.	12300	
		Iron City National Bank	" " "	1000	
		1st National Bank, Chicago	" " "	1500	
		1st Nat. Bank New Orleans	" " "	500	
		Circulation	" " "	160000	
				574538	50
			Balance bro't down	218471	84
Feb.	15	Circulation	Per Receiving Teller's C. B.	232000	
		Bills discounted	" " "	7900	
		Depositors	" " "	21164	
		Exchange	" " "	136	
				479671	84
			Balance bro't down	353071	84
Mar.	16	Circulation	Per Receiving Teller's C. B.	88000	
		Bills Discounted	" " " ,	18600	
		Depositors	" " "	6800	
		1st Nat. Bank, New Orleans	" " "	1200	
		1st Nat. Bank, Chicago	" " "	1600	
		Iron City Nat. Bank	" " "	1200	
				470471	84

Date		Account	Description	Dollars	Cts
1866. Dec.	5	Expense	P'd Root, Anthony & Co., for Stationery	150	
1867. Jan.	2	"	P'd Times & Tribune, Advertising	50	
Jan.	2	United States Bonds	" for 200 5/20 Bonds of $1000 each	200000	
	3	Bank Furniture	P'd Ashley & Son's bill	600	
	10		Balance to n/a	399238	50
				600038	50
Jan.	10	Depositors	Per Paying Teller's C. B.	7900	
		1st Nat. Bank, Chicago	" " "	500	
		1st " " New Orleans	" " "	1000	
		Foreign Bills of Exchange	" " "	44444	44
		Exchange	" " "	2222	22
		United States Bonds	" " "	300000	
			Balance to n/a	218471	84
				574538	50
Feb.	15	Depositors	Per Paying Teller's C. B.	18600	
		United States Bonds	" " "	100000	
		Iron City Nat. Bank	" " "	3564	
		1st Nat. Bank, Chicago	" " "	792	
		1st Nat. Bank, New Orleans	" " "	3528	
		Exchange	" " "	116	
			Balance to n/a	353071	84
				479671	84
Mar.	16	Depositors	Per Paying Teller's C. B.	10300	
		1st Nat. Bank, Chicago	" " "	1188	
		1st Nat. Bank, New Orleans	" " "	2352	
		Iron City Nat. Bank	" " "	1782	
		Foreign Bills of Exchange	" " "	22222	22
		Exchange	" " "	1189	11
			Balance carried forward	431438	51
				470471	84

1867.					
			Bal. bro't forward	431438	51
Apr.	15	Bills Discounted	Per Receiving Teller's C. B.	7200	
		Depositors	" " "	51100	
		1st Nat. Bank, New Orleans	" " "	8000	
		Iron City Nat. Bank	" " "	2000	
		1st Nat. Bank, Chicago	" " "	4000	
		Baring Bros. & Co.	" " "	26666	67
		Exchange	" " "	2666	67
			Certified Check unpaid	800	
				533871	85
			Balance bro't down	500606	85
May	14	Depositors	Per Receiving Teller's C. B.	12788	
		Discount and Interest	" " "	18000	
		Baring Bros. & Co.	" " "	40000	
		Exchange	" " "	4112	
		Iron City Nat. Bank	" " "	2	
		Bills Discounted	" " "	5700	
		1st Nat. Bank, Chicago	" " "	6900	
		1st Nat. Bank, Boston	" " "	2394	
				590502	85
			Balance bro't down	576799	10
June	12	Depositors	Per Receiving Teller's C. B.	18984	
		Baring Bros. & Co.	" " ".	20003	50
		Exchange	" " "	2116	
		Profit and Loss	" " "	2000	
		Discount and Interest	" " "	204	94
				620107	54
			Balance bro't down	603847	54

1867.						
Apr.	15	Circulation	Per Paying Teller's C. B.		500	
		Foreign Bills of Exchange	" " "		20000	
		Exchange	" " "		1290	
		Depositors	" " "		8500	
		Expense	" " "		2975	
			Balance to n/a		500606	85
					533871	85
			Certified Check out*		800	
May	14	Depositors	Per Paying Teller's C. B.		4903	75
		Iron City Nat. Bank	" " "		1980	
		Bank of Montreal	" " "		3564	
		1st Nat. Bank, Boston	" " "		2394	
		Exchange	" " "		62	
			Balance to n/a		576799	10
					590502	85
June	12	Depositors	Per Paying Teller's C. B.		8300	
		Iron City Nat. Bank	" " "		2772	
		1st Nat. Bank, Chicago	" " "		2970	
		Foreign Bills of Exchange	" " "		2000	
		Exchange	" " "		218	
			Balance to n/a		603847	54
					620107	54

* Checks are certified with the understanding that they are to be immediately paid into another bank, which will present them promptly for payment. If the holder uses his check for a distant remittance, if unpaid at the time of balancing this book it must be re-entered, as in this case.

FORM OF A POWER OF ATTORNEY TO TRANSFER STOCK.

For Value Received .... *hereby constitute and appoint irrevocably*

.... *true and lawful attorney for* ....

and in .... *name to transfer to* ....

....

.... *Shares in the Capital Stock of the*

CITY NATIONAL BANK OF NEW YORK.

Witness .... *hand and seal this* .... *day of* .... *18* ......

Witness present. .... (SEAL)

....

LETTER OF AUTHORITY TO SIGN BUSINESS PAPER.

NEW YORK, June 30, 1867.

SIR :—I have to-day authorized my Book-keeper, Mr. F. L. Rainbow, to sign my name to Promissory Notes, Checks, and Drafts; also, in like manner, to use my signature in accepting Orders, Drafts, and Bills of Exchange; also, in endorsing Promissory Notes, Checks, Drafts, and Bills of Exchange.

Very respectfully, yours,

W. B. ARCHER.

To the Cashier City National Bank, }
         New York. }

The above authority must, in every case, be strictly observed in form and extent, otherwise the validity of the act may be endangered.

JOURNAL,

CITY NATIONAL BANK,

JANUARY, 1867.

Although banks do not generally keep this book, we retain it to enable the uninitiated to understand more readily the process of arranging the contents of so many books for the General Ledger. When this book is kept, the General Ledger receives no entries from any other book.

1	Cash, Dr. To Sundries, per Gen'l. C. B. 1	300038	50		
1	To Capital Stock			300000	
3	" Discount & Interest . . .			38	50
	"				
3	Expense, Dr., . . .	200			
1	To Cash, per Gen'l. C. B. 1 . .			200	

Jan. 10, 1867.

1	Cash, Dr., per Gen'l. C. B. 1 .	300000			
1	To Capital Stock . .			300000	
	"				
1	Sundries, Dr. To Cash, per Gen'l. C. B. 1 .			200600	
1	United States Bonds . . .	200000			
2	Bank Furniture . . .	600			
	"				
1	Cash, Dr. To Sundries, per Gen'l. C. B. 1 . .	15300			
2	To Depositors			12300	
4	" Iron City Nat. Bank . . .			1000	
4	" First Nat. Bank, Chicago . .			1500	
4	" First Nat. Bank, New Orleans .			500	
	"				
1	Sundries, Dr. To Cash, per Gen'l. C. B. 1			56066	66
2	Depositors . .	7900			
4	First Nat. Bank, Chicago . .	500			
4	First Nat. Bank, New Orleans .	1000			
2	Foreign Bills of Exchange .	44444	44		
3	Exchange . . .	2222	22		
	"				
2	Bills Discounted, Dr. To Sundries, D. B. 1 .	12100			
2	To Depositors . . .			11958	87
3	" Discount & Interest . . .			89	13
3	" Exchange . . .			52	
	"				
1	Cash, Dr., per Gen'l. C. B. 1	160000			
3	To Circulation . . .			160000	
	"				
1	United States Bonds, Dr. .	300000			
1	To Cash, per Gen'l. C. B. 1			300000	

12.

4	Baring Brothers & Co., Dr.	44444	44		
2	To Foreign Bills of Exchange for Brown Brothers & Co., on G. Peabody . £10000 St'g.			44444	44

Feb. 15.

1	Cash. Dr. To Sundries, per Gen'l. C. B. 1 . .	261200			
3	To Circulation . . .			232000	
2	" Bills Discounted . .			7900	
2	" Depositors .			21164	
3	" Exchange .			136	
	"				
1	Sundries, Dr. To Cash, per Gen'l. C. B. 1			126600	
2	Depositors . . .	18600			
1	U. S. Bonds	100000			
4	Iron City Nat. Bank	3564			
4	First Nat. Bank, Chicago	792			
4	First Nat. Bank, New Orleans	3528			
3	Exchange . . .	116			

2	Bills Discounted, Dr. To Sundries, per D. B. 1 .	14400			
2	To Depositors			14267	60
3	" Discount & Interest			66	40
3	" Exchange			66	

March 16.

1	Cash, Dr. To Sundries, per Gen'l. C. B. 1 .	117400			
3	To Circulation			88000	
2	" Bills Discounted			18600	
2	" Depositors			6800	
4	" First Nat. Bank, New Orleans			1200	
4	" First Nat. Bank, Chicago			1600	
4	" Iron City Nat. Bank			1200	
1	Sundries, Dr. To Cash, per Gen'l. C. B. 1			39033	33
2	Depositors	10300			
4	First Nat. Bank, Chicago	1188			
4	First Nat. Bank, New Orleans .	2352			
4	Iron City Nat. Bank	1782			
2	Foreign Bills of Exchange	22222	22		
3	Exchange	1189	11		
2	Bills Discounted, Dr. To Sundries, per D. B. 1 .	7200			
2	To Depositors			7164	
3	" Discount & Interest .			36	
4	Baring Bros. & Co., Dr.	22222	22		
2	To Foreign Bills of Exchange, for Pollock & Gilmore, on R. Rankin & Co. . £5000 St'g.			22222	22

April 15.

1	Cash, Dr. To Sundries, per Gen'l. C. B. 2	101633	34		
2	To Bills Discounted			7200	
2	" Depositors			51100	
4	" First Nat. Bank, New Orleans			8000	
4	" First Nat. Bank, Chicago			4000	
4	" Iron City Nat. Bank			2000	
4	" Baring Bros. & Co.			26666	67
3	" Exchange .			2666	67
1	Sundries, Dr. To Cash, per Gen'l. C. B. 2			33265	
3	Circulation	500			
2	Foreign Bills of Exchange .	20000			
3	Exchange	1290			
2	Depositors	8500			
3	Expense	2975			
2	Bills Discounted, Dr. To Sundries, D. B. 1	7300			
2	To Depositors			7253	12
3	" Discount & Interest			34	88
3	" Exchange .			12	
4	Baring Brothers and Co., Dr.	20000			
2	To Foreign Bills of Exchange, for Betts & Turner, on Bold & Starkey . £4500 St'g.			20000	

1	Cash, Dr. To Sundries, per Gen'l. C. B. 2.		89896		
2	To Depositors			12788	
3	" Discount & Interest			18000	
4	" Baring Bros. & Co.			40000	
3	" Exchange			4112	
4	" Iron City Bank			2	
2	" Bills Discounted			5700	
4	" First Nat. Bank, Chicago			6900	
4	" First Nat. Bank, Boston			2394	
	"				
1	Sundries, Dr. To Cash, per Gen'l. C. B. 2			12903	75
2	Depositors		4903	75	
4	Iron City Nat. Bank		1980		
4	Bank of Montreal		3564		
4	First Nat. Bank, Boston		2394		
3	Exchange		62		
	"				
2	Bills Discounted, Dr. To Sundries, per D. B. 2		6200		
2	To Depositors			6062	30
3	" Discount & Interest			87	70
3	" Exchange			50	

June 12.

4	Baring Brothers & Co., Dr.		2000		
2	To Foreign Bills of Exchange, for Dyer & Morgan, on Swainson & Willis £450 St'g.			2000	
	"				
1	Cash, Dr. To Sundries, per Gen'l. C. B. 2		43308	44	
2	To Depositors			18984	
2	" Baring Brothers & Co.			20003	50
3	" Exchange			2116	
5	" Profit & Loss			2000	
3	" Discount & Interest			204	94
	"				
1	Sundries, Dr. To Cash, per Gen'l. C. B. 2			16260	
2	Depositors		8300		
4	Iron City Nat. Bank		2772		
4	First Nat. Bank, Chicago		2970		
2	Foreign Bills of Exchange		2000		
3	Exchange		218		
	"				
2	Bills Discounted, Dr. To Sundries, D. B. 2		9200		
2	To Depositors			9014	77
3	" Discount & Interest			167	23
3	" Exchange			18	

STOCK LEDGER,

CITY NATIONAL BANK,

1867.

1. This book records nothing but the number of Shares of the Capital Stock of the Company held by each shareholder, and the instalments that he has paid upon them. The entries are first obtained from the Instalment List. When transfers afterwards take place. they are posted to this Ledger from the Transfer Book.

2. The aggregate credits of this Ledger must always agree with the credit of the "Capital Stock" account in the General Ledger.

3. Keeping these accounts in alphabetical order enables us more easily to keep them so on the Dividend List.

R   257

I Dr.   **WM. B.**   **ARCHER.**   Cr.

				Shs.						Shs.	
						1866. Dec. 1867. Jan.	10 28 10	1st Instalment 2d " 3d "	2000	60000 40000 100000

J. C.   **BAKER.**

					1866. Dec. 1867. Jan.	5 21 9	1st Instalment 2d " 3d "	100	3000 2000 5000

BARCLAY,   **HOPE & CO.**

					1866. Dec. 1867. Jan.	1 27 9	1st Instalment 2d " 3d "	300	9000 6000 15000

ROBT.   **BANKS.**

					1866. Dec. 1867. Jan.	15 31 10	1st Instalment 2d " 3d "	600	18000 12000 30000

J. W.   **COX.**

					1866. Dec. 1867. Jan.	5 19 9	1st Instalment 2d " 3d "	100	3000 2000 5000

J. R.   **COMPTON.**

1867. Mar.	16	G. R. Duncan	10	1000	1866. Dec. 1867. Jan.	15 28 10	1st Instalment 2d " 3d "	30	900 660 1500

WILLIAM   **DRAPER.**

1866. Apr.	15	G. R. Duncan	20	2000	1866. Dec. 1867. Jan.	15 28 10	1st Instalment 2d " 3d "	20	600 400 1000
				2000					2000

GEO. R.   **DUNCAN.**

					1867. Mar. Apr.	16 15	J. R. Compton Wm. Draper	10 20	1000 2000

						Shs.	
		1866. Dec.	15	1st	Instalment	100	3000
		1867.	28	2d	"		2000
		Jan.	10	3d	"		5000

WM. H.   DUFF.

		1866. Dec.	6	1st	Instalment	100	3000
		1867.	21	2d	"		2000
		Jan.	9	3d	"		5000

JAMES   HARPER.

		1866. Dec.	5	1st	Instalment	500	15000
			18	1st	"	100	3000
			19	2d	"		10000
		1867.	30	2d	"		2000
		Jan.	9	3d	"		30000

WM.   HAY.

		1866. Dec.	9	1st	Instalment	200	6000
		1867.	21	2d	"		4000
		Jan.	9	3d	"		10000

RICHARD   IRVIN & CO.

		1866. Dec.	15	1st	Instalment	100	3000
		1867.	30	2d			2000
		Jan.	10	3d			5000

HARRIET   LENOX.

		1866. Dec.	10	1st	Instalment	50	1500
		1867.	25	2d	"		1000
		Jan.	9	3d	"		2500

ROBERT   LENOX.

		1866. Dec.	10	1st	Instalment	100	3000
		1867.	25	2d	"		2000
		Jan.	9	3d	"		5000

								Shs.	
					1866.				
					Dec.	15	1st Instalment	500	15000
					1867.	30	2d "		10000
					Jan.	10	3d "		25000

WM.   MAJOR.

					1866.				
					Dec.	18	1st Instalment	300	9000
					1867.	30	2d "		6000
					Jan.	10	3d "		15000

R. C.   ROOT.

					1866.				
					Dec.	10	1st Instalment	100	3000
					1867.	25	2d "		2000
					Jan.	10	3d "		5000

T. B.   SMITH.

					1866.				
					Dec.	18	1st Instalment	100	3000
					1867.	30	2d "		2000
					Jan.	10	3d "		5000

JOHN   WARD.

					1866.				
					Dec.	5	1st Instalment	500	15000
					1867.	19	2d "		10000
					Jan.	9	3d "		25000

SAMUEL   WARREN.

					1866.				
					Dec.	15	1st Instalment	100	3000
					1867.	30	2d "		2000
					Jan.	10	3d "		5000

RECEIVING TELLER'S CASH BOOK,

CITY NATIONAL BANK,

JANUARY, 1867.

Upon the left page are entered all amounts for the General Ledger; upon the right page, all amounts for the Depositors' Ledger, into which each Deposit is posted as indicated by the post-marks. We have passed the amounts of both sides into the General Cash Book. By comparing this book with the General Ledger, the titles of the accounts will be found so distinctly arranged upon it as to admit of direct posting without a Journal or General Cash Book.

261

* Iron City Nat. Bank.	Rec'd Check on 1st Nat. Bk., N.Y.		1000
1st Nat. Bk., Chicago.	" Draft on 9th Nat. Bk., N.Y.		1500
1st Nat. Bk., New Orleans,	" Draft on Chemical Nat. Bk.		500
Circulation,	" of U. S. Comptroller, per B. N. R. 1		80000
Circulation,	" " " "		80000
	G. C. B. 1		163000

February

Bills Discounted,			7900
	Rec'd Gregg & Hall, No. 1	2000	
	Mount, Joy & Co. 2	1000	
	G. W. Leeds, 3	1800	
	Hay & Wood, 4	1600	
	Bateman & Hill, 6	1500	
Circulation,			232000
	" of U. S. Comptroller, B. N. R. 1	200000	
	" " " "	32000	
Exchange,	" for sundry exchanges,		136
	G. C. B. 1		240036

* When posted direct to the General Ledger, insert the pages in this column.

1	R. Irvin & Co.			1500
		Dep'd Smith on Chemical Bk.	200	
		Draft on O. H. Bliss, Chicago	500	
		Bank Notes	800	
1	R. Lenox	" Bank Notes		1200
1	R. C. Root, Anthony & Co.			1600
		" Cluley on 9th Nat. Bk.	600	
		" Bank Notes	1000	
2	John Ward			1800
		" Bank Notes	1000	
		Moore on 1st Nat. Bank	400	
		Lawson on 4th Nat. Bank	400	
2	Harriet Lenox	" Bank Notes		1000
2	Harper & Bros.			2000
		" Draft on F. J. Herron, New Orleans	1000	
		Bank Notes	1000	
3	Barclay, Hope & Co.	" Bank Notes		800
3	Duff Brothers & Co.			1000
		" Coin	500	
		Robb on 3d Nat. Bk.	500	
3	J. Carver	" Bank Notes		600
4	Ryan & Dale	" " "		800
		G. C. B. 1		12300

15, 1867.

1	R. C. Root, Anthony & Co. Dep'd Bank Notes			900
1	R. Irvin & Co.			1800
		" Brown on 1st Nat. Bk.	1100	
		Bank Notes	700	
1	R. Lenox	" " "		1400
3	Duff Bros. & Co.	" " "		1000
5	A. B. Hunter	" " "		400
2	Harper & Brothers	" " "		2500
4	Ryan & Dale			3528
		" Coll. on Bates & Bell, Pittsburgh	3600	
		Less Exchange	72	
2	Harper & Bros.			784
		Coll. on W. S. Hunter, Chicago	800	
		Less Exchange	16	
1	R. Irvin & Co.			1552
		Coll. on J. Kane, New Orleans	1600	
		Less Exchange	48	
3	Barclay, Hope & Co.	Coll. Baker & Fox, City		1600
1	R. Irvin & Co.	" Joel Post, "		2400
3	Jas. Carver	" R. S. Davis, "		1200
4	Lyon & Haven	" J. B. Marks, "		2100
		G. C. B. 1		21164

Bills Discounted				18600	
Rec'd Patterson & Wild, No. 5			1200		
J. W. Loring	7		3000		
W. Page	8		3600		
Hay & Wood	9		2400		
R. Bruce	10		1800		
Hunter & Co.	11		3300		
J. Morton	12		1200		
J. Carver	13		2100		
1st Nat. Bk., New Orleans	ʺ	Draft on Ryan & Dale		1200	
1st Nat. Bk., Chicago	ʺ	Draft on R. C. Root, Anthony & Co.		1600	
Iron City Nat. Bk.	ʺ	Draft on Harper & Bros.		1200	
Circulation				88000	
of U. S. Comptroller, B. N. R. 1			40000		
ʺ ʺ ʺ			20000		
ʺ ʺ ʺ			10000		
ʺ ʺ ʺ			10000		
ʺ ʺ ʺ			8000		
G. C. B. 1				110600	

Bills Discounted				7200	
Rec'd Day & Martin,	No. 14		1500		
Hart & Bowman,	15		2400		
Duncan, Dunlap & Co.,	16		900		
Geo. Wilde,	17		2400		
1st Nat. Bk., New Orleans	ʺ	our Draft No. 1, favor W. B. Morgan		8000	
Iron City Nat. Bank	ʺ	ʺ ʺ 2, ʺ Kramer & Rahm		2000	
Baring Bros. & Co.	ʺ	ʺ Bill ʺ 1, at 60 days' sight			
		favor R. Banks & Co. £6000 St'g		26666	67
1st Nat. Bk., Chicago	ʺ	J. Astley & Co.		4000	
Exchange	ʺ	10 % prem. for our Bill No. 1		2666	67
G. C. B. 2				50533	34

2	John Ward				1500
		Dep'd S. Hill on Union Bk.		800	
		Bank Notes		700	
2	Harriet Lenox	"	"	"	1200
3	Barclay, Hope & Co.	"	"	"	1400
5	A. B. Hunter	"	"	"	1100
5	J. W. Burnham				1600
		"	"	700	
		Jas. Wood on 1st Nat. Bk.		900	
		G. C. B. 1			6800

1	R. Lenox				3000
		Dep'd Bank Notes		1000	
		Hill on 9th Nat. Bk.		2000	
1	R. C. Root, Anthony & Co.				5000
		"	Bank Notes	3600	
		"	Mackey on Chemical Bk.	1400	
2	John Ward	"	Bank Notes		2500
2	Harriet Lenox	"	"	"	1800
2	Harper & Brothers	"	"	"	5700
3	Duff Bros. & Co.	"	"	"	6500
3	J. Carver	"	"	"	2100
4	W. B. Archer	"	"	"	10000
4	Lyon & Haven	"	"	"	4350
5	Roy, Wade & Co.	"	"	"	3700
5	J. W. Burnham	"	"	"	1950
5	R. P. Duff	Certificate of Deposit No. 1*			2100
5	H. P. Ford	"	"	" 2	2400
		G. C. B. 2			51100

* See Form, p. 274.

Discount & Interest	Rec'd for May Coupons ⅚ bonds			18000
Baring Bros. & Co.	" " Bill No. 2 @ 60 days s'gt in			40000
	favor of C. Bell, £9000 St'g			
Iron City Nat. Bank	protest on A. J. Turner, No. 8, ret'd			2
Bills Discounted				5700
	" J. Barker & Co., No. 18		2400	
	S. Lewis & Co., 20		1500	
	J. W. Bliss 21		1800	
1st Nat. Bk., Chicago				6900
	" Baker & Hill		3600	
	Porter & Dick		2100	
	W. G. Ray		1200	
1st Nat. Bk., Boston	" Draft on Chemical Bank			2394
Exchange				4112
	" 10 % prem. on Bill No. 2		4000	
	sundry exchanges		112	
	G. C. B. 2			77108

Baring Bros. & Co.,				20003	50
	Rec'd of Stacy & Evans for No. 3 ret'd	20000			
	" for protest on do	3	50		
Profit & Loss	" 10% damages on do			2000	
Discount & Interest	" Interest on do			204	94
Exchange				2116	
	" 10% premium on do	2000			
	sundry exchanges	116			
	G. C. B. 2			24324	44

1	R. C. Root, Anthony & Co.				3000
		Dep'd Bank Notes		1400	
		Coin		1600	
3	Duff Brothers & Co.				2000
		Dep'd Bank Notes		1100	
		Coin		900	
2	Harriet Lenox	" "			1100
5	G. R. Duncan	Certificate of Deposit No. 3			1200
1	R. Irvin & Co.				784
		Coll. R. Glass & Co., Pittsburgh		800	
		Less Exchange		16	
2	Harper & Bros.				1176
		Coll. W. Payson, Pittsburgh		1200	
		Less Exchange		24	
1	R. Lenox	Coll. G. Wilde & Co., Montreal	2400		3528
		" J. Carter, "	1200	3600	
		Less Exchange		72	
		G. C. B. 2			12788

12, 1867.

4	Lyon & Haven				1300
		Dep'd Coin		700	
		Bank Notes		600	
5	A. B. Hunter				1200
		" Brown on 4th Nat. Bk.		900	
		Coin		300	
3	Duff Bros. & Co.				2100
		" Coin		1200	
		Jones on Winslow, Lanier & Co.		900	
2	Harriet Lenox	" Bank Notes			1800
1	R. C. Root, Anthony & Co.				2700
		" Coll. J. L. Dixon		1600	
		" Day & Martin		1100	
1	R. Lenox				4200
		" Coll. W. Burton		2400	
		Jas. Carver		1800	
4	W. B. Archer				2744
		" Coll. C. H. Ball, Pittsburgh,	800		
		" " J. Horne, "	2000	2800	
		Less Exchange		56	
4	Lyon & Haven				2940
		" Coll. W. Baker, Chicago		3000	
		Less Exchange		60	
		G. C. B. 2			18984

REGISTER OF SIGNATURES.

Date.	Name.	Place of Business.	Witness.
1867.			
	A.		
Jan. 10	W B. Archer	City	J. J. Jones.*
	B.		
Jan. 10	Barclay, Hope & Co., by A. C. Barclay . .	City	
Mar. 16	J W Burnham	"	
	C.		
Jan. 10	James Carver	City	
	D.		
Jan. 10	Duff Brothers & Co., by Wm. H. Duff . . .	City	
	Duff Brothers & Co., " T. C. Duff	"	
	Duff Brothers & Co., " R. P. Duff	"	
	H.		
Jan. 10	Harper & Brothers, by John Harper . . .	City	
	Harper & Brothers, " James Harper	"	
	I.		
Jan. 10	Richard Irvin & Co., by R. Irvin	City	
	L.		
Jan 10	Lyon & Haven, by Wm. M. Lyon	City	
	Lyon & Haven, " J. W. Haven	"	
	Robert Lenox	"	
	Harriet Lenox	"	
	R.		
Jan. 10	R. C. Root, Anthony & Co., by R. C. Root . .	City	
	R. C. Root, Anthony & Co., " J. Anthony, Jr.	"	
	R. C. Root, Anthony & Co., " A. S. Allison .	"	
	Ryan & Dale, " W. L. Ryan . .	"	
Feb. 15	Roy, Wade & Co., " J. C. Roy . .	"	
	W.		
Jan. 10	John Ward	City	

* In this book the Bank ought to have registered, in alphabetical order, the signatures of all persons keeping accounts with it; and these signatures should be witnessed by the Paying Teller, or some other officer of the Bank.

PAYING TELLER'S CASH BOOK,

CITY NATIONAL BANK,

JANUARY, 1867.

1. This book is of the same form as the Receiving Teller's Cash Book, the left page recording all transactions for the accounts of the General Ledger, and the right page for the Depositors' Checks paid and certified, and for Certificates of Deposit. Although we have passed the contents of this book into the General Cash Book, the Accountant will soon perceive that the arrangement of the Ledger titles enables him to post them direct from here as easily as from a Journal. When this mode of posting is adopted, no General Cash Book is required,—the balance of that account being obtained from the Cash account in the General Ledger.

269

1st Nat. B'k, Chicago	P'd Draft on O. H. Bliss			500	
1st Nat. B'k, New Orleans	" " " F. J. Herron			1000	
Foreign Bills of Exchange	" for Brown, Brothers & Co., on			44444	44
	G. Peabody for £10,000 St'g				
Exchange	" 5% Premium for do.			2222	22
U. S. Bonds	" for 300 5/20 Bonds of $1000				
	each			300000	
	G. C. B. 1			348166	66

Iron City Nat. Bank				3564	
	P'd Coll. Bates & Bell		3600		
	Less Exchange		36		
1st Nat. B'k, Chicago				792	
	" Coll. W. S. Hunter		800		
	Less Exchange		8		
1st Nat. B'k, New Orleans				3528	
	" Coll. Gregg & Hall	2000			
	" " J. Kane	1600	3600		
	Less Exchange		72		
U. S. Bonds	" for 100 5/20 Bonds of $1000				
	each	.		100000	
Exchange	" Sundry Exchanges			116	
	G. C. B. 1			108000	

1st Nat. B'k, Chicago				1188	
	P'd Coll. Patterson & Wild		1200		
	Less Exchange		12		
1st Nat. B'k, New Orleans				2352	
	" Coll. Hay & Wood		2400		
	Less Exchange		48		
Iron City Nat. B'k				1782	
	" Coll. R. Bruce		1800		
	Less Exchange		18		
Foreign Bills of Exchange	" for Pollock & Gilmore on R.				
	Rankin & Co., for £5000 St'g			22222	22
Exchange				1189	11
	" 5% Premium on ditto	1111	11		
	" Sundry Exchanges	78			
	G. C. B. 1			28733	33

2	Harper & Bros.	Paid Check		1800
3	Barclay, Hope & Co.	" "		1500
4	W. B. Archer	" "		1000
4	Lyon & Haven	" "		1200
1	Rich'd Irvin & Co.	" "		2400
		G. C. B. 1		7900

15th, 1867.

2	Harper & Bros.	Paid Check		2000
1	R. Irvin & Co.	" "		2100
1	R. C. Root, Anthony & Co.	" "		600
1	R. Lenox	" "	1500, 1000	2500
3	Duff Bros. & Co.	" "		1100
2	Harriet Lenox	" "		600
2	John Ward	" "	600, 500	1100
4	Lyon & Haven	" "	1500, 1000	2500
3	Jas. Carver	" "	300, 400, 600	1300
4	Ryan & Dale	" /	600, 200	800
4	W. B. Archer	" "	1400, 1600	3000
5	Roy, Wade & Co	" "		1000
		G. C. B. 1		18600

16th, 1867.

5	J. W. Burnham	Paid Checks	500, 700	1200
5	A. B. Hunter	" "	200, 100	300
5	Roy, Wade & Co.	" "	400, 600	1000
4	Ryan & Dale	" "	2000, 500	2500
3	J. Carver	" "	1600, 400	2000
3	Barclay, Hope & Co.	" "		1100
3	Duff Bros. & Co.	" "	1200, 1000	2200
		G. C. B. 1		10300

The left money column is used for short-extending checks where one depositor
draws a number on one day.

Circulation	P'd mutilated ret'd per B. N. R. 1			500
Foreign Bills of Exchange	" for Betts & Turner on Bold & Starkey for £4500 St'g			20000
Exchange				1290
	" 6% Premium for ditto	1200		
	" 1% disc't on our Dr'ft No. 1	80		
	" ½% " " " " " 2	10		
Expense				2975
	" Rent to April 1st	1000		
	" Salaries to April 1st	1975		
	G. C. B. 2			24765

May

Iron City Nat. B'k				1980
	P'd Coll. R. Glass & Co.	800		
	" " W. Payson	1200	2000	
	Less Exchange		20	
Bank of Montreal				3564
	" Coll. G. Wilde & Co.	2400		
	" " J. Carter	1200	3600	
	Less Exchange		36	
1st Nat. B'k, Boston				2394
	" Coll. J. Barker & Co.		2400	
	Less Exchange		6	
Exchange	" Sundry Exchanges			62
	G. C. B. 2			8000

June

Iron City Nat. Bank				2772
	P'd Coll. C. H. Ball	800		
	" " J. Horne & Co.	2000	2800	
	Less Exchange		28	
1st Nat. B'k Chicago				2970
	" Coll. W. Baker		3000	
	Less Exchange		30	
Foreign Bills of Exchange	" for Dyer & Morgan on Swainson & Willis, £450 St'g			2000
Exchange				218
	" 8% Premium on ditto	160		
	" Sundry Exchanges	58		
	G. C. B. 2			7960

1	R. Irvin & Co.	Paid Check		2000
1	R. Lenox	" "		1100
1	R. C. Root, Anthony & Co.	Certified Check		1000
2	Harriet Lenox	Paid "		600
3	Duff Brothers & Co.	Certified* "		800
5	A. B. Hunter	" "		1000
2	John Ward	Paid "		2000
		Paid		5700
		Certified		2800
		G. C. B. 2		8500

14th, 1867.

2	Harper & Bros.	Paid Checks	400, 500		900
2	Harriet Lenox	" "			700
2	John Ward	" "	300, 400, 700		1400
3	J. Carver	" "	200, 300		500
4	Ryan & Dale	" "	600, 800		1400
1	R. Lenox	" Protest on No. 8, ret'd			2
4	Lyon & Haven	" " " " 19			1 75
		G. C. B. 2			4903 75

12th, 1867.

2	Harriet Lenox	Paid Check			1300
2	Jno. Ward	" "	600, 500		1100
3	Duff Bros. & Co.	" "	200, 300		500
1	R. C. Root, Anthony & Co.	" "	400, 500		900
4	W. B. Archer	" "	300, 900		1200
5	R. P. Duff	Certificate of Deposit No. 1			2100
5	G. R. Duncan	" " " " 3			1200
		G. C. B. 2			8300

* See Form, Page 274.

	A.M.		P.M.	
"City National Bank" Notes			10000	
Legal Tender "	150000		150000	
National Bank "	160000		44500	
Gold	87000		10000	
Silver	2238	50	1871	84
Checks and Drafts			2100	
Memoranda				
	399238	50	218471	84
Receipts	175300			
Payments			356066	66
	574538	50	574538	50

A CERTIFICATE OF DEPOSIT.

No. 1. **City National Bank of New York,** *April 15, 1867.*

Robert P. Duff .... *has deposited in this Bank*

Five Thousand One Hundred *Dollars payable to his*
order on return of this certificate properly endorsed.

STAMP.

$2100. *Chas. P. Duff* CASHIER.

1. This certificate is negotiable either by blank or special endorsement. (See Entry, p. 265.)

A CERTIFIED CHECK.

No. 2. *New York, April 15, 1867.*

CITY NATIONAL BANK OF NEW YORK,

Pay to *Ourselves* *or Bearer,*

Eight Hundred *Dollars*

STAMP.

$800. *Duff Brothers & Co.*

THE

OFFERING BOOK,

CITY NATIONAL BANK,

JANUARY, 1867.

1. This is a memorandum of the business paper*offered to the Board of Directors for discount. The owner endorses his signature on each piece of paper. If rejected, it is returned to him. If accepted, it is numbered, and entered in the Book "Notes and Bills Discounted."

OFFERED THURSDAY, JANUARY 10, 1867.

Date.	Time.	Payer.	Where Payable.	Endorser.	Discounter.	Amount.	Memoranda.
1865.							
Dec. 1	2 months	Gregg & Hall	New Orleans	W. S. Haven	Harper & Bros.	2000	Accepted
Nov. 12	3 "	Mount, Joy & Co.	City	J. W. Burnham	Ryan & Dale	1000	Accepted
Dec. 14	60 days	G. W. Leeds	"	W. S. Murray	Barclay, Hope & Co.	1800	Accepted
14	60 "	Hay & Wood	"	Joel Post	James Carver	1600	Accepted
Nov. 14	4 months	J. W. Burnham	Chicago	R. Manly	Wm. Macgregor	900	Rejected
10	4 "	Patterson & Wild	City	R. C. Root	W. B. Archer	1200	Accepted
Dec. 14	60 days	Bateman & Hill	"	Hardy, Jones & Co.	Lyon & Haven	1500	Accepted
14	3 months	J. W. Loring	"	R. Banks	R. Irvin & Co.	3000	Accepted
1867.							
Jan. 9	90 days	May & Robertson	"	Cannon & Miller	Roy, Wade & Co.	800	Rejected
9	3 months	Buck & Massey		Geo. Wildes & Co.	A. B. Hunter	700	Rejected

OFFERED FRIDAY, FEBRUARY 15, 1867.

Date.	Time.	Payer.	Where Payable.	Endorser.	Discounter.	Amount.	Memoranda.
1865.							
Dec. 13	3 months	J. Wier & Co.	City	Jas. Beck & Co.	Wm. Macgregor	3000	Rejected
Nov. 13	4 "	Wm. Page	"	W. B. Archer	W. B. Archer	3600	Accepted
Oct. 8	5 "	Hay & Wood	New Orleans	Wm. Irons	R. Irvin & Co.	2400	Accepted
Sept. 9	6 "	R. Bruce	Pittsburgh	John Doe	Roy, Wade & Co.	1800	Accepted
1867.							
Feb. 13	6 "	M. Hunter & Co.	City	Duff Bros. & Co.	Duff Bros. & Co.	3300	Accepted
11	30 days	J. Morton	"	Lyon & Haven	R. Lenox	1200	Accepted
Jan. 12	60 "	J. Carver		J. W. Ryan	R. C. Root, Anthony & Co.	2100	Accepted
1866.							
Sept. 13	6 months	S. Hardy		R. Morris	Ryan & Dale	1800	Rejected
Nov. 20	4 "	Jno. Smith	St. Paul, Minn.	Wm. Pagan & Co.	Wm. Pagan & Co.	1100	Rejected
Sept. 30	6 "	W. Moody	Iowa City	J. Mills & Co.	Carter & Bates	1700	Rejected
Nov. 1	4 "	Birch & Woods	Mobile, Ala.	Wall & Birney	Wall & Birney	900	Rejected

OFFERED SATURDAY, MARCH 16, 1867.

Date.		Time.	Payer.	Where Payable.	Endorser.	Discounter.	Amount.	Memoranda.
1867.								
Jan.	12	3 months	Day & Martin	City	Smith & Beck	A. B. Hunter	1500	Accepted
Feb.	11	60 days	Hart & Bowman	"	Paul Cooper	J. W. Burnham	2400	Accepted
1866.								
Dec.	12	4 months	Duncan, Dunlap & Co.	"	Wm. Porter	Duff Bros. & Co.	900	Accepted
1867.								
Mar.	13	30 days	Geo. Wilde	"	J. Ward	John Ward	2400	Accepted
Jan.	3	90 "	Hiram Fish	Denver City, Col.	Walker & Best	Walker & Best	1700	Rejected
1866.								
Dec.	27	4 months	J. W. Moore	Austin, Texas	Turner & Reed	Turner & Reed	800	Rejected

OFFERED MONDAY, APRIL 15, 1867.

Date.		Time.	Payer.	Where Payable.	Endorser.	Discounter.	Amount.	Memoranda.
1867.								
Apr.	10	30 days	J. Barker & Co.	Boston	J. Carver	J. Carver	2400	Accepted
Feb.	11	3 months	J. Kane	City	R. Morris	Lyon & Haven	1600	Accepted
Jan.	11	4 "	S. Lewis & Co.	"	J. Barker	W. B. Archer	1500	Accepted
Mar.	12	60 days	J. W. Bliss	"	Porter & Hill	Ryan & Dale	1800	Accepted
Feb.	1	4 months	J. Dean	Nashville	J. K. Brookes	J. K. Brookes	1300	Rejected

It is deemed unnecessary to continue the form of this book further.

NOTES AND BILLS DISCOUNTED

No.	Drawer.	Endorser.	Payer.	Payable in
1	Harper & Bros.	W. S. Haven	Gregg & Hall	New Orleans
2	Note	J. W. Burnham	Mount, Joy & Co.	City
3	"	W. S. Murray	G. W. Leeds	"
4	"	Joel Post	Hay & Wood	"
5	W. B. Archer	R. C. Root	Patterson & Wild	Chicago
6	Note	Hardy, Jones & Co.	Bateman & Hill	City
7	"	R. Banks	J. W. Loring	"

NOTE.—1. All paper discounted by the Board is entered in this book. It is the property of the Bank, and differs from paper received for collection. Protested paper is registered in the "Protest" Book.

NOTES AND BILLS DISCOUNTED

No.	Drawer.	Endorser.	Payer.	Payable in
8	Note	W. B. Archer	Wm. Page	City
9	"	Wm. Irons	Hay & Wood	New Orleans
10	"	John Doe	R. Bruce	Pittsburgh
11	"	Duff Bros. & Co.	M. Hunter & Co.	City
12	"	Lyon & Haven	J. Morton	"
13	"	J. W. Ryan	J. Carver	"

NOTES AND BILLS DISCOUNTED

No.	Drawer.	Endorser.	Payer.	Payable in
14	Note	Smith & Beck	Day & Martin	City
15	"	Paul Cooper	Hart & Bowman	"
16	"	Wm. Porter	Duncan, Dunlap & Co.	"
17	"	J. Ward	Geo. Wildes	"

NOTES AND BILLS DISCOUNTED

No.	Drawer.	Endorser.	Payer.	Payable in
18	Note	J. Carver	J. Barker & Co.	* Boston (sent 1st Nat. B'k)
19	"	R. Morris	J. Kane	City
20	"	J. Barker	S. Lewis & Co.	"
21	"	Porter & Hill	J. W. Bliss	"

* Where we have only an occasional collection, it is unnecessary to open an account on the "Bills Remitted for Collection" Book. The above memorandum is sufficient. See P. T. C. B., 272, and R. T. C. B., 266.

Thursday, January 10, 1867. 1

Discounter.	Date.	Time.	Due.	Unexp. Time.	Rate of Exch.	Amount.	Int.	Exch.	Int. & Exch.	Net Proceeds.	L.	When Paid.
	1866		1867.									1867.
Harper & Bros.	Dec. 1	2 mos.	Feb. 4	25	2%	2000	8 33	40	48 33	1951 67	2	Feb. 15
Ryan & Dale	Nov. 12	3 ″	15	36		1000	6		6	994	4	15
Barclay, Hope	Dec. 14	60 ds.	15	36		1800	10 80		10 80	1789 20	3	15
J. Carver	14	60 ″	15	36		1600	9 60		9 60	1590 40	3	15
W. B. Archer	Nov. 10	4 mos	Mar. 13	62	1%	1200	12 40	12	24 40	1175 60	4	Mar. 16
Lyon & Haven	Dec. 14	60 ds.	Feb. 15	36		1500	9		9	1491	4	Feb. 15
R. Irvin & Co.	14	3 mos.	Mar. 17	66		3000	33		33	2967	1	Mar. 16 *
							89 13	52	141 13	11958 87		Dep'rs
										89 13		Int.
										52		Exch.
						12100				12100		Jour. 1 †

* Mar. 17 was Sunday.
† The Journal explains how to post these matters direct to General Ledger.

Friday, February 15, 1867.

Discounter.	Date.	Time.	Due.	Unexp. Time.	Rate of Exch.	Amount.	Int.	Exch.	Int. & Exch.	Net Proceeds.	L.	When Paid.
	1866.		1867.									
W. B. Archer	Nov. 13	4 mos.	Mar. 16	29		3600	17 40		17 40	3582 60	4	Mar. 16
R. Irvin & Co.	Oct. 8	5 ″	11	24	2%	2400	9 60	48	57 60	2342 40	1	16
Roy, Wade & Co	Sept. 9	6 ″	12	25	1%	1800	7 50	18	25 50	1774 50	5	16
Duff Bros. & Co.	1867. 13	6 ″	16	29		3300	15 95		15 95	3284 05	3	16
R. Lenox	Feb. 11	30 ds.	16	29		1200	5 80		5 80	1194 20	1	16
Root, Anthony & Co.	Jan. 12	60 ″	16	29		2100	10 15		10 15	2089 85	1	16
							66 40	66	132 40	14267 60		Dep'rs.
										66 40		Int.
										66		Exch.
						14400				14400		Jour. 2

Saturday, March 16, 1867.

Discounter.	Date.	Time.	Due.	Unexp. Time.	Rate of Exch.	Amount.	Int.	Exch.	Int. & Exch.	Net Proceeds.	L.	When Paid.
	1867.		1867.									
A. B. Hunter	Jan. 12	3 mos.	Apr. 15	30		1500	7 50		7 50	1492 50	5	Apr. 15
J. W. Burnham	Feb. 11	60 ds.	15	30		2400	12		12	2388	5	15
	1866.											
Duff Bros. & Co.	Dec. 12	4 mos.	15	30		900	4 50		4 50	895 50	3	15
	1867.											
John Ward	Mar. 13	30 ds.	15	30		2400	12		12	2388	2	15
							36		36	7164		Dep'rs.
										36		Int.
						7200				7200		Jour. 2

Monday, April 15, 1867.

Discounter.	Date.	Time.	Due.	Unexp. Time.	Rate of Exch.	Amount.	Int.	Exch.	Int. & Exch.	Net Proceeds.	L.	When Paid.
	1867.		1867.									
J. Carver	Apr. 10	30 ds.	May 13	28	½%	2400	11 20	12	23 20	2376 80	3	May 14
Lyon & Haven	Feb. 11	3 mos.	14	29		1600	7 73		7 73	1592 27	4	Prot'd
W. B. Archer	Jan. 11	4 ″	14	29		1500	7 25		7 25	1492 75	4	May 14
Ryan & Dale	Mar. 12	60 ds.	14	29		1800	8 70		8 70	1791 30	4	14
							34 88	12	46 88	7253 12		Depre.
										34 88		Int.
										12		Exch.
						7300				7300		Jour. 2

NOTES AND BILLS DISCOUNTED

No.	Drawer.	Endorser.	Payer.	Payable in
22	A. J. Pierce	J. W. Burnham	Hay & Wood	New Orleans
23	Harper & Bros.	J. Betts & Co.	J. R. Weldin & Co.	Pittsburgh
24	Note	Lyon & Haven	Davy, Jones & Co.	City
25	A. Stewart & Co.	J. W. Myers	J. Horne	Pittsburgh

NOTES AND BILLS DISCOUNTED

No.	Drawer.	Endorser.	Payer.	Payable in
26	Harper & Bros.	Harper & Bros.	W. G. Johnston & Co.	Pittsburgh
27	Note	J. Page	A. B. Weed	City
28	"	A. T. Howden	J. Gardner	"
29	J. West & Co.	Barclay, Hope & Co.	F. L. Rainbow	Pittsburgh
30	Note	R. Irvin & Co.	R. Banks	City

FOREIGN

1. This is a register of all Foreign Bills of Exchange usually bought by the President under (By-Board. But this paper, being usually bought at a premium, cannot be registered on "Bills Discounted"

Foreign Bills

When received.	No.	Drawers.	Drawees.	Endorsers.
1867.				
Jan. 10	1	Brown Brothers & Co.	George Peabody	Wm. Page
Mar. 16	2	Pollock & Gilmore	R. Rankin & Co.	Marks & Cowden
Apr. 15	3	Betts & Turner	Bold & Starkey	Stacy & Evans
June 12	4	Dyer & Morgan	Swainson & Willis	W. Martin

Discounter.	Date.	Time.	Due.	Unexp. Time.	Rate of Exch.	Amount.	Int.	Exch.	Int. & Exch.	Net Proceeds.	L.P.	When Paid.
	1867.		1867.									
John Ward	May 14	90 ds.	Aug. 15	93*	2%	1200	18 60	24	42 60	1157 40	2	
Barclay, Hope	14	60 "	July 16	63	1%	800	8 40	8	16 40	783 60	3	
Lyon & Haven	1	3 mos.	Aug. 4	82		2400	32 80		32 80	2367 20	4	
Roy, Wade & Co	14	90 ds.	15	93	1%	1800	27 90	18	45 90	1754 10	5	
							87 70	50	137 70	6062 30		Deprs.
										87 70		Int.
										50		Exch.
						6200				6200		Jour. 3

* In some States the law authorizes the banks to charge interest for the day of discount and day of payment. In New York the rule is as stated p. 45.

Wednesday, June 12, 1867.

	1867.		1867.									
Harper & Bros.	June 12	60 ds.	Aug. 14	63	1%	600	6 30	6	12 30	587 70	2	
J. W. Burnham	May 30	4 mos.	Oct. 3	113		1600	30 13		30 13	1569 87	5	
A. B. Hunter	June 1	3 "	Sept. 4	84		1800	25 20		25 20	1774 80	5	
Barclay, Hope	5	4 "	Oct. 8	118	1%	1200	23 60	12	35 60	1164 40	3	
R. Irvin & Co.	10	4 "	13	123		4000	82		82	3918	1	
							167 23	18	185 23	9014 77		Deprs.
										167 23		Int.
										18		Exch.
						9200				9200		Jour. 3

BILL BOOK.

Laws, Article X.) direction of the Board; or, if desired, each transaction may be submitted to the book without changing its form.

of Exchange.

Where drawn.	Dated.	Sight.	Payable in.	Amount.			When Remitted.	Memoranda.
	1867.			£	s.	d.	1867.	
New York	Jan. 10	60 days	London	10000			Jan. 12	Jour. 1 *
Montreal	Mar. 5	60 "	Liverpool	5000			Mar. 16	2
Toronto	Apr. 10	30 "	"	4500			Apr. 15	2
New York	June 12	60 "	London	450			June 12	3

* See also P. T. C. B. 1.

PROTESTED PAPER.

No.	No. of Bnct.	Date Protested.	Drawer.	Endorser.	Payer.	Amount.	Memoranda.
1	19	May 14	Note	R. Morris	J. Kane	1600	Paid June 12
2		15	Betts & Turner	Stacy & Evans	Bold & Starkey	£4500	

NOTE.—1. Some Banks open an account for "Protested Paper" belonging to the Bank in the Ledger. As paper of this kind, if paid at all, is generally promptly taken up by some of the parties, the registry and payment of it as above will be all the record necessary. But when the other method is preferred, the account in the Ledger will be debited for all protested paper, and credited for the same when paid.

2. Collection paper when protested is noted on that Register and returned to the owner, he at the same time refunding expenses of protest.

BANK-NOTE REGISTER,

CITY NATIONAL BANK,

JANUARY, 1867.

1. This book registers all Bank-notes received from the Comptroller of the Currency. As they are signed, they pass into the Receiving Teller's Cash Book as money. When mutilated, and returned to the Comptroller, they pass into the Paying Teller's Cash Book to credit of Cash and debit of " Circulation."

283

Issued.	Impres- sions.	Let- ter.	Date.	Treasury Number.	Bank Number.	Denomi- nation.	Amount.	Mem.
1867. Jan. 10	4000	A	1867. Jan. 5	324001 to 328000	1 to 4000	5s	20000	
	4000	B		324001 ″ 328000	1 ″ 4000	5s	20000	
	4000	C		324001 ″ 328000	1 ″ 4000	5s	20000	
	4000	D		324001 ″ 328000	1 ″ 4000	5s	20000	
							80000	R.T.C.B. 1
10	2000	A	Jan. 5	328001 to 330000	4001 to 6000	10s	20000	
	2000	B		328001 ″ 330000	4001 ″ 6000	10s	20000	
	2000	C		328001 ″ 330000	4001 ″ 6000	10s	20000	
	2000	D		328001 ″ 330000	4001 ″ 6000	10s	20000	
							80000	R.T.C.B. 1
Feb. 15	10000	A	Jan. 5	415001 to 425000	6001 to 16000	5s	50000	
	10000	B		415001 ″ 425000	6001 ″ 16000	5s	50000	
	10000	C		415001 ″ 425000	6001 ″ 16000	5s	50000	
	10000	D		415001 ″ 425000	6001 ″ 16000	5s	50000	
							200000	R.T.C.B. 1
15	800	A	Jan. 5	425001 to 425800	16001 to 16800	10s	8000	
	800	B		425001 ″ 425800	16001 ″ 16800	10s	8000	
	800	C		425001 ″ 425800	16001 ″ 16800	10s	8000	
	800	D		425001 ″ 425800	16001 ″ 16800	10s	8000	
							32000	R.T.C.B. 1
Mar. 16	500	A	Jan. 5	430001 to 430500	16801 to 17300	20s	10000	
	500	B		430001 ″ 430500	16801 ″ 17300	20s	10000	
	500	C		430001 ″ 430500	16801 ″ 17300	20s	10000	
	500	D		430001 ″ 430500	16801 ″ 17300	20s	10000	
							40000	R.T.C.B. 2
16	100	A	Jan. 5	430501 to 430600	17301 to 17400	50s	5000	
	100	B		430501 ″ 430600	17301 ″ 17400	50s	5000	
	100	C		430501 ″ 430600	17301 ″ 17400	50s	5000	
	100	D		430501 ″ 430600	17301 ″ 17400	50s	5000	
							20000	R.T.C.B. 2
16	25	A	Jan. 5	430601 to 430625	17401 to 17425	100s	2500	
	25	B		430601 ″ 430625	17401 ″ 17425	100s	2500	
	25	C		430601 ″ 430625	17401 ″ 17425	100s	2500	
	25	D		430601 ″ 430625	17401 ″ 17425	100s	2500	
							10000	R.T.C.B. 2
16	5	A	Jan. 5	430626 to 430630	17426 to 17430	500s	2500	
	5	B		430626 ″ 430630	17426 ″ 17430	500s	2500	
	5	C		430626 ″ 430630	17426 ″ 17430	500s	2500	
	5	D		430626 ″ 430630	17426 ″ 17430	500s	2500	
							10000	R.T.C.B. 2
16	2	A	Jan. 5	430631 to 430632	17431 to 17432	1000s	2000	
	2	B		430631 ″ 430632	17431 ″ 17432	1000s	2000	
	2	C		430631 ″ 430632	17431 ″ 17432	1000s	2000	
	2	D		430631 ″ 430632	17431 ″ 17432	1000s	2000	
							8000	R.T.C.B. 2

When and		How Retired.	Notes.	Treasury Number.	Bank Number.	Denomi- nation.	Amount.	Mem.
1867. Apr.	15	Sent to Washington	10	324001 to 324010	1 to 10	5s	50	Mutilated
			10	324051 ″ 324060	51 ″ 60	5s	50	*
			20	328001 ″ 328020	4001 ″ 4020	10s	200	
			20	328041 ″ 328060	4041 ″ 4060	10s	200	
							500	P.T.C.B. 2

FORM OF PROTEST FOR NON-PAYMENT.

UNITED STATES OF AMERICA.

Be it Known, *That on the day of the date hereof, I, W. B. Cook, Notary Public, by authority of the Commonwealth of Pennsylvania, duly commissioned and sworn, residing in the City of Pittsburgh, County of* Allegheny, *in the said Commonwealth, at the request of*

The Iron City National Bank,

exhibited the original Note whereof a true copy is on the other side written (the time therein specified for its payment having fully expired), To A. J. Turner, *and demanded payment thereof, which was* refused ....

....

whereof I duly notified the Maker and Endorser.

Whereupon *I, the said Notary, at the request aforesaid, Have* Protested, *and Do hereby solemnly* Protest, *against the Maker and Endorser of the said Note, and all others concerned, for all exchange, re-exchange, costs, damages and interests, suffered and to be suffered for want of Payment thereof.*

Thus Done and Protested. *at Pittsburgh, the 12th day of May, 1867.*

STAMP.	In Testimony Whereof, *I have hereunto set my hand and affixed my Notarial seal, the day and year above written.*

W. B. Cook, Notary Public

286

CITY COLLECTION REGISTER,

CITY NATIONAL BANK,

JANUARY, 1867.

1. Notes and Bills received for collection and payable in the City are registered in this book. In a limited business the payments may pass direct into the Receiving Teller's Cash Book. But, as the amounts never mature in the same order that they are entered, the dates of payment can be more conveniently brought into regular order on the "Passed Collection Register."

THE FOREIGN COLLECTION REGISTER

2. Records all paper falling due out of the City and which has to be forwarded to our agent in time for presentation on day of maturity. As forwarded, each is passed into the Book "Notes and Bills Remitted for Collection."

CITY NOTES AND BILLS

When received.		Payer.	Endorser.	Owner.
1867.				
Jan.	10	Baker & Fox	R. C. Root	Barclay, Hope & Co.
		Joel Post	J. W. Burnham	R. Irvin & Co.
		R. S. Davis	R. Barnes & Co.	Jas. Carver
		J. B. Marks	Paul Jones	Lyon & Haven
Mar.	3	Ryan & Dale	Jno. Taylor & Co.	1st Nat. Bk. New Orleans
		R. C. Root, Anthony & Co.	Wm. Black	1st Nat. Bk. Chicago
Apr.	25	Baker & Hill	J. W. Burnham	" " "
		Porter & Dick	Bailey & Coy	" " " .
		W. G. Ray	W Morris	" " "
May	14	J. L. Dixon	Paul Jones	R. C. Root, Anthony & Co.
		Day & Martin	G. A. Bayard	" "
		W. Burton	Joel Post	R. Lenox
		Jas. Carver	R. Lenox	"
		Wm. Beach	Harper & Brothers	Harper & Bros.
		H. J. Holmes	Barclay, Hope & Co.	Barclay, Hope & Co.
		Allen Park	" " "	" "
		A. B. Ryan	J. Hardy	J Carver
		J. W. Parker	J. Carter	"

FOREIGN NOTES AND BILLS

When received.		No.	Drawer.	On whom.	In favor of.	Payable in.
1867.						
Jan.	10	1	Bates & Bell	Note	A. Stewart & Co.	Pittsburgh
		2	Harper & Bros.	W. S. Hunter	Harper & Bros.	Chicago
		3	R. Irvin & Co.	J. Kane	R. Irvin & Co.	New Orleans
Apr.	15	4	Wm. Pagan	G. Wilde & Co.	R. Lenox	Montreal
		5	R. Manly	Jas. Carter	"	"
		6	R. Glass & Co.	Note	J. W. Burnham	Pittsburgh
		7	W. Payson	"	R. Dick & Co.	"
		8	A. J. Turner	"	R. Lenox	"
May	14	9	C. H. Ball	"	Wm. Hood	"
		10	J. Horne & Co.	"	Wm. Lyon	"
		11	Wm. Baker	"	Wm. White	Chicago
		12	J. Morton	J. C. Baker & Co.	A. B. Hunter	New Orleans
		13	Roy, Wade & Co.	W. S. Haven	Ourselves	Pittsburgh
		14	A. D. Walker	Note	R. Weston	Chicago
		15	Chas. Page	"	Lyon & Haven	Pittsburgh
		16	J. Butler	"	W. Watts	Chicago
		17	Myers & Hunter	"	J. Post	New Orleans

No.	Date		Time		Due		Amount	Memoranda
	1866.				1867.			
1	Aug.	12	6 months	Feb.		15	1600	Passed Feb. 15th
2	Oct.	12	4 "			15	2400	" 15th
3	Nov.	12	3 "			15	1200	" 15th
4	Dec.	14	60 days			15	2100	" 15th
5	Feb.	20	10 ds. s'gt.	Mar.		16	1200	" Mar. 16th
6		26	10 "			16	1600	" 16th
7		11	3 months	May		14	3600	" May 14th
8	Jan.	11	4 "			14	2100	" 14th
9	Mar.	12	60 days			14	1200	" 14th
10		9	3 months	June		12	1600	" June 12th
11	Feb.	9	4 "			12	1100	" 12th
12	Jan.	9	5 "			12	2400	" 12th
13	Feb.	9	4 "			12	1800	" 12th
14	Apr.	9	3 "	July		12	900	
15	Mar.	9	4 "			12	1200	
16		9	4 "			12	1800	
17	Apr.	9	3 "			12	1800	
18	Feb.	9	5 "			12	1500	

RECEIVED FOR COLLECTION.

Owner.	Date.		Time.	Due.		Amount.	Exchange.	Net Proceeds.	Memoranda.
	1866.			1867.					
Ryan & Dale	Dec.	12	60 days	Feb.	13	3600	36	3564	Passed Feb. 15
Harper & Bros.	Nov.	9	3 months		12	800	8	792	" 15
R. Irvin & Co.	Oct.	8	4 "		11	1600	32	1568	" 15
	1867.								
R. Lenox	Feb.	8	3 "	May	11	2400	24	2376	" May 14
R. Lenox	Jan.	8	4 "		11	1200	12	1188	" 14
R. Irvin & Co.	Mar.	10	60 days		12	800	8	792	" 14
Harper & Bros.	Feb.	9	3 months		12	1200	12	1188	" 14
R. Lenox	Jan.	9	4 "		12	1800	-	Ret'd	Protested
W. B. Archer	May	7	30 days	June	9	800	8	792	Passed June 12
W. B. Archer	Apr.	7	60 "		9	2000	20	1980	" 12
Lyon & Haven		7	60 "		9	3000	30	2970	" 12
A. B. Hunter	May	14	60 ds. sgt.	Aug.	27	2400			
Roy, Wade & Co.		14	60 "		22	1000			
Roy, Wade & Co.	Mar.	15	4 months	July	18	1500			
Lyon & Haven		15	4 "		18	800			
A. B. Hunter		15	4 "		18	1600			
Duff Bros. & Co.	Apr.	15	3 "		18	1100			

NOTES AND BILLS REMITTED FOR COLLECTION.

Iron City National Bank, Pittsburgh.

When sent.		No.	Payer.	Amount.	When due.		Memoranda.
1867.					1867.		
Feb.	1	1	Bates & Bell	3600	Feb.	13	Passed Feb. 15
Mar.	1	10	R. Bruce	1800	Mar.	12	R. T. C. B. Mar. 16
May	1	6	R. Glass & Co.	800	May	12	Passed May 14
		7	W. Payson	1200		12	" 14
		8	A. J. Turner	1800		12	Protested
	14	9	C. H. Ball	800	June	9	Passed June 12
		10	J. Horne & Co.	2000		9	" 12
		13	W. S. Haven	1000	60 ds. sgt.		

First National Bank of New Orleans.

When sent.		No.	Payer.	Amount.	When due.		Memoranda.
1867.					1867.		
Jan.	20	1	Gregg & Hall	2000	Feb.	4	R. T. C. B. Feb. 15
Feb.	1	3	J. Kane	1600		11	Passed Feb. 15
Mar.	1	9	Hay & Wood	2400	Mar.	11	R. T C. B. Mar. 16
May	14	12	J. C. Baker & Co.	2400	60 ds. sgt		.

First National Bank of Chicago.

When sent.		No.	Payer.	Amount.	When due.		Memoranda.
1867.					1867.		
Feb.	1	2	W. S. Hunter	800	Feb.	12	Passed Feb. 15
Mar.	1	5	Patterson & Wild	1200	Mar.	13	R. T. C. B. Mar. .
May	14	11	Wm. Baker	3000	June	9	Passed June 12

Bank of Montreal, Canada.

When sent.		No.	Payer.	Amount.	When due.		Memoranda.
1867.					1867.		
Apr.	25	4	Geo. Wilde & Co.	2400	May	11	Passed May 14
		5	Jas. Carter	1200		11	" 14

1. In our **Private** Bankers' Accounts, pp. 360 and 361, we give another form of this book. The above is the most convenient for a large foreign collection business.

2. All paper remitted to our agents for collection is entered upon this book.

3. After allowing sufficient time for the return of the paper, we enter our own in the "Receiving Teller's Cash Book," and Collections in the "Passed Collection Register," debiting at the same time our agent for the amount.

PASSED CITY AND FOREIGN

COLLECTION REGISTER.

CITY NATIONAL BANK,

JANUARY, 1867.

1. Banks generally keep a Passed City and a Passed Foreign Collection Register. To save space, we have entered both on this book, the use of which is explained in "City Collection Register," p. 287. When the business requires two Passed Collection Registers, this form will serve for both. Reference to the Receiving Teller's Cash Book explains the mode of posting them.

2. Sight Drafts sent us for collection are entered in this book without passing through "City Collection Register."

291

PASSED COLLECTIONS.

When passed.	No.	Paid by.	Where paid.	To whom paid.	Owner.	Amount.	Exchange.	Net proceeds.	Mem.
186? Jan.	10	1st National Bank	City	Ourselves	Iron City Nat. Bank	1000		1000	R.T.C.B
	9th	"	"	"	1st Nat. Bank, Chicago	1500		1500	"
		Chemical Nat. Bank	"	"	1st Nat. B'k, New Orleans	500		500	"
Feb.	15 1	Baker & Fox	"	"	Barclay, Hope & Co.	1600		1600	"
	2	Joel Post	"	"	R. Irvin & Co.	2400		2400	"
	3	R. S. Davis	"	"	James Carver	1200		1200	"
	4	J. B. Marks			Lyon & Haven	2100		2100	"
	1	Bates & Bell	Pittsburgh	Iron City Nat. Bank	Ryan & Dale	3600	72	3528	"
	2	W. S. Hunter	Chicago	First Nat. Bank	Harper & Brothers	800	16	784	"
	3	J. Kane	New Orleans	First Nat. Bank	R. Irvin & Co.	1600	48	1552	"
Mar.	16	Harper & Bros.	City	Ourselves	Iron City Nat. Bank	1200		1200	"
		Ryan & Dale	"	"	1st Nat. B'k, New Orleans	1200		1200	"
	5	Root, Anthony & Co.	"	"	" " Chicago	1600		1600	"
	6	J. Astley & Co.			R. Irvin & Co.	4000		4000	"
Apr.	15 6	R. Glass & Co.	Pittsburgh	Iron City Nat. Bank	R. Irvin & Co.	800	16	784	"
May	14 7	W. Payson	"	"	Harper & Brothers	1200	24	1176	"
	4	Geo. Wilde & Co.	Montreal	Bank of Montreal	R. Lenox	2400	48	2352	"
	5	Jas. Carter	"	"	"	1200	24	1176	"
	7	Baker & Hill	City	Ourselves	1st Nat. Bank, Chicago	3600		3600	"
	8	Porter & Dick	"	"	" " "	2100		2100	"
	9	W. G. Ray	"	"	" " "	1200		1200	"
June	12 10	J. L. Dixon	"	"	Root, Anthony & Co.	1600		1600	"
	11	Day & Martin			"	1100		1100	"
	12	W. Burton	"	"	R. Lenox	2400		2400	"
	13	Jas. Carver	"	"	"	1800		1800	"
	9	C. H. Ball	Pittsburgh	Iron City Nat. Bank	W. B. Archer	800	16	784	"
	10	J. Horse & Co.	"	"	"	2000	40	1960	"
	11	Wm. Baker.	Chicago	First Nat. Bank	Lyon & Haven	3000	60	2940	●

TICKLER,

CITY NATIONAL BANK,

JANUARY, 1867.

1. This book records the day of payment of all the business paper in the Bank. It is made up from the Discount Book and Collection Registers. One, and sometimes two pages have to be reserved for every day's business in the year. And in extensive business it is often convenient to have one book for discounted paper, and another for collections, and sometimes one for Foreign collections. To save room, we have entered all in one book, the form of which will serve for the others when the nature and extent of the business require them. Although a very important book, it is, strictly speaking, only a memorandum-book. from which payers are notified of the day upon which their paper falls due. The Directors also regulate their discounts by learning from it the amount of discounted paper falling due every day.

2. As paid, our own paper is marked "Entered," or "Paid." Collections are marked "Passed."

NOTES AND BILLS DUE February 4, 1867.

No.	Collected for.	Drawer.	Payer.	Endorser.	Payable in.	Amount.	Memoranda.
1	Ourselves	Harper & Brothers	Gregg & Hall	W. S. Haven	New Orleans	2000	Ent'd Feb. 15
			Due February 11th, 1867				
3	R. Irvin & Co.	R. Irvin & Co.	J. Kane	R. Irvin & Co.	New Orleans	1600	Passed Feb. 15
			Due February 12th, 1867				
2	Harper & Brothers	Harper & Brothers	W. S. Hunter	Harper & Bros.	Chicago	800	Passed Feb. 15
			Due February 13th, 1867				
1	Ryan & Dale	Note	Bates & Bell	A. Stewart & Co.	Pittsburgh	3600	Passed Feb. 15
			Due February 15th, 1867				
2	Ourselves	Note	Mount, Joy & Co.	J. W. Burnham	City	1000	Paid Feb. 15
3	"	"	G. W. Leeds	W. S. Murray	"	1800	15
4	"	"	Hay & Wood	Joel Post	"	1600	15
6		"	Bateman & Hill	Hardy, Jones & Co.	"	1500	15
1	Barclay, Hope & Co.	"	Baker & Fox	R. C. Root	"	1600	Passed Feb. 15
2	R. Irvin & Co.	"	Joel Post	J. W. Burnham	"	2400	15
3	J. Carver	"	R. S. Davis	R. Barnes & Co.	"	1200	15
4	Lyon & Haven	"	J. B. Marks	Paul Jones	"	2100	15
			Due March 11th, 1867				
9	Ourselves	Note	Hay & Wood	Wm. Irons	New Orleans	2400	Ent'd Mar. 16
			Due March 12th, 1867				
10	Ourselves	Note	R. Bruce	John Doe	Pittsburgh	1800	Ent'd Mar. 16
			Due March 13th, 1867				
5	Ourselves	W. B. Archer	Patterson & Wild	R. C. Root	Chicago	1200	Ent'd Mar. 16

NOTES AND BILLS DUE March 16th, 1867.

No.	Collected for.	Drawer.	Payer.	Endorser.	Payable in.	Amount.	Memoranda.
8	Ourselves	Note	Wm. Page	W. B. Archer	City	3600	Paid Mar. 16
11	"	"	M. Hunter & Co.	Duff Bros. & Co.	"	3300	" " 16
12	"	"	J. Morton	Lyon & Haven	"	1200	" " 16
13	"	"	J. Carver	J. W. Ryan	"	2100	" " 16
5	1st Nat. B'k, New Orleans	Jno. Taylor & Co.	Ryan & Dale	J. Taylor & Co.	"	1200	Passed " 16
6	1st Nat. B'k, Chicago	Wm. Black	R. C. Root, Anthony & Co.	Wm. Black	"	1600	" " 16
			Due March 17th, 1867				
7	Ourselves	Note	J. W. Loring	R. Banks	City	3000	Paid Mar. 16
			Due April 15th, 1867				
14	Ourselves	Note	Day & Martin	Smith & Beck	City	1500	Paid April 15
15	"	"	Hart & Bowman	Paul Cooper	"	2400	" " 15
16	"	"	Duncan, Dunlap & Co.	Wm. Porter	"	990	" " 15
17	"	"	Geo. Wilde	J. Ward	"	2400	" " 15
			Due May 11th, 1867				
4	R. Lenox	Wm. Pagan	G. Wilde & Co.	R. Lenox	Montreal	2400	Passed May 14
5	R. Lenox	R. Manly	J. Carter	R. Lenox	"	1200	" " 14
			Due May 12th, 1867				
6	R. Irvin & Co.	Note	R. Glass & Co.	J. W. Burnham	Pittsburgh	800	Passed May 14
7	Harper & Brothers	"	W. Payson	R. Dick & Co.	"	1200	" " 14
8	R. Lenox	"	A. J. Turner	R. Lenox	"	1800	Ret'd Prot'd 14
			Due May 13th, 1867				
18	Ourselves	Note	J. Barker & Co.	J. Carver	Boston	2400	Ent'd May 14
			Due May 14th, 1867				
19	Ourselves	Note	J. Kane	R. Morris	City	1600	Protested
20	"	"	S. Lewis & Co.	J. Barker	"	1500	Paid May 14
21	"	"	J. W. Bliss	Porter & Hill	"	1800	" " 14
7	1st Nat B'k, Chicago	"	Baker & Hill	J. W. Burnham	"	3600	Passed " 14
8	"	"	Porter & Dick	Bailey & Coy	"	2100	" " 14
9	"	"	W. G. Ray	W. Morris	"	1200	" " 14

295

NOTES AND BILLS DUE June 9th, 1867.

No.	Collected for	Drawer	Payer	Endorser	Payable in	Amount	Memoranda
9	W. B. Archer	Note	C. H. Ball	Wm. Hood	Pittsburgh	800	Passed June 12
10	"	"	J. Horne & Co.	Wm. Lyon	Chicago	2000	" " 12
11	Lyon & Haven	"	Wm. Baker	Wm. White	Chicago	3000	" " 12
			Due June 12th, 1867				
10	Root, Anthony & Co.	Note	J. L. Dixon	Paul Jones	City	1600	Passed June 12
11	"	"	Day & Martin	G. A. Bayard	"	1100	" " 12
12	R. Lenox	"	W. Burton	Joel Post	"	2400	" " 12
13	"	"	Jas. Carver	R. Lenox	"	1800	" " 12
			Due July 12th, 1867				
14	Harper & Brothers	Harper & Bros.	Wm. Beach	Harper & Brothers	City	900	
15	Barclay, Hope & Co.	Barclay, Hope & Co.	H. J. Holmes	Barclay, Hope & Co.	"	1200	
16	"	"	Allen Park	"	"	1800	
17	J Carver	Note	A. B. Ryan	J. Hardy	"	1800	
18	"	"	J. W. Parker	J. Carter	"	1500	
			Due July 16th, 1867.				
23	Ourselves	Harper & Brothers	J. R. Weldin & Co.	J. Betts & Co.	Pittsburgh	800	
			Due July 18th, 1867.				
14	Roy, Wade & Co.	Note	A. D. Walker	R. Weston	Chicago	1500	
15	Lyon & Haven	"	Chas. Page	Lyon & Haven	Pittsburgh	800	
16	A. B. Hunter	"	J. Butler	W. Watts	Chicago	1600	
17	Duff Bros. & Co.	"	Myers & Hunter	J. Post	New Orleans	1100	

296

The preceding entries are deemed sufficient to illustrate this book.

DEPOSITORS' LEDGER.

CITY NATIONAL BANK.

JANUARY, 1867.

1. This book contains no accounts but those of Depositors and Certificates of Deposit. We have adopted a new form which we think Banks will find very convenient in business, as it constantly shows the balance of each account. The accounts are never closed until the depositor desires his Pass Book balanced. His account is then footed, and the balance brought down into the new account. See Duff Brothers & Co.'s account, p. 300.

2. The aggregate balances of this Ledger must agree with the balance of the " Depositors' " account in the General Ledger.

RICHARD IRVIN & CO.

1867.			CHECKS.	DEPOSITS.		BALANCE.	
Jan.	10	Cash		1500			
		Discount No. 7		2967			
		Check	2400			2067	
Feb.	15	Cash		1800			
		Collection		1552			
		"		2400			
		Discount No. 9		2342	40		
		Check	2100			8061	40
Apr.	15	"	2000			6061	40
May	14	Collection		784		6845	40
June	12	Discount No. 30		3918		10763	40

ROBERT LENOX.

1867.			CHECKS.	DEPOSITS.		BALANCE.	
Jan.	10	Cash		1200			
Feb.	15	"		1400			
		Discount No. 12		1194	20		
		Checks	2500			1294	20
Apr.	15	Cash		3000			
		Check	1100			3194	20
May	14	Collections		3528			
		Protest on No. 8.	2			6720	20
June	12	Collections		4200		10920	20

R. C. ROOT, ANTHONY & CO.

1867.			CHECKS.	DEPOSITS.		BALANCE.	
Jan.	10	Cash		1600			
Feb.	15	"		900			
		Discount No. 13		2089	85		
		Check	600			3989	85
Apr.	15	Cash		5000			
		Certified Check	1000			7989	85
May	14	Cash		3000		10989	85
June	12	Collection-		2700			
		Checks	900			12789	85

1867.			Checks.	Deposits.	Balance.
Jan.	10	Cash		1800	
Feb.	15	Checks	1100		700
Mar.	16	Discount No. 17		2388	
		Cash		1500	4588
Apr	15	"		2500	
		Check	2000		5088
May	14	Discount No. 22		1157 40	
		Checks	1400		4845 40
June	12	"	1100		3745 40

HARRIET LENOX.

1867.			Checks.	Deposits.	Balance.
Jan.	10	Cash		1000	
Feb.	15	Check	600		400
Mar.	16	Cash		1200	1600
Apr.	15	"		1800	
		Check	600		2800
May	14	Cash		1100	
		Check	700		3200
June	12	Cash		1800	
		Check	1300		3700

HARPER & BROTHERS.

1867.			Checks.	Deposits.	Balance.
Jan.	10	Cash		2000	
		Discount No. 1		1951 67	
		Check	1800		2151 67
Feb.	15	Cash		2500	
		Collection		784	
		Check	2000		3435 67
Apr.	15	Cash		5700	9135 67
May	14	Collection		1176	
		Checks	900		9411 67
June	12	Discount No. 26		587 70	9999 37

DUFF BROTHERS & CO.

1867.			CHECKS.	DEPOSITS.	BALANCE.
Jan.	10	Cash		1000	
Feb.	15	"		1000	
		Discount No. 11		3284 05	
		Check	1100		4184 05
Mar.	16	Discount No. 16		895 50	
		Checks	2200		2879 55
Apr.	15	Cash		6500	
		Certified Check	800		8579 55
May	14	Cash		2000	10579 55
June	12	"		2100	
		Checks	500		12179 55
	30	Balance	12179 55		
			16779 55	16779 55	
June	30	Balance		12179 55	

BARCLAY, HOPE & CO.

1867.					
Jan.	10	Cash		800	
		Discount No. 3		1789 20	
		Check	1500		1089 20
Feb.	15	Collection		1600	2689 20
Mar.	16	Cash		1400	
		Check	1100		2989 20
May	14	Discount No. 23		783 60	3772 80
June	12	" " 29		1164 40	4937 20

JAMES CARVER.

1867.					
Jan.	10	Cash		600	
		Discount No. 4		1590 40	2190 40
Feb.	15	Collection		1200	
		Checks	1300		2090 40
Mar.	16	"	2000		90 40
Apr.	15	Discount No. 18		2376 80	
		Cash		2100	4567 20
May	14	Checks	500		4067 20

RYAN & DALE.

				Checks.		Deposits.		Balance.	
1867.									
Jan.	10	Cash				800			
		Discount No. 2				994		1794	
Feb.	15	Collection				3528			
		Checks		800				4522	
Mar.	16	"		2500				2022	
Apr.	15	Discount No. 21				1791	30	3813	30
May	14	Checks		1400				2413	30

W. B. ARCHER.

				Checks.		Deposits.		Balance.	
1867.									
Jan	10	Discount No. 5				1175	60		
		Check		1000				175	60
Feb.	15	Discount No. 8				3582	60		
		Checks		3000				758	20
Apr.	15	Discount No. 20				1492	75		
		Cash				10000		12250	95
June	12	Collections				2744			
		Checks		1200				13794	95

LYON & HAVEN.

				Checks.		Deposits.		Balance.	
1867.									
Jan.	10	Discount No. 6				1491			
		Check		1200				291	
Feb.	15	Collection				2100			
		Checks		2500				109	
Apr.	15	Discount No. 19				1592	27		
		Cash				4350		5833	27
May	14	Discount No. 24				2367	20		
		Protest on No. 19		1	75			8198	72
June	12	Cash				1300			
		Collection				2940		12438	72

The red figures indicate the balance overdrawn.

A. B. HUNTER.

			Checks.	Deposits.	Balance.
1867.					
Feb. 15	Cash			400	
Mar. 16	Discount No. 14			1492 50	
	Cash			1100	
	Checks		300		2692 50
Apr. 15	Certified Check		1000		1692 50
June 12	Discount No. 28			1774 80	
	Cash			1200	4667 30

ROY, WADE & CO.

			Checks.	Deposits.	Balance.
1867.					
Feb. 15	Discount No. 10			1774 50	
	Check		1000		774 50
Mar. 16	Checks		1000		225 50
Apr. 15	Cash			3700	3474 50
May 14	Discount No. 24			1754 10	5228 60

J. W. BURNHAM.

			Checks.	Deposits.	Balance.
1867.					
Mar. 16	Discount No. 15			2388	
	Cash			1600	
	Checks		1200		2788
Apr. 15	Cash			1950	4738
June 12	Discount No. 27			1569 87	6307 87

CERTIFICATES OF DEPOSIT.

				Checks.	Deposits.	Balance.
1867.						
Apr. 15	R. P. Duff,	No. 1			2100	
	H. P. Ford,	2			2400	4500
May 14	G. R. Duncan,	3			1200	5700
June 12	R. P. Duff,	1		2100		
	G. R. Duncan,	3		1200		2400

GENERAL LEDGER,

CITY NATIONAL BANK

JANUARY, 1867.

1. This book, like the Ledger in any other business, is the book which exhibits all the results of the business. In the present instance it is made up exclusively from the Journal. In a business in which that book is dispensed with, the Ledger is made up from the General Cash Book, as in our Private Banker's Books. But, as we stated, notes pp. 261 and 269, we have arranged the Receiving and Paying Tellers' Cash Books so as to admit of direct posting to this Ledger. When that mode of keeping the books is adopted, these two books will be auxiliaries to the Deposit and the General Ledger.

2. From this book the monthly and semi-annual statements are made out.

3. Having given indexes to all the Ledgers in the first three parts of this work, we omit them in the fourth part.

4. The Taxes on the profits, circulation, and deposits of the Bank, being payable in July and January, could not be practically exhibited here.

5. Before closing, a Trial Balance must be taken. We have made the closing entries on the face of the Ledger. Those who prefer journalizing them can do as we have done with our Rail Road accounts, pp. 334 and 335.

1 Dr.   **CAPITAL**   **STOCK.**   Cr.

1867.						1866.					
June	30	Balance	f.	5	600000	Dec.	31	Cash		1	300000
						1867.					
						Jan.	10	"		1	300000
					600000						600000
						June	30	Balance			600000

CASH   ACCOUNT.

1866.						1866.						
Dec.	31	Sundries	1	300038	50	Dec.	31	Expense	1	200	
1867.						1867.						
Jan.	10	Capital Stock	1	300000		Jan.	10	Sundries	1	200600	
		Sundries	1	15300				"	1	56066	66
		Circulation	1	160000				U.S. Bonds	1	300000	
Feb.	15	Sundries	1	261200		Feb.	15	Sundries	1	126600	
Mar	16	"	2	117400		Mar.	16	"	2	39033	33
Apr.	15	"	2	101633	34	Apr.	15	"	2	33205	
May	14	"	3	89896		May	14	"	3	12903	75
June	12	"	3	43308	44	June	12	"	3	16260	
							30	Balance	f.	5	603847	54
				1388776	28					1388776	28
June	30	Balance		603847	54						

UNITED STATES   BONDS.

1867.						1867.					
Jan.	10	Cash	1	200000		June	30	Balance	f.	5	600000
		"	1	300000							
Feb.	15	"	1	100000							
				600000							600000
June	30	Balance		600000							

1867.					1867.					
Jan.	10	Cash	1	7900		Jan.	10	Cash	1	12300	
Feb.	15	"	1	18600				Bills Discounted	1	11958	87
Mar.	16	"	2	10300		Feb.	15	Cash	1	21164	
Apr.	15	"	2	8500				Bills Discounted	2	14267	60
May	14	"	3	4903	75	Mar.	16	Cash	2	6800	
June	12	"	3	8300				Bills Discounted	2	7164	
	30	Balance	f 5	120352	91	Apr.	15	Cash	2	51100	
								Bills Discounted	2	7253	12
						May	14	Cash	3	12788	
								Bills Discounted	3	6062	30
						June	12	Cash	3	18984	
								Bills Discounted	3	9014	77
				178856	66					178856	66
						June	30	Balance		120352	91

FOREIGN BILLS   OF EXCHANGE.

1867.							1867.						
Jan.	10	Cash,	No. 1	1	44444	44	Jan.	12	Baring Bros. & Co. No. 1	1	44444	44
Mar.	16	"	2	2	22222	22	Mar.	16	"	2	2	22222	22
Apr.	15	"	3	2	20000		Apr.	15	"	3	2	20000	
June	12	"	4	3	2000		June	12	"	4	3	2000	
					88666	66						88666	66

BILLS   DISCOUNTED.

1867.						1867.					
Jan.	10	Sundries	1	12100		Feb.	15	Cash	1	7900	
Feb.	15	"	2	14400		Mar.	16	"	2	18600	
Mar.	16	"	2	7200		Apr.	15	"	2	7200	
Apr.	15	"	2	7300		May	14	"	3	5700	
May	14	"	3	6200		June	30	Balance	f 5	17000	
June	12	"	3	9200							
				56400						56400	
June	30	Balance		17000							

BANK   FURNITURE.

1867.					
Jan.	10	Cash	1	600	

U

1867.						1866.					
June 30	Profit & Loss	f 5	18724	78		Dec. 31	Cash	1	38	50	
						1867.					
						Jan. 10	Bills Discounted	1	89	13	
						Feb. 15	" "	2	66	40	
						Mar. 16	" "	2	36		
						Apr. 15	" "	2	34	88	
						May 14	Cash	3	18000		
							Bills Discounted	3	87	70	
						June 12	Cash	3	204	94	
							Bills Discounted	3	167	23	
			18724	78					18724	78	

EXPENSE   ACCOUNT.

1866.						1867.				
Dec. 31	Cash	1	200			June 30	Profit & Loss	f 5	3175	
1867.										
Apr. 15	"	2	2975							
			3175						3175	

EXCHANGE   ACCOUNT.

1867.						1867.				
Jan. 10	Cash	1	2222	22		Jan. 10	Bills Discounted	1	52	
Feb. 15	"	1	116			Feb. 15	Cash	1	136	
Mar. 16	"	2	1189	11			Bills Discounted	2	66	
Apr. 15	"	2	1290			Apr. 15	Cash	2	2666	67
May 14	"	3	62				Bills Discounted	2	12	
June 12	"	3	218			May 14	Cash	3	4112	
	30	Profit & Loss	f 5	4131	34		Bills Discounted	3	50	
						June 12	Cash	3	2116	
							Bills Discounted	3	18	
			9228	67					9228	67

CIRCULATION   ACCOUNT.

1867.						1867.				
Apr. 15	Cash	2	500			Jan. 10	Cash	1	160000	
June 30	Balance	f 5	479500			Feb. 15	"	1	232000	
						Mar. 16	"	2	88000	
			480000						480000	
						June 30	Balance		479500	

Dr.   IRON CITY   (Pittsburgh.) NATIONAL BANK.   Cr.   4

1867.						1867.					
Feb.	15	Cash	1	3564		Jan.	10	Cash	1	1000	
Mar.	16	"	2	1782		Mar.	16	"	2	1200	
May	14	"	3	1980		Apr.	15	"	2	2000	
June	12	"	3	2772		May	14	Protest	3	2	
						June	30	Balance	f 5	5896	
				10098						10098	
June	30	Balance		5896							

FIRST NATIONAL   (Chicago.)   BANK.

1867.						1867.					
Jan.	10	Cash	1	500		Jan.	10	Cash	1	1500	
Feb.	15	"	1	792		Mar.	16	"	2	1600	
Mar.	16	"	2	1188		Apr.	15	"	2	4000	
June	12	"	3	2970		May	14	"	3	6900	
	30	Balance	f 5	8550							
				14000						14000	
						June	30	Balance		8550	

FIRST NATIONAL   (New Orleans.)   BANK.

1867.						1867.					
Jan.	10	Cash	1	1000		Jan.	10	Cash	1	500	
Feb.	15	"	1	3528		Mar.	16	"	2	1200	
Mar.	16	"	2	2352		Apr.	15	"	2	8000	
June	30	Balance	f 5	2820							
				9700						9700	
						June	30	Balance		2820	

BARING   (London.)   BROS. & CO.

1867.								1867.						
Jan.	12	Foreign Bill,	No. 1	1	44444	44		Apr.	15	Cash,	No. 1	2	26666	67
Mar.	16	"	"	2	2	22222	22		May	14	"		2 3	40000	
Apr.	15	"	"	3	2	20000			June	12	"	for No. 3 ret'd.	3	20003	50
June	12	"	"	4	3	2000				30	Balance		f 5	1996	49
					88666	66							88666	66
June	30	Balance			1996	49								

BANK OF   (Montreal, Canada.)   MONTREAL.

1867.				
May	14	Cash	3	3564

FIRST NATIONAL   (Boston.)   BANK.

1867.						1867.				
May	14	Cash	3	2394		May	14	Cash	3	2394

5	Dr.	PROFIT			&			LOSS.		Cr.	
1867. June	30	Expense	f	3	3175		1867. June	12	Cash	3	2000	
		Dividend No. 1		5	18000			30	Discount & Interest	f 3	18724	78
		Surplus Capital		5	3681	12			Exchange	3	4131	34
					24856	12					24856	12

DIVIDEND No. 1.

							1867. June	30	Profit & Loss	f 5	18000	

SURPLUS CAPITAL.

							1867. June	30	Profit & Loss	f 5	3681	12

BALANCE ACCOUNT.

1867. June	30	Cash	f	1	603847	54	1867. June	30	Capital Stock	f	1	600000	
		U. S. Bonds		1	600000				Depositors		2	120352	91
		Bills Discounted		2	17000				Circulation		3	479500	
		Bank Furniture		2	600				1st Nat. Bk. N. Orleans		4	2820	
		Bank of Montreal		4	3564				1st Nat. Bk. Chicago		4	8550	
		Baring Bros. & Co.		4	1996	49			Dividend No. 1		5	18000	
		Iron City Nat. Bank		4	5896				Surplus Capital		5	3681	12
					1232904	03						1232904	03

DIVIDEND BOOK, CITY NATIONAL BANK.

Dividend No. 1, Three per cent., declared June 30, 1867.

Name.	No. of Shares.	Amount.	Date.	Received Payment.
Archer, W. B.	2000	6000		
Baker, J. C.	100	300		
Barclay, Hope & Co.	300	900		
Banks, Robert	600	1800		
Cox, J. W.	100	300		
Compton, J. R.	20	60		
Duff, Wm. H.	100	300		
Duff, P.	100	300		
Duncan, Geo. R.	30	90		
Harper, James	600	1800		
Hay, Wm.	200	600		
Irvin, Richard, & Co.	100	300		
Lenox, Harriet	50	150		
Lenox, Robert	100	300		
Mitchell, Thos.	500	1500		
Major, Wm.	300	900		
Root, R. C.	100	300		
Smith, T. B.	100	300		
Ward, John	500	1500		
Warren, Samuel	100	300		
	6000	18000		

1. When a stockholder calls for his dividend, the book-keeper fills a check for the amount, as follows:—

City National Bank,

Pay William B. Archer, Esq., or Bearer,

Six Thousand .... Dollars,

and charge Dividend No. 1.

$ 6000.₁₀₀

W. J. Parker,
General Book-keeper.

The date is then inserted in the "date" column above, and the drawer of the dividend inserts his signature in the "Received Payment" column, opposite the amount of his dividend.

2. Dividend Checks are charged to the Dividend Account, in the same manner that Depositors' Checks are charged to individuals. When all the dividends are paid, "Dividend No. 1," in the Ledger, will be balanced.

SEMI-ANNUAL STATEMENT OF CITY NATIONAL BANK, NEW YORK, FOR THE TERM ENDING JUNE 30, 1867.

ASSETS.

U. S. Bonds		600000	
Bills Discounted		17000	
Bank Furniture		600	
Bank of Montreal		3564	
Baring Bros. & Co.		1996	40
Iron City National Bank, Pittsburgh		5896	
Notes and Checks	$420000.54		
Coin	23847.		
310			
Treasury Notes	160000		
	$603847.54		
Less our own Notes on hand	40000.	563847	54
		1192904	03

LIABILITIES.

Capital Stock		600000	
Depositors		120352	91
First National Bank, New Orleans		2820	
" " Chicago		8550	
Dividend No. 1		18000	
Surplus Capital		3681	12
Circulation	$479500.		
Less our Notes on hand	40000.	439500	
		1192904	03

STANDING LEDGER.

RICHARD IRVIN & .CO.

Date.		Payable by.	As discounter.	As payer.	As endorser.	Due.		Mem.
1866.						1867.		
Dec.	14	J. W. Loring	3000		·	Mar.	17	Paid
Oct.	8	Hay & Wood	2400				11	"
1867.								
June	10	R. Banks	4000			Oct.	13	

LYON & HAVEN.

1866.					*	1867.		
Dec.	14	Bateman & Hill	1500			Feb.	15	Paid
1867.								
Feb.	11	J. Morton			1200	Mar.	16	"
	11	J. Kane	1600			May	14	Protested

1. Some call this the "Blue Book." The form and two illustrations which we give will fully explain its use and importance to the President and Directors. In business it is indexed, which enables them to refer to it and see at once what every borrower is liable for as promisor or endorser.

2. The entries are made from the Discount Book as the notes are entered on that book.

REGISTER OF STOCKS.

Purchased.		Due.		Description.	Amount.	Interest is due.	Remarks.
1867.		1881.					
Jan'y.	2	Feb.	25	100 Bonds U.S. 5/20s of $1000 each, 3d Series, Nos. 19001 to 19100	100000	May 1 and Nov. 1	
Jan'y.	2	1881. Feb.	25	100 Bonds U.S. 5/20s of $1000 each, 4th Series, Nos. 1201 to 1300	100000	May 1 and Nov. 1	
Jan'y.	10	1881. Feb.	25	300 Bonds U.S. 5/20s of $1000 each, 4th Series, Nos. 20001 to 20300	300000	May 1 and Nov. 1	
Feb.	15	1881. Feb.	25	100 Bonds U.S. 5/20s of $1000 each, 4th Series, Nos. 30001 to 30100	100000	May 1 and Nov. 1	

This book records all stocks and bonds the property of the bank, and when the interest is payable.

QUESTIONS FOR EXAMINATION ON NATIONAL BANK ACCOUNTS.

1. When is the General Cash Book a book of original entry? (N. 1, p. 247.)
2. What is it made up from? (N. 1, p. 247.)
3. What should its balance agree with? (N 1, p. 247.)
4. Do banks generally keep a Journal? (N. 1, p. 253.)
5. When it is kept, what book receives all its entries from it? (N. 1, p. 253.)
6. What does the Stock Ledger record? (N. 1, p. 257.)
7. Where are its entries first obtained? (N. 1, p. 257.)
8. Upon what book are the transfer entries first recorded? (N. 1, p. 257.)
9. What must the aggregate credits of the Stock Ledger agree with? (N. 2, p. 257.)
10. Why are its accounts kept in alphabetical order? (N. 3, p. 257.)
11. Where do the amounts of the Receiving Teller's Cash Book pass when a General Cash Book is kept? (N. 1, p. 261.)
12. When no General Cash Book or Journal is kept, where are the contents of this book posted? (N. 1, p. 261.)
13. What is the use of the Signature Book? (N. 1, p. 268.)
14. Who should witness the signatures? (N. 1, p. 268.)
15. Where is the balance of Cash on hand found when no General Cash Book is kept? (N. 1, p. 269.)
16. How can a Certificate of Deposit be negotiated? (N. 1, p. 274.)
17. What is the use of the Offering Book? (N. 1, p. 275.)
18. Where are the Accepted Notes and Bills entered? (N. 1, p. 275.)
19. What is done with Rejected Notes and Bills? (N. 1, p. 275.)
20. What is done with Discounted Paper when protested? (N. 1, p. 278.)
21. What is done with Protested Collection Paper? (N 2, p. 282.)
22. Where do we enter all paper remitted for collection? (N. 2, p. 290.)
23. Where do we enter Discounted Paper when collected? (N. 3, p. 290.)
24. Where do we enter collections when paid? (N. 3, p. 290.)
25. What do we record in the Foreign Bill Book? (N. 1, p. 280.)
26. Why not enter them on the Discount Book, as we do all other paper belonging to the bank? (N. 1, p. 280.)
27. Where are all Notes and Bills entered when received for collection? (N. 1 and 2. p. 287.)
28. What is the Tickler used for? (N 1, p. 293.)
29. What accounts are kept in the Depositors' Ledger? (N. 1, p. 297.)
30. When are they closed? (N. 1, p. 297.)
31. What must the aggregate balances of this Ledger agree with? (N. 2, p. 297.)
32. How are overdrawn balances indicated? (N 1, p. 301.)
33. What Ledger exhibits the results of the business? (N. 1, p. 303.)
34. What book are the Monthly and Semi-monthly Statements made from? (N. 2, p 303.)
35. What account do we debit for the Dividend Checks? (N. 2, p. 309.)
36. How will the account "Dividend No. 1" stand when all are paid? (N. 2, p. 309.)

RAIL ROAD ACCOUNTS.

JANUARY, 1867.

313

REMARKS.

The following set of Rail Road accounts illustrates in a condensed form the construction and equipment of the road, the commencement of its operations, and the declaration of the first dividend. Part of the earnings are carried to credit of the STOCK, part to the DIVIDEND, and part to the SURPLUS CAPITAL.

The forms of Manifests, Bills of Lading, &c. are among the best in use; but Rail Road and Express Companies vary all these forms to adapt them to changes in business.

RAIL ROAD ACCOUNTS.

CONSTRUCTION AND EQUIPMENT DAY BOOK,

PENNSYLVANIA RAIL ROAD,

JANUARY, 1867.

1. This book is ruled with a date and voucher column on the left: the next two are for the titles of the account and the items of expenditure. To the right of these are eleven money columns, each of which has its representative account in the General Ledger. Compare and see.

2. The figures in the Voucher column are the numbers which are endorsed upon them as they are filed away for future reference.

3. When the footings are brought forward to the end of the month, bring them under the amount in the Depot column on the left. From the aggregate footing make the Journal entry. See Journal entry of January 31.

4. The Incidentals should be designated "Construction Incidentals," in the Journal, as there is another account of the same name in Operating Expenditures.

5. The entries in this book are made from the vouchers, and are, as the Journal entry indicates, cash payments.

Date.		Vouchers	What Account.	For what paid.		Depots.
1866.						
Jan.	4	1	Surveying	Pd. E. H. Heastings 1 mo.'s Salary to Jan. 1st		
	8	2	Land	" J. Cartwright, for Right of Way, per Deed M'ch **4, 1866**		
	9	3	Incidental Exps.	" W. S. Haven, for Blank Books		
	12	4	Grading	" Jacob Ring, Excavating 21000 yds. @ 10¢ $2100		
				Less 20% retained 420		
	14	5	Depots	" Passal and Hay, building Freight Depot at Harrisburg		6000
	15	6	Road Building	" Knap, Ward & Co., for R.R. Iron		
	16	7	Bridging	" Carpenter & Co., Bridging Wood Run, **per Contract**		
	18	8	Tunneling	" Hall & Oxley, for Tunneling Bills Hill, " "		
	19	9	Locomotives	" Pillow & Lens, for Locomotive and Tender "Locomotive"		
			do.	" " " " " " " "Driver"		
		10	Cars	" Kirk & Rhodes, for 5 Freight Cars, @ $500 each		
	21	11	Fencing	" Burns & Shell, for Fencing 350 Rods, @ $1.00		
		12	Incidental **Exps.**	" H. Greeley, for Advertising		
		13	do.	" J. G. Bennett, "		
		14	Fencing	" G. Wood, for Fencing 160 Rods, @ $1.00		
		15	Cars	" Kirk and Rhodes, for 3 Passenger Cars, at $2000 each		
		16	Depots	" J. Burchinell, for Freight and Passenger Depot at Altoona,		
				per Contract		7600
	22	17	Road **Building**	" R. Driver, Laborers' Pay-Roll for Dec. 1866		
		18	Lands	" Adam Oaks, for 40 Acres, per Deed Jan. 14, **1867**		
		19	Surveying	" W. Maxwell's Traveling Expenses		
		20	Bridging	" Oliver Birch, for 9000 ft. Oak Lumber, @ 20¢		
		21	Depots	" Boyd & Murdoch, for Freight Depots at Pittsburgh, per		
				Contract		9400
		22	Grading	" Excavating on Section 14, 4000 yds., @ 10 $400		
				" " 15, 3000 " @ 20 600		
				" " 16, 2500 " @ 20 500		
				$1500		
				Less 20% retained, 300		
		23	Incidental Exps.	" Telegraphing for one month		
	24	24	Bridging	" F. Freeman, Bridging Red Run, **Sec. 31**		
		25	Tunneling	" Piper & Wood, Tunneling Coal Hill, " 27		
		26	Grading	" Murphy & Hill, Grading Roads Hill, " 21		
		27	Locomotives	" Sterling & Brown, for Locomotive and Tender "Velocity"		
		28	Surveying	" J. Camp, 4 mos.' Salary to date		
		29	Cars	" Painter & Carpenter, for 2 Pass. Cars, @ $2200, per Contract		
		30	Lands	" R. Stone, for Right of Way, 100 ft. wide, per Deed Jan. 23, 1867		
		31	Road Building	" Freight & Duty on R.R. Iron received per Ship from Li-		
				verpool		
		32	Fencing	" Samuel Graves, for 1600 Rods, @ 75¢		
		33	Depots	" J. & A. Patterson, for Building Depot at Pittsburgh, per		
				Contract		1300
	26	34	Incidental **Exps.**	" W. S. Haven, for Binding and Stationery		
		35	do.	" Daily Commercial, for Advertising to date		
		36	Depots	" Carpenter & Co., for Building New Office at Pittsburgh Pas-		
				senger Depot		270
		37	Cars	" Kirk & Rhodes, 6 Cars, @ $400, **per** Contract		
				Amounts carried forward		24570

Road Building.	Lands.	Surveying.	Grading.	Bridging.	Tunnelling.	Locomotives.	Cars.	Fencing.	Incidental.
	700	100							130
			1680						
4400				1300					
					3800	7000			
						7000	2500	350	
									40
								160	35
							6000		
1500	800	80							
				1800					
			1200						65
				4900	4400				
			170			6600			
		80					4400		
	850								
3100								1200	
									330
									70
							2400		
9000	2350	260	3050	8000	8200	20600	15300	1710	670

Date.	Vouchers.	What Account.	For what paid.		Depots.
1867.			Amounts bro't forward,		24570
Jan. 26	38	Lands	Pd. J. Banks, for Procuring Right of Way		
	39	Bridging	" Hiram Hill, for Material delivered on Sec. 1		
	40	do.	" W. Stone, for Bridging " 1		
	41	Grading	" R. Baker & Sons, Excavating, as follows,—viz.:		
			31000 yds. on Sec. 18, 19, 20, @ 10¢	$3100	
			1500 " " 18, 19, 20, @ 20¢	300	
				3400	
			Less 20% retained	680	
	42	Lands	" R. Banks, for Right of Way 100 feet wide, per Deed May 7, 1866.		
28	43	do.	" Commission of Appraisement, for services		
	44	Road Building	" for Switch Ties, 80, @ 20		
	45	Incidental Exps.	" J. K. Smith, 1 mo.'s Salary to date		
	46	do.	" R. Roberts, 1 " do. do.		
	47	Surveying	" W. Morris, 3 " do. do.		
	48	do.	" R. Manley, 3 " do. do.		
	49	Lands	" J. Wood, Right of Way 100 ft. wide, per Deed May 7 1866		
31	50	Road Building	" Freight and Duties on R.R. Iron from Liverpool		
	51	do.	" Driver's Pay-Roll for Jan.		
	52	Grading	" A. Wood, Grading Farmer's Hill		
	53	Bridging	" D. Haven, for Bridging Wood Creek		
	54	Locomotives	" Archer & Co., for Locomotive and Tender "Ajax"		
	55	Cars	" Kirk & Rhodes, 6 Passenger Cars, @ $2200		
	56	Incidental Exps.	" Team Hire this month		
	57	do.	" "Morning Post" for Notice to Stockholders		
	58	Fencing	" Robert Hall, for 1600 Rods, @ $1.00		
	59	Depots	" Carpenter & Co., for Building Freight Depot at Pittsburgh		11500
	60	Surveying	" R. Patterson, Horse Hire		
			Total amount pd. for Depots		36070
			" Road Building		20100
			" Lands		6090
			" Surveying		1100
			" Grading		8100
			" Bridging		14800
			" Tunneling		8200
			" Locomotives		27600
			" Cars		28500
			" Fencing		3310
			" Incidentals		1200
			Journal 1. Total .		155070

Road Building.	Lands.	Surveying.	Grading.	Bridging.	Tunneling.	Locomotives.	Cars.	Fencing.	Incidental.
9000	2350 110	200	3050	8000 460 940	8200	20600	15300	1710	670
			2720						
16	1300 440								80 150
		450 300							
8484 2600	1890		2330	5400		7000	13200		230 70
								1600	
		90							
20100	6090	1100	8100	14800	8200	27600	28500	3310	1200

Date.	Vouchers.	What Account.	For what paid.	Depots.
1867. Feb. 1	61	Incidental Exps.	Pd. Dispatch, for Advertising	
"	62	Depots	" J. & A. Patterson, Building Depot at East Liberty	5000
	63	Road Building	" R. R⁵ Spike Co., for bill of Spikes	
	64	Lands	" Z. Wainwright, per Deed May 7, 1866	
28	65	Surveying	" W. Moore and Assistants, to date	
	66	Depots	" R. Shrum, Building Depot at Greensburg	8000
	67	Grading	" J. Dignam, for Grading 93750 yds. @ 10 $9375 Less 20% retained 1875	
	68	Bridging	" Cox & Co., Bridging Turtle Creek	
	69	Tunneling	" Ames & Co., for Tunnel at Greensburg	
	70	Locomotives	" Baldwin & Co., for Locomotive and Tender "Kiskiminitas"	
"		do.	" " " " " " " "Allegheny"	
"		do.	" " " " " " " "Altoona"	
	71	Depots	" D. Wood, Building Depot at Johnstown	10000
	72	do.	" S. Maple " " " Lancaster	8000
	73	Road Building	" Laborers' Pay-Roll for Feb.	
	74	Bridging	" for Bridges from Greensburg to Altoona, per Contract	
	75	Cars	" Kirk & Rhodes, for 8 Passenger Cars, @ $2000	
"		do.	" " " " 3 Baggage " @ 500	
	76	Fencing	" J. Post, for 700 Rods, @ $1.00	
	77	Incidental Exps.	" J. Daub, painting signboards, per Contract	
			Total amount pd. for Depots	31000
			" Road Building	18000
			" Lands	1100
			" Surveying	900
			" Grading	7500
			" Bridging	14800
			" Tunneling	8200
			" Locomotives	22200
			" Cars	17500
			" Fencing	700
			" Incidentals	800
			Journal 2. Total	122700

Road Building	Lands.	Surveying.	Grading.	Bridging.	Tunneling.	Locomotives.	Cars.	Fencing.	Incidental.
									270
4500	1100	900							
			7500	800	8200	7000 8000 7200			
13500				14000			16000 1500	700	530
18000	1100	900	7500	14800	8200	22200	17500	700	800

FORM OF A LOCAL BILL OF LADING.

PENNSYLVANIA RAIL ROAD COMPANY.

C. A. CARPENTER, FREIGHT AGENT, PITTSBURGH, PA.

Received, Pittsburgh, ... 186 , of ....
the following packages, in apparent good order, marked as per margin, which we promise to deliver in like good order, the incidental dangers of the Rail Road, Fire in Cars and in Stations, excepted, at .... *Station, the Owner or Consignee paying Freight and Charges, in par funds, as per Tariff Rates.*

It is agreed, and is part of the Consideration of this Contract:

1. That all goods received for transportation shall be properly packed, and distinctly marked with the name of the consignee and the Station where and to whom consigned.
2. That the Pennsylvania Rail Road Company shall not be responsible for the melting of Ice; decay or perishable articles from heat or cold; or for any loss, injury, or damage from the dangers of rail road transportation, explosions, fire in stores, depots, or in transit, leakage, breakage, theft, or from any cause whatever, unless the same be proved to have occurred from the fraud or gross negligence of said Company or its servants; nor liable for any damage to glass or fragile articles, unless herein specially insured. And when goods are intrusted to any other Company or person (which said Pennsylvania Rail Road Company is hereby authorized to do), such Company or person so selected shall be regarded exclusively as the Agent of the owner, and as such alone liable; and the Pennsylvania Rail Road Company shall not in any event be responsible for the negligence or non-performance of any such Company or person; nor in any event shall the Pennsylvania Rail Road Company be liable for any loss or damage unless the claim therefor shall be presented in writing to the Agent of said Company within five days after the time when said property has or ought to have been delivered. The goods transported shall be subject to a lien—and may also be retained—for all arrearages of freight and charges due on other goods by the same consignee or owner.
   Freight to be paid upon the weight of goods as ascertained by the Company's scales.
3. Storage will be charged on goods allowed to remain over twenty-four hours in the Depots or Warehouses of said Company.
4. All articles consigned will be charged therewith.
5. Gun-Powder, Gun-Cotton, Friction Matches, and like combustibles, are not received or transported under this contract.
6. Goods at private turnouts shall be at the owner's risk until attached to, and until after they are detached from the train.
7. All articles will be at the risk of the owner as the several "Way Stations" and Platforms where Depot Buildings have not been established by the Company, from the moment such articles are delivered from the cars as directed or ordered.
8. Freight carried by this Company must be removed from the Station to which it is consigned during business hours on the day of its arrival, or it may be stored at owner's risk and expense, and in the event of its destruction or damage from any cause while in the depot of the Company, it is agreed that said Company shall not be liable to pay any damages therefor.
9. The responsibility of the Company under this Bill of Lading to commence upon the shipment of the goods from this Station, and to terminate when unloaded from the cars.

MARKS.	ARTICLES.

FORM OF A THROUGH BILL OF LADING.

PENNSYLVANIA RAIL ROAD COMPANY.

C. A. CARPENTER, Freight Agent, Pittsburgh, Pa.   S. B. KINGSTON, Jr., Freight Agent, Philadelphia, Pa.
WILLIAM BROWN, Agent, N. C. R. W. Co., Baltimore.

H. H. HOUSTON, GENERAL FREIGHT AGENT, PHILADELPHIA.

Received, Pittsburgh, ... 186 , of ....
the following packages, in apparent good order, marked as per margin, to be transported to .... and delivered at the FREIGHT STATION at ....

UPON THE FOLLOWING CONDITIONS.

The Owner or Consignee to pay freight as per specified rates, and charges, in par funds, upon the goods as they from time to time arrive. It is agreed, and is part of the consideration of this contract, that the Company will not be responsible for leakage of Liquids, breakage of Glass or Queensware, the injury or breakage of Looking Glasses, Glass Show Cases, Picture Frames, Store Castings or Hollow Ware, nor for injury to the hidden contents of Packages, nor for the loss in weight or alteration of Grain or Coffee in bags, or Rice in sleeves, nor for the decay of perishable articles, nor for damages arising to any article carried from the effects of heat or cold, nor for the loss of Nuts in bags, or of Lemons or Oranges in boxes, unless covered by canvas, or loss or damage to Goods occasioned by Providential causes, or by Fire from any cause whatever, while in transit or at Stations, unless the additional charge of five cents per one hundred pounds be added to the following rates, in consideration of the Company insuring the Goods safe to Philadelphia or Baltimore, against all hazard, by instructions of owners or shippers before shipping.
The Company will not be responsible for damage on Tobacco, unless it is proved to have occurred during the time of its transit between Pittsburgh and Baltimore, or Philadelphia, and of this, notice must be given within thirty hours after the arrival of the same.
Freight is to be paid upon the weight as ascertained by the Company's Scales at Pittsburgh.
If delivered to any point beyond Philadelphia or Baltimore, the same may be intrusted or delivered in the cars of this Company, or otherwise, to any other Rail Road or Transportation Company, or Agent; and such Rail Road or Transportation Company, or Agent so selected, shall be regarded exclusively as the Agent of the owner or consignee, and shall be entitled to the benefits of the Conditions and Provisions of this, and of such Bill of Lading as they may deliver therefor; and the Pennsylvania Rail Road Company shall not, in any event, be responsible for the negligence or non-performance of any such Company or Agent, nor shall such Company or Agent be liable for any loss or injury except upon its or their respective routes, and while such merchandise is in their respective custody.
That the Owner or Consignee hereby assumes all risks from leakage, and loss by Fire, while in transit or at Depots, or in Stations, or on board Boats, from any cause whatever; and all dangers and delays of Rail Road and Water Transportation between Pittsburgh and point of destination; and in any chain or demand, suit at law or equity, against this Company or Transportation Company or Agent, for loss or damage thereby, this Bill of Lading shall be deemed and taken as a release in full therefor.
Whatever responsibility is assumed, under this Bill of Lading, shall begin when the merchandise is loaded into the cars of the Company, and cease when unloaded therefrom, or intrusted or delivered as aforesaid, and which it is agreed shall constitute a delivery.
The Owner or Consignee will have his or their Agent or Employees to receive said merchandise, as the same from time to time arrives and is delivered as aforesaid; but if not then removed, the same will remain at place of unloading, at the Owner's risk, or be removed, at the option of the Company, to such place of deposit as it may select, at the risk and cost of the Owner or Consignee.
Said merchandise may be retained for all arrearages of freight and charges due this Company on other goods by the same Consignee or Owner.
Nor shall any Company or Agent hereunder be liable, by reason of any responsibility hereby assumed, for any loss or damage to such merchandise, unless the claim be presented in writing at the office of the Agent at the point receipted to, within ten days after the time when the same has been or ought to have been delivered.
In case of loss or damage to any property herein mentioned, from such cause as would render the Carriers liable, it is expressly agreed that they shall have the benefit of any insurance that may have been or may be effected upon, or on account of said property, and the Owner, Consignee, and Shipper severally agree that it shall be so inserted in the policy.
Notice.—In accepting this Bill of Lading, the Shipper, or other Agent of the owner of the property carried, expressly accepts and agrees to all its conditions, stipulations, and exceptions.

MARKS.	ARTICLES.

322

RAIL ROAD ACCOUNTS.

OPERATING EXPENDITURES,

PENNSYLVANIA RAIL ROAD,

JANUARY, 1867.

1. The headings of the columns will sufficiently explain the use of this book.

2. Its ten money columns have also their representatives in the General Ledger, which will explain themselves.—Refer to them.

3. The final footing at the end of the month is made and Journalized like the last book.

Date.			What Account.	For what paid.
1857.				
Mar.	1	1	Incidental Exps.	Pd. W. G. Johnston & Co., for Blanks and Stationery
		2	Track Repairs	" Whitmore, Wolff, Duff & Co., for Spikes
		3	Fuel	" James Oak, for his Bill of Wood
		4	Station	" Wm. Ward, 1 mo.'s Salary as Supt.
		5	Trains	" Pay-Roll for Feb'y.
		6	Engines	" Mitchell, Stevenson & Co., for Castings
		7	Cars	" Kirk & Rhodes, for Glass
		8	Station	" W. Darsie, 1 mo.'s Salary
		9	Shop	" Craig & Co., for 3 Stoves
		10	Buildings	" Carpenter & Co., for Repairs to Pittsburgh Depot
		11	Oil & Waste	" Childs & Co., for 5 Bales 1500 lb. Cotton
		12	Incidental Exps.	" W. S. Haven, for Printing Cards and Way Bills
		13	Fuel	" Darlington Coal Co., for 400 Tons Coal, @ $2.00
		14	Station	" Salaries for Feb'y
		15	Trains	" Trains, Pay-Roll for Feb'y.
		16	Shop	" Geo. Dexter (Foreman), Salary to date
		17	do.	" Blacksmiths' Pay-Roll for Feby.
		18	Engines	" Warden & Son, Cylinder Head for Locomotive "Driver"
		19	Cars	" Kirk & Rhodes, for Bill of Locks, &c.
		20	Track	" Bell & Ward, for New Switch at Altoona
		21	Buildings	" Boyd & Murdoch, Repairs to Office
		22	Oil & Waste	" Fleming & Bros., Bill of Oil
		23	Incidental Exps.	" R. M. Riddle, for Advertising to date
		24	Fuel	" J. A. Reams' Bill of Wood
	4	25	Train	" Brakesman's Pay-Roll for last month
		26	do.	" Conductor's " " "
		27	Station	" Laborers' " " "
		28	Shop	" Machinists' " " "
	5	29	Station	" Watchman's Wages
	6	30	Engines	" Craig & Co., Repairing Pipe and New Pipe for "Velocity"
		31	Cars	" Jas. Sawyer, for Oak Plank
		32	Incidental Exps.	" Daily Post, for Advertising
		33	do.	" J. Bailey & Co., "
		34	Track	" Pay-Roll for M'ch 4
		35	do.	" " " " " 6
	8	36	Fuel	" J. Day, 150 Tons Coal delivered at Johnstown
		37	Incidental Exps.	" W. S. Haven's Bill for Printing Tickets
	10	38	Oil & Waste	" F. Sellers & Co., for Oil
		39	do.	" B. C. & J. H. Sawyer, 1200 lb. Grease, @ 8¢
		40	Incidental Exps.	" W. G. Johnston & Co., for Office Stationery
		41	Building	" Hugh Beatty, for Painting Depot at Pittsburgh
	15	42	Cars	" E. Edmunson & Co., for Upholstering
		43	Engines	" Paine & Co., for New Spark-Catcher for "Ajax"
	16	44	Station	" W. White, 1 mo.'s Salary as Freight Agent at Pittsburgh
		45	do.	" D. Hill, " " Passenger " " "
	18	46	Trains	" A. Black, 1 mo.'s Salary as Freight Conductor
	19	47	Shop	" J. Woodwell & Co., for Tools
				Amounts carried forward

Station.	Shop.	Trains.	Engines.	Cars.	Track.	Buildings.	Oil & Waste.	Fuel.	Incidentals
					180				130
								120	
150		1600	190						
200	45			30		80			
							150		370
								800	
160	80	940							
	420		60	170					
					120	220			
							250		
								180	110
		560							
		440							
140	1365								
30			150	190					
					95				120
					75				110
								300	
							350		60
							96		
									30
				110		180			
			130						
180									
120		50							
	390								
980	2300	3650	530	500	470	480	846	1400	930

Date.	Vouchers.	What Account.	For what paid.
			Amounts bro't forward
1857. Mar. 19	48	Shop	Pd. J. Gardiner, for Horse Hire 1 month
	49	Track	" Repairs on Division No. 7, in Feby.
	"	do.	" " " " " 9, " "
20	50	Buildings	" Masons' Bill at Philadelphia
24	51	Cars	" for 14 Water Coolers, @ $5
	52	do.	" Wilson & Co., Bill of Lamps and Fitting
26	53	Trains	" Watson's Salary as Passenger Conductor
	54	**do.**	" Gray's " " " "
27	55	Incidental Exps.	" H. Turner, for Trunk Lost
	56	do.	" Kay & Co., Freight "
28	57	Fuel	" A. Bell, for Wood
	58	Oil & Waste	" B. L. Fahnestock & Co., for Oil
29	59	Station	" Wilson, Freight Agent at **Altoona, Salary for this month**
	60	do.	" Hay, Passenger " " " " " "
30	61	Shop	" G. Dexter (Foreman), Salary for this month
	62	do.	" Blacksmiths' Pay-Roll for this month
	63	Trains	" Brakesman's " " "
31	64	Oil & Waste	" for Rags and Tallow
	65	Fuel	" Baird & Sons, 700 Tons Coal, @ $2
	66	Trains	" Fireman's Pay-Roll for this month
	67	Shop	" Machinist's " " "
	68	Station	" W. N. Davis, Salary for this month
	69	Engines	" Machinists at Philadelphia
	70	Cars	" Warren & Lee, of "
	71	Track	" for New Rail on Secs. 17, 18, 19, & 24
	72	Buildings	" for Enlarging Office at Pittsburgh
	73	Station	" Secretary & Clerks' Pay-Roll at Philadelphia

           Amount pd. for Stations this month
           "   " " Shop   "   "
           "   " " Trains   "   "
           "   " " Engines "   "
           "   " " Cars   "   "
           "   " " Track   "   "
           "   " " Buildings "
           "   " " Oil & Waste "
           "   " " Fuel   "   "
           "   " " Incidentals "

    Jour. 2. Total Operating Expenditures for March

Station.	Shop.	Trains.	Engines.	Cars.	Track.	Buildings.	Oil & Waste.	Fuel.	Incidentals.
980	2300	3650	. 530	560	470	480	846	1400	930
	30				440				
					160				
						320			
				70				*	
				60					
		60							
		60							90
								80	210
							204		
140									
110	80								
	420								
		530					55		
		980						1400	
	1475								
200			3670						
				4470					
					3330				
						1360			
1670									
3100	4305	5280	4200	5100	4400	2160	1105	2880	1230
4305									
5280									
4200									
5100									
4400									
2160									
1105									
2880									
1230									
33760									

FORM OF WAY MANIFEST.

PENNSYLVANIA RAIL ROAD.

No. _____ *186* .

Manifest of Merchandise, *forwarded from* _____ *to* _____ ,

No.CAR.	CONSIGNOR.	MARKS.	CONSIGNEE.	DESCRIPTION OF ARTICLES.	WEIGHT.	RATE.	AMOUNT OF FREIGHT.	EXPENSES.	PREPAID.	TO BE COLLECTED.

☞ N.B.—In all cases where the Price charged for Transportation is less than the Tariff Rates, the authority for so making the same must be attached to or stated in the Manifest, and also entered in the Freight Forwarded Book.

_____ *Agent.*

328

FORM OF THROUGH MANIFEST.

No. _____

Manifest of Merchandise *forwarded by* PENNSYLVANIA RAIL ROAD COMPANY, *from Pittsburgh, consigned to Philadelphia.*

No. CARS.	MARKS.	CONSIGNEE.	ARTICLES.	WEIGHT.	RATE.	FREIGHT.	EXPENSES.	PREPAID.	TO BE COLLECTED.	REMARKS.

RAIL ROAD ACCOUNTS.

OPERATING RECEIPTS,

PENNSYLVANIA RAIL ROAD,

JANUARY, 1867.

1. The headings of the columns of this book fully explain their use. Its three money columns have their representatives in the General Ledger.

2. There are four columns used in Rail Road Accounts; but, as I cannot see any use for the fourth column for totals, I have used only three of them, bringing the aggregate into the Freight column at the end of the month, from whence they are journalized. See Journal entry, March 31st.

329

I OPERATING RECEIPTS OF P. R. R. FOR MARCH, 1867.

Date.		Name.	Station.	Freights.	Passages.	Mails
1867. Mar.	1	Geo. Brown	Greensburg	560	1900	
		J. W. Vann	Blairsville	340	700	
		Hiram Fish	Cresson	180	240	
		J. Scott	Altoona	760		
		W. Wills	Harrisburg	860		
		R. Weed	Lancaster	640		
		J. Powers	Philadelphia	970		
		W. Ryan	Conductor		712	
		J. Hilton	do.		680	
		B. Ray	do.		518	
		C. King	do.		670	
		R. Howe	do.		530	
		U.S. Mail	Pittsburgh to Philadelphia			1460
		do.	" " Altoona			340
		do.	" " Greensburg			490
		do.	" " Lancaster			710
		do.	" " Harrisburg			800
	15	J. Powers	Philadelphia	2200		
		R. Weed	Lancaster	1890		
		W. Wills	Harrisburg	1860		
		J. Scott	Altoona	1790		
		Hiram Fish	Cresson	1110		
		J. W. Vann	Blairsville	1370		
		Geo. Brown	Greensburg	1630		
		H. Lee	Pittsburgh	2150		
		C. Dickson	Philadelphia		2770	
		R. Bill	Lancaster		2630	
		J. Watson	Pittsburgh		2690	
		W. King	Harrisburg		2540	
		B. Hagan	Altoona		2512	
	31	R. Weed	Lancaster	4700		
		J. Powers	Philadelphia	6300		
		W. Wills	Harrisburg	4970		
		Geo. Brown	Greensburg	1770	1400	
		J. Scott	Altoona	1860		
		J. W. Vann	Blairsville	1300	260	
		Hiram Fish	Cresson	1100	500	
		J. Watson	Pittsburgh		2590	
		R. Bill	Lancaster		2610	
		C. Dickson	Philadelphia		2470	
		B. Hagan	Altoona		2330	
		W. King	Harrisburg		2840	
		U.S. Mail	Pittsburgh to Johnstown			190
			Freight	40310	34092	3990
			Passage	34092		
			U.S. Mail	3990		
		Journal 2.	Receipts for this month	78392		

RAIL ROAD ACCOUNTS.

JOURNAL,

PENNSYLVANIA RAIL ROAD,

JANUARY, 1867.

1. This book serves for a Journal and General Day Book. The first three entries are original, and are first recorded in this book.

2. These books are kept by the Secretary, who debits and credits the Treasurer for all receipts and payments of money. Some Companies employ a Treasurer, who, under instructions from the board, takes charge of all the revenues of the Company, and pays out all their expenditures, reporting the same to the board. For some Companies the banker is their only Treasurer.

3. The first entry in March, and the second and third entries on the 31st, are original.

4. When the Journal is posted, compare and check the Journal and Ledger, then take off a trial sheet and prepare to close the Ledger, and make a dividend. For this purpose open the six accounts on page 6 of the Ledger.

5. The four entries on Journal, page 3, we obtain from the Ledger; but the same accounts may be closed on the face of the Ledger without a Journal entry, as we do in Mercantile Books. I have followed the practice of Rail Road Accountants.

6. You will see that the Operating Account finally closes into Profit & Loss with a net gain of $44,632. Of this the Directors divide 5% on the paid-up Capital of $300,000, and place $20,000 to the credit of the Shareholders on the Stock Ledger. See Journal, p. 4. The surplus is carried to the credit of Surplus Capital, or Contingent Fund, as it is sometimes called.

7. The Dividend must be carried to the credit of the Dividend Account; and as the stockholders draw their Dividends, that account is Dr., and Cash, or the Bank Account, is credited.

8. The entries for closing the Ledger and making the Dividend are all made on pages 3 and 4 of the Journal, from which they are posted to the Stock and General Ledger. See posting to Stock Ledger from first entry in the Journal.

1	Treasurer, Dr.			100000	
1	To Capital Stock, for 1st Instalment paid by Shareholders				100000
1	R. Fulton 1200 Shares of $100 ea. Cash 10% $12000				
1	T. Graham 500 do 100 ″ do 5000				
1	D. Martin 800 do 100 ″ do 8000				
1	A.T.Howden 1000 do 100 ″ do 10000				
1	J. Carver 900 do 100 ″ do 9000				
2	A. Bowman 1000 do 100 ″ do 10000				
2	W. M. Lyon 1500 do 100 ″ do 15000				
2	G.R.Duncan 1500 do 100 ″ do 15000				
2	W. H. Duff 600 do 100 ″ do 6000				
2	R. Banks 1000 do 100 ″ do 10000				
	Shares, 10000 First Instalment, $100000				

15.

1	Cash, Dr.			170000	
1	To Treasurer, for Check				170000

31.

1	Sundries, Dr. To Bonds Payable				600000
1	Treasurer, for n/p, received of W. Dumas & Co. for sales			540000	
1	Discount, for 10% Discount on above sales			60000	

1	Sundries, Dr. To Cash				155070
	Paid for Construction & Equipment this month				
2	Depots			36070	
2	Road Building			20100	
2	Lands			6090	
2	Surveying			1100	
2	Grading			8100	
3	Bridging			14800	
3	Tunneling			8200	
3	Locomotives			27600	
3	Cars			28500	
3	Fencing			3310	
3	Construction Incidentals			1200	

Feb. 1.

1	Treasurer, Dr.			200000	
1	To Capital Stock, for 2d Instalment paid by Shareholders				200000
1	R. Fulton 1200 Shares of $100 ea. Cash 20% $24000				
1	T. Graham 500 do 100 ″ do 10000				
1	D. Martin 800 do 100 ″ do 16000				
1	A.T.Howden 1000 do 100 ″ do 20000				
1	J. Carver 900 do 100 ″ do 18000				
2	R. Banks 1000 do 100 ″ do 20000				
2	A. Bowman 1000 do 100 ″ do 20000				
2	W. M. Lyon 1500 do 100 ″ do 30000				
2	G.R.Duncan 1500 do 100 ″ do 30000				
2	W. H. Duff 600 do 100 ″ do 12000				
	Shares, 10000 Second Instalment, $200000				

1	Cash, Dr.	120000	
1	To Treasurer, for Check		120000

28.

1	Sundries, Dr. To Cash		122700
	Paid for Construction & Equipment this month		
2	Depots	31000	
2	Road Building	18000	
2	Lands	1100	
2	Surveying	900	
2	Grading	7500	
3	Bridging	14800	
3	Tunneling	8200	
3	Locomotives	22200	
3	Cars	17500	
3	Fencing	700	
3	Construction Incidentals	800	

March 1.

3	Sundries, Dr. To Bills Payable		169080
2	Road Building, for notes to E. Dudley & Co., at 6, 8, 9, 12, and 18 months, for R. R. Iron	160000	
4	Interest, for amount added in notes	9080	

31.

1	Sundries, Dr. to Cash		33760
	Paid Operating Expenses this month		
4	Station	3100	
4	Shop	4305	
4	Train	5280	
5	Engines	4200	
5	Cars	5100	
5	Track	4400	
5	Buildings	2160	
5	Oil & Waste	1105	
5	Fuel	2880	
5	Operating Incidentals	1230	

1	Cash, Dr.	52400	
1	To Treasurer, for Check		52400

4	Interest, Dr.	18180	
1	To Cash, Pd. Int. for 6 mths. on $600,000 Bonds, $18,000		18180
	1% Exchange 180		

1	Treasurer, Dr. to Sundries	78392	
4	To Freights, for Receipts for this month		40310
4	" Passages " " " "		34092
4	" Mails " " " "		3990

333

6	Construction & Equipment, Dr. To Sundries		525030	
2	To Depots	To close acc't		67070
2	Road Building	do		198100
2	Lands	do		7190
2	Surveying	do		2000
2	Grading	do		15600
3	Bridging	do		29600
3	Tunneling	do		16400
3	Locomotives	do		49800
3	Cars	do		46000
3	Fencing	do		4010
3	Construction & Equipment Incidentals	do		2000
4	Interest	do		27260
1	Discount	do		60000
6	Operating, Dr. To Sundries		33760	
4	To Stations	To close acc't		3100
4	Shop	do		4305
4	Train	do		5280
5	Engines	do		4200
5	Cars	do		5100
5	Track	do		4400
5	Building	do		2160
5	Oil & Waste	do		1105
5	Fuel	do		2880
5	Operating Incidentals	do		1230
6	Sundries, Dr. To Operating			78392
4	Freights	To close acc't	40310	
4	Passages	do	34092	
4	Mails	do	3990	
6	Operating, Dr.		44632	
6	To Profit & Loss, for gain			44632

6	Profit & Loss, Dr. To Sundries	44632	
6	To Dividend No. 1		15000

For 5% on $300000, payable in Cash to Shareholders

R. Fulton	5% on $36000 paid in		$1800
T. Graham	15000	″	750
D. Martin	24000	″	1200
A. T. Howden	30000	″	1500
J. Carver	27000	″	1350
R. Banks	30000	″	1500
A. Bowman	30000	″	1500
W. M. Lyon	45000	″	2250
G. R. Duncan	45000	″	2250
W. H. Duff	18000	″	900

$300000 Cash Div'nd, $15000

1	To Capital Stock		20000

For $2 pr Sh'e on 10000 Sh's to credit of Sharehold's

1	T. Graham	$2 on 500 Shares		$1000
1	D. Martin	″ 800	″	1600
1	R. Fulton	″ 1200	″	2400
1	A. T. Howden	″ 1000	″	2000
1	J. Carver	″ 900	″	1800
2	R. Banks	″ 1000	″	2000
2	A. Bowman	″ 1000	″	2000
2	W. M. Lyon	″ 1500	″	3000
2	G. R. Duncan	″ 1500	″	3000
2	W. H. Duff	″ 600	″	1200

Shares, 10000 Stock Div'nd, 20000

6	To Surplus Capital		9632
	For amount of gain undivided		

PENNSYLVANIA RAIL ROAD COMPANY'S

PETROLEUM BILL OF LADING.

OWNER'S RISK OF FIRE.

H. H. HOUSTON,	C. A. CARPENTER,
General Freight Agent, Philadelphia.	*Freight Agent, Pittsburgh.*

Received,...................Station,...................186 , of...................

...................Barrels, said to contain...................and marked...................

to be transported to...................Consignee, at

...................at...................Cents (freight for this and connecting Companies

or Agents) per one hundred pounds, subject to the following Conditions and Agreement:—

First.—The owner or consignee shall pay freight and charges thereon at specified rates at time of delivery, as the same from time to time arrives.

Second.—This merchandise may be carried in Box-Cars, Covered Skeleton-Cars, or on open Platform-Cars; if destined beyond the line of the Philadelphia & Erie, Northern Central, or Pennsylvania Rail Roads, it may be transported by water, in boats, barges or lighters, or it may be entrusted or delivered in the Cars of this Company, or otherwise, to any other Railroad, or Transportation Company, or Agent; and such Rail Road, or Transportation Company, or Agent so selected, shall be regarded exclusively as the AGENT of the owner or consignee, and shall be entitled to the benefit of the Conditions and Provisions of this, and of such Bill of Lading as they may deliver therefor; and the Pennsylvania Rail Road Company, Lessee Philadelphia and Erie Railroad, shall not be, in any event, responsible for the negligence or non-performance of any such Company or Agent, nor shall such Company or Agent be liable for any loss or injury except upon its or their respective routes, and while such merchandise is in their respective custody.

Third.—That the owner or consignee, in *consideration of the extremely hazardous nature of such merchandise, which is not covered by any extra charge for transportation,* hereby assumes all risk from leakage, evaporation, *and loss by fire,* while in transit, or at Depots or in Stations, or on board boats, vessels or lighters, from any cause whatever, and all dangers and delays of Rail Road and Water Transportation between the place of shipment and final delivery; and in any claim or demand, suit at law or equity, against this Company or Transportation Company or Agent, for loss or damage thereby, this Bill of Lading shall be deemed and taken as a release in full therefor.

Fourth.—Whatever responsibility is assumed under this Bill of Lading shall begin when the merchandise is loaded into the cars of the Company at the above station, and cease when unloaded therefrom, or entrusted or delivered as aforesaid, and which, it is agreed, shall constitute a delivery.

Fifth.—The owner or consignee will have his or their agent or employees to receive and remove the said merchandise as the same from time to time arrives and is delivered as aforesaid; but if not then removed, the same will remain at place of unloading, or be removed, at the option of the Company, to such place of deposit as it may select, at the risk and cost of the owner or consignee.

Sixth.—Said merchandise may be retained for all arrearages of freight and charges due this Company on other goods by the same consignee or owner.

Seventh.—Nor shall any agent hereunder be liable, by reason of any responsibility hereby assumed, for any loss or damage to such merchandise, unless the claim therefor be presented in writing at the Office of the General Freight Agent of the Pennsylvania Rail Road Company in Philadelphia, above mentioned, within ten days after the time when the same has been or ought to have been delivered.

Eighth.—In case of loss or damage to any property herein mentioned, from such cause as would render this Company liable, it is expressly agreed that they shall have the benefit of any insurance that may have been or may be effected upon, or on account of said property, and the owner, consignee and shipper severally agree that it shall be so inserted in the policy, and the measure of such loss or damage shall be the market price of such property at the time and place of shipment.

...................*Agent*

RAIL ROAD ACCOUNTS.

STOCK LEDGER,

PENNSYLVANIA RAIL ROAD COMPANY.

JANUARY, 1867.

1. This Ledger has an account opened in it for every shareholder. The rulings and headings explain themselves. No accounts are kept in this Ledger but those of the shareholders, and in business it must have an index in the usual form. When a shareholder transfers the whole or only part of his stock (a thing that occurs daily), the Secretary makes an original entry on the Transfer book, from whence it is posted to this. See Transfer Ledger from J. Carter to T. Graham $27520, and to R. Manly, $1280. While the Directors are preparing the dividend, they generally give notice, ten days before declaring it, that no stock will be transferred until after it is declared. The holders of the stock up to that day are entitled to the dividend unless otherwise agreed upon by the purchaser; but the purchaser buys the interest in the surplus capital with the stock.

2. When you take a trial balance off your General Ledger before closing, and when making the dividend, you must also take off from the Stock Ledger a list of the Shareholders, with the amount paid by each. The aggregate amount must agree with the credit of the Capital Stock in the General Ledger. In this instance it is $300000.

3. This Ledger is never closed; but the individual accounts in it are closed when they transfer all the stock in J. Carver's account.

W   337

1 Dr.   **THOMAS**   **GRAHAM.**   **Cr.**

	P. Shares.				1867.			P.	Shares.	%	
					Jan.	2	Treasurer	1	500	10	5000
					Feb.	1	"		"	20	10000
					Mar.	31	Profit and Loss	4	"	2	1000
					Apl.	6	J. Carver f.	1	860	32	27520

R.   **FULTON.**

					1867.						
					Jan.	2	Treasurer	1	1200	10	12000
					Feb.	1	"		"	20	24000
					Mar.	31	Profit and Loss	4	"	2	2400

DAVID   **MARTIN.**

					1867.						
					Jan.	2	Treasurer	1	800	10	8000
					Feb.	1	"		"	20	16000
					Mar.	31	Profit and Loss	4	"	2	1600

A. T.   **HOWDEN.**

					1867.						
					Jan.	2	Treasurer	1	1000	10	10000
					Feb.	1	"		"	20	20000
					Mar.	31	Profit and Loss	4	"	2	2000

JAMES   **CARVER.**

1867.							1867.						
Apr.	2	R. Manly	f.	2	40	1280	Jan.	2	Treasurer	1	900	10	9000
	6	T. Graham		1	860	27520	Feb.	1	"		"	20	18000
							Mar.	31	Profit and Loss	4	"	2	1800
						28800							28800

					1867.			P.	Shares.	%	
	P. Shares.				Jan.	2	Treasurer	1	1000	10	10000
					Feb.	1	"		"	20	20000
					Mar.	31	Profit & Loss	4	"	2	2000

A.   ·   BOWMAN.

			1867.						
			Jan.	2	Treasurer	1	1000	10	10000
			Feb.	1	"		"	20	20000
			Mar.	31	Profit & Loss	4	"	2	2000

WM. M.   LYON.

			1867.						
			Jan.	2	Treasurer	1	1500	10	15000
			Feb.	1	"		"	20	30000
			Mar.	31	Profit & Loss	4	"	2	3000

GEO. R.   DUNCAN.

			1867.						
			Jan.	2	Treasurer	1	1500	10	15000
			Feb.	1	"		"	20	30000
			Mar.	31	Profit & Loss	4	"	2	3000

WM. H.   DUFF.

			1867.						
			Jan.	2	Treasurer	1	600	10	6000
			Feb.	1	"		"	20	12000
			Mar.	31	Profit & Loss	4	"	2	1200

ROBERT   MANLY.

			1867.						
			Apr.	2	J. Carver	f 1	40	32	1280

339

DIVIDEND BOOK.

PENNSYLVANIA RAIL ROAD COMPANY.—Dividend No. 1.

Ledger Folio.	Name of Shareholders.	Amount paid up.	Rate of Dividend.	Amount.	Date.	Received the sums set opposite our names.
	Banks, Rob't	30000	5 %	1500		
	Bowman, A.	30000	5 %	1500		
	Carver, J.	27000	5 %	1350		
	Duncan, G. R.	45000	5 %	2250		
	Duff, Wm. H.	18000	5 %	900		
	Fulton, R.	36000	5 %	1800		
	Graham, T.	15000	5 %	750		
	Howden, A. T.	30000	5 %	1500		
	Lyon, W. M.	45000	5 %	2250		
	Martic, D.	24000	5 %	1200		
		300000		15000		

Paying the dividends is explained p. 309

RAIL ROAD ACCOUNTS.

GENERAL LEDGER,

PENNSYLVANIA RAIL ROAD.

1. This book and the Stock Ledger are generally opened at once, as all entries relating to the shareholders have to be posted into that Ledger, and this one also. See the posting to both, January 2

2. This Ledger, in business, must have an Index, but it need not be written here. The Bonds Payable account is the same as the Bills Payable account, and may be posted to that account, but it is better to follow the established custom.

3. All the accounts which you closed into Construction & Equipment account represent property, and the debit side of that account stands in the debit side of the Balance account as assets of the company.

4. Operating accounts are of the same nature as Profit & Loss, into which they finally close. Dividend and Surplus Capital are both accounts representing liabilities, and are entered in the credit of the Balance account.

5. All the accounts that close into Construction & Equipment and Operating account remain closed, and the unoccupied space below them may be used for a new account without a new heading.

6. By comparing these Books before writing, the student who is well versed in Double Entry Book-keeping will have no trouble in understanding them.

7. Surplus Capital is a reserve fund to enable the directors to make uniform dividends when business is unfavorable.

1 Dʀ.   **CAPITAL**   **STOCK.**   Cʀ.

				1867.				
				Jan.	2	Treasurer	1	100000
				Feb	1	″		200000
				Mar.	31	Profit & Loss	4	20000

TREASURER'S   ACCOUNT.

1867.					1867.				
Jan.	2	Capital Stock	1	100000	Jan.	15	Cash	1	170000
	31	Bonds Payable		540000	Feb.	15	″	2	120000
Feb.	1	Capital Stock		200000	Mar.	31	″		52400
Mar.	31	Sundries	2	78392			Balance	f 6	575992
				918392					918392
		Balance		575992					

CASH   ACCOUNT.

1867.					1867.				
Jan.	15	Treasurer	1	170000	Jan.	31	Sundries	1	155070
Feb.	15	″	2	120000	Feb.	28	″	2	122700
Mar.	31	″		52400	Mar.	31	″		33760
							Interest		18180
							Balance	f 6	12690
				342400					342400
		Balance		12690					

BONDS   PAYABLE.

					1867.				
					Jan.	31	Sundries	1	600000

DISCOUNT   ACCOUNT.

1867.					1867.				
Jan.	31	Bonds Payable	1	60000	Mar.	31	Constr. & Equip.	3	60000

342

1867. Jan.	31	Cash	1	36070	1867. Mar.	31	Constr. & Equip.	3	67070
Feb.	28	"	2	31000					
				67070					67070

ROAD   BUILDING.

1867. Jan.	31	Cash	1	20100	1867. Mar.	31	Constr. & Equip.	3	198100
Feb.	28	"	2	18000					
Mar.	1	Bills Payable		160000					
				198100					198100

LANDS   ACCOUNT.

1867. Jan.	31	Cash	1	6090	1867. Mar.	31	Constr. & Equip.	3	7190
Feb.	23	"	2	1100					
				7190					7190

SURVEYING   ACCOUNT.

1867. Jan.	31	Cash	1	1100	1867. Mar.	31	Constr. & Equip.	3	2000
Feb.	28	"	2	900					
				2000					2000

GRADING   ACCOUNT.

1867. Jan.	31	Cash	1	8100	1867. Mar.	31	Constr. & Equip.	3	15600
Feb.	28	"	2	7500					
				15600					15600

BRIDGING.

1867.					1867.				
Jan.	31	Cash	1	14800	Mar.	31	Constr. & Equip.	3	29600
Feb.	28	"	2	14800					
				29600					29600

TUNNELING   ACCOUNT.

1867.					1867.				
Jan.	31	Cash	1	8200	Mar.	31	Constr. & Equip.	3	16400
Feb.	28	"	2	8200					
				16400					16400

LOCOMOTIVE   ACCOUNT.

1867.					1867.				
Jan.	31	Cash	1	27600	Mar.	31	Constr. & Equip.	3	49800
Feb.	28	"	2	22200					
				49800					49800

CARS   ACCOUNT.

1867.					1867.				
Jan.	31	Cash	1	28500	Mar.	31	Constr. & Equip.	3	46000
Feb.	28	"	2	17500					
				46000					46000

FENCING   ACCOUNT.

1867.					1867.				
Jan.	31	Cash	1	3310	Mar.	31	Constr. & Equip.	3	4010
Feb.	28	"	2	700					
				4010					4010

CONSTRUCTION   INCIDENTALS.

1867.					1867.				
Jan.	31	Cash	1	1200	Mar.	31	Constr. & Equip.	3	2000
Feb.	28	"	2	800					
				2000					2000

BILLS   PAYABLE.

					1867.				
					Mar.	1	Sundries	2	169080

1867.					1867.				
Mar.	1	Bills Payable	2	9080	Mar.	31	Constr. & Equip.	3	27260
	31	Cash		18180					
				27260					27260

FREIGHT   ACCOUNT.

1867.					1867.				
Mar.	31	Operating	3	40310	Mar.	31	Treasurer	2	40310

PASSAGE   ACCOUNT.

1867.					1867.				
Mar.	31	Operating	3	34092	Mar.	31	Treasurer	2	34092

U. S. MAIL   SERVICE.

1867.					1867.				
Mar	31	Operating	3	3990	Mar.	31	Treasurer	2	3990

STATION   SERVICE.

1867.					1867.				
Mar.	31	Cash	2	3100	Mar.	31	Operating	3	3100

SHOP   SERVICE.

1867.					1867.				
Mar.	31	Cash	2	4305	Mar.	31	Operating	3	4305

TRAIN   SERVICE.

1867.					1867.				
Mar.	31	Cash	2	5280	Mar.	31	Operating	3	5280

1867. Mar.	31	Cash	2	4200	1867. Mar.	31	Operating	3	4200

CAR   REPAIRS.

1867. Mar.	31	Cash	2	5100	1867. Mar.	31	Operating	3	5100

TRACK ✳   REPAIRS.

1867. Mar.	31	Cash	2	4400	1867. Mar.	31	Operating	3	4400

BUILDING   REPAIRS.

1867. Mar.	31	Cash	2	2160	1867. Mar.	31	Operating	3	2160

OIL   &   WASTE.

1867. Mar.	31	Cash	2	1105	1867. Mar.	31	Operating	3.	1105

FUEL   ACCOUNT.

1867. Mar.	31	Cash	2	2880	1867. Mar.	31	Operating	3	2880

OPERATING   INCIDENTALS.

1867. Mar.	31	Cash	2	1230	1867. Mar.	31	Operating	3	1230

Dr.			**PROFIT**		&		**LOSS.**		Cr.	**6**
1867.					1867.					
Mar.	31	Sundries	4	44632	Mar.	31	Operating	3	44632	

CONSTRUCTION & EQUIPMENT.

1867.								
Mar.	31	Sundries	3	525030				

BALANCE ACCOUNT.

1867.					1867.					
Mar.	31	Treasurer	f 1	575992	Mar.	31	Capital	f 1	320000	
		Cash		12690			Bonds Payable		600000	
		Constr. & Equip.	6	525030			Bills Payable	3	169080	
							Dividend No. 1	6	15000	
							Surplus Capital		9632	
				1113712					1113712	

OPERATING ACCOUNT.

1867.					1867.					
Mar.	31	Sundries	3	33760	Mar	31	Sundries	3	78392	
		Profit & Loss		44632						
				78392					78392	

DIVIDEND No. 1.

					1867.					
					Mar.	31	Profit & Loss	4	15000	

SURPLUS CAPITAL.

					1867.					
					Mar.	31	Profit & Loss	4	9632	

QUESTIONS FOR EXAMINATION ON RAIL ROAD ACCOUNTS.

1. Where are the totals of the Construction & Equipment Day Book carried to? (N. 3, p. 315.)
2. What are the entries of this book made from? (N. 5, p. 315.)
3. Where are the total amounts of the money columns of the Operating Expenditures represented? (N. 2, p. 323.)
4. Where are the aggregates of the Operating Receipts carried to? (N. 2, p. 329.)
5. What entries originate upon the Journal? (N. 1, p. 331.)
6. Who is supposed to keep the books of the company? (N. 2, p. 331.)
7. How does the Secretary keep his account with the Treasurer? (N. 2, p. 331.)
8. What is done after the contents of the Journal are posted into the General Ledger? (N. 4, p. 331.)
9. What accounts are to be opened preparatory to closing the Ledger? (N. 4, p. 331.)
10. Where are the closing entries of the Ledger made? (N. 5, p. 331.)
11. How is the total gain divided? (N. 6, p. 331.)
12. What accounts are kept in the Stock Ledger? (N. 1, p. 337.)
13. How are transfers of stock made? (N. 1, p. 337.)
14. When is the transfer of stock prohibited? (N. 1, p. 337.)
15. If a sale of stock is made while the transfer book is closed, who is entitled to the Dividend? (N. 1, p. 337.)
16. What must be done when you take a Trial Balance off the General Ledger? (N. 2, p. 337.)
17. What must the aggregate amount of the credits of the Stock Ledger agree with? (N. 2, p. 337.)
18. When are the accounts in this Ledger closed? (N. 3, p. 337.)
19. When is the General Ledger opened? (N. 1, p. 341.)
20. Is there any difference between "Bonds Payable" and "Bills Payable"? (N. 2, p. 341.)
21. What do the accounts closing into "Construction & Equipment" represent? (N. 3, p. 341.)
22. What is the nature of Operating Accounts? (N. 4, p. 341.)
23. Into what account do they close? (N. 4, p. 341.)
24. Are "Dividend" and "Surplus Capital" effects, or liabilities? (N. 4, p. 341.)
25. What is done with the accounts closed into Construction & Equipment after the books are closed? (N. 5, p. 341.)
26. What is "Surplus Capital"? (N. 7, p. 341.)

PRIVATE BANKER'S ACCOUNTS.

1867.

PRELIMINARY REMARKS.

Although the principles of Bank Accounts have been fully illustrated in our set of National Bank Accounts, the business of the Private Banker differs in so many particulars from that of the Joint Stock Company that we think the following set of books, expressly adapted to this particular business, will prove useful in perfecting the business man's education

CASH BOOK,

PRIVATE BANKER'S ACCOUNTS.

NOVEMBER, 1867.

1. Bankers generally make this book perform the office of Cash Book and Journal. The arginal pages indicate the direct posts to the General Ledger, which is made up from this book.

2. The aggregate monthly receipts and payments are posted from the right-hand money columns.

351

1867								
Nov.	2	To P. Duff	Rec'd in full for his capital		1	20000		
		" Wm. Hay	" " " " " "		1	10000		
		" W. Wood	" " " " " "		1	10000		
		" Depositors	" per Deposit Register	P. 1	2	2200		
		" Discount	" Discount Book	1	3	158	92	
	7	" Depositors	" Deposit Register	1	2	1900		
		" Discount	" Discount Book	1	3	69		
	8	" Depositors	" Deposit Register	1	2	2200		
		" Discount	" Discount Book	1	3	25		
	9	" Depositors	" Deposit Register	1	2	3260		
		" Discount	" Discount Book	1	3	39	70	
	10	" Depositors	" Deposit Register	1	2	3049		
	16	" do.	" do. do.	1	2	5985		
		" Discount	" Discount Book	1	3	62	47	
	23	" Depositors	" Deposit Register	1	2	2900		
		" Discount	" Discount Book	1	3	154	57	
		" Bills Receivable	" for Discount No. 3		2	5600		
	30	" Depositors	" per Deposit Register	2	2	6630		
		" Bills Receivable	" for Discount No. 2		2	4000		
		" Discount	" per Discount Book	1	3	110		78343 66
						78343	66	
			Balance			26533	66	
Dec.	4	To Discount	Rec'd per Discount Book	2	3	1260		
	7	" Depositors	" Deposit Register	2	2	8815		
		" Discount	" Discount Book	2	3	75	50	
	14	" Depositors	" Deposit Register	2	2	9960		
		" Bills Receivable	" for Discount No. 4		2	2800		
		" do. do.	" " No. 5		2	4200		
		" Discount	" per Discount Book	2	3	2618	60	
	21	" Depositors	" Deposit Register	2	2	2700		
		" Discount	" Discount Book	2	3	80	80	
	28	" Depositors	" Deposit Register	2	2	1410		
		" Discount	" Discount Book	2	3	143	84	
		" Bills Receivable	" for Discounts No. 8, 9, and 10		2	3600		
	29	" Discount	" per Discount Book	2	3	306		
	30	" Depositors	" Deposit Register	2	2	890		
		" Discount	" Discount Book	2	3	200		
	31	" Depositors	" Deposit Register	2	2	13910		
		" Discount	" Discount Book	2	3	113	34	
		" Duff Brothers & Co.	" for draft on them		3	1000		
		" Thomas Thompson & Co.	" " " do.		3	6000		
		" Bills Receivable	" Discount No. 7		2	3800		
		" do. do.	" " " 1		2	5000		68883 08
						95416	74	
			Balance			6737	74	

1867						
Nov.	2	By Depositors	Pd. per Check Register	1	2	1000
		" Bills Receivable	" for Notes 1, 2, 3, and 4		2	17400
		" Discount	" per Discount Book	1	3	20
	7	" Depositors	" Check Register	1	2	675
		" Discount	" Discount Book	1	3	37
	8	" Depositors	" Check Register	1	2	1600
		" Discount	" Discount Book	1	3	12
	9	" Depositors	" Check Register	1	2	2400
		" Bills Receivable	" for Note 5		2	4200
		" Discount	" per Discount Book	1	3	15
	10	" Depositors	" Check Register	1	2	1100
	11	" Bills Receivable	" for Note 6		2	1600
	16	" Depositors	" per Check Register	1	2	1300
		" Discount	" Discount Book	1	3	75
	23	" Depositors	" Check Register	1	2	7920
		" Bills Receivable	" for Notes 7, 8, 9, and 10		2	7400
		" Discount	" per Discount Book	1	3	105
	30	" Depositors	" Check Register	1	2	4920
		" Discount	" Discount Book	1	3	31
			. Balance carried down			26533 66	51810
						78343 66

Dec.	4	By Depositors	Pd. per Check Register	2	2	560
		" Discount	" Discount Book	1	3	15
	7	" Depositors	" Check Register	2	2	360
		" Discount	" Discount Book	2	3	24
		" Bills Receivable	" for Note 11		2	3800
	14	" Depositors	" per Check Register	2	2	430
		" Bills Receivable	" for Notes 12, 13, and 14		2	4500
	21	" Depositors	" per Check Register	2	2	2850
		" Discount	" Discount Book	2	3	56
		" Bills Receivable	" for Notes 15 and 16		2	5600
	28	" Depositors	" per Check Register	2	2	3640
		" Discount	" Discount Book	2	3	12
		" Bills Receivable	" for Notes 17, 18, 19, and 20		2	12600
		" Duff Brothers & Co.	" Retaining n/p of Note No. 10		2	1188
	29	" Bills Receivable	" for Notes 21 and 22		2	24000
	30	" do. do.	" " " 23, 24, and 25		2	15000
		" R. P. Duff	" Retaining n/p of Note No. 19		4	130
	31	" Depositors	" per Check Register	2	2	6700
		" Discount	" Discount Book	2	3	50
		" Bills Receivable	" for Notes No. 26,27,28,29,30,&31		2	1254
		" T. F. Shephard	" Retaining n/p of Note No. 10		4	960
		" T. Thompson & Co.	" do. " " " 1		3	4950	88673
			Balance carried down •			6737 74
						95416 74

A

PRIVATE BANKER'S

PITTSBURGH, Nov. 2, 1867.

1867.					
Nov.	2	Wilson, Childs & Co		1	400
		R. S. Carson		1	600
		W J Murphy		1	500
		Wm Payne		1	700
			C. B. 1		2200
Nov.	7	Wm. Payne		1	300
		J. R. Weldin		2	600
		R. Banks		2	400
		Jas. Wood		2	600
			C. B. 1		1900
Nov.	8	Chas. Page		2	700
		W. Stoner		2	240
		R. S. Carson		1	260
		R. Banks		2	1000
			C. B. 1		2200
Nov.	9	Wm. Payne	Note 2	1	300
		R. S. Carson	3	1	260
		R. Banks	6	2	1000
		J. Pillow		3	1700
			C. B. 1		3260
Nov.	10	J. R. Weldin	Note 5	2	600
		W. J. Murphy	4	1	500
		Robt. Knox		3	749
		Jas. Watt		3	450
		Geo. Draper		3	750
			C. B. 1		3049
Nov.	16	Jas. Wood	Note 7	2	2000
		W. Hay		3	1475
		John Hatch		4	760
		White & Edwards		4	1750
			C. B. 1		5985
Nov.	23	Chas. Page		2	450
		Jones & Hatch		4	750
		Rich & Gray		4	460
		Hay & Wood		5	500
		Wm. Payne		1	40
		Certificate of Deposit	No. 1	5	700
			C. B. 1		2900

DEPOSIT REGISTER.

PITTSBURGH, Nov. 30, 1867.

1867.					
Nov.	30	Chas. Page	Note 8	2	470
		Wm. Hay		3	1000
		R. S. Carson		1	1400
		Wm. Stoner		2	560
		Hay & Wood		5	700
		Certificate of Deposit	No. 2	5	1000
		" "	" 3	5	600
		" "	" 4	5	900
			C. B. 1		6630
Dec.	7	Wilson, Childs & Co.	Note 1	1	400
		James Pillow	12	3	7800
		Hay & Wood		5	615
			C. B. 1		8815
Dec.	14	James Watt	Note 15	3	3000
		R. Knox	14	3	3960
		Jones & Hatch		4	1000
		Certificate of Deposit	No. 5	5	2000
			C. B. 1		9960
Dec.	21	Geo. Draper	Note 11	3	2600
		Wm. Stoner		2	100
			C. B. 1		2700
Dec.	28	Jno. Hatch	Note 16	4	200
		White & Edwards	17	4	150
		Rich & Gray	18	4	500
		Hay & Wood	20	5	560
			C. B. 1		1410
Dec.	30	Jones & Hatch	Note 19	4	130
		W. Payne		1	360
		R. Martin		5	400
			C. B. 1		890
Dec.	31	Wm. Hay	Note 10	3	960
		R. Banks		2	550
		H. P. Ford & Co.		5	600
		Wilson, Childs & Co.		1	3200
		W. Stoner		2	4800
		W. Payne		1	3800
			C. B. 1		13910

1. In this book enter all receipts of money received on deposit account and for Certificates of Deposit. The daily amounts are carried to the Cash Book, and the particulars are posted into the Depositors' Ledger.

1867. Nov.					
Nov.	2	W. Payne		1	400
		Wilson, Childs & Co.		1	400
		W. J. Murphy		1	200
			C. B. 1		1000
	7	R. S. Carson		1	375
		Robt. Banks		2	200
		Jas. Wood		2	100
			C. B. 1		675
	8	J. R. Weldin		2	700
		C. Page		2	600
		W. Payne		1	300
			C. B. 1		1600
	9	R. S. Carson	Note 6, Collection Register	1	1000
		R. Banks		2	600
		W. Stoner		2	200
		James Pillow		3	600
			C. B. 1		2400
	10	Wm. Payne		1	200
		W. J. Murphy		1	700
		Robt. Knox		3	200
			C. B. 1		1100
	16	Jas. Watt		3	400
		Geo. Draper		3	200
		Jas. Wood		2	500
		Wm. Hay		3	200
			C. B. 1		1300
	23	Jones & Hatch		4	400
		White & Edwards		4	800
		John Hatch	Certificate of Deposit No. 1	4	700
		Rich & Gray		4	20
		Hay & Wood		5	400
		C. Page	Note 3 Discounted	2	5600
			C. B. 1		7920
	30	John Hatch		4	840
		White & Edwards	Certificate of Deposit No. 2	4	1000
		Wm. Payne	" " " 3	1	600
		Wilson, Childs & Co.		1	1000
		R. S. Carson		1	1480
			C. B. 1		4920

1. This book records the payment of all Checks and Certificates of Deposit. Transfer the amounts daily to the Cash Book, and post the particulars to the Deposit Ledger.

CHECK REGISTER. 2

PITTSBURGH, Dec. 4, 1867.

1867. Dec.				
4	Hay & Wood		5	400
	R. S. Carson		1	160
		C. B. 1		560
7	Jones & Hatch		4	200
	Wm. Payne		1	160
		C. B. 1		360
14	R. Martin		5	300
	Rich & Gray		4	130
		C. B. 1		430
21	Wm. Hay		3	500
	Wilson, Childs & Co.		1	200
	R. Knox		3	150
	Certificate of Deposit No. 5		5	2000
		C. B. 1		2850
28	R. Knox		3	400
	Jones & Hatch		4	240
	White & Edwards		4	2400
	Certificate of Deposit No. 3		5	600
		C. B. 1		3640
31	Wm. Stoner		2	5000
	Wilson, Childs & Co.		1	700
	do. do.		1	300
	Certificate of Deposit No. 1		5	700
		C. B. 1		6700

PRIVATE BANKER'S

NOTES & BILLS

WHEN REC'D.		DISCOUNTED FOR.	DRAWER.	ON WHOM DRAWN.	IN WHOSE FAVOR.
1867.					
Nov.	2	Jno. Scott	Simon Payne	Wm. Young	Jno. Jones
		R. Banks	Thos. Gains		S. Myers
		S. White	Chas. Page		S. White
		S. Smith	W. Hay	J. S. Ward	Good & Bacon
	9	T. Rhodes	S. Barrett		T. Rhodes
	11	Good & Little	S. Wise		J. S. Duncan
	23	Moss & Howard	R. Goodwill		Moss & Howard
		Rhodes & Verner	M. Thompson		Rhodes & Verner
		G. R. White	A. Mason		G. R. White
		W. Payne	C. Ralston	T. C. Duff	S. Stevens
Dec.	7	J. Taylor	Jno. Eastman		E. D. Jones
	14	S. Barrett	W. Hare		S. Barrett
		D. A. Carston	Simon Payne		D. A. Carston
		Jno. Hawkins	Hay & Wood		Jno. Hawkins
	21	Hay & Wood	Jas. May		Hay & Wood
		J. Watt	Rogers & Co.	E. Lynch	J. Dally
	28	J. Pillow	Ragan & Morse		J. Pillow
		R. Banks	T. A. Craig		R. Banks
		S. Simpson	M. Love		S. Simpson
		W. Wells	C. Page		W. Wells
	29	R. Smith	J. Brown		Henry Rigg
		E. Waltby	Adrian & Co.	Jno. Kerr	E. Waltby
	30	Thos. Anderson	C. Rhea		C. Gipner
		D. Fox	W. F. Smith	Wm. Cook	J. C. Young
		W. Langdon	W. Langdon		Ourselves
	31	B. F. Swan	L. C. Donnell	G. L. Ryder	S. J. Grant
		J. M. Smith	G. W Holmes		R. B. Wilson
		R. Root	J. Hoag		M. Die
		Jno. Black	S. Green	D. Hall	D. White
		R. P. Murry	L. Bradley		V. B. Smith
		J. Higgins	J. Vinsonhaler	A. D. Walker	H. S. Kerr

1. Enter all discounted paper as above; the Discounts in the Discount Book, the payments in the Cash Book, and the day of maturity in the Tickler.

DISCOUNTED.

Where Payable.	No.	Date.		Time.	When Due.		Amount.	Memoranda.
		1867.			1867.			
Chicago	1	Sept.	25	3 months	Dec.	28	5000	Paid Dec. 31
City	2		28	60 days	Nov.	30	4000	" Nov. 30
"	3	Oct.	21	30 "		23	5600	" " 23
Philadelphia	4	Nov.	7	1 month	Dec.	10	2800	" Dec. 14
City	5	Sept.	7	3 months			4200	Protested Dec. 10, pd. Dec. 14
"	6	July	11	5 "		14	1600	" Dec. 14
"	7		18	5 "		21	3800	" Dec. 21, pd. Dec 31
"	8	June	25	6 "		28	600	Paid Dec. 28
"	9	Sept.	26	90 days		28	1800	" Dec. 28
New York	10	Nov.	18	30 "		21	1200	" Dec. 28
					1868			
City	11	Aug.	1	6 months	Feb.	4	3800	
"	12	July	10	6 "	Jan.	13	800	
"	13	Sept.	1	5 "	Feb.	4	3000	
"	14		28	4 "	Jan.	31	700	
"	15	Dec.	1	3 "	Mar.	4	1600	
St. Louis	16		20	3 "		23	4000	
City	17		15	90 days		18	2000	
"	18		5	60 "	Feb.	6	4000	
"	19		20	3 months	Mar.	23	3000	
"	20	Oct.	15	5 "		18	3600	
"	21	Dec.	5	60 days	Feb.	6	4000	
Chicago	22		20	90 "	Mar.	23	20000	
City	23		15	3 months		18	5000	
New Orleans	24		"	90 days		"	4000	
City	25		20	3 months		23	6000	
New York	26	Nov.	3	90 days	Feb.	4	225	
City	27	Dec.	1	3 months	Mar.	4	140	
"	28		30	60 days		3	170	
Cincinnati	29		3	3 months		6	360	
City	30		15	3 "		18	125	
St. Louis	31	Sept.	15	6 "		18	234	

PRIVATE BANKER'S
NOTES & BILLS

WHEN REC'D.		COLLECTED FOR.	DRAWER.	ON WHOM DRAWN.	IN WHOSE FAVOR.
1867. Nov.	2	Wilson, Childs & Co	Jas. Moultrie	H. Jones	S. Stinson
		W Payne	S. Girty	J. Gray	J. Shepler
		R. S. Carson	J. S. Duncan		R. S. Carson
		W. J. Murphy	S. Stevens		Thos. McCabe
		J. R. Weldin	S. Crites	F. Wallace	J. R. Weldin
	3	R. Banks	R. Carson		Thos. Smith
	7	Jas. Woods	S. R. Moultrie		Jas. Woods
	10	C. Page	Jno. Easton	C. J. Logan	R. Sanders
	15	W. Stoner	W. Roy		J Getty
	20	W. Hay	J. Dalton	A. Martin	R. Jones
	30	Geo. Draper	Ditto & Knox		Geo. Draper
Dec	1	Jas. Pillow	Stein & Dawson		Jas. Pillow
	4	S. Barrett	W. Hare		S. Barrett
		R. Knox	J. Moultrie	Jno. Milton	R. Good
		J. Watt	S. Barrett		F. Garrett
	21	Jno. Hatch	R. Knox		Jno. Hatch
		White & Edwards	Jones & Langdon		White & Edwards
		Rich & Gray	S. Girty		Rich & Gray
		Jones & Hatch	Brady & Stein	S. Grant	T. Fairbanks
		Hay & Wood	R. Roy		J. Goodall
	28	Ross & Childs	J. Riggs		S. Lowry
	30	R. Banks	Thos. King	F. Johnson	R. Banks

1. This book records all paper received for collection. Record its maturity at the same time on the Tickler. When collected, pass it to the credit of the owner on the Deposit Register.

PRIVATE BANKER'S
NOTES & BILLS

WHEN.		REMITTED TO.	PLACE.	DRAWER.	IN WHOSE FAVOR
1867. Nov	2	S. Ripley	Philadelphia	S. Girty	J. Shepler
		T. Thompson & Co.	Chicago	S. Crites	J. R. Weldin
	13	Duff Bros. & Co.	New York	Jno. Easton	R. Sanders
	25	R. P. Duff	Cincinnati	Jas. Moultrie	S. Stinson
Dec.	1	S. Ripley	Philadelphia	W. Hay	Good & Bacon
	4	Geo. McCallum	St. Louis	Jas. Moultrie	R. Good
	15	Duff Bros. & Co.	New York	C. Ralston	S. Stevens
	20	T. F. Shepard	New Orleans	J. Dalton	R. Jones
		R. P. Duff	Cincinnati	Brady & Stein	T. Fairbanks
1868. Jan.		T Thompson & Co.	Chicago	Simon Payne	Jno. Jones
	25	Duff Bros. & Co.	New York	Thos. King	R. Banks
		do	"	L. C. Donnell	S. J. Grant
Feb.	25	T. Thompson & Co.	Chicago	Adrian & Co.	E. Waltby
Mar.	1	R. P. Duff	Cincinnati	Samuel Green	D. White
	10	T. F. Shepard	New Orleans	W. F. Smith	J. C. Young
		G. McCallum	St. Louis	J. Vinsonhaler	H. S. Kerr
	15	do	"	Rogers & Co.	J. Dally

2. Ten or fifteen days before the maturity of foreign paper, forward it to your agent, transferring it from the Tickler to this book. When he notifies you of its payment, debit him; or, if he remits the proceeds, enter it to credit of the owner on Deposit Register.

COLLECTION REGISTER. 1
RECEIVED FOR COLLECTION.

Where Payable.	No.	Date.		Time.	When Due.		Amount.	Memoranda.
		1867.			1867.			
Cincinnati	1	Oct.	2	60 days	Dec.	4	400	Paid Dec. 7
Philadelphia	2		5	30 "	Nov.	7	300	Nov. 9
City	3		6	1 month		9	260	9
"	4	Aug.	7	3 months		10	500	10
Chicago	5	Sept.	5	2 "		8	600	10
City	6	July	6	4 "		9	1000	9
"	7	Sept.	14	60 days		16	2000	16
New York	8	Aug.	20	3 months		23	470	30
City	9		29	90 days		30	560	Ret'd Protested Nov. 30
New Orleans	10	July	25	5 months	Dec.	28	980	Paid Dec. 31, less $20
City	11		18	5 "		21	2600	21
"	12	Nov.	4	30 days	1868.	7	7800	7
"	13	July	10	6 months	Jan.	13	100	
					1867.			
St. Louis	14	Oct.	12	60 days	Dec.	14	4000	Paid Dec. 14, less $40
City	15		11	2 months			3000	14
"	16	Feb.	25	10 "		28	200	28
"	17			10 "			150	28
"	18	Nov.	25	1 "			500	28
Cincinnati	19	Sept	26	90 days			140	30, less $10
City	20	Oct.	26	60 days	1868.		560	28
"	21		30	90 "	Jan.	31	800	
New York	22		28	3 months			3000	

FOREIGN COLLECTION REGISTER.
REMITTED FOR COLLECTION.

Collected for.	No.	Date.		Due.		Amount.	Memoranda.
		1867.		1867.			
W. Payne	2	Oct.	5	Nov.	7	300	Received Nov. 9
J. R. Weldin	5	Sept.	5		8	600	Rec'd 10
C. Page	8	Aug.	20		23	470	Rec'd 30
Wilson, Childs & Co.	1	Oct.	2	Dec.	4	400	Rec'd Dec. 7
Ourselves	4	Nov.	7		10	2800	Rec'd 14
R. Knox	14	Oct.	12		14	4000	Rec'd 14, less $40
Ourselves	10	Nov.	18		21	1200	Rec'd 28, less $12
W. Hay	10	July	25		28	980	Rec'd 31, less $20
Jones & Hatch	19	Sept.	26			140	Rec'd 30, less $10
Ourselves	1		25	1868.		5000	Rec'd 31, less $50
R. Banks	22	Oct.	28	Jan.	31	3000	
Ourselves	26	Nov.	3	Feb.	4	225	
do	22	Dec.	20	Mar.	23	20000	
do	29		3		6	360	
do	24		15		18	4000	
do	31	Sept.	15		18	234	
do	16	Dec.	20		23	4000	

PRIVATE BANKER'S

DISCOUNTS.

RECEIVED.

1867.			
Nov.	2	Note 1	46 67
		" 2	18 67
		" 3	19 60
		" 4	17 73
		Exchange	45
		"	10
		"	1 25
		C. B. 1	158 92
Nov.	7	Exchange	23
		"	17
		"	8
		"	21
		C. B. 1	69
Nov.	8	Exchange	10
		"	7
		"	3
		"	5
		C. B. 1	25
Nov.	9	Note 5	21 70
		Exchange	18
		C. B. 1	39 70
Nov.	16	Note 6	7 47
		Exchange	45
		"	10
		C. B. 1	62 47
Nov.	23	Note 7	16 47
		" 8	35
		" 9	10
		" 10	5 60
		Exchange	56 50
		"	31
		C. B. 1	154 57
Nov.	30	Exchange	40
		"	17
		"	22
		"	31
		C. B. 1	110

PAID.

1867.			
Nov.	2	Exchange	10
		"	3
		"	5
		"	2
		C. B. 1	20
Nov.	7	Exchange	25
		"	2 50
		"	4 75
		"	1 25
		"	3 50
		C. B. 1	37
Nov.	8	Exchange	3
		"	4
		"	5
		C. B. 1	12
Nov.	9	Exchange	5
		"	10
		C. B. 1	15
Nov.	16	Exchange	45
		"	17
		"	2
		"	11
		C. B. 1	75
Nov.	23	Exchange	25
		"	37
		"	22
		"	21
		C. B. 1	105
Nov.	30	Exchange	10
		"	3 50
		"	11 50
		"	4 75
		"	1 25
		C. B. 1	31
Dec.	4	Exchange	10
		"	2
		"	3
		C. B. 1	15

1. This is a record of all discounts received and paid and all sums received and paid for exchanging money. The amounts are daily passed into the Cash Book.

DISCOUNTS.

1867.		RECEIVED.			1867.		PAID.	
Dec.	4	Exchange	625		Dec.	7	Exchange	3
		"	635				"	7
		C. B. 1	1260				"	4
							"	10
Dec.	7	Note 11	37 37				C. B. 1	24
		Exchange	25 13					
		"	13		Dec.	21	Exchange	16
		C. B. 1	75 50				"	3
							"	15
Dec.	14	Exchange	525				"	28
		Note 12	4				C. B. 1	56
		Exchange	522 40					
		Note 13	26		Dec.	28	F. C. R., Note 10	12
		Exchange	504				C. B. 1	
		Note 14	5 60					
		Exchange	526		Dec.	31	F. C. R., Note 1	50
		"	505 60				C. B. 1	
		C. B. 1	2618 60					
Dec.	21	Note 15	19 47					
		" 16	61 33					
		C. B. 1	80 80					
Dec.	28	Note 17	26 67					
		" 18	26 67					
		" 19	42 50					
		" 20	48					
		C. B. 1	143 84					
Dec.	29	Note 21	26					
		" 22	280					
		C. B. 1	306					
Dec.	30	Note 23	65					
		" 24	52					
		" 25	83					
		C. B. 1	200					
Dec.	31	Note 26	1 31					
		" 27	1 47					
		" 28	1 76					
		" 29	4 20					
		" 30	1 60					
		Draft 1	10					
		Note 31	3					
		Draft 2	90					
		C. B. 1	113 34					

Treasurer's Department.

Register's Office.

$1000

$1000

No. 1941.

No. 1941.

It is hereby certified that

The United States of America

R. P. DUFF,

One Thousand Dollars

LOAN OF FEB. 25, 1862.

Registered this

25, 1862.

Register of the Treasury.

Treasurer,

Washington, May 1, 1862.

$30.   Act of Feb. 25, 1862. $30.

The United States of America

Will pay the bearer

THIRTY DOLLARS,

For Six Months' Interest, due May 1, 1880, upon Bond 1941.

L. E. Chittenden,
Reg. of the Treas.

$1000.

$30.   Act of Feb. 25, 1862. $30.

The United States of America

Will pay the bearer

THIRTY DOLLARS,

For Six Months' Interest, due Nov. 1, 1860, upon Bond 1941.

L. E. Chittenden,
Reg. of the Treas.

$1000.

$30.   Act of Feb. 25, 1862. $30.

The United States of America

Will pay the bearer

THIRTY DOLLARS,

For Six Months' Interest, due May 1, 1881, upon Bond 1941.

L. E. Chittenden,
Reg. of the Treas.

$1000.

$30.   Act of Feb. 25, 1862. $30.

The United States of America

Will pay the bearer

THIRTY DOLLARS,

For Six Months' Interest, due Nov. 1, 1861, upon Bond 1941.

L. E. Chittenden,
Reg. of the Treas.

$1000.

TICKLER,

PRIVATE BANKER'S ACCOUNTS,

NOVEMBER, 1867.

1. In business there is generally a whole page of this book appropriated for each day of the month. And some bankers keep one Tickler for discounted paper, and another for collections. But we think the following form will serve without any inconvenience for both classes of paper.

2. As the notes are paid, they pass into the Cash Book ; or, if collections, to the Deposit Register. Protested notes, like No. 9, are returned to the owner, who must pay any expenses that are incurred.

365

NOTES DUE Nov. 7, 1867.

No.	For whom collected.	Drawer's name.	Endorser.	Where payable.	Amount.	Memoranda.
2	Wm. Payne	S. Girty	J Sheplar Nov. 8	Philadelphia	300	Paid Nov. 9
5	J. R. Weldin	S. Crites	Nov. 9	Chicago	600	Paid Nov. 10
3	R. S. Carson	Jno. S. Duncan	Thomas Smith Nov. 10	City	260	Paid Nov. 9
6	R. Banks	R. Carson		"	1000	" 9
4	W. J. Murphy	S. Stevens	Thos. McCabe Nov. 16	City	500	Paid Nov. 10
7	Jas. Woods	S. R. Moultrie	Nov. 16	City	2000	Paid Nov. 16
8	C. Page	John Easton	R. Sanders Nov. 23	New York	470	Paid Nov. 30
3	Ourselves	Chas. Page		City	5600	Charged Nov. 23
9	W. Stoner	Wm. Roy	J. Getty Nov. 30	City	560	Protested and Ret'd Nov. 30
2	Ourselves	Thos. Gaines	S. Myers Dec. 4	"	4000	Paid Nov. 30
1	Wilson, Childs & Co.	Jas. Moultrie	S. Stinson Dec. 7	Cincinnati	400	Paid Dec. 7
12	Jas. Pillow	Stein & Dawson	Dec. 10	City	7800	Paid Dec. 7
4	Ourselves	Wm. Hay	Good & Bacon Dec. 14	Philadelphia	2800	Paid Dec. 14
5	"	S. Barrett		City	4200	" " 14
14	R. Knox	J. Moultrie	R. Good	St. Louis	4000	Paid Dec. 14, less $40
15	J. Watt	S. Barrett	F. Garrett	City	3000	" " 14
6	Ourselves	S. Wise	J. S. Duncan	"	1600	Protested

NOTES DUE Dec. 21, 1867.

No.	For whom collected.	Drawer's name.	Endorser.	Where payable.	Amount.	Memoranda.
11	Geo. Draper	Ditto & Knox		City	2000	Paid Dec. 21
10	Ourselves	C. Ralston	S. Stevens	New York	1200	Paid " 28
7	"	R. Goodwill		City	3800	Paid " 31
			Dec. 28			
10	W. Hay	J. Dalton		New Orleans	980	Paid Dec. 31, less $20
16	Jno. Hatch	R. Knox	R. Jones	City	200	Paid " 28
17	White & Edwards	Jones & Langdon		"	150	Paid " 28
18	Rich & Gray	S. Girty		Cincinnati	500	Paid " 28
19	Jones & Hatch	Brady & Stein	T. Fairbanks	Cincinnati	140	Paid " 30, less $10
20	Hay & Wood	R. Roy	J. Goodall	City	500	Paid " 28
1	Ourselves	Simon Payne	John Jones	Chicago	5000	Paid " 31, less $50
8	"	M. Thompson		City	600	Paid " 28
9	"	A. Mason		"	1800	Paid " 28
13	S. Barret	W. Hare	Jan'y 13, 1868	City	100	
12	Ourselves	W. Hare		"	800	
21	Ross & Childs	J. Riggs	Jan'y 31	City	800	
22	R. Banks	Thos. King	S. Lowry	New York	3000	
14	Ourselves	Hay & Wood		City	700	
11	Ourselves	Jno. Eastman	Feb'y 4 E. D. Jones	City	3800	
13	"	Simon Payne		"	3000	
26	"	L. C. Donnell	S. J. Grant	New York	225	
21	Ourselves	J. Brown	Feb'y 6 Henry Riggs	City	4000	
18	" "	T. A. Craig		"	4000	
28	Ourselves	J. Hoag	March 3 Martin Die	City	170	

NOTES DUE March 4th, 1868.

No.	For whom collected.	Drawer's name.	Endorser.	Where payable.	Amount.	Memoranda.
27	Ourselves	G. W. Holmes	R. B. Wilson	City	140	
15	"	Jas. May		"	1600	
29	Ourselves	Saml. Green	March 6	Cincinnati	360	
			D. White			
			March 18			
17	Ourselves	Ragan & Morse		City	2000	
20	"	C. Page	C. Gipner	"	3000	
23	"	C. Rhea	J. C. Young	"	5000	
24	"	W. F. Smith	V. B. Smith	New Orleans	4000	
30	"	L. Bradley	H. S. Kerr	City	125	
31	"	J. Vinsonhaler	March 23	St. Louis	234	
16	Ourselves	Roger & Co.	J. Dalley	St. Louis	4000	
19	"	M. Love		City	3000	
22	"	Adrian & Co.	Ourselves	Chicago	20000	
25	"	W. Langdon		City	6000	

368

DEPOSITOR'S LEDGER,

PRIVATE BANKER'S ACCOUNTS.

NOVEMBER, 1867.

1. The new form which we gave of this Ledger in our set of National Bank accounts will also be found convenient for the private banker's business. But we retain the old form n this set, leaving it for the accountant to choose for himself.

2. There are no accounts kept in this Ledger but those of the depositors and certificates of deposit. It is composed wholly from the Deposit and Check Registers. The accounts are never balanced except when the customer hands in his pass-book to be balanced.

3. The aggregate balances of this Ledger must agree with the balance of the Depositor's account in the General Ledger.

1 Dr.   WILSON,   CHILDS & CO.   Cr.

1867.					1867.				
Nov.	2	Cash	1	400	Nov.	2	Cash	1	400
	30	"	1	1000	Dec.	7	Note 1	2	400
Dec.	21	"	2	200		31	Cash	2	3200
	31	"	2	700					
		"	2	300					
		Balance		1400					
				4000					4000
					Dec.	31	Balance		1400

         R. S.   CARSON.

1867.					1867.				
Nov.	7	Cash	1	375	Nov.	2	Cash	1	600
	9	Note 6	1	1000		8	"	1	260
	30	Cash	1	1480		9	Note 3	1	260
Dec.	4	"	2	160		30	Cash	2	1400

         W. J.   MURPHY.

1867.					1867.				
Nov.	2	Cash	1	200	Nov.	2	Cash	1	500
	10	"	1	700		10	Note 4	1	500
Dec.	31	Balance		100					
				1000					1000
					Dec.	31	Balance		100

         WILLIAM   PAYNE.

1867.					1867.				
Nov.	2	Cash	1	400	Nov.	2	Cash	1	700
	8	"	1	300		7	"	1	300
	10	"	1	200		9	Note 2	1	300
	30	Certif. of Dep. No. 3	1	600		23	Cash	1	40
Dec.	7	Cash	2	160	Dec.	30	"	2	360
	31	Balance		3840		31	"	2	3800
				5500					5500
					Dec.	31	Balance		3840

1867.					1867.				
Nov.	8	Cash	1	700	Nov.	7	Cash	1	600
Dec.	31	Balance		500		10	Note 5	1	600
				1200					1200
					Dec.	31	Balance		500

ROBERT   BANKS.

1867.					1867.				
Nov.	7	Cash	1	200	Nov.	7	Cash	1	400
	9	"	1	600		8	"	1	1000
Dec.	31	Balance		2150		9	Note 6	1	1000
					Dec.	31	Cash	2	550
				2950					2950
					Dec.	31	Balance		2150

JAMES   WOOD.

1867.					1867.				
Nov.	7	Cash	1	100	Nov.	7	Cash	1	600
	16	"	1	500		16	Note 7	1	2000

CHARLES   PAGE.

1867.					1867.				
Nov.	8	Cash	1	600	Nov.	8	Cash	1	700
	23	Note 3	1	5600		23	"	1	450
						30	Note 8	2	470
					Dec.	31	Balance		4580
				6200					6200
Dec.	31	Balance		4580					

WILLIAM   STONER.

1867.					1867.				
Nov.	9	Cash	1	200	Nov.	8	Cash	1	240
Dec.	31	"	2	5000		30	"	2	560
	31	Balance		500	Dec.	21	"	2	100
						31	"	2	4800
				5700					5700
					Dec.	31	Balance		500

3 Dr.   **JAMES**   **PILLOW.**   Cr.

1867.					1867.				
Nov.	9	Cash	1	600	Nov.	9	Cash	1	1700
Dec.	31	Balance		8900	Dec.	7	Note 12	2	7800
				9500					9500
					Dec.	31	Balance		8900

        ROBT.   **KNOX.**

1867.					1867.				
Nov.	10	Cash	1	200	Nov.	10	Cash	1	749
Dec.	21	"	2	150	Dec.	14	Note 14	2	3960
	28	"	2	400					
	31	Balance		3959					
				4709					4709
					Dec.	31	Balance		3959

        JAMES   **WATT.**

1867.					1867.				
Nov.	16	Cash	1	400	Nov.	10	Cash	1	450
Dec.	31	Balance		3050	Dec.	14	Note 15	2	3000
				3450					3450
					Dec.	31	Balance		3050

        GEORGE   **DRAPER.**

1867.					1867.				
Nov.	16	Cash	1	200	Nov.	10	Cash	1	750
					Dec.	21	Note 11	2	2600

        WILLIAM   **HAY.**

1867.					1867.				
Nov	16	Cash	1	200	Nov.	16	Cash	1	1475
Dec.	21	"	2	500		30	"	2	1000
	31	Balance		2735	Dec.	31	Note 10	2	960
				3435					3435
					Dec.	31	Balance		2735

JOHN HATCH (Dr. / Cr.)

1867.				1867.			
Nov.	23	Certif. of Dep. No. 1	1	700	Nov.	16	Cash	1	760
	30	Cash	1	840	Dec.	28	Note 16	2	200

WHITE & EDWARDS

1867.					1867.				
Nov.	23	Cash	1	800	Nov.	16	Cash	1	1750
	30	Certif. of Dep. No. 2	1	1000	Dec.	28	Note 17	2	150
Dec.	28	Cash	2	2400		31	Balance		2300
				4200					4200
Dec.	31	Balance		2300					

JONES & HATCH

1867.					1867.				
Nov.	23	Cash	1	400	Nov.	23	Cash	1	750
Dec.	7	"	2	200	Dec.	14	"	2	1000
	28	"	2	240		30	Note 19	2	130
	31	Balance		1040					
				1880					1880
					Dec.	31	Balance		1040

RICH & GRAY

1867.					1867.				
Nov.	23	Cash	1	20	Nov.	23	Cash	1	460
Dec.	14	"	2	130	Dec.	28	Note 18	2	500
	31	Balance		810					
				960					960
					Dec.	31	Balance		810

1867					1867.				
Nov	23	Cash	1	400	Nov.	23	Cash	1	500
Dec.	4	"	2	400		30	"	2	700
					Dec.	7	"	2	615
						28	Note 20	2	560

ROBERT   MARTIN.

1867.					1867.				
Dec.	14	Cash	2	300	Dec.	30	Cash	2	400

H. P.   FORD & CO.

					1867.				
					Dec.	31	Cash	2	600

CERTIFICATES   OF DEPOSIT.

1867.						1867.					
Dec.	31	Cash,	No. 1	2	700	Nov.	23	Cash,	No. 1	1	700
							30	"	" 2	2	1000
Dec.	28	"	" 3	2	600			"	" 3	2	600
								"	" 4	2	900
Dec.	21	"	" 5	2	2000	Dec.	14	"	" 5	2	2000

GENERAL LEDGER,

PRIVATE BANKER'S ACCOUNTS.

1. When there is no Journal kept, this book is posted exclusively from the Cash Book. It has no other auxiliary.

2. It is closed whenever the partners desire to divide the profits or see the results of their business.

375

1867.						1867.					
Dec.	31	Balance	f	4	22482	87	Nov.	2	Cash	1	20000	
							Dec.	31	Profit & Loss	f	4	2482	87
					22482	87					22482	87
							Dec.	31	Balance		22482	87

WM.   **HAY.**

1867.							1867.					
Dec.	31	Balance	*	f	4	11241	43	Nov.	2	Cash	1	10000	
								Dec.	31	Profit & Loss	f	4	1241	43
						11241	43					11241	43
								Dec.	31	Balance		11241	43

W.   **WOOD.**

1867.						1867.					
Dec.	31	Balance	f	4	11241	44	Nov.	2	Cash	1	10000	
							Dec.	31	Profit & Loss	f	4	1241	44
					11241	44					11241	44
							Dec.	31	Balance		11241	44

CASH   **ACCOUNT.**

1867.						1867.					
Nov.	30	Sundries	1	78343	66	Nov.	30	Sundries	1	51810	
Dec.	31	″	1	68883	08	Dec.	31	″	1	88679	
							″	Balance	f	4	6737	74
				147226	74					147226	74
Dec.	31	Balance		6737	74						

1867.					1867.				
Nov.	2	Cash	1	1000	Nov.	2	Cash	1	2200
	7	"	1	675		7	"	1	1900
	8	"	1	1600		8	"	1	2200
	9	"	1	2400		9	"	1	3260
	10	"	1	1100		10	"	1	3049
	16	"	1	1300		16	"	1	5985
	23	"	1	7920		23	"	1	2900
	30	"	1	4920		30	"	1	6630
Dec.	4	"	1	560	Dec.	7	"	1	8815
	7	"	1	360		14	"	1	9960
	14	"	1	430		21	"	1	2700
	21	"	1	2850		28	"	1	1410
	28	"	1	3640		30	"	1	890
	31	"	1	6700		31	"	1	13910
		Balance	f 4	30354					
				65809					65809
					Dec.	31	Balance		30354

BILLS   RECEIVABLE.

1867.					1867.				
Nov.	2	Cash	1	17400	Nov.	23	Cash	1	5600
	9	"	1	4200		30	"	1	4000
	11	"	1	1600	Dec.	14	"	1	2800
	23	"	1	7400			"	1	4200
Dec.	7	"	1	3800		28	"	1	3600
	14	"	1	4500		31	"	1	3800
	21	"	1	5600			"	1	5000
	28	"	1	12600			Balance	f 4	68354
	29	"	1	24000					
	30	"	1	15000					
	31	"	1	1254					
				97354					97354
Dec.	31	Balance		68354					

1867.						1867.					
Nov.	2	Cash	1	20		Nov.	2	Cash	1	158	92
	7	"	1	37			7	"	1	69	
	8	"	1	12			8	"	1	25	
	9	"	1	15			9	"	1	39	70
	16	"	1	75			16	"	1	62	47
	23	"	1	105			23	"	1	154	57
	30	"	1	31			30	"	1	110	
Dec.	4	"	1	15		Dec.	4	"	1	1260	
	7	"	1	24			7	"	1	75	50
	21	"	1	56			14	"	1	2618	60
	28	"	1	12			21	"	1	80	80
	31	"	1	50			28	"	1	143	84
		Profit & Loss f	4	4965			29	"	1	306	
							30	"	1	200	
							31	"	1	113	34
				5417	74					5417	74

DUFF   (New York.)   **BROTHERS & CO.**

1867.						1867.					
Dec.	28	Cash	1	1188		Dec.	31	Cash	1	1000	
								Balance f	4	188	
				1188						1188	
Dec.	31	Balance		188							

THOMAS   (Chicago.)   **THOMPSON & CO.**

1867.						1867.				
Dec.	31	Cash	1	4950		Dec.	31	Cash	1	6000
		Balance f	4	1050						
				6000						6000
						Dec.	31	Balance		1050

1867. Dec.	30	Cash		1	130		1867. Dec.	31	Balance	f	4	130
Dec.	31	Balance			130							

THOMAS F.   (New Orleans.)   SHEPHERD

1867. Dec.	31	Cash		1	960		1867. Dec.	31	Balance	f	4	960
Dec.	31	Balance			960							

PROFIT   &   LOSS.

1867. Dec.	31	P. Duff	f	1	2482	87	1867. Dec.	31	Discount	f	3	4965	74
		W. Hay		1	1241	43							
		W. Wood	*	1	1241	44							
					4965	74						4965	74

BALANCE   ACCOUNT.

1867. Dec.	31	Cash	f	1	6737	74	1867. Dec.	31	Depositors	f	2	30354	
		Bills Receivable		2	68354				Thompson & Co.		3	1050	
		Duff Bros. & Co.		3	188				P. Duff		1	22482	87
		R. P. Duff		4	130				Wm. Hay		1	11241	43
		T. F. Shepherd		4	960				W. Wood		1	11241	44
					76369	74						76369	74

QUESTIONS FOR EXAMINATION ON PRIVATE BANKER'S ACCOUNTS.

1. What office does the Cash Book perform? (N. 1, p. 351.)
2. Into what book are its contents posted? (N. 1, p. 351.)
3. Where are the aggregate monthly receipts and payments posted from? (N. 2, p. 351.)
4. What is entered in the Deposit Register? (N. 1, p. 355.)
5. Where are the daily amounts carried to? (N. 1, p. 355.)
6. Into what book do we post the particulars? (N. 1, p. 355.)
7. What does the Check Register record? (N. 1, p. 356.)
8. Where are the amounts transferred? (N. 1, p. 256.)
9. How often? (N. 1, p. 356.)
10. Where do we post the particulars? (N. 1, p. 356.)
11. What is entered on the Bill Book? (N. 1, p. 358.)
12. Where are the discounts entered? (N. 1, p. 358.)
13. Where do we enter the payments? (N. 1, p. 358.)
14. Where do we record the maturity of discounted paper? (N. 1, p. 358.)
15. What does the Collection Register record? (N. 1, p. 360.)
16. What is done with the net proceeds of collections? (N. 1, p. 360.)
17. When are Foreign Notes or Bills remitted for collection? (N. 2, p. 360.)
18. When you are notified by your agent of the payment of a collection, how is it entered? (N. 2, p. 360.)
19. What is recorded in the Discount Book? (N. 1, p. 362.)
20. When and where are the amounts carried to? (N. 1, p. 362.)
21. How many Ticklers are kept by some Bankers? (N. 1, p. 365.)
22. How do we enter the notes as they are paid? (N. 2, p. 365.)
23. What is done with protested paper? (N. 2, p. 365.)
24. Who pays the expenses of a Protest? (N. 2, p. 365.)
25. What accounts are kept in the Depositor's Ledger? (N. 2, p. 369.)
26. What books is it composed from? (N. 2, p. 369.)
27. When are the accounts in it balanced? (N. 2, p. 369.)
28. What must the aggregate balances agree with? (N. 3, p. 369.)
29. Where are the contents of the General Ledger posted from? (N. 1, p. 375.)
30. When is it closed? (N. 2, p. 375.)

380

SELECTED PROBLEMS IN ACCOUNTS.

PROBLEM I.

W., X., Y., and Z. bought of A. on joint account, each ¼, $20000 worth of sugars, for which W. as manager of the sales gave his note to A. at four months, indorsed by the other partners; and each partner made conforming entries in his books. Afterward, A. offers W. 5 per cent. discount off the face of his notes, to cash them, which W. on conferring with X. and Y. agrees to, Z. being a resident of Philadelphia, to which place he had returned after entering into the above transaction. W. pays his own share and half of Z.'s in cash, less the 5 per cent. discount. X. pays his own share and one-fourth of Z.'s, less the 5 per cent. discount, in a draft at sight on C., of New York, which A. accepts in payment at ¾ per cent. premium; X. allowing him 1 per cent. brokerage on the face of the draft for negotiating it. Y. pays his own share and ¼ of Z.'s, less 5 per cent. discount, in a draft at 60 days' sight upon Z., which A. accepts in payment at 2½ per cent. discount, drawn for such sum as will cover the transaction, and 1 per cent. brokerage on the face of the draft, which A. charges for negotiating it. On advice of this second arrangement, Z. makes conforming entries in his books. Afterward W. orders him to invest the amount which he had advanced for him in the above transaction in bills on New Orleans, and remit, on W.'s account, to B., of that place. This was done in bills at 2½ per cent. discount, which closed the account, and covered ¼ per cent. brokerage on the face of the bills, which Z. charged for investing.

Required the correct amounts and the correct Journal entries of W., X., Y., and Z., in each of the above transactions.

PROBLEM II.

A., B., and C. purchased the machinery and hull of an old steamer called the "Vixen," for $10000, of which A. paid $4000, B. $3400, and C. $2600. They afterward sold ¼ of the purchase to D. for $2000 cash, which they divided and drew out of the concern in such proportions as left them all ¼ owners. In these proportions as owners, and with this machinery, they built the steamer "Volante." In addition to their shares in the machinery, A. paid in cash $1261, B. $1320, C. $1410, and D. $1430. After running fifteen months, the boat was sunk and lost. The accounts on her books then stood as follows:

	Debits.	Credits.
Steamer "Volante"	$14894.83	
Steamer "Vixen"	164.35	$265.39
Freight account	270.67	35803.04
Passage *v*		28375.17
Wages *v*	21923.88	
Fuel *v*	11843.02	
Expense *v*	24134.27	104.01
Bills Payable		8450.
Bar account	130.30	363.71

Effects saved from the wreck realized $2860. C. and D.'s shares were uninsured. A had $4000 and B. $3000 insured on their shares, valued at $5000 each. The amounts insured when recovered, and the amount realized by the owners from the wreck, were applied in discharging the above claims against the vessel. Each owner was ¼ gain or loss. Required the settlement of the transaction between them. Also, the division of D.'s purchase-money between A., B., and C.

PROBLEM III.

A., B., and C. agree to do business in partnership, on the following terms: C. is to manage the business, and to have a commission equal to half the net gain on the business for the management of it. A. pays in $2600 capital, B. $1400, C. $1200. C. draws out $2400. At the end of the year they have cash on hand, $3000; merchandise, $2400. They owe $500. Their expense account is Dr. for $600. The gain or loss to be divided equally.

Required the balance due each; also, the amount of C.'s commission.

SELECTED PROBLEMS.

PROBLEM IV.

C. is manager of a joint speculation in flour with D. and E., of which C. and D. are each ¼ and E ½ proprietors. C. takes $12,000 worth of the joint property to his private account, and pays the other two partners their respective shares of the same, as follows, viz.:

He pays D. $1500 in merchandise, and gave his (C.'s) note for $1000, and gave up his (D.'s) own note which he held against him for $500. He paid E. his ½ ($6000)—$3000 in flour belonging to the Company, and $3000 in his (C.'s) draft on F., of New York, at 90 days' sight, at 2½ per cent. discount for such sum as will cover the $3000 and ¾ per cent. brokerage on the face of the draft, which E. charges for negotiating it.

Required C.'s Journal entry, with the correct amounts composing it.

PROBLEM V.

Robert Morris and myself are doing business on joint account. As manager of the sales, I keep the account in my own private books, under the title of 1st Co. sales, each partner ½ gain or loss. On the same conditions, I purchase on my note, $10,500 worth of merchandise to ship on joint account with R. Morris, to New Orleans. R. Morris puts into the shipment out of his own store, 400 barrels flour at $6.00, and I have also put in 600 barrels of flour at $6.00, which I had on hand belonging to the 1st Co. sales. I have paid insurance and other expenses upon the shipment, in cash, $660.

Required my Journal entry for the joint shipment; also, Morris' Journal entry, when he receives my invoice of the same.

PROBLEM VI.

J. Day, F. Howe, and J. King, owners of steamer "Albatross."

J. Day is one-fourth, F. Howe one-fourth, J. King one-half, owners: after running the boat for eighteen months, it appeared by her books that

J. Day paid in $2400, drew out $1158
F. Howe „ 2690, „ 1212
J. King „ 4950, „ 2750

The boat was then sunk and entirely lost. King had his share insured for $3000, which he recovered, and applied in discharging the debts of the boat.

The boat owes $650, and the only effects that remain are—cash, $820, and debts due the boat, $550.

Required the settlement between the owners of the boat.

PROBLEM VII.

On the 1st of January, 1846, A., B., C., and D. purchase the steamer "Velocity" for $8000, each to share one-fourth of the gain or loss in running her. They pay for her as follows:—

A... $1440
B... 1465
C... 1485
D... 1610
                                                    ———
                                                    $6000

which sums were placed to the credit of their respective accounts on the vessel's books

For the balance of $2000 they gave their joint note, which was afterwards taken up with funds earned by the boat.

At the end of six months, D. sells out his interest, as it then stood upon the books, to C., who paid him for the same out of his own private funds. The remaining owners some time afterwards sold the vessel for $6500; and, after discharging all claims against them, they have cash and other effects left amounting to $6450. The books were kept by Single Entry, and no settlement took place since the commencement of their connection. Their accounts now stand upon their Ledger as follows:—

A.'s account debited for sums withdrawn, $2050, and credited for sums paid in, $2255
B.'s   "   "   "   1640,   "   "   "   2060
C.'s   "   "   "   1750,   "   "   "   2110
D.'s   "   "   "   1965,   "   "   "   2090

No interest to be computed in the settlement. **Required the division** of the above $6450 between A., B., and C.

PROBLEM VIII.

On January **1**, 1867, Brewer, Malt & Co., of Pittsburgh, sent their clerk, W. Porter, to Louisville, to establish an agency for selling their ales. On 30th June following, the agency was discontinued, and they rendered the following account to Porter, the items of which both parties agree are correct, but Porter thinks the balance is not correct. Is it so? or, what is the correct balance?

MR. WALTER PORTER

Dr.   In Account with BREWER, MALT & CO.,   Cr.

1867.				1867.			
Jan.	1	To Cash advanced.......	191	Feb.	1	By Cash paid for Barley	1508
		" Invoice of Ales.......	297	Mar.	1	" Cash paid for Hops...	1007 50
	30	" Cash..................	389	May	1	" Paid Rent.............	260
		" Invoice of Ale.......	298	June	30	" Paid Expenses........	40
June	30	" Cash for sales.........	2938 50			" Salary.................	690
		" Ale returned....	810			" Ale returned.........	810
						" Balance due..........	608
			4923 50				4923 50
		To Bal. due B., M. & Co.	608				

PROBLEM IX.

Lea & Preston purchase of J. Stanley ⅓ of the steamer "Herald," which is ½ his paid-up capital (at his credit on the books) of $6500, for which they pay him $4000. They have an account against the boat for repairing machinery of $1250, which it is agreed is to stand as part payment; the balance they pay Stanley in cash. Required the Journal entry to introduce the new owners into the books.

INDEX.

INDEX.

z   385

INDEX.

INDEX.

INDEX TO NATIONAL BANK BOOKS.

INDEX.

INDEX TO RAIL ROAD BOOKS.

INDEX TO PRIVATE BANKER'S BOOKS.

RECONMENDATIONS.

THE FOLLOWING RECOMMENDATIONS INDICATE THE **PUBLIC** SENTIMENT **IN** REFERENCE **TO** THIS WORK.

Extract from the official report of a Special Committee of Merchants of the Chamber of Commerce of the city of New York :

CHAMBER OF COMMERCE, NEW YORK, Feb. 6, 1849.
At a regular meeting of the Chamber, held this day, the following report was presented, accepted, and a copy ordered to be transmitted to Mr. Duff. The committee to whom was referred the subject of Mr. Duff's work on Book-keeping, *Report,* That they have examined the work submitted to them, and deem the favorable opinions which have already been expressed by gentlemen of competent authority, and prefixed to its pages, well deserved, and in this case very properly bestowed.

Respectfully submitted,
(Signed)
CHARLES M. LEUPP, *Merchant.*
LEOPOLD BIERWIRTH, *do.*
ROBERT KELLY,
President of the Board of Education.

Extract from the Minutes.
PROSPER M. WETMORE, *Secretary.*

Extract from a report of a Special Committee of Merchants and Accountants, appointed by the Board of Managers for the American Institute, to examine this work :
" Your committee are so favorably impressed with the proposed improved method of Mr. Duff, that they unanimously concur in the opinion of its utility, and that the public would be benefited by adopting it."
I certify that the foregoing is a true copy of a Report of a Special Committee, made to and adopted by the American Institute of the city of New York.
GURDON J. LEEDS, *Recording Secretary.*

" It contains much matter that is important and interesting to the merchant and man of business, to whom it will be found highly useful." C. O. HALSTEAD,
Late President of Manhattan Bank, N. Y.

" It is by far the most complete work of the kind I have ever seen."
JAMES B. MURRAY,
President Exchange National Bank, Pittsburgh.

" I differ entirely from those who think the counting-house the best place to learn Book-keeping in. From this work it is learned in its application to every form of business, untrammelled by the peculiar details of any one kind of business."
THOMPSON BELL,
President Commercial Bank of Pittsburgh.

" No other work upon Book-keeping, so far as my knowledge of them extends, explains the subject with so much clearness and simplicity." F. W. EDMONDS,
Late Cashier Mechanics' Bank, Wall Street, N. Y.

RECOMMENDATIONS.

"It gives a clear insight into this science through all its gradations, from the simple style of the retailer to that required for the most varied and complicated commercial business."

A. S. FRASER,
Cashier Seventh Ward Bank, N. Y.

"I graduated in Duff's College in about half the time that I expected. His admirable system leaves out nothing essential, nor puts in any thing superfluous."

J. R. COMPTON,
Cashier of the Niagara Bank, Lockport, N. Y.

"I admire your system of Book-keeping. Since I acquired a knowledge of it, some years since, through Mr. David Parsons, I have put it in practice in different branches of business, and have always found it work like a charm. I have recommended it to my friends as containing all that is necessary to make the most thorough accountant."

R. LAMB,
Cashier People's Bank, Bellefontaine, Ohio.

"Duff's Book-keeping is, without doubt, the best adapted to a business education ever published. Students save about half the time and labor required by other systems."

JOHN J. JONES,
Book-keeper First National Bank, Wheeling, Va.

"The new method of checks and balances will, if carried out, prevent errors, or, if made, they will be more readily found than by any other system."

DAVID L. BROWN,
Late Book-keeper to the Merc. and Manuf. National Bank, Pittsburgh.

"It is in every way calculated to impart that knowledge necessary for the experienced book-keeper. Every thing is made plain and easy to be understood."

J. CAROTHERS,
Formerly Banker, Wood Street, Pittsburgh.

"Your work on Book-keeping is the most clear and comprehensive that I have met with."

JOHN SNYDER,
Late Cashier Bank of Pittsburgh.

"It is evident that you have brought to the study of Book-keeping a clear head which has lost none of that clearness by the long cultivation of an accurate science. It is impossible to make the subject of accounts more easy of comprehension to the young beginner; and, what is often still more difficult, you have made it so to the old learner."

W. H. DENNY,
Late Cashier of the Merchants' and Manufacturers' National Bank, Pittsburgh.

"I knew little or nothing of Book-keeping when I entered your College. Since leaving it I have had charge of the books of this banking firm for nearly six years, and have kept them without difficulty. During my leisure hours I settled up the books of a mercantile firm, and have met with nothing but what was fully explained in your course of instruction."

M. HUNNINGS,
Of the firm of Kramer & Rahm, Bankers, Pittsburgh.

"I took charge of the books of this extensive banking-house immediately on leaving your classes, and have every evidence that I give them perfect satisfaction."

J. W. DAVITT,
Of the firm of Kramer & Rahm, Bankers, Pittsburgh.

"My tuition fee in Duff's College and the study of his new system of accounts was among the best investments I ever made."

C. E. BABCOCK,
Book-keeper State Bank of Iowa, Fort Madison.

RECOMMENDATIONS.

"An experience of nine years in business has not yet brought any transaction into my hand so difficult as many of your class exercises." E. SPAHR,

Book-keeper to the National Bank of Commerce, Pittsburgh.

The following letter indicates the perfection of the course of study in this old and popular institution:

"With no previous knowledge of accounts, nor practice in any kind of book-keeping, except a course of study in Duff's College, from his system of Book-keeping, I took charge of the books of this bank. This treatise certainly combines the most comprehensive system of science and practice in accountantship now before the public. It is so judiciously diversified that it fits the student for keeping accounts in any kind of business."

FRED. L. RAINBOW,

Book-keeper Mechanics' National Bank, Pittsburgh.

"I consider this treatise the most comprehensive and complete system of Book-keeping that I have met with." T. B. DICKSON,

Individual Book-keeper Merc. and Manuf. National Bank, Pittsburgh.

"I readily concur in all that is said of this work by other competent judges. No writer upon Book-keeping has had the advantage of such an extensive and varied experience in business. I have known him, personally, for upwards of twenty years; a great part of that time as an extensive American and European merchant, as an extensive ship-owner, and as a bank director, &c., and in all these departments he has borne the reputation of the highest order of business talents. Every thing said or written by such a person, on the subject of business, is of interest, not only to young men designed for business, but for those already engaged in it." JOHN W. BURNHAM,

Merchant, No. 8 South Street, New York.

"You have made good use of your long experience as a merchant in making plain many of those matters of business, the want of due comprehension of which so often occasions serious difficulties in the counting-house. The accuracy and conciseness manifested throughout the whole work, bear testimony to the great care and labor you have bestowed upon it." RICHARD IRVIN,

Merchant, 98 Front Street, New York.

"Mr. Duff is a man of rare qualifications for business,—a man that will go through with whatever he takes in hand. His system of Book-keeping should be studied by every one who has any thing to do with dollars and cents." JOHN McD. TAYLOR,

Merchant, Union Street, New Orleans.

"Mr. Duff is a merchant of the first respectability." J. LANDIS,

Merchant, New Orleans.

"Mr. Duff has been recommended to me as a merchant of the highest respectability." O. H. BLISS,

Merchant, New Orleans.

"I have always pronounced your system the most thorough and diversified course of training for business, before the public. The most experienced accountant will recognize, in your plan of rectifying deranged books, a new and most ingenious method of bringing order out of confusion." ANGUS CAMPBELL,

Book-keeper to Burdett & Choate, Wholesale Commission Merchants, Memphis, Tenn.

RECOMMENDATIONS.

"Your system of accounts is *excelsior*. Every man that studies it as you direct cannot help going into business a first-class accountant, and with a good general business knowledge that it will take years to acquire by practice. Your Bank Check Book is an improvement of great value in all large houses."

W. D. ELLIOTT,
Book-keeper to Smith, Sherwood & Co., Merchants,
St. Louis, Mo.

"I have been thirty years a practical book-keeper, and during my practice I have never before met with a work which so fully explains the whole subject of accounts; in fact, it is the first treatise that I have seen from which a thorough practical knowledge of the science can be obtained."

JOHN CAMPBELL,
Merchant, 53 John Street, New York.

"There is no other system of Book-keeping in use that so thoroughly and practically elucidates this part of a business education; and your impressive and interesting lectures on business, commercial law, banking, &c., will be useful to me through life."

T. H. ADAMS,
Book-keeper for McElroy, Dickson & Co., Merchants, Pittsburgh.

"With no previous knowledge of accounts, except your course of study, I took charge of the books of this extensive business, and have kept them satisfactorily for nearly eight years. To obtain the best business education, I say go at once to the best college, which I am positive is yours."

CHARLES F. WELLS,
Book-keeper for B. L. Fahnestock & Co., Importers and
Wholesale Druggists, Pittsburgh, Pa.

"With no other education than I got in a common country school, your instruction in Book-keeping enabled me to take charge of the books of an extensive firm in Wood Street, and finally of the books of this department of the Railroad Company, which I have now kept successfully for eight years."

J. K. SMITH,
Book-keeper, Treasurer of the Pittsburgh, Fort Wayne
& Chicago Railroad Co.

"I have tested the thorough business training I received in your excellent establishment, by many years' successful practice in some of the largest firms in the city."

SIMON JOHNSTON,
Druggist, Pittsburgh.

"The accountant who keeps his books upon your system will have the advantage of improvements which are not found in any other system."

HARVEY M. COWAN,
Late Book-keeper to Messrs. J. Woodwell & Co.,
Hardware Merchants, Pittsburgh.

"At the age of seventeen I graduated in your College. I have since kept books in banks in Springfield, Illinois, and St. Louis, Missouri, until my health compelled me to return to this vicinity, where I am keeping the books of this extensive firm. It is due to you to say, that the longer I have practised upon it, the more I am satisfied that your judiciously arranged and diversified course of study is superior to all others that I have seen, in preparing a young man for any branch of business."

T. K. BABCOCK,
Book-keeper to the Cambria Iron Works, Johnstown, Pa.

"Although the books I am keeping are widely different from what I studied with you, yet that complete knowledge of the principles of the science which I obtained in your classes has enabled me to conduct every thing successfully."

GEO. W. JACKSON,
Book-keeper to the N. W. Virginia R. R. Co., Grafton, Va.

RECOMMENDATIONS.

" We have used your Book-keeping for eight years. During this time I have examined every other work I could hear of, but have found none so judiciously arranged and so comprehensive in all that relates to an accountant's education. This fact is also attested by numbers who had first studied other systems and afterward graduated with us."

T. H. POLLOCK,
Principal Pollock's Commercial College, Chestnut Street, Philadelphia, Pa.

" I do not hesitate to say that this is the most perfect work that I ever examined on the subject."

T. H. TUTTLE,
Banker, Philadelphia.

" Your system of accounts is in every way thorough, without any superfluous matter. Since leaving your Institution I have met many of your pupils who express the same opinion."

JOHN S. WILSON,
Of Messrs. Kilgore, Wilson & Co., Merchants, Philadelphia.

" I believe your system to be the best now taught."

B. McKENNA,
Of A. Diamond & Co., Booksellers and Stationers, Philadelphia.

" Book-keeping, as elucidated by your system, is the most thorough and complete extant. Since I studied with you, I have had seven years' experience in the practice of it."

CHARLES FITCH,
Book-keeper to Messrs. Allibone & Jenks, Merchants, Philadelphia.

" I believe your course of study to be far superior to that given in Eastern cities, in this branch of education."

B. K. JAMISON,
Book-keeper to Messrs. R. J. Ross & Co., Bankers, Philadelphia.

" My present business brings before me nearly every system of Book-keeping in use, and it is to your admirable system of accounts, and your masterly manner of teaching it, that I owe my qualification for effecting the intricate settlements brought into my hands by this business."

JAMES FULTON,
Adjuster of Fire Insurances, 424 Chestnut Street, Philadelphia.

" Since graduating in your College, I have settled several sets of complicated books. I am now satisfied that I have mastered the science under your instruction, and recommend all who desire to become expert and scientific accountants, to go at once to your establishment."

J. A. STEELE,
Book-keeper to Messrs. Sledge & Cress, Merchants, Chappell Hill, Texas.

" I shall ever regard your instruction in Book-keeping, and your impressive and interesting lectures upon business, as my most valuable preparation for my present business. Your system of accounts can never be excelled. It prepares one for every kind of business."

R. J. BROWN,
Of Brown & Brother, Druggists, Leavenworth City, Kansas.

" I say from experience, that no one who graduates in your system of Book-keeping, as you teach it, will have any trouble in keeping any kind of books."

S. M. RANKIN,
Of Sample & Rankin, Bankers, Keokuk, Iowa.

' I had no idea that your course of instruction was so much a course of practice until I applied it in business. Your system of Book-keeping has business letters, accounts, invoices, notes, acceptances, checks, &c., so thoroughly interwoven with the exercises in Book-keeping, that I have met with nothing in business that your excellent course of training has not fully prepared me for.'

JAMES H. SMITH,
Book-keeper for Smith & Baker, Wool Merchants, Newark, Ohio.

RECOMMENDATIONS.

"I experienced no difficulty in applying your excellent instruction to immediate practice, particularly your six-columned Journal, which proves to be a great economizer of time and labor, and a safeguard against error."

M. S. STOKES,
Book-keeper to Messrs. R. S. Hollins & Co., Merchants, Nashville, Tenn.

"We take pleasure in testifying to the truth of Mr. Stokes' statements in regard to your system of Book-keeping, and fully concur with him in recommending it to the public as safe, accurate, and easily comprehended."

R. S. HOLLINS & CO.

"Your six-columned Journal is a model of accuracy and brevity, not likely soon to be improved upon; and your method of rectifying deranged books is a most valuable appendage to your system, that I have not seen nor heard of elsewhere."

A. J. McCLELLAND,
Book-keeper, Cumberland Iron Works, Tenn.

"I found no difficulty in applying your system to practice. Your six-column Journal saves a large amount of writing, and is, therefore, better adapted to my business than any other system of Book-keeping that I have seen."

P. J. FLINDALL,
Merchant, Trenton, Canada West.

"I am getting on finely with the books and the business of this firm. Success to your valuable Institution and to all who avail themselves of the advantages of your instruction from your system of Book-keeping—the best of all systems extant."

R. C. ARMSTRONG,
Book-keeper to Messrs. Hibbert & Son, Merchants, Louisville, Ky.

"I advise all my friends to enter your well-organized Institution. It is certainly headquarters for a thorough commercial education."

WM. B. MORGAN,
U. S. Treasury, Washington, D. C.

"With no previous knowledge of accounts or business but what I learned in less than eight weeks under that able and systematic course of instruction for which your establishment has been so long and so justly celebrated, I have since kept books for several years in two mercantile establishments; I have several times successfully rectified deranged books, changing the Single Entry Ledger into Double Entry, &c. Since 1861, my position in this Department required the greatest skill and accuracy in Book-keeping, the duties being more varied and changeable than in any other Bureau in the Department. Few of your graduates have had their proficiency more thoroughly tested than mine; and I say to all desiring a thorough business education, by no means miss your College and your lectures upon business. I speak of their value from experience."

THOS. GLEN JONES,
U. S. Treasury Department, Washington, D. C.

"Duff's Book-keeping is an excellent text-book for schools. Its teachings are very lucid, while it embraces many points of interest to be found in no other work on Book-keeping extant."

J. R. WEBSTER,
Teacher of Book-keeping, Central High School, Baltimore.

"After a year's trial of it in my classes, I find the instruction conveyed by your Book-keeping is more complete and practical than any other I have used."

JOHN SHEPHERD,
Late Teacher of Book-keeping, Columbia College, N. Y

"Having ascertained that Duff's system of business accounts is the best in use, we have introduced it as a text-book in this college."

JOHN K. STEWART,
Late Professor of Book-keeping, Southern Commercial College, Richmond, Va.

RECOMMENDATIONS.

"The crowning excellence of your system of Book-keeping is the judicious abridgment of all unnecessary details and repetitions, reducing the time of study to about half that required in other Commercial Colleges. And my employer says he has never seen a person direct from College that went ahead with all their books so promptly and accurately as I have."   WILSON S. ROOSE,
                    Book-keeper for Ignatz & Herzog, Merchants, Chicago, Ill.

"I have had no difficulty with my books. I see now the great advantage and superiority of your well-arranged system of instruction in Book-keeping."
                    WM. M. HORGAN,
                    Book-keeper to J. B. Shay, Merchant, Chicago, Ill.

"I have already successfully tested the value of your admirable rules for settling old business books and opening new ones from them, and now readily subscribe to all that your former graduates have said of the superiority of your system of Book-keeping."
                    D. C. BERGUNDTHAL,
                    Book-keeper for S. W. Prather, Merchant, Wheeling, W. Va.

"I believe your system of accounts, and manner of teaching it, unequalled by any in use."   R. T. KITTS,
                    Book-keeper to McCullough, Morris & Co., Wholesale Grocers,
                            Cincinnati, Ohio.

"Without any previous knowledge of business books except a course of study from Duff's Book-keeping, I have kept the books of this extensive business for about three years. In my opinion, a more complete system of science and business practice has never been printed."
                    W. L. KEEPERS,
                    Book-keeper, Raccoon Iron Works, Greenupsburg, Ky.

"Duff's system of accounts is the most perfect I have seen. It contains many improvements, abbreviations, and guards against errors which I have not seen nor heard of elsewhere."   JAMES H. McCLOY,
                    Book-keeper W. McClintock's Carpet Warehouse, Pittsburgh.

"I fully concur in all that I have heard in commendation of your system of merchants' accounts. Many years' experience in keeping books in this and other houses, since I studied it, enables me to say that I consider it decidedly the best work of the kind in use."
                    JAMES E. DICKSON,
                    Book-keeper for Mitchell, Stevenson & Co., Iron Founders
                            and Merchants, Pittsburgh.

"This work comes to us with such high recommendations, from parties well able to judge of its merits, that we have no hesitation in cordially inviting attention to it as a work of great utility to merchants."—*New York Albion.*

"Evidently the production of one thoroughly versed in the art and science of accounts, and artistic in his views and manner of elucidating them."—*Journal of Commerce.*

"Numerous as are the publications already before the public on this important branch of mercantile education, we think, from the emphatic testimonials appended to the work, that Mr. Duff has succeeded in effecting a more ready and desirable method of teaching and reducing to practice this great essential in the conduct of mercantile affairs."—*New York Evening Express, October 30.*

RECOMMENDATIONS.

FROM THE PITTSBURGH GAZETTE.

"DUFF'S BOOK-KEEPING.—This has become the standard work upon commercial science. No work yet published so thoroughly unfolds the whole subject. We are informed that it is the only work yet published in this country which exemplifies the merchant's private Ledger,—an arrangement by which the results of the business cannot be known by the principal Ledger; an arrangement which mercantile men, conducting a large business, know the value of. No possible good can arise from a needless exposure of any man's business."

"We have in a former number spoken of Mr. Duff's new and excellent treatise upon merchants' accounts, published by the Messrs. Harpers. Every merchant will prize it as an indispensable addition to his library; and there are but few accountants so old, or so wise, as not to derive valuable information from it."—*Hunt's Merchants' Magazine, N. Y.*

"A few weeks' study in Duff's College prepared me for keeping the books of this extensive firm. I have seen no other system so complete." EDWIN REEDER,
Book-keeper to the Waterbury & Detroit Copper Co.,
Detroit, Mich.

"Duff's Book-keeping is so much of a self-instructor, that I graduated in twenty-one days, and have kept books ever since without difficulty." R. NEEL, JR.,
Merchant, Looneyville, N. Y.

"During my former occupation of a teacher of Book-keeping, few persons took greater pains to compare different treatises upon this science, with a view to select the most thorough and comprehensive; and I state, without hesitation, that Duff's Book-keeping will impart a more perfect and practical knowledge of the science, in less time, with less labor to the learner, and with less trouble to the teacher, than any treatise that has yet appeared upon the subject." C. C. COCHRAN,
General Book-keeper for B. A. Fahnestock's Son & Co.,
Wholesale Druggists, Pittsburgh.

"My brother and a number of my young business friends having at different times been educated for business from Duff's Book-keeping, and they all having afterwards proved to be highly accomplished accountants and business men, I therefore infer that this branch of education is brought to full perfection in this work." JAMES ROBB,
President Keystone Savings-Bank.
Pittsburgh, Pa.

"Duff's system of Merchants' Accounts exhibits in a clear, compact, and condensed form, without being superficial, all the essentials of a thorough education in Book-keeping." GEO. R. DUNCAN,
Book-keeper Iron City National Bank, Pittsburgh.

"I am recommending all my friends to your Commercial College. My course of study, from your excellent treatise on merchants' accounts, prepared me for keeping the books of this banking-house." WILLIAM H. SELLERS,
Book-keeper to Austin, Elder & Fletcher, Bankers,
Chambersburg, Pa.

"I prefer your Book-keeping and plan of instruction to any I have seen in the colleges in this city. I have no trouble in keeping our books." JAMES WILSON,
Book-keeper to C. H. Grant & Co., Merchants,
Philadelphia.

RECOMMENDATIONS.

" I now hold a clerkship of the first class in this department. I esteem it a privilege to commend what I have reason to regard as the best Commercial College in America. Since graduating, I have had my educational attainments thoroughly tested in a number of commercial offices; and it is due to your splendid system of business accounts to say that its judiciously diversified exercises have enabled me to fill every position I have held to the satisfaction of my employers." SAMUEL M. BRYAN,

Treasury Department, Washington, D.C.

" I am now a clerk in the counting-room of these extensive mills, for which I was fitted mainly by the excellent business education I received in your college. I now fully concur in all that your other numerous students have said of the superiority of your system of Book-keeping and business education." N. D. HOOPER,

Clerk Salisbury Mills, Amesbury, Mass.

" I have had charge of this bank as cashier since 1st October last, and for my ability to discharge the duties of this responsible office you are entitled to the credit. The few months spent in your noble educational establishment studying your admirable system of accounts has been of great value to me." L. W. VALE,

Cashier First National Bank, Mount Pleasant, Iowa.

DUFF'S MERCANTILE COLLEGE,

No. 37 FIFTH STREET, PITTSBURGH, PA.

FOUNDED IN 1840,

AND

INCORPORATED BY THE LEGISLATURE OF PENNSYLVANIA WITH PERPETUAL CHARTER.

THE BUSINESS MAN'S FAVORITE COLLEGE FOR THE LAST

TWENTY-SEVEN YEARS.

It is believed to be the only institution of the kind in America founded and conducted by an experienced merchant. Our course of original lectures upon the details of

ACTUAL BUSINESS

are; to one going into business on his own account, worth more than his tuition fee, and may save him thousands of dollars in experimental knowledge, that will take him years to acquire in business. In these lectures we have no competitors, as none but an experienced merchant can impart the practical information which they contain. It will also be found that our system of accounts is, with one exception, the only modern one in use, including comprehensive exercises in

BUSINESS WITH FOREIGN COUNTRIES.

Our system of instruction, thus extended into fields of business wholly omitted by others, enables us to present our students with a valuable collection of

BUSINESS FORMS

in every department of inland and foreign business. Regular lectures upon the

LAWS OF BUSINESS

are delivered to the classes. One of the most accomplished and experienced teachers of Business and Ornamental

PENMANSHIP

is in constant attendance on the classes.

For Terms and all other Particulars, send for our Pamphlet Circular, pp. 75.

ADDRESS

P. DUFF & SON,

399   PITTSBURGH, PA.

EXTRACTS FROM THE CHARTER

OF

DUFF'S MERCANTILE COLLEGE.

The preamble of the Act, after reciting the circumstances connected with the establishment of the Institution by the proprietor, in 1840, proceeds:—

"And having, through his professional labors and publications upon commercial science, greatly improved and enlarged the facilities for obtaining a thorough mercantile education, in order to give increased efficiency and permanence to his laudable efforts in promoting the cause of Commercial education, and thereby advancing the ends and purposes of commerce, it is hereby proposed that his Academy be incorporated. Therefore,

"SECTION 1. *Be it enacted by the Senate and House of Representatives of the Commonwealth of Pennsylvania, in General Assembly met, and it is hereby enacted by the authority of the same,* That there be, and hereby is erected and established, in the County of Allegheny, in this Commonwealth, a College for the education of merchants, and others, in the various branches of literature and science immediately connected with a thorough mercantile education, by the name, style, and title of 'DUFF'S MERCANTILE COLLEGE OF PENNSYLVANIA,' to be permanently located in the city of Pittsburgh, in said county of Allegheny."

(SECTIONS 2, 3, 4, and 5 relate to the government of the College,—its liabilities, privileges, &c.)

"SECTION 6. That the President, Professors, and Tutors for the time being, of said College, shall constitute the Faculty of said College, and shall have power to grant and confirm such degrees in the sciences taught in the College, to such students and graduates of the College, and others, when, by their proficiency and learning, professional eminence, or other meritorious distinction, they shall become entitled thereto, as they may see fit, and to grant graduates, or persons on whom such degrees may be conferred, diplomas, or certificates.

"SECTION 7. No religious sentiments shall be accounted a disability to hinder or debar students from entering the College, prosecuting their studies, and receiving diplomas or certificates, or in any manner to abridge their privileges or immunities as students in any department of said College."

(SECTIONS 8, 9, and 10 relate to the By-Laws, Conveyances, &c.)

(Signed)   **JOHN CESSNA,** *Speaker of the House of Representatives.*

BENJ. MATTHEWS, *Speaker of the Senate.*

Approved the eleventh day of March, one thousand eight hundred and fifty-one.

WM. F. JOHNSTON, *Governor of Pennsylvania.*

Pennsylvania, ss.:

I do hereby Certify, that the foregoing is a true and correct copy of the original Act of the General Assembly, entitled, "An Act to Incorporate Duff's Mercantile College of Pennsylvania," as the same remains on file in this office.

SECRETARY'S OFFICE.

[L.S.]   Witness my hand and the seal of the said office at Harrisburg, this 25th day of April, 1851.

A. L. RUSSELL, *Secretary of the Commonwealth.*